PEASANT DREAMS & MARKET POLITICS

PITT SERIES IN RUSSIAN AND EAST EUROPEAN STUDIES
Jonathan Harris, Editor

PEASANT DREAMS & MARKET POLITICS

Labor Migration and the Russian Village, 1861–1905

Jeffrey Burds

UNIVERSITY OF PITTSBURGH PRESS

Published by the University of Pittsburgh Press, Pittsburgh, Pa. 15261
Copyright © 1998, University of Pittsburgh Press
All rights reserved
Manufactured in the United States of America
Printed on acid-free paper
10 9 8 7 6 5 4 3 2 1

Library of Congress Cataloging-in-Publication Data
Burds, Jeffrey.
    Peasant dreams and market politics : labor migration and the
Russian village, 1861–1905 / Jeffrey Burds.
        p.   cm. — (Pitt series in Russian and East European studies)
        Includes bibliographical references (p.) and index.
        ISBN 0-8229-4049-3 — ISBN 0-8229-5655-1 (pbk.)
        1. Peasantry—Russia—History—19th century. 2. Peasantry—
Russia—History—20th century. 3. Village communities—Russia—
History. 4. Migrant labor—Russia—History. 5. Russia—Rural
conditions. 6. Russia—Economic conditions—1861–1917. I. Title.
II. Series: Series in Russian and East European studies.
HD1536.R9B848   1998
305.5'633'094709034—dc21   97-33876

A CIP catalog record for this book is available from the British Library.

Frontispiece: A Russian Beggar [*Nishchii*]. While the world outside of their native villages was a land of opportunity for Russian peasant youth, it was also the place to send old, sick, unproductive villagers without family who otherwise would become a burden on the commune. Lacking social insurance and unable to find work, these marginalized peasants normally made a living by begging alms, backmarket trade, or petty theft. *Photograph by N. Svishchova-Paola. Late nineteenth century. Courtesy of the Russian State Archive of Kinofoto Documents in Krasnogorsk.*

Material from "The Social Control of Peasant Labor in Russia: The Responses of Village Communities to Labor Migration in the Central Industrial Region, 1861–1905," in *Peasant Economy, Culture, and Politics in European Russia, 1800–1921*, ed. Esther Kingston-Mann and Timothy Mixter (1991), is used by permission of Princeton University Press. Material from "A Culture of Denunciation: Patterns of Religious Anathematization in Rural Russia, 1860–1905," *Journal of Modern History* (1996), is used by permission of the University of Chicago Press. Cambridge University Press has kindly authorized the use of a map from Maureen Perrie, *The Agrarian Policy of the Russian Socialist-Revolutionary Party from its Origins through the Revolution of 1905–1907* (1976).

For my mother, Faith Somers,
And her husband, George Somers,
And in memory of my father,
Albert Burds, whose sojourn
From Iowa farmer's son to Detroit factory worker
Inspired this study.

The concept of culture I espouse . . . is essentially a semiotic one. Believing, with Max Weber, that man is an animal suspended in webs of significance he himself has spun, I take culture to be those webs, and the analysis of it to be therefore not an experimental science in search of law but an interpretive one in search of meaning. It is explication I am after, construing social expressions on their surface enigmatical.

—Clifford Geertz, "Thick Description: Toward an Interpretive Theory of Culture"

The irruption of modern capitalism into peasant society . . . has always had cataclysmic effects on that society. When it comes suddenly . . . its effect is all the more disturbing.

—Eric Hobsbawm, *Primitive Rebels*

CONTENTS

Preface xi

The Politics of Reputation: Toward an Anthropology of the Personal 1

Part I. Emancipation, Interregnum, and Rural Crisis 11

    Chapter 1. The Roots of Ambivalence: Peasant Labor Migration as a Threat to Village Security 17

Part II. In Defense of Peasant Patriarchalism: Institutional Responses to Peasant Labor Migration 41

    Chapter 2. Autocratic Authority and the Peasant "Little Community": State Agents, Village Officials, and Community Opinion 45

    Chapter 3. The Social Control of Peasant Labor: The Alliance of Family and Community 51

    Chapter 4. The Sociology of Class: Peasant Communes and Market Brokers 89

    Chapter 5. The Logic of Solidarity: Migrants and Villagers 118

Part III. Legacies: *Otkhod* and Russian Popular Culture 141

    Chapter 6. A Culture of Acquisition: The Genesis of Mass Consumer Culture in Rural Russia 143

    Chapter 7. A Culture of Denunciation: Patterns of Religious Anathematization in Rural Russia 186

Appendix 221

Abbreviations 223

Notes *225*

Glossary *279*

Bibliography *281*

Index *307*

PREFACE

THIS STUDY IS BASED SUBSTANTIALLY on over three years of research in Russian central and provincial archives, many collections that (before 1989) had never been used by any researcher, Russian or Western. I focused particularly on a systematic review of unpublished material in the Central State Historical Archives for Moscow City which was, until 1917, the main repository for state, institutional, and religious archives of Moscow City and Province. This research was supplemented with substantial work in police archives preserved in the prerevolutionary collections of the State Archives of the Russian Federation (Moscow), the Museum of the Ministry of Internal Affairs (Moscow), and the Russian State Historical Archive (Petersburg). I have also drawn extensively from work in what is perhaps the finest collection of material on the history of Russian village social life and ethnography, the nearly eighteen hundred files preserved in the Tenishev collection at the Russian State Museum of Ethnography in St. Petersburg. These were supplemented by the rich collections of the Manuscripts Division of the State Russian Library (Moscow), and the collections of the State Historical Museum (Moscow). Visits to museum and archival collections in Dmitrov, Iaroslavl, Kostroma, Nerekhta, Perm, Chusovoi, and Tver were invaluable not only for supplementing sources, but also in providing me with the opportunity to stroll through contemporary and reconstructed villages and provincial towns. In this respect, I gained precious insights into the history and social life of the Russian peasantry when I was invited to take part in two month-long expeditions in Perm Oblast and the Crimea in summer and autumn 1990.

Every author incurs debts in the course of writing a book, and this is especially so in my case. At Yale, Robert Jackson graciously taught me to allow life experience to inform my scholarly writing. Paul Bushkovitch and Peter Gay played important roles in the early conceptualizations of the dissertation, while Ivo Banac and John Merriman oversaw the work to its completion, providing limitless support and friendship along the way. John's family—Carol,

Laura, and Christopher—brought me periodic and healthy reminders of the sunshine I was missing as I sat in drab and dusty libraries and archives.

James C. Scott was variously the inspiration, straw man, friend, frustrating questioner, and chief mentor of the project from beginning to end. It is no exaggeration when I say I could not have completed this work without him and his wife, Louise Scott. Little did I know early in my graduate career that shoveling sheep shit in Durham, Connecticut, was Scotty's idea of an apprenticeship in peasant studies. To say that Scotty was a unique mentor with a wonderfully idiosyncratic style of inspiring students is just to scratch the surface of a precious enigma.

Mark von Hagen and Gregory Freeze played critical roles in the dissertation stage. Greg's particularly generous efforts to comment on early drafts contributed toward refocusing my thoughts on several key issues. Greg also provided invaluable direction on my terrified first steps into Russian archival research.

At the University of Rochester, I am grateful for support received from several colleagues: Tom Gibson, William Hauser, Emil Homerin, Larry Hudson, Elias Mandala, Perez Zagorin, and, particularly, Brenda Meehan. Much of the reconceptualization of my dissertation, especially several new sections in parts 2 and 3, took place in the highly charged and inspiring atmosphere of the Rochester History Department. I am especially grateful to students in my advanced seminar on European popular culture in 1991 and 1992, who helped me to develop a deeper appreciation for cultural contexts.

I am also grateful to the staffs of the Slavonic Library in Helsinki, Finland, and the interlibrary loan departments at Yale University and the University of Rochester who rescued me countless times in helping to locate particularly esoteric titles.

Financial support for this research has been generously provided from numerous foundations and agencies. While I was a graduate student at Yale University, a slew of Yale fellowships and a Whiting Fellowship in the Humanities provided crucial support. Dissertation research fellowships from the International Research and Exchanges (IREX) Board and a Fulbright-Hays award enabled me to spend eighteen months doing archival and field research in that most special time from 1989 to 1990, when many of the unpublished materials and finding aids used in this study were made available to Western researchers for the first time. A postdoctoral fellowship in Russian and Soviet Studies from the Joint Committee on Soviet Studies of the Social Science Research Council enabled me to return to Russia for several short visits from 1991 to 1993, while a junior faculty leave from the University of Rochester helped to support the final leg of research and writing in 1993–1994.

In Russia, I am grateful to archivists and librarians at several institutions, notably the Central State Historical Archive for Moscow City; the State Archive of the Russian Federation; the Russian State Archive of Literature and Art; the Museum of the Revolution, Moscow; the Russian State Archive of Ancient Acts, Moscow; the infinitely patient staff of *pervyi zal* at the Russian State Library; the annex of newspaper and dissertation collections of the Russian State Library in Khimki; the manuscripts division in both the main and annex collections of the Russian State Library; the State Historical Museum in Moscow; the State Historical Library in Moscow; the Gorkii Library of Moscow State University; historical museums in Dmitrov, Nerekhta, Perm, and Chusovoi; the Russian State Archive of the Economy; the state archives of Iaroslavl, Perm, and Tver oblasts. In St. Petersburg, I am grateful to the staff of the Central State Historical Archive for assistance in the collections of the Ministry of Internal Affairs. Valentina Ivanova of the State Museum of Ethnography in St. Petersburg was extraordinarily generous in guiding me through the invaluable materials of the Tenishev collection.

In addition, I am grateful to several others who have in one way or another helped me along the way: F. G. Bailey, Andrei Batalov, Leonid Borodkin, Bill Chase, Boris Dadonov, S. V. Dimidov, Olia Edel'man, Sheila Fitzpatrick, Stephen Frank, Arch Getty, Leopold Haimson, Nikolai Iakovlev, John Kachur, R. F. Khoklov, Esther Kingston-Mann, Vladimir Kozlov, Hiroaki Kuromiya, Boris Litvak, David Luebke, Kim Markowski, Burton Miller, Tat'iana Mironova, Sam Ramer, Slava Riabov, Matt Scruton, Scott Seregny, Vera Shevzov, Andrei Sokolov, Richard Stites, Carmine Storella, Wilton and Iryna Tifft, Lynne Viola, James Von Geldern, the late Allan Wildman, and Ellie Zavadskaia. And words cannot express the gratitude I feel toward Jonathan Harris and Catherine Marshall of the University of Pittsburgh Press, who have been so enthusiastic and supportive about the manuscript. I am also grateful to artist Bill Nelson of Accomac, Virginia, for redrawing the excellent map that appears in chapter 5.

Two people deserve special thanks for the extra-special assistance they rendered to me. Throughout the years since we met in the mid-1980s, Tim Mixter has represented for me the epitome of integrity and scholarship, with his undaunting support and superhuman efforts to read and re-read my written work. Anyone who works in Russian peasant studies today knows that Tim is the guiding force who has brought so many of us together, the clearinghouse who has helped us all to make our work so much better. Early on, Tim evidently saw in my work a lot more promise than I ever could, and whatever I have achieved here has a lot to do with Tim's friendship, patience, and support.

And in Russia back in 1989, I was rescued from floundering by a generous scholar and friend, Leonid Romanovich Vaintraub, who thankfully adopted me and throughout these years has patiently taught me most of what I know about archival research in the former Soviet Union. Lenia, his wife Lena, and their two daughters Tanya and Olia have provided me and my family with a Russian home during the many years we have had to spend away from our own.

Throughout the work of writing and rewriting this manuscript, my wife Orysia and our daughter Ivanna Christina have been constant sources of strength and support. This book seems a small compensation indeed.

Author's note: All Russian terms have been transliterated according to the Library of Congress system. In addition, all references have been presented in their modern Russian versions: archaicisms such as, for example, "ie" and "ago" have been replaced by their modern forms "e" and "ogo." Likewise, modern rules were enforced in spelling: "obespechennost," not "obezpechennost"; "issledovanie," not "izsledovanie"; "otechestvennye," not "otechestvennyia." Finally, the soft ending has been dropped in the text: Iaroslavl instead of Iaroslavl', Tver not Tver'; it is retained in the notes and the bibliography.

Dates correspond to the Gregorian calendar in use in Russia before 1917. Dates are therefore twelve days behind the standard Western calendar in the nineteenth century, and thirteen days behind in the twentieth century.

The Politics of Reputation

TOWARD AN ANTHROPOLOGY
OF THE PERSONAL

RURAL RUSSIA DURING THE LAST THREE GENERATIONS of the Old Regime was a society in flux, a peripatetic world in which traditional relationships and traditional ways of doing things were profoundly transformed. This transformation was observable not just in myriad individual relationships, but more broadly, it was represented in the thoroughgoing transformation of the totality of village social relations. Sweeping changes in the structure of the Russian economy had a telling impact on the contours of everyday life.

This book is an introduction to the labyrinth of village social institutions and community relations during the period of Russia's transformation from a traditional to a commodity economy. Focusing on the nexus of family and community in the Central Industrial Region (Moscow and the surrounding radius of roughly three hundred kilometers), I have explored the responses of peasant households and communes to two primary forces that corresponded to the development of the commodity economy in the Russian countryside: periodic economic crises, and threats by "outsiders" (state agents, hiring brokers, and market middlemen).

I have placed particular emphasis on the mediating role of the peasant commune in the Central Industrial Region from the abolition of serfdom in 1861 to the dawn of the Stolypin reforms in 1906. All over European Russia, the peasant commune served in varying degrees and permutations four distinct, yet often overlapping and conflicting roles: (1) the commune functioned as an extension of the state apparatus, responsible as a collective for the fulfillment of dues and obligations and for the general maintenance of order according to the norms of peasant customary law; (2) the commune was a mitigator, an organization of families associated by shared proximity, tradition, kinship, religious, economic, and cultural bonds which in practice served and protected the interests of villagers from the inroads of outsiders, both distinct (such as state agents, creditors, market middlemen) and amorphous (such as commoditization and wage labor); (3) the commune was a broker, the principal mediator (with *volost* authorities) between locally controlled resources (in labor, raw materials, land) and outside agents; and (4) the commune was a safety net: the same forces that bound peasants to their community also served as a form of insurance (however unpredictable) to protect against failure in the outside world.[1]

In the Central Industrial Region, in particular, a very high rate of peasant labor migration for nonagricultural side-earnings became the chief catalyst that bonded these four elements together to generate a distinct regional form of peasant community. Significant before 1861, rates of migration for side-earnings would skyrocket throughout the Central Industrial Region following the abolition of serfdom.

The convergence of forces had three key components. The Russian state sought to coopt the peasant commune in order to expropriate the cash earnings of peasant-workers through state taxation and redemption dues, while avoiding the pitfalls of Western-style proletarianization. In its efforts to subordinate the peasant commune to state control, the state followed a carrot-and-stick strategy: while vigorously pursuing the insuperable task of imposing a rule of law in the countryside, state policy also upheld and extended the status of village patriarchal authorities, who were likewise threatened, yet dependent upon, the vital lifeline provided by the departure of household members for outside earnings to the urban and industrial centers. The attitude of the village hierarchy was one of ambivalence: migration for earnings was an "inescapable evil, which appears as the necessary consequence of the absence of local industry and the insufficient size of allotment lands."[2]

This was the essential ingredient in the regional crisis of peasant economy:

Regions and guberniyas of European Russia. Reproduced from Maureen Perrie, *The Agrarian Policy of the Russian Socialist-Revolutionary Party* (Cambridge: At the University Press, 1976), p. xii.

the overriding task of primary village institutions (commune, household, family) was somehow to integrate into a *changing* conception of community a large proportion of village members who would spend most of their adult lives in wage-earning positions outside the village. In the West, these forces had often led to a clear social division of labor between peasants and proletarians; in Russia, all the way up to the time of the Revolution, the ranks of the nonagricultural work force continued to be filled to a large degree by fresh labor recruits from the countryside. In the interregnum that marked the period, opportunists—cognizant of their capacity to exploit the breach to their advantage—stepped in to assist cash-hungry villages fending off state tax agents on the one hand, and peasant families threatened by a pervasive sense of insecurity in the commodity economy, on the other.

The structure of this book corresponds directly with this scheme. In part 1 (chapter 1), I analyze the Russian migration phenomenon, the principal factors behind its development, and the impact of labor migration on peasant communities in the Moscow region. In part 2 (chapters 2–5), I evaluate the operation of rural institutions and various informal networks and associations in the countryside. Chapters 2–3 look at state and village efforts to regulate peasant labor migration. In chapter 4, I move to a revised interpetation of the roles and social positions of opportunists and middlemen—the so-called "kulak problem"—with a close analysis of evolving patron-client associations and the transformed structure of rural economic relations in order to gain a deeper understanding of the context and parameters of intracommunity exploitation by village insiders. And in chapter 5, I focus on peasant migrant experience and summarize the overall impact of these various developments on patterns of peasant subsistence strategies in the Moscow region between the abolition of serfdom and the First World War. In part 3 (chapters 6–7), I introduce a new set of problematica for interpreting the transformation of village social relations during the last half of the nineteenth century, focusing in particular on the filters through which peasants largely experienced the forces of change. Chapter 6 is devoted to the study of the subtle but profound transition from a peasant culture based on need to a *culture of acquisition,* the development of a conspicuous consumer consciousness, with its numerous honeycomb effects on the whole structure and content of village popular and material culture. In chapter 7, I analyze the remarkable correlation between patterns of peasant religious anathematization and the labeling of peasant outmigrants as "heretics" in a rapidly emerging *culture of denunciation.*

The Social Significance of Commoditization

My principal task in this study is to evaluate the transformation of the totality of social relations in the Russian countryside associated with the metamorphosis of peasant labor and products into commodities. A hint at the profound social meaning of the new set of opportunities and constraints imposed by the transition to a system of market exchange was suggested by Georg Lukacs in his now classic essay, "Reification and the Consciousness of the Proletariat": "The essence of commodity structure . . . is that a relation between people takes on the character of a thing and thus acquires a 'phantom objectivity,' an autonomy that seems so strictly rational and all embracing as to conceal every trace of its fundamental nature: the relation between people. . . . What is at issue *here* . . . is the question: how far is commodity exchange together with its structural consequences able to influence the *total* outer and inner life of society?"[3] The development of a commodity economy entailed a transition from a network of social relationships founded on highly contextualized, local, and *personal relations* to one where personal relationships were increasingly subordinated to impersonal, structural forces.

In reality, of course, that transition was hardly so universal, clearcut, or complete: if the essence of commoditization and urbanization theories rests on the presumption of a movement of control from local to nonlocal agencies (hence, the appearance of social forces as having a "phantom objectivity"), then that process was nonetheless accompanied in popular perceptions by the personalization or anthropomorphization of those agencies. Outsiders (especially, state agents and market middlemen) operated by coopting local power structures, while insider-opportunists buttressed their personal authority through a subtle process of self-legitimization founded on their relationships with outsiders; they became "hingemen" or experts at mediating the enormous gulf between the village and the outside world. Anthropologists and historians have long noted the power of that gulf to undermine initiatives toward or from the village: even the best-laid plans of conscientious bureaucrats have been defeated by what is nominally labeled "village intransigence," or what James Scott called "everyday forms of peasant resistance." In contrast, even highly unpopular dictators have retained authority precisely because they managed to render charismatic village rebels utterly impotent in regions outside their own personal domains.[4]

My underlying focus is on the inertia of tradition in the inherited cultural framework of the village "little community"—the deeply imbedded, highly tenacious, multistranded context within which small changes in rural economic relations inevitably take place. Recognition of the cultural influences on the peasant's perception of ongoing structural relations must be the starting point for any serious attempt to reconstruct an anatomy of peasant social relations. This view was succinctly expressed in James Scott's article on the role of the "little tradition" in agrarian revolt:

> Compared with . . . the proletariat, the political culture of the peasantry is strongly influenced by factors which are not purely a consequence of its relationship to the means of production. To put it somewhat differently, the proletariat has to create its class subculture in a new environment while the peasantry, like traditional artisans, inherits a far greater residue of custom, community, and values which influences its behavior. Theories of peasant politics that do not take this cultural dimension into account are likely to misconstrue the meaning of both peasant passivity and peasant jacqueries.[5]

The principal factor that distinguishes proletarian culture is precisely this quality of "uprootedness," in contrast to the peasantry, for whom class relations are always intermeshed with and glossed over by inherited sociocultural forms. As fruitful as class analysis has been for the study of social movements, historians of Russia must develop new paradigms for interpreting social conflict that restore the varying roles of politics, culture, kinship, and religion to their rightful place alongside economic factors in the dynamics of social change. To put it somewhat differently, *power* in the village is founded not just on economic supremacy—wealthy peasants as the least marginalized element in a community of peasants living on the margin—but on a whole host of noneconomic factors as well.[6]

Against the "Species Peasant" of Traditional Russian Historiography

Historians have interpreted the hybrid condition of the Russian peasant economy in widely varying ways. Following Lenin, the predominant tendency in Soviet historiography emphasized the growing social division of labor between agriculture and industry, and therefore portrayed the mixed economy or "bifurcated peasant household" as a transitional phenomenon with little lasting or intrinsic historical significance. Cottage manufacturers *(kustari)* and migrating peasant-workers *(otkhodniki)* were portrayed as de facto extensions of the proletarian labor category, reflecting a conceptual framework that implicitly rejected any claim that the influence of the village community was historically (or politically) relevant. Typical of the underlying perspective was Lenin's position in *The Development of Capitalism in Russia*, first published in 1899:

> The development of commodity economy *eo ipso* means the divorcement of an ever-growing part of the population from agriculture, i.e., the growth of the industrial population at the expense of the agricultural population. . . . Thus one cannot conceive of capitalism without an increase in the commercial and industrial population at the expense of the agricultural population, and everybody knows that this phenomenon is revealed in the most clear-cut fashion in all capitalist countries.[7]

This theoretical formulation of the complete division of industrial from agricultural labor was upheld by successive Soviet analysts who focused in particular on the more active, educated, and skilled strata of the labor movement: large factories employing more than a thousand workers (which contained 44 percent of the total industrial labor force and accounted for nearly 90 percent of all strike activity) and on the growing numbers of "hereditary" industrial laborers—that is, those "workers" whose fathers also did some sort of factory work. In Soviet historiography, emphasis was placed on the purely legal character of the ties between industrial workers and their villages, an impression upheld by the evidence only if one arbitrarily chooses to identify "peasantness" with the seasonal return for field work observed among declining proportions of urban and industrial workers in the nineteenth and early twentieth centuries.[8]

In contrast, Western historians of Russian labor have stressed the proximity —geographic, legal, economic, social, and emotional—of factory and urban workers to their native villages. In emphasizing the Russian industrial labor force's "almost exclusively rural origins and . . . *the persistence of its peasant characteristics* and . . . its links with village society," Olga Crisp has succinctly summarized the mainstream perspective of scholars in the West:

> Above all it must be borne in mind that the time-span over which the [Russian] labour force could develop was relatively short. Industrial growth on any appreciable scale was a matter of not more than three decades, which was not more than a lifespan of one generation. Consequently it would not be reasonable to expect that within so short a time there could have developed a class of industrial workers with a working-class ancestry, specialized skill, and a mentality all its own. Even though eventually in a few large industrial centres . . . a core of factory workers made its appearance whose life-style and expectations were entirely shaped by the factory, they were constantly swamped by masses of new arrivals from the countryside as industry expanded. Moreover, even though the evidence

is strong that a proportion of workers with a fairly long record of factory work had made its appearance by around 1900, and though there were many workers whose parents were also workers, there is still much uncertainty as to the extent to which a typical Russian worker actually ended his life in the working-class environment or how often his son started his life there. There is evidence ... that workers, even of the most industrialized cities, resumed their life in the village, often from the age of forty and usually by the age of fifty, and that many of their offspring tended to spend their childhood, usually up to the age of fifteen, in the village, usually with their paternal grandparents, even when they happened to be born in factory maternity wards, and even though their mothers might have continued working in the factory.[9]

Until recently, and with rare exceptions, Western observers have depicted the Russian industrial labor force as mere "peasants in the factory" who were concerned less with labor organization than subsistence, less with politics than economics. Western scholars have pointed to the persistence of the dual economy based in the village—that is, of a predominantly small-farm peasant economy consisting of single-family households, each of which sent one or more family members outside the village for either year-round or seasonal earnings in order to augment equally unpredictable and generally insufficient agricultural receipts.[10] Similarly, stressing that industrial labor had not made a complete break with the village, Western historians have often identified work stoppages, strikes, and labor violence as varying forms of peasant *buntarstvo*—the defensive and spontaneous rowdiness and rebelliousness one would expect from *muzhiki* in a jacquerie; that is, hardly proletarian consciousness![11] Theodore Von Laue summed up the mainstream opinion: the Russian labor movement was typically peasant-workers "applying their village sense of social justice to the factory or city."[12]

In the most recent full-length study of the links between peasants and proletarians, Robert Johnson has retained the amorphous and convenient category of *species peasant*. He argues that *zemliachestvo*—in this context, the concentration of peasant-workers from the same village or region in a single factory, working-class ghetto, or skill—was the principal organizing factor in the Moscow labor movement prior to 1905. While observations of the peasant roots of working-class activism are certainly warranted, it is hardly sufficient merely to indicate "peasant origins" as a sociological category, without any further effort to examine the village world and village experience of peasant-workers. Peasant origins and peasant decisions to migrate need to be contextualized.[13]

While Soviet historiography tended to dismiss altogether the village as a factor in the broad social movement that preceded the Revolution, numerous

Western attempts to redress this hermeneutic flaw, restricted for the most part to the closely related field of Russian labor history, have likewise been marred by their own failures to penetrate into the "mysterious" village origins so often used to account for certain key features of Russian factory organization and working-class consciousness.[14]

This study represents, then, a needed corrective, a recontextualization of Russian peasant labor migration, a restoration of village social relations as the ground for understanding and interpreting peasant experience outside the village. The primary concern is not the "peasantness" that profoundly influenced the history of Russian urban development and the evolution of the Russian labor movement, but rather the ways in which peasant experience of nonvillage life affected a whole spectrum of village and nonvillage social relations.

An Alternative View of "Peasantness": Community and the Role of Reputation in Village Society

Any consideration of peasant labor migration must begin with the decision to leave the village commune. And here, the intricate webs that bound peasant-workers to their communities are of greatest importance. One of the most distinctive characteristics of village social relations is the means by which a peasant community imposes a kind of orthodoxy on its members. In the form of community opinion, the community becomes something far greater than the mere sum of its parts: mores and norms are dictated; behavior is proscribed; deviants and rebels are punished; potential scofflaws are intimidated.

Historians and anthropologists have long recognized the enormous authority wielded by village communities over their members. Scholars have placed overriding emphasis on the personal element in village social relations. As the noted historian of the Russian peasantry Boris Mironov has perceptively argued, "The rural commune was a small social grouping, that is, a group based on personal contacts, where all members [of the community] knew each other well. This gave to it exclusive rights and opportunities for the regulation of peasant behavior. Within [the peasant commune was] the strictest social control, a censorship of morals, from which in practice it was impossible to escape."[15]

In a host of ways, then, village communities were dominated by complex networks of personal contacts, relationships that continued to exert powerful influence on a peasant's life even when he left the village for outside labor. The village community was a universe in which "everyone had a right to know what everyone else was doing."[16] Or, as the social anthropologist F. G. Bailey has so eloquently put it:

> It is hard to mind your own business if you live in a village. . . . Everyday life is lived in small communities, where everyone knows about everyone else, or, if they do not actually know about a particular other person, they know who will be able to talk about him. These are "face-to-face" or—as a cynical Indian anthropologist put it—"back-to-back" societies. These phrases do not mean that everyone is constantly in everyone else's presence: only that there is a fund of common knowledge about all the members of the community, and that it is not too difficult for anyone in the community to have access to it. This fund, in fact, is made up of reputations.[17]

Whether a peasant lived and worked in or away from the village, he or she was subjected to a host of judgments and constraints by neighbors and fellow villagers.

As useful as class analysis may be for understanding social movements and the anatomy of social conflict, in everyday experience structural factors such as class or socioeconomic status often yield to more phenomenological factors, deeply influenced by religious belief, superstition, kinship, and a multitude of local-specific factors: namely, an individual's reputation. The important point to keep in mind is that when peasants and peasant-workers rendered judgments about the cataclysmic changes in the world around them, they did so not in terms of the abstract forces of commoditization, urbanization, or revolutionism, but rather in the highly personalized terms of their everyday lives. In a village community, "The small politics of everyone's everyday life is about reputations; about what it means to 'have a good name'; about being socially bankrupted; about gossip and insult and 'one-upmanship'; in short, about the rules of how to play 'the social game.'"[18]

The politics of reputation meant first and foremost that peasant communities coped with threats both internal and external by anthropomorphizing them: the momentous forces of urbanization and modernization were identified with individual agents of change, most notably, peasants who migrated for needed side earnings. And, as we shall see, the individual agents themselves were subjected to the strictest forms of social control.

I

EMANCIPATION, INTERREGNUM, AND RURAL CRISIS

How can a commune resist, pounded as it is by state exactions, plundered by trade, exploited by landowners, and undermined from within by usury!
 What threatens the life of the Russian commune is neither a historical inevitability nor a theory; it is state oppression, and exploitation by capitalist intruders whom the state has made powerful at the peasants' expense.
—KARL MARX, SECOND DRAFT OF A LETTER TO VERA ZASULICH, FEBRUARY/MARCH 1881

"MY DEPARTURE [FROM MY NATIVE VILLAGE] was marked by some ceremony.... In the morning, father gathered the whole family in the cottage and lit the lamp in front of the holy icons. Everyone sat in solemn silence along the benches, and waited. Then father rose and began to offer prayers before the icon. His example was followed by the entire family. At the end of the prayers, father appealed to me in a farewell sermon, once again reminding me not to forget God, to respect my elders, to serve the boss honestly, and—in particular—always to take care of [those at] home."¹ In this way the sixteen-year-old peasant Semën Kanatchikov left his village for apprenticeship at a machine factory in Moscow, which lay some 120 kilometers to the east.² It was winter 1895. Semën had anxiously awaited this moment for over two years, ever since he had finished (at age thirteen) a rudimentary education at a primary school in a nearby village. His departure had been delayed by his father's hesitation: "Father did not want to let me 'go free' *[otpustit menia 'na vol'iu']* to Moscow, for there I, without fatherly supervision, might break off from the family and become spoiled. His dream was to keep me in the village, to make a good peasant of me."³ For two years, while his father remained stubbornly intransigent, Kanatchikov was further schooled in peasant work—plowing, harrowing, mowing, threshing, and wood-cutting. "Hold on to the land, sonny," his father would often say, "the land is your benefactress-provider."⁴ But the gradual erosion of old bases of support for the large extended household (nine to ten members), and the death of his mother—who died as much from the exhaustion of having given birth to at least twelve children as from the sorrow with having only four survive through infancy and childhood—wore down his father's resistance. Semën found life in the village unendurable and more insistently pressed for the needed parental consent. Meanwhile, his father increasingly recognized the need to augment family income with outside earnings. And so, permission was granted, on the strict condition that Semën stick to the ways of the village.

The ceremony described by Kanatchikov was typical, ritually uniting the departing member's future with his past life, ceremonially reaffirming his ties to the family and the village world. As an oft-quoted proverb said, only "when the earth takes the parents [do] the children get their freedom."⁵ Appeals were made on the basis of the four main principles of the village patriarchal moral economy: religion, family, obedience and respect for authority (one's elders), and, above all, responsibility. At base, traditional Russian village culture and economy were grounded on the presumption that the younger members of the household would work to support the rest. As local sources dried up in the wake of the development of factory industry, and as state exactions grew—making it next to impossible for peasant families throughout the Central Industrial Region to live either wholly off the land *or* from outside wage-earnings alone—the shift to wage labor away from the village split families and threatened to undermine traditional arrangements. The dualism in Kanatchikov's description is apt: against the background of his father's apprehensions and exhortations are the son's anxious expectations.⁶

Introduction   13

The farewell ceremony was in its essence an extension of the "sorrowful repast" traditionally celebrated by Russian peasants in the event of a family or village member's induction into military service.[7] The parallels are significant, for the peasant labor-migrants were in an important sense soldiers of the village guard: they were members of the village community, armed with strong communal defenses and sent out beyond the native environs to defend the fiscal, organizational, and spiritual vitality of an institution under siege. The old order was at war with the new, the village patriarchal system with the onslaught of the market economy, and the migrating peasant-workers were expected to fight on the front lines.

At almost exactly the same time Semën Kanatchikov was making his way to Moscow, Fëdor Samoilov—a peasant from the village of Gomylenka, near Lezhnevo in Suzdal District, Vladimir Province—was taking his own first uneasy steps in the Russian Manchester, Ivanovo-Voznesensk. The textile town lay some twenty kilometers north of his native village, but even such short distances posed considerable obstacles.

Quite a different scene accompanied Samoilov's departure from the village, but the story leading up to this point is intrinsically the same. Sometime during the winter of 1893, the nearby factory at which Samoilov's father had been working burned down. The industrial downturn at this time, combined with a repeated series of bad harvests, had created a general hardship throughout the Central Industrial Region, making it difficult to find substitute employment. Quite abruptly and unexpectedly, the Samoilov family found itself cast into a state of extreme hunger and destitution. By some good fortune, the elder Samoilov picked up a job as a sawyer in a neighboring forest, and the family somehow managed to make it through to the summer and the autumn harvest. The following winter (1894), as economic recovery reached full force, Samoilov's father succeeded in landing a job as a textile weaver in Ivanovo-Voznesensk. But the work required him to stay at the factory year-round, making it difficult for his family—which had divided from a larger household about a decade earlier[8]—to maintain the village allotment. So, too, was the fact that the family's living situation had not greatly improved. Consequently, when Fëdor—the eldest of three sons aged thirteen, eleven, and five—reached working age in 1895, the decision was made to move the entire family to the nearest town.[9] But such a momentous decision did not come easily.

> Finding no exit from this situation, father and mother started to talk about moving the family to the town of Ivanovo-Voznesensk. Mother first began to

insist on moving. She did not know whether it would be better, but seized on moving, just as a drowning man clutches at straws. My brother and I also begged father to take us to the town. Town life seemed interesting and prosperous to us. But father was indecisive. Having worked in the factory since he was young, he knew town life better than us, and understood that living there with a family would not be easy. After a long period of wavering, father finally decided to move to town. In the fall of 1895, having collected a negligible harvest, we sold our cow, boarded up our small cottage, and—taking leave of our native home—departed.[10]

The sentiments expressed by Fëdor and his brother were typical: for the younger village generation, unattuned to the hardships imposed by the depersonalized world "out there" away from the village, nothing could have seemed better or a greater adventure than exploring the world beyond the village. Peasant children were accustomed to hearing stories from more seasoned fellow villagers—*zemliaki* who had served in the army or worked "on the side" in younger years. Later, wiser with age, having families of their own and sobered by their experiences of town and factory life, their attitudes would usually come to resemble the apprehensions of their fathers.

Faced with the exitlessness *(beziskhodnost)* of village poverty, the Samoilov family hoped to offset the expense of family living in the city by placing at least three members in wage-earning positions. Fëdor, like Semën Kanatchikov, was overwhelmed with anticipation of the new life that lay before him. He thought with joy of how he was being spared the seemingly endless drudgery of field work.[11]

But, having already loaded their wagon with all their earthly possessions, a significant event took place as they were leaving their village. Just as the family farewell ceremony for the young Kanatchikov emphasized his responsibilities, his mutual interdependence with family and village, a final exchange between the departing Samoilov family and their neighbors is a good illustration of the not-so-subtle ways in which the village collective reminded Fëdor's father of his and his family's obligations to their native community. Their wagon was surrounded by friends in the village, who apparently showed some surprise at the imminent departure. Asked about his destination, the elder Samoilov prevaricated—preferring to emphasize his family's needs, the impossibility of remaining in the village. The villagers were evidently concerned about his intentions toward the peasantry: did he plan to abandon the community? Samoilov and his family were permitted to leave only after his expressed assurance that he would not "forsake the village, and never will do so." But he was mocked for thinking that town life was better than village living: "It will not be better [in the town], so the road to the village is not closed."[12]

The words were prophetic, rooted in the wisdom of collective experience: a few years later, unable to support the entire family in the city even with three workers, the Samoilov family returned to their native village, leaving Fëdor alone as an apprentice in an Ivanovo textile factory.[13] The Samoilovs had learned firsthand the impossibility of living without both the land and side-earnings.

The self-preserving, self-perpetuating character of the village community made its members frown on threats against it—the greatest of which was, as in this case, resettlement and potential abandonment by an entire family. As another proverb powerfully expressed: "Die, but do not leave your father's land." The departure of an entire family was not only a step toward the cultural disintegration of the village community, it was also in a very real sense a direct challenge to the economic integrity of the entire community. As we shall see, the principle of mutual responsibility for redemption dues and fiscal obligations meant that such whole-family departures could potentially undermine the economic security of the entire village, since any unpaid receipts would fall to the responsibility of those who remained. Thus, while the typical *obshchina* in the Central Industrial Region might have tolerated and even encouraged temporary "migration for side-earnings" as a means of sustaining the fiscal and institutional vitality of the village, there were formidable constraints against the permanent resettlement of productive members away from the native community. In this way, village communities in the Central Industrial Region stood in stark contrast to those in, for instance, the Central Agricultural Region, where the overwhelming reliance on agricultural earnings coupled with high population growth and land scarcity led communities to encourage whole-family resettlement as a means of contributing to the position of those who remained. The overwhelming majority of migrants to Siberia—the *pereselentsy*—who composed an almost continuous stream throughout the last half of the nineteenth century in search of a better life, were peasants from predominantly chernozem areas.[14] For those in the Central Industrial Region, the hope of a better life lay not in Russia's Siberian frontier, but in the towns, industrial settlements, and factories.

These two case studies of the family- and village-based forces acting upon migrants to keep them in line, to actively integrate them into the village community when counterforces aggressively and sometimes quite successfully undermined and severed those traditional relationships, serve as an introduction to the myriad complex networks that enmeshed peasants from the nonagricultural regions "working on the side." While every community functioned differently, each with its own specific sets of rewards and punishments, the legal, institutional, cultural, and—to a large extent—economic context of the collective experiences of migrants and villagers alike overlapped in real ways. The logic of existing networks that tied peasant-workers to their villages derived from three independent yet intrinsically related and interrelated sources: (1) *community:* the forces brought to bear by state, *volost* and village institutions, and community members through legal, illegal, and extralegal mechanisms and sanctions (the system of tax assessment and collection, passport regulations, corporal punishment, the rural credit and hiring markets, apprenticeship); (2) *household/family:* the pressures exerted by household members, dominated by concerns about subsistence, dependence, kinship, and religion (marriage patterns, passport manipulation, cultural and religious norms); and (3) *individual:* peasant-workers' sense of isolation and alienation in the outside world, their concerns about security against market downturns, their own social, cultural, and family connections to the village.

Inevitably, in the phenomenology of everyday life, these various forces overlapped to such a degree as to have been indistinguishable, an irreducible totality that shaped and defined the actors as much as it was shaped and defined by them.

1   The Roots of Ambivalence

PEASANT LABOR MIGRATION AS A
THREAT TO VILLAGE SECURITY

FAR MORE THAN ANY OTHER SECTOR of the Russian Empire, the villages in the Central Industrial Region maintained a hybrid economy that blurred the now-familiar distinctions between subsistence and capitalist forms. Because they lived in an area of poor soil and a short, irregular growing season, peasants in this region had by the nineteenth century become habituated to meeting individual, household, and village subsistence requirements by supplementing village agriculture with a wide variety of predominantly nonagricultural jobs that augmented their typically meager agricultural earnings on village allotments. Here, as elsewhere, a complex set of social relations had evolved that sustained and perpetuated those schemes and associations.

The central unifying element in traditional peasant culture was the concept of the patriarchal household, or *domokhoziaistvo*. There were three primary village institutions: the conjugal dyad or married couple *(tiaglo)* as the base productive unit; the peasant household *(dvor)*; and the peasant commune or assembly *(obshchina)*. *Domokhoziaistvo* refers to the organizational element which linked all three.

The ideal of the extended, joint-family household was imposed under serfdom through the strict enforcement of the principle of *nerazdel'naia sem'ia*—the indivisible or immutable family unit.[1] The household, not the simple family or individual member, became the basic unit responsible as a collectivity *(podatnaia edinitsa)* for various obligations and duties. "Every peasant, including the adult independent worker, was regarded not as a self-sufficing, solitary person, but rather as a dependent part of a *naturally created community*—that is, of the peasant family, of the peasant *dvor.*"[2]

In his position as household chief, the *domokhoziain* was responsible for the fulfillment of all community and estate duties—fiscal, labor, and military—as well as personally responsible for the activities of all the members of his household. He was as a result granted extensive powers not just over the management of the family economy, but also over its "inseparable members" *(neotdelennye chleny),* who were in principle and often in practice subordinated to the will of the family patriarch—the peasant household head. "To him belongs not only the parental power, but also the power of the *domokhoziain,* who manages the entire family economy according to his own discretion."[3] On his part, the *domokhoziain* was obligated to provide subsistence and security *(obespechenie)* for the members of his household. "To the remaining members of the family belongs only the right to receive upkeep from the father and, in relation to the [household] property *[imushchestvo],* they have only a right to its use."[4] Within the peasant household, conjugal relations were subordinated to patrilineal ones. Simple family heads, normally the sons of the *domokhoziain,* brought their wives and raised their families within the multiple-family environment of the extended patriarchal household.

The chief of the extended household thus drew his power from two theoretically independent but, in practice, intrinsically related sources: his dual position as family chief (the *starik-otets* or elder-father) and as household manager. Another leading expert on peasant organization, Aleksandr Leont'ev, concurred: "The entire family makes use of the allotment, but the eldest member of the family—the *domokhoziain*—manages its use."[5]

Similarly, within each village there was an elder-overseer *(starosta),* who was elected and advised by an association of village *domokhoziaeva* in the village assembly. "In this manner, the *obshchina* is a composite juridical person. It . . . is composed from the aggregate of [the community's] juridical persons—the *domokhoziaistvo.*"[6] Just as the *domokhoziain* was responsible for all obligations of each of his household members, all of the households of the village community were mutually responsible for dues and obligations imposed by the landlord and the state. This system—*krugovaia poruka* or mutual responsibility

—was designed to ensure the prompt fulfillment of dues and obligations.[7] "Overall the system reflected a social strategy which did not reckon with social entities smaller than the *dvor* . . . the family/household. In this respect it was completely consistent with the Russian concept of serfdom, which until its abolition in 1861 deprived bonded peasants of any semblance of a civic identity, and regarded them exclusively as units of tribute and taxation."[8]

As a strategy for peasant subsistence, the patriarchal moral economy rested on the capacity of the *domokhoziaistvo*—elder members of the household and community—to exploit the labor product of the young. For only in this way could a member of the community be assured of support during the less autonomous years of infancy, childhood, sickness, and old age. As several historians have convincingly demonstrated, the entire social structure of the village patriarchal system was designed to deprive junior members of any political power until they themselves had reached an age in which they too, by virtue of their position in the village, would seek to uphold the status quo.[9]

Well suited to the strategies for social control that predominated under serfdom, the patriarchal hierarchy was the principal institution that came under siege when market relations developed and—after the abolition of serfdom in 1861—the state institutions that relied on peasant patriarchal social structure for their maintenance of internal order were removed. Viewed from this perspective, in this study I will analyze the evolution of traditional peasant economic strategies as such hierarchies and their associated institutions and customs were called upon to meet the exigencies imposed by Russia's rapid shift to a commodity economy during the last half of the nineteenth century. Of considerable importance for the Central Industrial Region were the potentially devastating effects on the surrounding village economy associated with the rapid growth of factory industry and the regional centralization of trade.[10] In particular, ever larger proportions of the peasantry were forced to seek their incomes in wage labor away from their native villages.

The Logic of the Russian Fiscal System

The peasant demand for outside sources of cash income was only exacerbated by the abolition of serfdom in 1861. The chief explanation lies in the fact that Russia's fiscal system during the last half of the nineteenth century was founded on a critical contradiction. Despite the presence of a well-developed industry and the predominance of nonfarm earnings among peasant households in the Central Industrial Region, taxes were most often based on land, on the size of peasant allotments.[11] While imposing a tax based primarily on land, the state nonetheless recognized that peasants in the non-black-earth areas would migrate for outside earnings in order to fulfill those cash obligations. This policy was in keeping with procedures established prior to the Emancipation, when noble landlords in the northern and central forest regions by and large imposed cash dues on their serfs, thereby generating a system of estate administration that was virtually indifferent to alternative forms of peasant labor.[12] All over European Russia, the cost of redeeming the land far exceeded its real market value: the size of allotments was reduced *(otrezki)* and the best land was held back by landlords or sold at a profit to outside buyers. The general pattern was one in which peasant families could not make a living off their allotments alone and were compelled to rent additional land or to work as wage laborers. In the Central Agricultural Region, such terms were imposed deliberately, so as to ensure a large, inexpensive pool of wage laborers for demesne agriculture.[13] In the nonchernozem zones to the north, however, the terms of redemption were a direct reflection of the comparatively poor quality of land: noble income had long been derived not so much from demesne agriculture as from the earnings of serf laborers in nonagricultural occupations. Artificially high redemption costs were a reimbursement to the landed nobility for their lost labor income *(obrok,* or quitrent payments). For instance, in twelve Moscow districts, the average annual obligation on an individual parcel was 10.45 rubles, while the mean rent for the same size and quality of parcel was 3.6 rubles, a difference of nearly 300 percent![14] The noted Soviet historian P. A. Zaionchkovskii calculated the ratio of payments for the land versus income derived from it for six non-black-soil provinces, finding that the typical redemption price for land in central non-black-earth districts was 1–2 times its actual value among former state peasants, and 2–2.5 times for former manorial peasants. (See table 1.1.)

Table 1.1. Proportion of Redemption Dues to Land Values in Six Non-Black-Earth Provinces, 1860s
(in percentages)

Province	Former State Peasants	Former Manorial Peasants (with a full holding)
Kostroma	146	240
Pskov	130	213
Smolensk	166	220
Tver	244	252
Viatka	97	200
Vladimir	168	276

Source: P. A. Zaionchkovskii, *Otmena krepostnogo prava v Rossii,* 3d ed. (Moscow, 1968), pp. 301–02.

The Russian fiscal system operated on the presumption that peasants in the nonchernozem areas would turn to sources outside agriculture to supplement their earnings and fulfill state obligations.[15] Two other factors—a steady increase in rural tax burdens throughout most of the last half of the nineteenth century, and a rapid population growth—gave further impetus to these developments.

For estate administrators before the abolition of serfdom, as for the state agents who gradually supplanted them after 1861, the principal concern in non-black-earth areas was not the land, but the payments for it, payments that far exceeded the land's real productive value. This condition posed a serious challenge to rural institutions throughout the Central Industrial Region. To compensate for the inevitable discrepancy between land values and labor power, the assessment of allotments was as a rule determined by the "economic significance of the allotment," in connection with the "greater or lesser side-earnings of locals."[16] In this way, communes in the non-black-earth districts translated state exactions on village land into a modified, village-based income tax. Rarely were land distribution or tax assessment schemes founded on the number of revised souls or even according to the number of souls actually present.[17] The system left enormous room for arbitrariness.

The Growth of Peasant Labor Migration

To meet the excessive obligations of state taxes and redemption dues, peasants in the Central Industrial Region were compelled to depart for earnings outside their native villages. Tables 1.2 and 1.3 contain comprehensive data on the rapid growth of Russian peasant labor migration *(otkhodnichestvo)* from 1861 to 1910.[18]

Taking European Russia as a whole, the number of issued passports grew in inverse proportion to the distance from the center, with the percentage of issued passports declining in definite concentric rings as one moved away from Moscow. The Central Industrial Region (Moscow and six surrounding provinces) held the absolute and proportionally highest number of issued passports. In 1896, for every hundred souls (both sexes) of the general village population, 20.5 passports were issued in Kaluga Province; 20.4 in Vladimir; 18.4 in Tver; 17.9 in Riazan; 17.0 in Iaroslavl; 16.6 in Moscow; and 14.4 in Tula.[19] This corresponded to 30 to 40 percent of the peasant adult males in these regions. This central core of high migration was bordered on the east by Kostroma and Nizhnii Novgorod, and to the west, Smolensk, where there was

Table 1.2. Peasant Labor Migration in 43 Provinces of European Russia, 1861–1910

Regions and Provinces	Average Annual Number of Issued Passports (in thousands)					
	1861–70	1871–80	1881–90	1891–1900	1902	1906–10
I. Nonagricultural/Industrial	**850.7**	**2,060.9**	**2,455.1**	**3,203.9**	**3,871.4**	**4,572.5**
North and Northwest	296.4	669.5	740.6	1,037.2	1,293.7	1,443.5
Arkhangel	14.0	34.1	33.0	42.9	49.0	52.1
Vologda	16.2	63.0	70.4	109.0	140.2	160.2
Olonets	8.9	27.6	32.5	46.3	48.1	51.9
St. Petersburg	40.3	84.0	104.5	151.2	193.3	175.2
Novgorod	34.1	95.9	98.0	141.7	182.6	214.1
Pskov	13.4	25.8	32.1	64.0	98.3	128.3
Smolensk	58.6	115.6	123.5	157.2	191.2	219.6
Tver	110.9	223.5	246.6	324.9	391.0	442.1
Central Industrial Region	510.2	1,281.8	1,541.0	1,902.9	2,225.4	2,684.7
Iaroslavl	71.9	142.4	149.7	188.7	233.9	239.8
Moscow	108.1	199.9	236.9	374.9	458.0	536.9
Vladimir	54.9	200.3	231.2	294.7	368.9	388.7
Kostroma	39.7	138.4	171.8	183.5	10.9	282.1
Kaluga	78.1	172.3	205.4	257.2	284.2	313.5
Nizhnii Novgorod	37.2	116.1	143.4	18.7	203.0	210.6
Tula	46.1	109.3	139.8	221.7	267.1	293.8
Riazan	74.2	203.1	262.8	363.5	399.4	419.3
Belorussia	44.1	109.6	173.5	263.8	352.3	444.3
Vitebsk	22.7	39.2	57.5	97.0	148.4	166.7
Minsk	8.7	27.6	57.5	77.8	94.7	99.3
Mogilev	12.7	42.8	58.5	89.0	109.2	178.3
II. Southern Agricultural	**117.1**	**421.3**	**816.9**	**1,204.2**	**1,398.9**	**1,551.7**
Ukraine	116.4	413.2	796.9	1,152.9	1,306.3	1,439.3
Poltava	24.6	83.7	139.0	193.8	221.4	195.5
Kharkov	18.6	63.9	122.9	175.7	231.2	244.4
Chernigov	19.4	65.1	102.7	149.5	188.1	201.1
Kiev	10.1	46.8	138.6	235.9	244.4	295.1
Volynia	8.0	31.6	61.2	85.7	15.5	110.5
Podolia	6.4	30.6	78.8	109.0	117.9	132.6
Kherson	12.1	40.3	65.8	89.5	103.3	113.9
Ekaterinoslav	11.5	29.7	56.1	71.0	135.5	80.8
Taurida	5.7	21.5	31.8	42.8	49.0	65.4
North Caucasus	0.7	8.1	20.0	51.3	92.6	112.4
Don Oblast	0.7	8.1	20.0	51.3	92.6	112.4
III. Central Agricultural	**244.7**	**968.9**	**1,297.1**	**1,572.2**	**2,213.8**	**2,319.3**
Central Chernozem	126.8	412.0	558.8	620.4	952.7	1,011.6
Voronezh	24.3	127.7	155.8	14.4	222.5	252.4
Kursk	32.1	110.1	165.0	245.4	272.7	240.0
Orel	35.5	85.3	122.7	193.3	221.6	267.9
Tambov	34.9	88.9	115.3	167.3	235.9	251.3
Volga	117.9	556.9	738.3	951.8	1,261.1	1,307.7
Astrakhan	4.2	29.0	53.6	71.9	77.3	90.8
Saratov	14.4	69.4	107.3	143.9	176.1	143.7
Samara	6.8	31.6	34.6	51.4	129.6	111.0
Penza	24.0	77.9	91.1	123.8	153.3	147.9
Simbirsk	15.6	92.5	133.5	137.8	166.1	171.5
Kazan	15.0	89.4	108.9	145.6	199.5	219.2
Viatka	31.8	143.6	174.1	220.2	268.4	310.7
Ufa	6.1	23.5	35.2	57.2	90.8	112.9
IV. Eastern Agricultural	**20.9**	**119.6**	**161.3**	**231.1**	**291.5**	**328.1**
Ural	20.9	119.6	161.3	231.1	291.5	328.1
Perm	13.8	80.8	121.0	192.0	228.9	252.4
Orenburg	7.1	38.8	40.3	39.1	62.6	75.7
Total	**1,233.4**	**3,570.7**	**4,730.4**	**6,211.4**	**7,775.6**	**8,771.6**

Source: Adapted from L. E. Mints, *Otkhod krest'ianskogo naseleniia na zarabotki v SSSR* (Moscow, 1925), pp. 16–18.

Table 1.3. Peasant Labor Migration as a Proportion of Village Population, 1861–1910

Regions and Provinces	Proportion of Issued Passports to Local Peasant Population					
	1861–70	1871–80	1881–90	1891–1900	1902	1906–10
I. Nonagricultural/Industrial						
North and Northwest						
Arkhangel	5.9	13.0	11.3	12.6	14.7	13.8
Vologda	1.8	6.1	6.0	8.2	10.4	10.7
Olonets	3.2	9.1	9.6	12.4	13.4	13.2
St. Petersburg	8.6	17.9	21.8	28.9	27.6	23.0
Novgorod	4.5	11.6	10.5	13.1	13.4	14.2
Pskov	2.0	3.3	3.6	6.2	8.7	10.4
Smolensk	6.3	11.2	10.3	11.2	12.6	13.0
Tver	8.0	14.6	14.4	16.7	22.6	23.0
Central Industrial Region						
Iaroslavl	9.1	17.0	16.4	18.9	24.1	23.1
Moscow	10.0	18.0	20.4	29.9	33.9	34.2
Vladimir	4.8	16.0	16.7	19.1	26.1	24.2
Kostroma	3.9	12.3	13.8	13.1	7.6	20.0
Kaluga	8.8	17.2	18.3	20.5	25.8	25.4
Nizhnii Novgorod	3.1	8.8	9.6	11.0	13.1	12.0
Tula	4.2	8.8	9.9	14.3	20.1	20.0
Riazan	5.4	12.7	14.3	17.5	22.7	20.5
Belorussia						
Vitebsk	3.5	5.0	6.0	8.3	10.8	10.9
Minsk	1.1	2.8	4.6	4.9	10.0	4.1
Mogilev	1.6	4.5	5.0	6.0	6.5	9.1
II. Southern Agricultural						
Ukraine						
Poltava	1.4	4.2	5.9	7.0	8.2	6.3
Kharkov	1.2	3.6	5.9	7.2	9.9	9.2
Chernigov	1.4	4.2	5.7	6.9	8.3	8.0
Kiev	0.6	2.5	6.1	8.5	7.2	7.8
Volynia	0.6	2.0	3.2	3.7	0.5	3.2
Podolia	0.4	1.7	3.6	4.2	3.9	4.1
Kherson	1.2	3.3	4.4	4.8	4.8	5.0
Ekaterinoslav	1.2	2.4	3.7	3.9	6.3	3.2
Taurida	1.4	4.2	4.8	4.9	3.8	5.0
North Caucasus						
Don Oblast	0.1	0.5	1.1	2.3	3.7	4.0
III. Central Agricultural						
Central Chernozem						
Voronezh	1.3	5.7	6.1	7.4	8.5	8.0
Kursk	1.8	5.3	7.0	9.2	11.9	10.0
Orel	2.6	5.3	6.7	9.2	11.6	12.2
Tambov	1.9	4.2	4.7	5.9	8.8	8.2
Volga						
Astrakhan	1.9	10.8	15.9	17.6	8.3	9.0
Saratov	0.9	3.8	5.2	6.1	7.7	6.0
Samara	0.4	1.6	1.5	1.9	4.6	3.4
Penza	2.1	6.1	6.2	7.6	10.6	10.0
Simbirsk	1.4	7.5	9.3	8.6	10.8	10.0
Kazan	1.0	5.3	5.6	6.7	9.2	9.2
Viatka	1.5	5.8	6.1	6.9	8.5	8.8
Ufa	0.5	1.7	3.2	3.0	3.9	4.3
IV. Eastern Agricultural						
Ural						
Perm	0.6	3.2	4.3	6.1	7.5	7.0
Orenburg	1.2	5.6	4.9	4.1	3.9	4.3

Source: Adapted from L. E. Mints, *Otkhod krest'ianskogo naseleniia na zarabotki v SSSR* (Moscow, 1925), pp. 22–24.

an average of 10 to 13 passports per hundred. To this second group also belong two far northern provinces, Arkhangel and Olonets.

A third group of provinces, still with marked levels of peasant *otkhod*—7 to 10 passports per hundred souls, or 14–20 percent of the adult male population— consisted of Novgorod and Vologda in the north, Orlov, Kursk and Voronezh to the south, Penza and Simbirsk to the east of the central region. The remaining provinces of European Russia had a significantly lower proportion of issued passports: 3 or less per hundred souls in Volynia, Bessarabia, Taurida, the Don Region, Samara, Ufa, and Orenburg.

While it is difficult to determine with precision the total number of peasant labor migrants, most estimates for the 1890s (based on issued passports) agree on a figure near 2 million for the nine provinces in the Central Industrial Region, more than 6 million for the whole of European Russia.[20] This corresponded in the Central Industrial Region to more than 14 percent of the total rural population: more than a third of all adult peasant males, at least one member of every peasant household, were involved in some form of work that took them away from their villages for extended periods each year.[21]

The rate of growth in peasant migration for outside earnings was reflected in data from several provinces. In Iaroslavl Province, in 1802, there were 65,000 peasant passports issued, representing 9 percent of the peasant population. During the early 1870s, the proportion had risen to 14 percent. By 1901, there were 201,000 passports issued, or 20–21 percent of the registered village population. These figures represent a growth of over 300 percent in absolute numbers over the course of a century, while the rate of migration grew twice as fast as the general population.[22] In Kostroma, the number of issued passports more than doubled between 1853 and 1900 (from 96,834 to 209,203).[23] In Smolensk Province, the rate of *otkhod* "constantly and significantly grew" in the years 1875–1895, so that by the end of the century, in six key districts of Smolensk Province, 42.5 percent of all adult peasant males were involved in side-work.[24]

Passport data likewise reflected a distinct sexual division of labor in the Russian countryside. While men's *otkhod* had more or less stabilized by the 1890s, women's *otkhod* showed a marked increase near the end of the century —reflecting new restrictions on child labor, greater mechanization (which enabled women to replace men in what had been heavy manual labor), and a marked shift in village social structure. Despite such increases, males outnumbered females by three to one in Iaroslavl Province (172,864 to 62,871), five to one in Smolensk Province in 1895 (140,000 to 26,000). Moreover, 30.7 percent of the women's passports in Iaroslavl Province were issued for "noneconomic" reasons: the largest portion, 28.6 percent, enabled wives to visit their

The Roots of Ambivalence   25

An artel of peasant migrant laborers on the road to nonagricultural side work. From John Foster Fraser, *Russia of Today* (London, 1915), following p. 104.

husbands. The remainder (2.1 percent) were for religious pilgrimages. As a result, *otkhod* remained throughout the two generations preceding 1905 a predominantly male phenomenon: as late as 1897, males outnumbered females in the hired labor category by almost six to one.[25]

The drainage of young peasant males from the countryside was reflected in the census figures for 1897 (table 1.4). The gender deficit was even more apparent in the provinces with the highest proportions of hired laborers and servants, the Central Industrial and Baltic regions. The statistics in table 1.5 vividly illustrate the developing trend. The data reflect the general pattern of migration in the Central Industrial Region throughout the nineteenth century: husbands and sons migrated for earnings while wives, elders, and children occupied the village allotment and engaged in any other forms of economic activity available in their vicinity. As one contemporary summed it up: "The Russian worker is born and raised on the peasant homestead in the village. The adolescent or adult worker leaves for the town, to the factory—for earnings. In old age, if the difficult conditions of work and life in the town don't kill him, he returns to his native village, to his home."[26] For Kostroma, the cycle of the male peasant-worker's life typically took this form: "Usually children, aged 11 to 14 years, are sent away for an apprenticeship . . . , in 3 to 6 years made skilled craftsmen, then return home, start a family, which manages the rural economy, while they themselves lead a migrating life *[brodiachnaia*

Table 1.4. Women per 1,000 Men in European Russia, 1897

	Age	
	20–29	30–39
In rural areas	1,187	1.074
In towns	654	868
Total	1,065	1,046

Source: Prokopovich, "Krest'ianstvo i poreformennaia fabrika," p. 270.

Table 1.5. The Rural-Urban Gender Disparity, 1897

	Men Aged 20–29 (in percent)	Women Per 1,000 Men
European Russia		
Town population	22.3	653
Rural population	14.9	1,187
Rural, by province		
Moscow	14.3	1,395
Riazan	14.0	1,497
Tula	14.0	1,524
Kaluga	13.8	1,751
Kostroma	13.8	1,465
Vladimir	13.7	1,495
Iaroslavl	13.3	1,760
Tver	13.2	1,507

Source: Prokopovich, "Krest'ianstvo i poreformennia fabrika," p. 271.

zhizn] until old age."[27] In peasant household inventories preserved in the 1880s from northwest Kostroma Province, for four villages with migration rates varying from 38–78 percent of the male adult population, 66 percent of all adult males worked on the side and nearly two-thirds (64 percent) of all households had no adult males present for most of the year.[28]

Besides profound contrasts in gender, age was another important factor reflected in patterns of peasant labor migration for side-earnings. Among male *otkhodniki* in Iaroslavl, half of the children aged twelve and one-half to thirteen were in apprenticeships away from the village; 70 percent of the adolescents (aged fourteen to seventeen) and 73 percent of all males eighteen to twenty were in side-work. In the highest migration districts—Uglich and Rybinsk—56 percent of all males eighteen to sixty were in *otkhod*. Among men, two-thirds of all *otkhodniki* were married, as compared to three-fourths of all women.

Peasant agriculture in the Central Industrial Region normally fell to the lot of those who remained—married women, elderly family members, or outsiders hired in to replace absent family members. The demographic, statistical, and qualitative evidence is all united on this point. In Pokrov District, Vladimir

Province, for instance: "Nonvillage side-earnings represent for us the main source for the family's well-being, since here the land is worked by just women and elders."[29]

The impact of peasant labor migration on agriculture in the Central Industrial Region was enormous. A study conducted at the turn of the century in five districts of Vladimir Province—household inventories of 100,000 peasant households with more than one-half million peasants—noted the following patterns throughout the Central Industrial Region: peasant-workers of all types

> return home only to rest, and have only the vaguest understanding of the land, which is worked by women, to whom the statistics on all questions about the peasant agricultural economy refer. Only 16.2 percent of men of working age are employed in agriculture alone, and more than half of all [male] workers have broken from the land. And among those 16 percent who are employed only in agriculture, a full half are aged 51–60—that is, peasants who have been rejected from industrial activity. The best plowmen of the village are directed to the town and the factory. Fully ¾'s of the peasant labor-migrants are in the prime of strength and health, at ages less than 40. From age 41 there begins a rapid decline in the proportion of out-migration, and for those older than 56 we meet among workers on the side only 1 in 100 people. Between [the ages of] 40–45, the peasant migrant laborer is worn out and returns to the village in order to pick at the exhausted, loamy soil with his weak arms.[30]

It was not without significance that peasant labor-migrants permanently returned to settle in their native villages precisely at the average age of thirty-five to forty, namely, the time when in traditional households peasant males were inheriting the mantle of patriarchal authority in the village.[31]

Otkhodnichestvo and Peasant Family Structure

The sheer magnitude of the migration phenomenon not only reflected a profound transformation of the traditional village world, but eventually did itself become a major agent of change in the Russian countryside. D. N. Zhbankov, a statistician and *zemstvo* physician commenting on the impact of migration throughout the Central Industrial Region, concluded that the growing networks of peasant-workers traveling to and from the village exerted a "powerful influence on the entire life of the rural population, on its economic and social conditions, family relations, development, habits, customs, and finally, on health—both for the migrants and for that part of the population which is left at home."[32] The growth and persistence of a large number of peasant households based simultaneously in the farm and nonfarm economies generated a "third" culture—neither fully traditional, nor fully urbanized—to a large degree unparalleled in other European peasant societies, where the absence of mutually reinforcing legal and cultural bonds to the land often facilitated a more rapid and complete division of labor into peasants and proletarians.

The tensions created by this growing dichotomy between village and work place intersected at three key junctures, each of which underscored the growing insecurity of dependent family members who remained in the village: (1) old versus young, as the growth of wage labor threatened to undermine the foundations of the traditional patriarchal economy; (2) male versus female, since labor migration in the Central Industrial Region was primarily a male phenomenon, with males outnumbering females by almost six to one in hired labor as late as 1897; and (3) community versus household, since growing strains on smaller and weakened peasant households in the Central Industrial Region led families to rely increasingly on the village commune for redistributing the products of wage labor back to the village.

The Threat to Communal Security

Fields have remained unsown, taverns have sprung up everywhere, idle beggars living without passports have become a common sight.[33]

Essential as it was for popular well-being and industrial development, peasant labor migration posed an enormous challenge to Russian institutions at all levels: the state, the community, and the migrant's household. For the state, a more mobile population hindered efforts at monitoring, controlling, and taxing the rural population, upon whom the overwhelming burden of fiscal solvency fell. As a district tax inspector from Moscow Province complained in the 1890s: "Work in factories and shops, significantly raising the tax-paying ability of the population, in actuality exerts an unfavorable influence on tax receipts.... The earnings received, with rare exceptions, are left in the taverns and factory stores; only a negligible part of those earnings reach home, which scarcely suffice for keeping a family."[34] For state tax authorities, the primary task lay in expropriating the product of peasant labor, a task that became extremely complicated when the bulk of peasant income was derived from cash wages earned outside the village. Russia's outmoded tax system therefore placed an enormous, and unpredicted, burden on the local village administration and the police. Theirs was the unenviable task of keeping track of labor-migrants and ensuring that they fulfilled their fiscal responsibilities.

However, the difficulty of keeping track of *otkhodniki* was not merely a matter for state concern. Migration posed a direct threat to whole communities in two ways. First, rising out-migration fundamentally altered the internal dynamics of the patriarchal peasant household, challenging the traditional capacity of elders and family chiefs to reallocate the labor products of junior family members. Second, unrestricted whole-family departures increased the proportion of fixed state dues for the remaining households, threatening to plunge villagers into greater hardship.

THE THREAT TO PATRIARCHALISM

As the primary foundation of family subsistence in the Central Industrial Region gradually shifted from local and household-based production to non-local wage labor, the hierarchical structure of the traditional peasant family was fundamentally undermined. This report from Vladimir Province in 1899 vividly illustrates the intergenerational tensions that developed in peasant households of high-migration villages:

> With the change in the form of obtaining a means for living, family relations are also changing in the countryside. When the whole family works together, earnings are likewise made together. When only individual members of the household begin to acquire a means independently, each on his own, then naturally there appears the desire to retain hold of that which has been earned for oneself personally and only for one's own [immediate] family. Hence, there are constant complaints on the part of elders about [household] divisions, about the fact that the young forget the home. When the junior members of the family become the main breadwinners in the peasant household, their role in the family also changes. Elders have already ceased to enjoy the absolute authority they wielded in earlier times. "When the young grow up," laments one correspondent, "they don't obey their elders [any more], but only behave defiantly."[35]

Families remaining at home expressed an uneasy confidence in those household members who left the village for earnings: particularly the youth—"who become accustomed to the easy, wild life" away from the village—were, it was feared, all too ready to abandon their responsibilities at home.[36] *Otkhodnichestvo* had strained the patriarchal hierarchy of the traditional village economy.

As villagers in Pokrov District, Vladimir Province, complained: "Outside labor tears the people away from agriculture; . . . young people working in the factories have completely lost touch with agriculture and they don't even know how to handle a plow or a scythe."[37] Several observers noted the growing preference among village youths to break permanently with the village.[38] In Melenki District, Vladimir Province, "As a consequence of insufficient land, soil exhaustion, and the impossibility of expanding purchased landholding due to the pressure of nearby factories, the villages have been ruined. Two-thirds to three-fourths of the youths leave for the factories, where they live fairly well, while the majority of those who remain in the village are old folks who grew up under serfdom."[39]

The departure of younger peasants for outside work reversed the traditional hierarchy and precipitated deep tensions within the peasant household. The direct effects of *otkhodnichestvo* and wage labor on the structure of family life were vividly illustrated in this contemporary report:

> Several members of the [peasant] family—sons, brothers, nephews—who have returned from military service or work outside the village, where they have been on several occasions, having become habituated to a more independent life, with easier work, are beginning to feel burdened by heavy peasant labor and their subordinate status as younger members of the family, and [therefore] work poorly, obey poorly, and are dissatisfied with everything. Finally, they declare directly that they do not want to live at home anymore, and will accordingly leave for "the side" and not return, if only they are given their share.[40]

The tensions were not only economic, but also disclosed a profound dissatisfaction with peasant ways, a village *kulturkrise* of potentially shattering proportions.

Migration and Moral Corruption

> По своей деревне стыдно, а по чужой не видно
>
> *[What's shameful in your own village won't be seen if it's done somewhere else.]*
>
> PEASANT SAYING IN KALUGA PROVINCE, 1890s[41]

Few questions were so clearcut in peasant popular attitudes as the general agreement that life outside the village corrupted peasants. *Otkhodniki* were, it was generally agreed, "spoiled" in two very Russian meanings of the term.

The Roots of Ambivalence 31

First, they were "spoiled" in the sense of *izbalovannyi*: they were enticed by delusions of imminent prosperity, by the wealth of consumers' goods, by the comparatively easy life of nonvillage labor, by the absence of the guiding hand of strict patriarchal authority in their lives. An excellent illustration of this pervasive attitude was described by the *zemstvo* correspondent Nedokhodovskii from Il'inskaia *volost*, in Kaluga Province, written in 1896: "The earnings of dyers, metal workers, caretakers, and others are decent enough, but very little ends up at home. Much is spent on fancy dress: 'topcoats,' jackets, trousers, waistcoats, high boots with galoshes, and so on, and for women—[town-style] dresses, cosmetics.... In general, there is among factory workers an extreme disgust toward the village: only children are kept down by women between the factory and the village." Another report from a village priest in 1896 repeated the general anxiety: "The people of our village have grown lazy: they are careless toward agriculture and yearn for Moscow, where they have grown accustomed to living freely and showing-off.... They have good jobs, but ... the people spend a lot on wine, on good appearances, on luxurious clothing and footwear..., as a consequence of which little money makes its way home."[42]

Young migrant workers were thought particularly vulnerable to the seductions of life away from the village. In 1888, a peasant correspondent in Podol'sk District, Moscow Province, wrote disparagingly:

> Many of these so-called [peasant-workers] ... have become attracted to the excessive use of strong drinks. This is especially [true] of the young generation, which in former times was ashamed of [such behavior], but now has come to be proud of it. Let's take for example the holidays, when the youth come home. No longer evident are those innocent and decent village amusements of an earlier generation, popular songs and dances of a proper kind. Although they still exist, they already do not have the same appearance [as before]. The songs that are sung are more indecent. In round dances it is evident that a large number of the village lads are drunk, affected and with cigarettes in their teeth. Today's youth stroll along the streets, brazen in their drunken state, with harmonicas and indecent songs, ashamed neither [in front of members of the opposite] sex nor [their] elders. Obedience to parents and elders has almost completely fallen away. Drunkenness, luxurious attire, and willfulness are everywhere taking root deeper and deeper.[43]

It was popularly believed that the "free atmosphere, the easy, high-paying work" in the town or factory enticed all *otkhodniki*, but especially the youth, and made it all too easy for them to neglect their responsibilities to religion and family.[44]

For those dependents who remained in the village, the alleged moral degeneration of young peasant-workers was directly reflected in their carelessness with money. *Otkhodniki* were said to "spend a lot on clothes and in general live wastefully." It was generally believed that their "side-earnings would suffice to make every peasant rich, if [they were spent] on a peasant's budget. . . . Every *otkhodnik* wastes 6 rubles a month just on food,—at home this money would feed a whole family." "They drink tea with wheat bread twice a day, while for the *muzhik*"—who must save his money—"lentil cake is better than wheat." *Otkhodniki* "waste a lot on clothes, watches, accordions, and other 'appurtenances of the toilet.'"⁴⁵

While most young peasants were generally thought to be "spoiled" in this first sense, there were only a few in every village who were generally believed to suffer from a far more insidious form of moral decadence: a condition usually described by the Russian word *isporchennyi*, meaning corrupted, immoral. Charges of spiritual laxness, decadence, and immorality were inseparably linked in popular perceptions of peasant labor-migrants. A village priest from Iur'ev-Pol'skii District, Vladimir Province, complained at the end of the 1890s:

> Migration to the factory exerts a corrupting influence on the workers and their families. A departing youth, lacking any of the supervision of family elders and having for himself a steady flow of money and free time, does not concern himself with the household, gets into the habit of undesirable vices, debauchery, a loss of morality, indifference to religion and to the rites of the Church. On Good Friday, a worker thinks nothing about duty until [he is] disgracefully drunk, gorging himself with sausage, playing the accordion, dancing and singing various songs. It's a fact! Of course, this exists in a minority [of cases], but it exists. . . . For several years they do not go to confession and do not partake of the blessed Sacraments; nineteen, twenty, twenty-two-year-olds refuse to get married, but instead prefer to live together conjugally outside the law.⁴⁶

Labor-migrants were identified as potentially more corrupted members of the community in every way: they were considered to be more likely to neglect religious duty; they showed a greater propensity toward celebration and rabble-rousing, and were thought to be wastrels of vitally needed family resources; they were considered to be more sexually profligate.

The profoundly distinct moral universe of peasant-workers was revealed in a written confession that was mailed to her village priest by one peasant woman who lived and worked in Moscow city during the mid-nineteenth century. The confession survived because it had been interdicted by the Moscow police. For the modern reader, her litany of sins is a lesson in the profound distance that separates our moral universe from the world of the nineteenth-century Russian peasant. But even for contemporaries, the list was just one example of the decadent moral universe of a corrupted peasant-worker. Her list of sins included, among other things, an admission of having breast-fed another woman's child as well as a kitten; playing kissing games with men and kissing men at *khorovody* (round dances); seducing a priest and surreptitiously kissing a priest; wearing men's clothes; swinging on a swing; telling fortunes; despairing and asking God for death; gazing at the sacred image while thinking lascivious thoughts; smearing herself with badger fat, probably with incantations in a popular ritual for inducing abortion.[47]

Regardless of one's perspective or social position, the "Russian peasant *away from the village*, . . . the peasant decontextualized, severed from his native cultural milieu"[48] was a potential threat to all: in various ways, the entire system in Old Regime Russia worked to uphold the imperatives of rooting the peasant-migrant to his native village and regulating the behavior of peasants who worked away from their families and communities.

In everyday life, concerns about economy were inextricably linked with issues of moral supervision. Time and again, the same sad story was heard: money that should have been sent back to the village was being wasted on debauchery, vodka, gambling, and other seductions.

> The departure of workmen has increased [in our village]. . . . Their earnings in Moscow this year were generally good, and if they had been used exclusively for the improvement of village agriculture, then it would now be in a prosperous position. In actuality, almost all of the earnings remain in Moscow, at the saloons for the upkeep of our national tavern industry. Moreover, having grown accustomed to the free and easy life and the cheerful ways of passing the time in the city's hangouts, the workman begins to look with disdain on the village; as a result, the appearance in the village of boarded-up homes and neglected fields.[49]

The threat of abandonment was great, the fate of families left in the village particularly precarious. A correspondent from the village of Krivtsino, Iur'ev District, Vladimir Province, reported this somber account: "With the abandonment of the farm and with the sale of the farming implements comes the decline [of the household], and those who remain in the village, who often sit without even a piece of bread, receive no assistance from those living on the side."[50] Villagers offered a number of explanations for this abandonment, but almost all of these came down to the temptations associated with industrial and urban life and the corruption of traditional values, the decadence and wastefulness it engendered.

Regardless whether the growing independence of *otkhodniki* posed any real threat to the livelihood of family members in the village, the *perception* of vulnerability to those departing for side-earnings was sufficient to dictate a policy of strict control over migrants. Such regulation was regarded as both a moral and an economic imperative. Family members who lived in the village, dependent on the steady flow of cash from peasant-worker earnings, were threatened by a pervasive sense of insecurity. The overriding concern was to avoid the utter hopelessness of scenes like this one, from a report on a village in Klin District, Moscow Province, in the 1880s:

> The majority of men and adolescents live in Moscow at the factories. At home are found only women and elders and therefore the land is worked in such a way that agriculture is in a most lamentable condition: in every home there is one poor cow and two chickens, one horse for every two households. Cottages stand without farmyards (not to mention gardens and kitchen gardens), the roofs are thatched. Peasants living in Moscow send scarcely half of the taxes, and the family struggles with need year-round, living half-starved. And those peasants who remain in the village, seeing around themselves decline in everything, cool toward agriculture and spend time in the taverns, which have grown to at least two in almost every village.[51]

There was a profound popular ambivalence toward migration for outside earnings: this "necessary evil" clearly provoked a deep-seated crisis among the elder generations of dependent family members who remained at home.

Household Divisions and the Declining Resilience of Peasant Households

The direct evidence of a growing cultural crisis was the marked proliferation in the rate of peasant household divisions *(semeinye razdely)* in the decades immediately following the abolition of serfdom. A Russian governmental report concluded in the 1870s that "family divisions have increased with each year [since the abolition of serfdom] and it has reached the point that not only two brothers, but even a father and son break off into separate households."[52] According to data provided by the Russian Ministry of Internal Affairs, during the years 1861–1882, there was an average of 116,229 peasant household divisions annually. In the years 1874–1884, the average number of annual divisions had jumped to 140,355, so that by 1884, 52.4 percent of all peasant households in thirty-seven provinces of European Russia had only one or no adult male worker in the family.⁵³ The abolition of serfdom had removed many of the mechanisms that had sustained artificially large households in most areas. As N. K. Brzheskii observed, "There is no doubt that the restraining influence of serfdom has been considerably undermined by the peasant's need for economic independence, a fact manifested with particular force in the first years after the [1861] reform. According to the testimony of peasants, they all or almost all have divided, and the village assembly did not impede the divisions. An immediate consequence of the abolition of serfdom was the break-up of large families into smaller ones, composed of persons connected by intimate blood ties."⁵⁴ The opinion of contemporary experts was solidly supported by impressionistic evidence of peasants themselves. A village correspondent from Iaroslavl lamented in the 1890s: "Twenty to thirty years ago, there weren't such efforts to divide."⁵⁵ Also, from a village in Kovrov District, Vladimir Province: "Here, nearly 30 percent of burned-down houses are not rebuilt. After a family division, all those who detach from the household without exception go to the factory."⁵⁶

Several local studies documented the growing trend. A survey conducted in Moscow Province, for instance, revealed that the number of peasant households had grown by more than 40 percent between 1857 and 1877, while the population had expanded by only 8 percent. Although there was heated contemporary debate over whether the rise reflected or caused the general rural decline, all sides were agreed that this growth correlated to an increase in household divisions and the decline of the traditional strength of peasant household chiefs.⁵⁷

In early 1883, Andrei Isaev, a well-known Populist lecturer in political economy at St. Petersburg University, conducted an invaluable survey of 112 cases of family division in a village in Iaroslavl Province. The majority—fifty-seven families (50.9 percent)—consisted of the division between brothers, probably representing the traditional twenty-year cycle of household divisions following the deaths of elders who had ascended to their positions around the time of the Great Reform. The crisis in traditional peasant culture was, however, reflected in the extremely large rate of previously unprecedented divisions of sons from fathers—occurring in 42 cases (37.5 percent).⁵⁸

The accelerated splintering of large, multiple-family households after 1861 was reflected in the 1897 census. A regional analysis of household size, reproduced in table 1.6, shows the relative impact of household divisions on peasant families in the Central Industrial Region. On the whole, peasant households

Table 1.6. Peasant Household Size in European Russia, 1897

Zone/Region	Distribution of Peasant Households (based on proportion to total in European Russia)	Average Number of Inhabitants per Household
Nonagricultural Zone	18.94	6.2
Moscow	5.09	6.04
Northwest	5.66	6.9
Upper Volga	8.19	5.8
Middle Agricultural Zone	35.03	6.7
Oka River	6.37	6.8
Central Agricultural	11.16	6.9
Middle Volga	7.90	6.3
Left-Bank Ukraine	9.60	6.9
Western Zone	16.48	9.5
Baltic	0.51	13.5
Belorussia-Litov	6.90	9.5
Right-Bank Ukraine	9.07	7.7
Steppe Zone	18.48	7.8
South Steppe	10.69	8.8
Southeast Steppe	7.79	9.1
North and Northeast Zone	11.07	6.1
Northeast	8.17	6.0
North	2.90	6.3

Source: P. G. Ryndziunskii, *Krest'iane i gorod v kapitalistecheskoi Rossii vtoroi poloviny XIX veka* (Moscow, 1983), pp. 22–23. Based on the 1897 census.

had an average of 1–2 fewer member-workers than households in any other region of European Russia, excluding the north and northeast. The earlier picture of the elder-patriarch managing a multiple-family unit gave way to the simple family head as chief in his own household of five or six members.[59] As an observer in Shuia District, Vladimir Province, remarked: "Now, since family divisions have become so common, the large [peasant] household has become very rare."[60]

While contemporaries debated the impact of this proliferation in household divisions,[61] the growing rate was unquestionably a sign of the intergenerational conflict which *otkhodnichestvo* and wage labor had exacerbated. Disputing the "personal differences" frequently cited by peasants when asked to explain divisions, several contemporary observers detected the problem in the breakdown of the traditional hierarchy of the patriarchal family:

> [Family divisions] are not only due to the arbitrariness of the elder members of the family, which in earlier times was far worse, not only to their drunkenness and dissipation, and not only do women's quarrels provoke them. All this merely serves as a pretext for the division. The main reason for the majority of family di-

visions among young peasant *domokhoziaeva* appears to be the aspiration to structure their lives independently and self-sufficiently from others. Furthermore this is a product of the ever-more-widespread awareness among peasant youth that they have personal rights equal to those of other family members, and of their confidence in their own capabilities.[62]

V. Dadonov, a Populist analyst who lamented the disintegration of peasant culture he saw in the villages outside the textile town of Ivanovo-Voznesensk, offered a rare glimpse into the changing popular culture associated with the peasant youth of high-migration areas. Telltale signs of a "generation gap" that threatened the old patriarchal system were visible. This representative experience occurred in the mid- to late-1890s:

> Meeting with peasant-workers, I nearly always led up to a conversation about the factory and the peasant. I was interested in learning how they resolve this question—so much discussed in our literature—how they themselves had become interested [in factory work]. Nearly always the answer received was unfavorable to the peasant way of life. On the question addressed to young lads and girls on which is better, devoting oneself to the farm or working in the factory, which is easier and more pleasant—I always received one answer: to work in the factory is both easier and more pleasant than plowing, sowing, cutting, and mowing.
> —Well, and when you yourself become the household chief, will you carry on the management [of the village allotment]? I posed this question to several young lads, and always received the same response:
> —No, I will stay at the factory, and the land will be given back [to the commune].[63]

Dadonov also observed considerable peer pressure among village youth favoring migration: "All the young and the majority of household chiefs one finds at the factory. For an adolescent *[molodoi]* boy or girl to remain home is considered shameful and those working at the factory regard such deviants *[iskliucheniia]* with a certain degree of contempt."[64] Such attitudes were found to predominate in most high-migration districts by the late 1880s and 1890s.[65]

The attractiveness of urban culture to village youth, and the tensions it created, was particularly well documented by D. N. Zhbankov in his observations of high-migration districts in northwest Kostroma Province: "Once a boy has been trained in *Piter,* he will without fail work on the side: the great ease and profitability of a trade in the capital, the total unfamiliarity with agricultural work among all of the young *pitershchiki,* all the fascinations of life in the capital, and, finally, habit and the example of departing comrades—all this compels every inhabitant of Chukloma and Soligalich to rise with the spring tide and ride the crest of the huge wave moving hence toward St. Petersburg, Moscow, and other centers."[66] This was indeed a marked contrast to first-generation *otkhodniki*, who often had to be forced by their parents to leave the village for earnings to help supplement the family income.[67]

For Kanatchikov, it was his father's frequent beatings of him, his mother, and his family that made him rejoice in his departure from the village. In his first days as a young apprentice in Moscow, he recalled his initial longing for the comparative security of his native village: "But another, stronger feeling—the consciousness of my independence, my desire to mix with [new] people, to become independent and proud, to live according to my own personal wishes and not on the caprice and will of my father—gave me courage and determination."[68]

The Threat of Whole-Family Departures

Weakened by divisions and by increasing, long-term departures of adult male workers for outside earnings, peasant households in the Central Industrial Region became more dependent than ever on the village commune to ensure family security: only the village commune could harness the resources necessary to redistribute peasant-workers' wage earnings from the work place back to the village.

A separate cause for concern for the community-at-large was the increasing trend toward whole-family resettlement. Since fiscal obligations were imposed collectively on whole communities, not individuals or households, each departure from the community threatened to raise the already excessive obligations of the households that remained. This report from Moscow Province in 1882 delineated the growing trend:

> Such *Riazan'tsy*, who—in their own words—have come "for earnings," are met rather more frequently in the factories of Moscow District than they were in former times. The workers themselves explain that this influx of workers from Smolensk and Kaluga Provinces to Moscow factories [is due to] the poor quality of land in those provinces and the insufficient size of allotments—as a result of which, had they remained home, they would not have had the means for the payment of taxes. Overwhelmed by concerns about their "daily bread," they emigrate with their entire families and settle somewhere near a factory. Meanwhile, the land—in the best cases—is worked by some members of the family who have remained home. And not infrequently it is hired out for a negligible price or simply given back to the village commune. On the whole, the desire to relinquish

the land completely is found rather frequently among these workers, since the land is giving them no profits whatsoever and only augments the items of expense in their extremely modest budgets, keeping them completely under its burden.[69]

Particularly in the 1870s and 1880s, the burden of the land and the enticements of urban life were sufficient to encourage widespread whole-family resettlement. As tax reforms in the mid-1880s reduced land burdens—especially in the Central Industrial Region, where annual fiscal obligations were reduced by at least 20–30 percent per household (see the appendix below)—and the cost of urban living skyrocketed, it became virtually impossible to live either wholly off the land or entirely from outside earnings. Growing restrictions on child labor in industry (from the 1880s) further diminished the productive capacity of working-class households.[70]

While the rate of growth of whole-family departures therefore declined by the 1890s, whole-family migration nonetheless showed a strong and steady increase. In Tver Province, for instance, the number of issued family passports increased from 16,808 families in 1893 to 18,046 families in 1896.[71] This growth in peasant whole-family departures was directly associated with abandonment of village ties. For example, of the 47,376 peasant families with family passports in Moscow Province during the late 1890s, 35,177 had no cottage in the village whatsoever: this represented 14.3 percent or one in seven of all peasant households in the province.[72] Communes were therefore faced with the considerable challenge of extracting dues from whole families absent from the village.

II

IN DEFENSE OF PEASANT PATRIARCHALISM
Institutional Responses to Peasant Labor Migration

Just as industrialization was grafted onto preestablished societal and political structures, so the feudal elements reconciled their rationalized bureaucratic and economic behavior with their pre-existent social and cultural praxis and mind-set. In other words, the old elites excelled at selectively ingesting, adapting, and assimilating new ideas and practices without seriously endangering their traditional status, temperament, and outlook.

—ARNO MAYER, *THE PERSISTENCE OF THE OLD REGIME*

IN SPITE OF WIDESPREAD EVIDENCE of considerable strains in Russian village life in the Central Industrial Region during the last three generations of the Old Regime, the Russian peasant commune proved itself to be quite resilient as an institutionalized scheme for the collective defense of peasant interests and the collective fulfillment of peasant obligations in the rapidly expanding commodity economy. In the sociocultural relations of the village, evolving concepts of community accommodated the migration phenomenon rather than being overwhelmed by it. From an anthropologist's point of view, this was no mean feat: peasant collective definitions of community were quickly adapted from a traditional sensibility of shared space—of community life founded on a proximity between neighbors—to a new identity that incorporated a more dynamic notion of *svoi* and *chuzhoi*—of insider-versus-outsider relations that had little to do with spatial criteria. Village communities coped with skyrocketing rates of migration for side earnings by profoundly redefining local conceptions of community and identity.

The transition was neither direct nor universal: hardship was great, family and community relations were strained to their utmost. Yet there is a persuasive body of evidence suggesting that the village community remained cohesive, central in the hearts and minds of a large number of *otkhodniki* and villagers alike. In the early years after the abolition of serfdom, when land obligations in the Central Industrial and northern regions were so excessively out of proportion with land values, retaining ties with the village was indeed an enormous burden, and a lot of community arm-twisting was applied against those who threatened to abandon their obligations. Later, as the reforms of the 1880s brought land obligations more closely in line with their real productive values, and as the restrictions on child labor plus the increase in the costs of urban living made whole-family resettlement more difficult, the coercive element became a less significant factor in village relations. The coercive formulas were, of course, to reappear, with the tsarist bureaucratic initiative to bypass the peasant commune in order to wean peasants of their "irrational faith" in "kulak-dominated" community defense schemes in the Stolypin reforms introduced in 1906.[1]

The transition from serfdom in Russia was a bureaucratic nightmare. While previously the day-to-day administrative rule of the state was greatly assisted by an apparatus that relied in large part on the manorial system, the abolition of serfdom signaled a moving away from this traditional arrangement.[2] From the very beginning, the 22 million new citizens—44.5 percent of the general population—were not absorbed into the existing civil system, but rather were classified (with former state and appanage peasants) into an independent estate or *soslovie* with its own distinct set of laws and procedures. The Emancipation statute's disproportionate reliance on *krest'ianskoe samoupravlenie*—peasant self-government through the rural commune—was essentially an admission by the tsarist autocracy of its inability to govern in the countryside. The period 1861–1881, in particular, marked an interregnum of imperial state power in the rural areas. As always, autocratic authority was sacrosanct, but only on an ad hoc basis; without undertaking extraordinary measures, the state could not make its unmitigated will felt in the normal, day-to-day life of the majority of peasants.[3] The main domestic autocratic initiative throughout the period 1861 to 1905 lay in bridling this hydra of peasant autonomy.[4]

Essentially, the reliance on a system that preserved many of the vestiges of serfdom was unsatisfactory to all sides, leading to conflicts and reversals in policy between different branches of government. Piecemeal and contradictory, state policy nonetheless had the effect of raising to a statutory level peasant customary law *(obychnoe pravo)* founded on the principles of patriarchal authority.

The hybrid apparatus that resulted from the abolition of serfdom and in response to commoditization of products and labor consisted of a hodgepodge of local solutions in which a number of groups fought to make their presence felt in the countryside: the state's interminable frustration at the imposition of civil discipline and the rule of law; entrepreneurs seeking to exploit the confusion for their own personal gains; peasants and peasant families trying desperately to make ends meet.

In their struggle to respond to the dual crises posed by the need for cash for fulfillment of excessive tax and redemption dues and the corollary threat of abandonment by members overburdened by such responsibilities, village institutions fell back on a number of traditional arrangements. The structures, institutions, and practices that had been imposed under serfdom proved rather well-suited for extension into the post-Emancipation era. The strength of these traditional arrangements was augmented by several new legislative initiatives. Temporary and limited alliances were forged between *volost* and village authorities with two groups in particular: (1) state authorities, who sought to uphold peasant patriarchalism as part of their strategy to maintain internal order and encourage prompt fulfillment of peasant obligations; and (2) outside employers, who exploited village structures to optimize control and reduce wages of peasant-workers (since ties to the land could be counted on for support during industrial downturns).

Chapters 2 and 3 focus on the operation of this hybrid apparatus: the conflicts and patterns of the commune's dual roles as both extension of the state apparatus and as mitigator and defender of community interests. The uneasy relationship between village authorities and state agents will be the main theme of chapter 2. Communal strategies for social control of *otkhod-*

niki will be the theme of chapter 3. The relationship between peasant officials and market agents (employers and creditors)—the commune as broker—will be discussed in chapter 4. In chapter 5, we will reverse the perspective, and investigate the factors in migrant experience outside the village which facilitiated and encouraged peasant-workers to uphold family and village ties while living and working outside their villages.

2 Autocratic Authority and the Peasant "Little Community"

STATE AGENTS, VILLAGE OFFICIALS, AND COMMUNITY OPINION

LACKING THE APPARATUS FOR DIRECT CONTROL in the countryside, Russian state agents were forced to operate through existing institutions —particularly, the peasant commune. The thrust of state policy throughout the postreform period (prior to the Stolypin reforms in 1906) was therefore to support communal efforts to regulate *otkhodniki*. Essentially, the state sought to coopt communal forms of social control by aligning its own initiatives with the interests of the traditional village hierarchy.

To reduce the likelihood of desertion, village and household patriarchs were extended enormous control over household members. The gist of these shared interests was reflected in a *volost* court resolution in Moscow Province from the 1860s: "The father is the total master in the home; the sons have no kind of individual property outside of the life of the father, and only with his blessing are they able to separate. Frequently, the *volost* court receives a petition from the son requesting apportionment of part of the property of the father, but such petitions are always ignored. Parental power must be observed and upheld, and besides, while the sons live with the father they pay their taxes more punctually."[1]

Patriarchalism was the cultural and legal basis that endowed village communities with considerable leverage over departing members. This tactic of implementing legal solutions to strengthen the vitality of traditional hierarchies was applied throughout European Russia. Only in the Central Industrial Region, however, did regionally specific conditions facilitate the development of an apparatus sufficiently powerful and far-reaching to enforce such regulations.[2]

State Officials and the Village "Little Community"

In their efforts to collect taxes, district and *volost* officials would either work through the village commune and its elected representatives or—in some cases—circumvent the structure of the official hierarchy and apply measures directly against delinquent households. Working through existing village institutions was always an uphill climb. It should not be surprising that one rarely saw the peasant commune apply coercive measures on its own initiative, without the prompting of *volost* authorities or the district police. It is clear that communes were often forced to play the role of reluctant executors of state authorities against community members.[3] Charges of negligence or excessive leniency abounded and were frequently cited as the principal reasons for the growing arrears in most areas.[4]

While there was enormous state pressure to enjoin the vigorous fulfillment of duty, to transform local officials into mere executors of instructions passed down from above, village opinion represented a mighty counterbalance in the struggle for the sympathies of local village officials: powerful community pressures aimed precisely at mitigating the effects of efficient civil administration. The far-reaching character of local influence can often be underestimated by outside observers. Innumerable opportunities presented themselves in the everyday lives of peasants. Acts ranged from the ever-popular *nepovinovenie*—obstinate refusal to carry out instructions passed down from above—through bribes to elders with the hope of influencing the award of family property during a household division,[5] to the much more serious intimidation of local forest guards through arson and murder.[6] The enormous influence of "insider" pressures on village officials was colorfully illustrated in this report from Moscow Province, where the level of arrears had quadrupled in the period 1884–1893, so that accumulated arrears in 1894 were almost double the annual assessment: "The only village elders who manage to serve several terms are those who do not disturb fellow villagers with demands for the payment of taxes. If the elder were to take it into his head to enact measures against delinquents, [local peasants] would not only not reelect him, but would most likely burn him alive. *Volost* elders likewise only pursue their own personal goals."[7] For officials who actually pursued energetic measures for the collection of taxes, the state power of seizure and sale of a delinquent's property was undermined through unannounced yet communitywide and enormously effective boycotts of public auctions.[8]

More sophisticated forms of resistance were also applied to undermine state authority in the countryside. For instance, the election or recall of communal officials was a serious affair, as demonstrated in Kostroma Province during the 1860s: "In those communes where the village elders did not resort to harsh measures in punishment, according to either the power granted to them by the law or by orders of the authorities, a larger part [of these] former elders were elected for a new three-year term. In the opposite cases, . . . several of those who had already shown too much boldness [in the use of harsh measures] were dismissed from their duties."[9] The same pattern was observed in the selection of tax collectors in Viatka Province.[10]

In Moscow and Nizhnii Novgorod Provinces, popular noncompliance thwarted the effectiveness of state authorities to collect tax obligations. Communitywide opposition among both rich and poor peasants had effectively undermined the state's capacity to collect taxes in these two provinces where peasant earnings through side-work were among the very highest. In both provinces, arrears more than quadrupled from below-average levels in 1884 to extraordinarily high levels in 1893 (from 51.5 percent to 197 percent arrears in Moscow, from 27.4 percent to 223.8 percent arrears in Nizhnii Novgorod). Likewise, these two provinces showed disproportionately high levels of noncompliance among wealthy peasants.[11]

In other areas of the Central Industrial Region, however, the story was somewhat different. To counter little-community resistance to tax collection, state authorities had a variety of ways of making pressure felt. Tsarist bureaucrats usually began with direct pressure against village officials. Written correspondence between higher officials and authorities in delinquent villages was voluminous. Descriptions left by local peasant officials, and the sheer volume of the archival records of *volost* authorities, reveal the degree to which peasant officials were inundated by a virtual hailstorm of communications from state bureaucrats. Writing at the end of the 1890s, a *volost* clerk from Kaluga Province,

F. Lashmanov, was highly critical of existing procedures, which placed undue strain on beleaguered peasant officials. He listed twenty-two different Russian state agencies with which he regularly exchanged correspondence![12]

The next step was for state authorities to escalate pressure from mere written warnings. Usually, this consisted of a summons of *volost* or village officials to appear in the district police headquarters. In Tula Province, village elders were obligated to appear before the district police chief at least once per month. In Iaroslavl, a monthly written report from the *volost* elder sufficed.[13] In autumn months when efforts for the exaction of taxes were particularly energetic, village elders were often expected to report twice a month in person at *volost* offices.[14]

In most cases, however, local officials neglected or evaded such summonses, acts of insubordination that sometimes provoked further action, usually an official's formal reprimand *(vygovor)*, then fines, arrest, and even removal from office. (Rural peasant officials were legally exempted from corporal punishment.) Usually, insubordinate village officials were first arrested and held until they agreed to work with state agents to press for receipts. Arrest was normally accompanied by fines against the officials themselves, for laziness *(lenost)*, excessive leniency *(sniskhozhdenie, potvorstvo)*, or negligence of duty *(neradivnost)*. Note that fines were used almost exclusively against either negligent officials or rich peasants seeking to evade payments and were not often applied (in cases of tax arrears) against delinquent households. Fines were, in practice, strictly a mechanism for maintaining administrative control among peasant officials and not—as has sometimes been argued—a major factor in the ruination of peasant well-being.[15]

Removal from office *(smeshchenie, smeshanie)* was particularly common in the early years after the abolition of serfdom. The tsarist regime's frustration with its elected village representatives is sharply reflected in the data on recalls imposed against elected *volost* elders. In the year preceding mid-1864, for instance, among 210 *volost* elders in the whole of Kostroma Province, "there were dismissed from duty by declarations of the peace-mediators and assemblies 56 *[volost]* elders, 1 [village] elder and one *[volost]* clerk. Among these, 14 persons were dismissed due to illness, 20 for embezzlement of communal funds and bribe-taking, 17 for failure to collect taxes *[neizyskanie obrokov]* and negligence of duty *[nerasporiaditel'nost po sluzhbe]*, 5 for drunkenness, and 2 for impertinence *[derzost]*." The figures indicate that in the course of a single year, adjusting to exclude cases of dismissal on the basis of illness, one-fifth or 20 percent of all *volost* elders in Kostroma Province were dismissed from office by state executive order.[16]

One fact is especially revealing of the attitudes of state officials toward the autonomy of village institutions. While district authorities were sometimes quite ruthless in their pursuit of tax evaders, negligent officials, and those who absconded with state funds, overzealous or corrupt peasant officials who exploited the system for personal gain in the name of the state were often left unhindered, their activities considered outside the jurisdiction of state authorities. Evidently, the Russian state preferred to uphold local hierarchies of village elites, not to oppose them. In Riazan Province, for instance, several cases of bias and graft were uncovered in which the property of tax delinquents was sold at a fraction of its worth to inside buyers. In such cases, state authorities did nothing, reasoning that "no authority is considered to have a right to interfere in these activities of the commune, carried out in the name of *krugovaia poruka*," the statutes that made all commune members responsible for the state debts of each household in the commune.[17]

The Carrot and the Stick: The Struggle of State Officials to Coopt Local Support

In their efforts to empower communal institutions, state officials on the one hand vigorously pursued the collection of taxes and arrears, convinced of the "stubbornness and unwillingness of peasants to pay dues without coercive measures."[18] On the other, they endowed peasant communal institutions with powerful sanctions for expropriating those obligations from community members.

State authorities had a variety of ways of applying pressure. In several districts of Tver Province, for instance, the "village and *volost* authorities or the police force the village commune to take these measures [for the fulfillment of obligations], threatening otherwise recovery through *krugovaia poruka*."[19] This was the state's trump card, since the threat of redistribution of arrears posed a direct challenge to the economic well-being of most villagers, but especially to village elites. Typical was the pattern in Vladimir Province: in Gorokhovets and Vladimir Districts, local village assemblies avoided use of coercive measures. But in most districts, police and *volost* authorities "forced village communes to observe the punctual payment of taxes, and sometimes even resorted to extraordinary measures" as defined in article 188 of the Emancipation statute: (1) compensate for arrears through the seizure of the delinquent's personal immovable property; (2) hire out the delinquent, or his family members, for work, deducting the wages for communal use; (3) designate a guardian for the delinquent household; (4) sell the delinquent's movable property; (5) sell part of the delinquent's immovable property, which is not considered to be essential to the farmstead; (6) seize the delinquent's allotment.[20]

Designed to encourage peasant fiscal accountability, these enhanced sanctions were wielded in equal measure by communal authorities to coerce the fulfillment of a negligent *otkhodnik*'s family obligations. The apparatus evolved into an imperfect hybrid of bureaucratic initiative and cooptation of "little community" norms founded on concerns about subsistence and family security. In this lay both the principal strength and weakness of Russian state fiscal policy in the countryside. The key tension consisted of the commune's conflicting roles as both an extension of the state apparatus and as a cultural entity. The gist of this tension was best described by N. K. Brzheskii, the leading contemporary authority on peasant taxation in Russia: "Village authorities, who are inclined as a general rule to be overindulgent toward taxpayers, do not bring in taxes until [there is] an insistence on the part of the police; but once the police have started to act, the sternest measures are employed, quite often at a time when peasants have no money for paying taxes."[21]

The threat of their own expropriation led stable peasant households to develop powerful tactics for ensuring at least the appearance of a vigorous effort toward the fulfillment of dues and obligations.

3 The Social Control of Peasant Labor

THE ALLIANCE OF FAMILY AND COMMUNITY

Collective responsibility forces each [member of the peasant commune] to remember if he does not squeeze the poor peasant then he must pay for him and it is this which makes the village commune pitiless.
   COUNT VORONTSOV-DASHKOV, MINISTER OF
   THE IMPERIAL COURT AND DOMAINS, 1900[1]

IN THE CONTEXT OF THE Russian fiscal system, abandonment or nonfulfillment of obligations by some households threatened to increase the already excessive dues of every other household in the village. In their efforts to prevent or alleviate such developments, all villagers—rich and poor, solvent and delinquent—pursued a wide variety of manipulative schemes to keep *otkhodniki* tied to the village and to extract from them the earnings their outside income could provide.[2] Under the threat of arbitrary intervention by state officials, village communes—acting by-and-large on their own initiative—adopted distinct procedures to facilitate the successful redistribution of migrant earnings from the work place to the village.[3]

As we have seen, the pressure was particularly great in non-black-earth areas, where the disproportionate relation between depressed land income and excessive state dues threatened the solvency of whole communities in the event of nonpayment, abandonment, or desertion. The terms of the abolition of serfdom and state fiscal policies since the 1860s had redefined the status of the repartitional commune in the Central Industrial Region: excessive dues had transformed the peasant commune into a mechanism for the redistribution of burden *(tiagota)*.

As a result, there was a marked aversion against accumulating allotment lands among peasants in non-black-earth districts. Typical was this report from Pogorelovskaia commune in Kineshema District, Kostroma Province, in 1880: "Cases of the use of supplementary reapportionments *[krugovaia poruka]* do not take place, nor are there cases of the deprivation of delinquents of land, nor does one find anyone desiring to take this land for themselves, [since this would mean] taking on all of the taxes belonging to it."[4] This aversion to taking on additional allotments—those given up to the commune *(upalye nadely)* and those seized for nonpayment of dues *(otobrannye nadely)*—may be contrasted to procedures in areas where agriculture was more profitable. In the Central Agricultural Region, for instance, fellow villagers were often eager to expand land-holdings through the communal right of expropriation of holdings of less productive fellow villagers.[5] The function and role of peasant communes evolved distinctly in each region of European Russia.

Communes in the Central Industrial Region aggressively fought to bind peasant-workers to the land and, in this way, to their families and communities. As the governor from Vladimir Province reported at the beginning of the 1880s: in non-black-earth regions "resettlement is made particularly inconvenient until the end of the redemption operation, since on poor land, after having released working hands, the village commune frequently proves to be incapable of liquidating redemption debts."[6] Communes in the Central Industrial Region were generally unwilling to permit families to break their connections with the village completely. As one commune in Moscow Province reasoned in a resolution from late in the century: "If peasants were [permitted to] leave the commune, then there would no longer be a sufficient number of persons for the payment of state taxes and arrears."[7]

Communal Efforts to Expropriate Earnings from Otkhodniki in the Central Industrial Region

Given the inevitable difficulty of finding others to take land at a price that exceeded its productive value, tenancy agreements throughout the Central Industrial Region developed a distinct regional form. The typical procedure was one in which the allotment's owner *(vladelets)*, unable to work the land profitably, endeavored to minimize his own losses by sharing the fees with renters. Normally, the *otkhodnik* simply signed over the land to a family member, another member of the community, or to the disposition of the entire commune. In this process, the migrant usually agreed to pay the difference between the taxes (and redemption payments) and the actual market price that could be obtained through land utilization. The logic was obvious: in non-black-earth districts "it is more advantageous to pay part of the taxes, and be without any allotment, than it is to take the land and carry all of the taxes."[8] As a rule, to guarantee fulfillment of obligations, communes insisted that land be given up for village use, and that the *otkhodnik* pay the annual dues—a departure fee which was known in the village as an *otpusknoe* or *spusta*. Typical was this case in Vladimir Province during the late nineteenth century:

> One village in Suzdal District, where land income exceeds the payments attached to it and where those leaving for the factory previously gave their land up for rent and even received for it a small payment, there was recently passed a resolution whereby no one could give his allotment up for rent without the permission of the *mir*. In this way, peasant-workers have been kept from exploiting their land, having been coerced either to pay all the taxes or to give it up to the commune, paying for it seven rubles per year. Likewise, the commune will not give its authorization for the [complete] redemption of the allotment. In such a way, the village commune does with great success extract kopecks from its members.[9]

This procedure was founded on the commune's right, granted in paragraph 130 of the Emancipation statute, to restrict any peasant household's dispossession of the land.[10] In Vladimir Province, the practice of restricting the free transfer of allotment lands originated in the highly industrialized Shuia District and then rapidly spread southward through Suzdal and other districts, under the cognizance and active encouragement of local officials, whose interests evidently overlapped with those of peasants unable to afford the dues on additional peasant land.[11]

Despite the emergence of a wide variety of local and distinct innovations, published and unpublished sources reveal that the procedures for temporarily giving up one's allotment were quite similar throughout the Central Industrial Region. As a *zemstvo* correspondent in Vladimir Province explained in 1899:

> Very frequently, peasant-workers completely break every connection with their homes, living at the factory by themselves, away from their families. Those fellow villagers who remain in the village are perfectly cognizant that their situation is most unfavorable, and begin a subtle struggle with departing workers, in order to compel them to part with their good earnings. . . . Assessing such workers certain duties which are to the advantage of the community is practiced extensively.[12]

V. Dadonov observed this pattern among peasant-workers from villages around Ivanovo-Voznesensk during the 1890s:

> The land of a departing member of the community enters into the direction of the commune with the obligation to return it to the owner in the event of his return, and the commune pays for him all of the taxes [assigned to the land]. But those whose families remain in the village do not usually want to make a final break in their connection with the land, and in this case have already personally hired out to someone (usually at the price of two rubles per allotment of 3¼–4 *desiatiny*) and forests and hayfields are disposed of by themselves: if they are rented out or otherwise, the lease payment rises to seven rubles.[13]

Despite his break with the village, the departing adult male worker usually remained responsible for the payment of obligations on the land: "The commune obliges the departing member to pay 3 rubles annually as a 'departure fee,' and if the departing member leaves a hut in the village, even if it is boarded up, he adds 1–2 rubles more."[14] In Suzdal District, this departure fee ranged from seven to ten rubles annually per one-soul allotment, versus eight to sixteen rubles plus natural labor duties if the *otkhodnik* worked the land himself.[15] Popularly, peasants dubbed this charge the *guliatskii obrok*, or "wanderer's tax."

> In Dmitrov District [Moscow Province], village communes collect from peasants—who have left the land, who have given up the peasantry, and those who work in industrial occupations on the side—the so-called *guliatskii obrok*, at a rate of 3 to 25 rubles per worker, depending on how much need the community has for the land. The *guliatskii obrok* goes for the payment of assessed taxes for the commune. . . .
>
> The *guliatskii obrok* is assessed in villages with factory and migrant earnings, and also in villages with low-income allotments. . . . In Dmitrov District, the average level of all assessed taxes per worker [varies] from 9 to 11 rubles; it is signi-

ficantly higher in villages where the population has increased slightly or even decreased since the revised census of 1857. . . .

Where peasants value the land, the level of the *guliatskii obrok* is lower than assessed payments. There are cases where such landless peasants must pay only the communal dues. Likewise, [there are cases] where, as a result of a low number of workers, peasants are not able to manage with an allotment, they neglect and mortgage part of the field, [and] the *guliatksii obrok* is not infrequently higher than the sum of dues on the land.[16]

In Nizhnii Novgorod, the *guliatskii obrok* ranged from 38 to 63 percent of the annual assessment for a single-soul allotment. Sometimes, however, the *guliatskii obrok* exceeded annual obligations on the land, a charge that villagers usually encouraged, since an *otkhodnik*'s absence from the village freed him from onerous "natural duties" (such as road work, police duty, etc.).[17] By the third quarter of the nineteenth century, such a departure fee was typically designated in a written agreement with the commune signed prior to the *otkhodnik*'s departure. Here is an example of the standard agreement common throughout the Central Industrial Region:

> 1874, November 13, I, the undersigned, from Moscow Province, Volokolamsk District, the village of Kurvinnaia, gave this receipt to my community . . . [acknowledging] that I, Grigor'ev, will give up land for communal use—a three-soul allotment, for which I, Grigor'ev, pledge myself to pay 21 rubles each year. . . . [T]he aforesaid money should be sent annually by the first of April, not including passports, for which I should send separately.[18]

The written contract was an important assurance to the commune as well as to the migrant, for whom the guarantee of a right to his allotment was a safety net during economic downturns, illness, and old age: "The farmstead remains usually in the ownership *[vladenie]* of the departing peasant household chief, since he gives up the field land only for a time, and not forever."[19] The legal standing of such written agreements was amply demonstrated in the years following the Stolypin reforms in 1906. Even among peasant families in Moscow Province who had lived and worked outside their villages for fifteen to thirty-five years, a large number returned to their native communities and successfully reclaimed their long-neglected allotments as personal disposable property.[20]

Available data suggest that the majority of peasants departing for side-earnings, by choice or through pressure of the village assembly, gave their land up to the commune rather than dispose of it in private rental agreements with individual fellow villagers. In practice, village communes in the Central Industrial Region vigilantly restricted the right to transfer communal resources to outside agents. In Dorogobuzh District, Smolensk Province, from a cross-sample of 500 heads of peasant households working "on the side" in 1889, 339 gave their land up to the commune, while 161 peasant heads transferred it to other individuals in the village.[21] Communes, moreover, encouraged written and formal legal procedures so as to protect the village from inevitable disputes over who was responsible for paying dues on the land. In Suzdal District, Vladimir Province, as in the majority of other districts, all rental contracts had to be approved by the commune.[22]

In Sychëvka District, Smolensk Province, in extreme cases where delinquent allotments were seized, communes refused to recognize transactions in which peasant tax delinquents had given the land over to someone else. They seized the allotments for the commune, with the renter of the land suffering damages.[23] Likely tenants were in this way encouraged to secure prior approval of the commune, while *otkhodniki* were encouraged to pay the departure fees and then turn the land over to the disposition of the commune. Land was then rented at reduced rates (more closely reflecting the actual productive value of the land) or, in the absence of interested renters, it was redistributed among selected households. In this way, villages in the non-black-earth region raided the cash economy for receipts that were used to subsidize the ailing village economy.

The Passport System

Communes imposed the terms of full or partial fulfillment of land obligations on *otkhodniki* through their power, shared with *volost* authorities, to manipulate the issuing of internal passports.[24] "To live without a passport is impossible," remarked the peasant Klimov from Vereia District, Moscow Province, after his forced return from Moscow to his native village in 1887.[25] This vestige of serfdom, strengthened after the 1861 abolition, was a powerful mechanism that extended the control of local authorities far beyond the village boundaries. Ultimately, the passport system placed the power to allocate peasant labor firmly in the hands of village and household chiefs. As the Governing Senate, the highest body responsible for interpreting legal precedent in autocratic Russia, resolved on 3 March 1892: "To the peasant household chief, as the person who is responsible for the punctual payment of the taxes of the household, belongs the right to give his consent or refusal for the issuing of passports to an inseparable member of the family or to make an agreement conditional upon the fulfillment of certain obligations."[26] The first of a series of regulations on internal passports, dated 3 June 1894, raised this widely accepted principle of peasant customary law to the statutory level: "Passports will be issued and renewed for inseparable members of peasant families, even if they have come of age, only with the consent of the head of the peasant household."[27]

Even as late as 1903, during the heated discussions in the Editing Commission of the Basic Committee on the Needs of the Rural Economy, the president of the commission, A. S. Stishinskii, vigorously objected to proposals to reform the passport system. He argued that passport restrictions should be retained on the basis of two overriding concerns. First, the passport was a guarantee for the prompt payment of taxes and communal dues. Second, the passport was a means of fortifying the patriarchal peasant family which, for Stishinskii and many of his contemporaries, was "the sole connecting link, the sole basis for the preservation of the authority of the household chief."[28] From the 1861 Emancipation until the dawn of the Stolypin reforms, tsarist policy in the countryside rested firmly on the presumption that state interests coincided directly with those of the patriarchal hierarchy of the traditional village.[29]

State efforts to uphold the legal authority of household patriarchs, and to preserve the principle of the *nerazdel'naia sem'ia*—the indivisible family unit—represented nothing more than the affirmation of peasant customary law. In his analysis of *volost* court proceedings in the area around Iaroslavl, the famed ethnographer E. I. Iakushkin summarized the general practice that he observed: "An adult son is able to leave the home for earnings. The passport, however, is issued each time only with the permission of the father, the elder-*domokhoziain,* under conditions which oblige payment of a fixed sum of money to the family [father] for the payment of taxes and for the fulfillment of needs. In the event of carelessness [on the part] of the son who has departed for earnings, if he stops sending money home because of negligence, or because he has himself received little compensation, the *volost* court recognizes the right of the father to demand the return *[vysylka]* of the son to the native village."[30] By and large, peasant courts upheld the authority of the household chiefs over household labor power, recognizing that to issue a son a passport without the father's authorization only "encourages . . . the young peasant generation toward nonpayment of duties and toward disobedience of parental power."[31]

Official restriction *(zaderzhka* or *stesnenie)* of passports was extensive throughout the Central Industrial Region, common in all but one district each in Moscow and Vladimir Provinces, the majority of districts in Riazan, Tver, Kaluga, Iaroslavl, and Kostroma, and large parts of the remaining provinces in the non-black-earth north.[32] Usually, *otkhodniki* were required as a condition for the issuing of a passport, to pay the current year's tax, or part of the arrears.³³ As we have seen, many communes simply merged passport fees with taxes (and bribes or "remuneration for services" to local officials) into a single "departure fee" which had to be paid before an *otkhodnik*'s passport could be issued or renewed. Very often, communes or *volost* officials demanded a written agreement or leave-contract *(podpiska)* in which the departing worker formally identified his responsibilities and provided a schedule of payment.³⁴

Passport restrictions were applied differently from district to district. In Iaroslavl Province, for example, where accumulated arrears were low, payment of all or part of the arrears was a strict precondition for the release of a passport in five districts. In Iaroslavl District, however, this demand was strictly applied only to those who would be away from the village for long periods of time; officials were more lenient toward those leaving for shorter periods, durations of less than a year.³⁵ In some districts, the use of passport restrictions as a means of extracting taxes and arrears required a formal resolution from the communal assembly, "depending on the person."³⁶ In several districts, the restrictions on passports applied not only to the heads of peasant households, but also to family members.³⁷

As a rule, local officials were lenient in most cases; those peasant-workers who failed to come up with the requisite funds were often granted passports for shorter periods, from one to six months, the renewal of which would depend on the *otkhodnik*'s prompt payment from earnings sent back to the village.³⁸ Such short-term passports would, it was hoped, keep *otkhodniki* on a tighter rein, so as to encourage more responsible behavior. In Kostroma, "short-term passports are issued to tax delinquents in all districts, with the exception of reliable *[blagonadezhnye]* persons."³⁹ In Vasil'ii District, Nizhnii Novgorod Province, authorities "issue a short-term passport to those in arrears, with the stipulation that long-term passports not be sent until the receipt of a payment toward arrears."⁴⁰ Likewise in Iaroslavl Province: "A passport is not issued to a tax delinquent in the majority of districts, or it is issued by the police at the place of residence only on payment of arrears. . . , or—if the arrears have not been completely paid off, in place of the annual passport, [they issue] a six-month or one-month [passport]. In several *volosti* of Myshkino District, they do not renew a passport even for members of the delinquent's family."⁴¹ By and large, passport restrictions were imposed subjectively, depending on the perceived character of the person (or family) departing for earnings. Typical of the general pattern observed, the *volost* elder in Sharapinskaia *volost,* Zvenigorod District, Moscow Province, reasoned this way: he issued short-term passports principally to "unreliable persons who had shown themselves to be careless in the payment of duties and *who had lost his trust.*"[42]

The widespread use of short-term passports as a means of encouraging fulfillment of obligations is reflected in the data on passports issued in the Central Industrial Region during the late nineteenth century. For the whole of European Russia, despite the fact that even in agricultural areas average *otkhod* was two to six months annually, the overwhelming majority of passports were short-term: an average of 49.5 percent of all passports issued in the years 1890–1896 were for three months or less; while one in four (26.9 percent) were for six months; and slightly less than one in four (23.7 percent) were for a year or more.[43] In the Central Industrial Region, where *otkhod* played a particularly significant role in gross peasant incomes, and where migrants' absence for earnings was increasingly year-round, the proportion of long-term passports was even lower. The data from Kostroma Province in 1887 were typical: just over half of all issued passports (50.3 percent) were for periods of three months or less; a third (31.58 percent) were for six months; and less than one in five of all passports (18.12 percent) were for a year or more. The growing awareness among *volost* and village authorities of the need to restrict passports was reflected in the changing proportion of long- versus short-term passports: between 1869 and 1887, the proportion of passports for a year or more declined from less than one in four (23.8 percent) to less than one in five (18.2 percent); in the same period, the proportion of one-month passports rose from 38.73 percent to 46.84 percent.[44] Evidently, during this period communes had learned the efficacy of manipulating passports to regulate *otkhodnik* behavior and to encourage the prompt fulfillment of obligations.[45] (See table 3.1.)

Of course, communal authorities were not unaware that the rigid enforcement of a policy denying passports to those in arrears could be self-defeating in a context where peasant income relied overwhelmingly on cash sent from wages earned outside the village. In parts of Kaluga Province, therefore, "passports were issued without hindrance *[bezprepiastvenno]:* otherwise, due to the absence of local earnings, arrears would only increase. The renewal of passports for those absent is sometimes delayed due to their nonpayment of assessed taxes."[46] In some areas, the need for outside earnings exceeded the risk of desertion, and communes did not restrict passports. The reasoning behind these decisions reveals, however, that such cases did not represent a rejection, but rather a reorientation of the commune's basic coercive strategy. In four districts of Tula Province, for instance, where peasant agriculture was more

Table 3.1. Passport Term in 43 Provinces of European Russia, 1861–1890

Regions and Provinces	1861–1870 (in percent)			1871–1880 (in percent)			1881–1890 (in percent)		
	1–3 Months	6 Months	12 Months	1–3 Months	6 Months	12 Months	1–3 Months	6 Months	12 Months
I. Nonagricultural/Industrial	**12.5**	**43.4**	**44.1**	**36.9**	**29.9**	**33.1**	**38.7**	**29.9**	**31.4**
North and Northwest	17.1	41.5	41.4	38.2	30.1	31.7	38.1	29.0	32.9
Arkhangel	17.4	35.6	47.0	39.7	26.2	34.1	38.7	28.6	32.7
Vologda	30.0	34.2	35.8	67.6	17.2	15.2	65.2	19.6	15.2
Olonets	12.5	46.2	41.3	48.0	25.6	26.4	57.4	21.7	20.9
St. Petersburg	2.3	36.7	61.0	21.2	29.7	49.1	20.2	26.8	53.0
Novgorod	32.2	42.8	25.0	49.5	29.0	21.5	44.5	27.7	27.8
Pskov	2.0	38.8	59.2	14.1	34.5	51.4	19.4	29.3	51.3
Smolensk	24.5	48.4	27.1	32.0	42.9	25.1	28.9	42.7	28.4
Tver	15.8	49.2	35.0	33.7	35.4	30.9	30.6	35.4	34.0
Central Industrial Region	13.6	44.9	41.6	40.3	32.4	27.3	38.5	34.2	27.3
Iaroslavl	7.3	29.3	63.4	27.3	23.7	49.0	26.9	23.9	49.2
Moscow	10.8	44.1	45.1	22.1	39.7	38.2	17.6	43.3	39.1
Vladimir	21.1	47.6	31.3	58.9	27.8	13.3	54.3	30.8	14.9
Kostroma	23.6	40.6	35.8	63.1	21.4	15.5	66.0	21.8	12.2
Kaluga	9.2	50.8	40.0	32.2	40.1	27.7	30.9	42.4	26.7
Nizhnii Novgorod	15.4	49.7	34.9	55.8	27.9	16.3	55.0	27.6	17.4
Tula	7.6	55.0	37.4	23.3	46.6	30.1	19.6	48.1	32.3
Riazan	13.6	41.8	44.6	39.9	32.0	28.1	37.8	35.7	26.5
Belorussia	6.9	43.8	49.3	32.2	27.4	40.4	39.6	26.5	34.0
Vitebsk	0.2	51.9	47.9	20.0	34.1	45.9	29.5	32.2	38.3
Minsk	8.2	37.6	54.2	38.2	19.6	42.2	50.1	18.6	31.3
Mogilev	12.3	41.8	45.9	38.4	28.4	33.2	39.1	28.6	32.3
II. Southern Agricultural	**7.9**	**47.6**	**44.5**	**48.4**	**22.6**	**29.0**	**57.9**	**19.4**	**22.8**
Ukraine	6.2	42.4	51.5	43.1	23.7	33.2	56.9	19.6	23.5
Poltava	13.8	59.1	27.1	58.3	27.5	14.2	67.7	19.1	13.2
Kharkov	3.6	62.2	34.2	59.3	24.8	15.9	70.5	16.1	13.4
Chernigov	0.4	58.6	41.0	44.1	33.8	22.1	48.1	31.9	20.0
Kiev	1.6	36.4	62.0	35.0	22.5	42.5	64.0	16.2	19.8
Volynia	0.6	21.7	77.7	38.5	8.9	52.6	54.2	11.3	34.5
Podolia	0.3	31.0	68.8	24.6	23.4	52.0	54.6	16.8	28.6
Kherson	15.6	40.9	43.5	42.6	27.9	29.5	51.9	21.4	26.7
Ekaterinoslav	1.7	43.8	54.5	37.3	25.5	37.2	50.3	24.6	25.1
Taurida	17.8	27.7	54.5	48.2	18.6	33.2	50.7	19.1	30.2
North Caucasus	9.7	52.8	37.5	53.7	21.5	24.8	58.9	19.1	22.0
Don Oblast	9.7	52.8	37.5	53.7	21.5	24.8	58.9	19.1	22.0
III. Central Agricultural	**22.1**	**44.5**	**33.4**	**62.0**	**22.7**	**15.3**	**63.1**	**21.9**	**14.9**
Central Chernozem	18.0	46.7	35.3	53.7	27.3	19.1	55.4	26.0	18.4
Voronezh	14.5	52.7	32.8	73.2	15.8	11.0	74.1	14.0	11.9
Kursk	20.3	50.5	29.2	52.7	32.1	15.2	58.2	25.6	16.2
Orel	20.9	45.4	33.7	41.7	33.9	24.4	41.3	36.3	21.4
Tambov	16.3	38.2	45.5	47.0	27.3	25.7	48.1	28.0	23.9
Volga	26.2	42.3	31.6	70.3	18.1	11.6	70.8	17.8	11.4
Astrakhan	29.3	42.0	28.7	79.8	10.5	9.7	82.2	8.3	9.5
Saratov	12.9	43.0	44.1	64.5	18.5	17.0	63.5	19.3	17.2
Samara	45.0	29.2	25.8	71.7	15.6	12.7	63.7	20.0	16.3
Penza	21.3	45.8	32.9	60.5	26.7	12.8	57.4	28.2	14.4
Simbirsk	25.3	44.9	29.8	72.5	17.9	9.6	76.5	16.1	7.4
Kazan	20.4	35.4	44.2	72.2	15.6	12.2	73.0	17.0	10.0
Viatka	31.8	39.2	29.0	74.1	15.2	10.7	74.8	15.9	9.3
Ufa	23.3	58.7	18.0	66.7	25.1	8.2	75.5	17.7	6.8

Table 3.1. (continued)

Regions and Provinces	1861–1870 (in percent)			1871–1880 (in percent)			1881–1890 (in percent)		
	1–3 Months	6 Months	12 Months	1–3 Months	6 Months	12 Months	1–3 Months	6 Months	12 Months
IV. Eastern Agricultural	34.6	39.6	25.8	78.0	14.4	7.7	78.6	14.0	7.5
Ural	34.6	39.6	25.8	78.0	14.4	7.7	78.6	14.0	7.5
Perm	21.0	47.4	31.6	82.0	10.6	7.4	81.5	11.3	7.2
Orenburg	48.2	31.8	20.0	73.9	18.2	7.9	75.7	16.6	7.7
Average passport term, 43 provinces	15.9	43.3	40.9	48.8	25.6	25.6	52.3	24.5	23.2

Source: Adapted from L. E. Mints, *Otkhod krest'ianskogo naseleniia na zarabotki v SSSR* (Moscow, 1925), p. 29.

extensive, passports were issued and renewed regardless of fulfillment of fiscal obligations, because it was believed that "land serves as a sufficient guarantee of payment."[47] In Smolensk Province: "Since the peasant workers who depart with passports on the side usually leave at home members of their own families who are responsible for the punctual payment of duties, or give up their land to the commune or to individual fellow villagers, in a large proportion of districts village communes do not inhibit them in receiving passports."[48] In effect, communal members were usually satisfied if at least part of an *otkhodnik*'s family remained hostage in the village.

Otkhodniki and Families: Expropriating Earnings from Town to Country

State and village officials applied considerable pressure on migrants' families as a means of extorting earnings from absent members. In Danilov District, Iaroslavl Province, the absent delinquent's family was subjected to arrest, and the movable property was distrained.[49] Distraint *(opis)*—the authorized seizure of peasant property pending payment of taxes or arrears—was one of the most common mechanisms for coercing villagers to fulfill obligations.[50] Generally, the threat of distraint was the first step. This gave households with arrears the opportunity to raise the needed money, either by pressuring household members working on the side, selling off property on their own (usually for a better price than public debt auctions), or borrowing from relatives, neighbors, or local tradesmen. The second step, the actual seizure of property, usually consisted of the distraint of unessential movable property first—samovars, holiday or town clothing, watches—and only later moved to livestock, sheds, and farm equipment.[51] In most cases, the temporary seizure of property led to

Table 3.2. Cases of Distraint and Public Sale of Peasant Property
for Tax Arrears in Tver Province, 1889–1892

Year	Distraints (no. cases)	Sales (no. cases)	Sales/Distraints (in percent)
1889	2,435	232	9.5
1890	1,410	209	14.8
1891	1,234	120	9.7
1892	1,516	250	16.5

Source: Russia, Ministerstvo Finansov, *Sushchestvuiushchii poriadok vzimaniia okladnykh sborov s krest'ian*, vol. 2 (Moscow, 1895), p. 89.

payment of at least part of a peasant household's arrears. The overwhelming numerical disparity between cases of distraint and actual sales of property reveals the degree to which seizure and the threat to auction movable property were used to coerce cooperation in the payment of obligations, and not as a means of covering a household's delinquent obligations. The data in table 3.2 from Tver Province were typical for most of the Central Industrial Region.

Between 1889 and 1892, peasant movable property was seized for arrears in 6,595 cases in rural Tver Province for a general sum of arrears of 148,158 rubles. Yet sales were eventually held in only 811 of those cases—that is, in approximately 10–15 percent (per year) of all cases in which property was seized. Of all the money collected toward arrears during this period, more than two-thirds (59,896 rubles) was paid by peasants to release property prior to sale, while less than one-third (24,895 rubles) was collected as a result of the public sale of the seized property; together, the two procedures brought in almost 60 percent of the total arrears.[52] In short, the seizure of property alone was usually a sufficient mechanism for extracting payments; actual sale was comparatively rare.[53]

Only in Vladimir Province did the majority of cases of distraint lead to the public sale of peasant property to cover arrears. But even here, the amount gained through sale was considerably less than the amount of accumulated arrears. This is reflected in table 3.3.

Table 3.3. Seizure and Sale of Peasant Movable Property
for Tax Arrears in Vladimir Province, 1887–1893

District	Number of Distraints	Number of Villages	Arrears (in rubles)	Number of Insolvency Sales	Amount Gained (in rubles)
Suzdal	1,474	33	990	1,441	423
Iur'ev	473	40	28,351[a]	436	5,420
Aleksandrov	181	65	68,521	116	3,178
Melenkov[b]	7	7	2,248	—	747

[a]No figures for 1889–90.
[b]1892 only.

Source: Russia, Ministerstvo Finansov, *Sushchestvuiushchii poriadok vzimaniia okladnykh sborov s krest'ian*, vol. 2 (Moscow, 1895), p. 53.

In Vladimir Province, more than 90 percent of all distraints of peasant movable property were followed by sales: however, less than 10 percent of attached arrears were collected in this way (compared to almost 17 percent in Tver from sale alone). It is clear from the data that in Vladimir Province not only the threat of sale, but actual sale of peasant movable property had ceased to be effective mechanisms for coercing payments. Distraint and sale in Vladimir Province had become more punitive than fiscal. At the same time, excessive expropriation of peasant property had prompted widespread noncompliance: there were several documented cases in which, despite repeated distraints, public auctions rendered negligible results. In Melenki District, for instance, in what appear to have been deliberate boycotts, buyers ceased to show up at local debt auctions.[54]

The relative effectiveness of community strategies that exerted pressure on *otkhodniki* through family members was powerfully illustrated in an exchange of letters between a peasant-worker in St. Petersburg and his wife who lived in their village in northwestern Kostroma Province. The effectiveness of passport manipulation as an instrument of control is evident in the husband's initial pleading:

> You did not write, my dear Anna Zinov'evna, whether you received the money. I sent 15 rubles on 21 August. You wrote [asking whether I would be returning] to the village, but I don't think so because money is short and it is bad to be without money in the village, but I thank you for the intention. If there is not great hardship, then write and I will come to the village. I remain alive and well. I inform you dear wife, Anna Zinov'evna, I beg you: would it be impossible to send an annual passport, because I don't have much time left. My brother had to pay 4 rubles for an expired passport *[ot"srochka]*. And if you send an annual passport so that I won't need to get one in the spring, then I will come to the village. I will winter [here] reluctantly, as I would rather [come back] to the village. Please, tell me about everything in detail. How is the horse now, since she had the colt? I think my coming home would be impossible. I could move timber on the water for household expenses, but I don't think I could winter there. Send a passport because I don't have much time. An expired passport is too costly. A passport is not to be wasted even in spring. Please write soon about everything. Farewell. To your health. You never write. Send a letter soon.[55]

The wife, who was illiterate, dictated a letter to a fellow villager in response, which included these passages:

> Dear husband Polien Petrovich, you have written that I should send you an annual passport. I will not send a passport [because] I have no money and the

village elder won't issue a travel permit. He is asking about the taxes. If you send money I will send you the passport. My dear husband Polien Petrovich, you ask for an account of the horse, but the horse I have has never been able to pull a winter carriage well. My dear husband Polien Petrovich, you inquire about needs [*nuzhda*]. I have no needs, and there is no money. If you decide to come to the village, then bring money for expenses, and if you remain to winter in *Piter*, then send a little more money. . . . Farewell. We remain alive and well, and wish the same for you. My dear husband Polien Petrovich, the harness is completely in tatters, so that riding is impossible.[56]

Such were the coercive forces applied when the distance between work place and village prevented frequent visitations by family members. In the majority of cases, however, such distances were not prohibitive: mothers, fathers, children, or wives would visit the work place often "to make sure her husband doesn't drink or gamble away all of the earnings."[57] It should not be surprising that a high proportion (28.6 percent) of women's passports in Iaroslavl Province at the turn of the century were issued so that wives could check up on their husbands at work.[58]

"Dear Most Esteemed Elder": Kowtowing to Authority

From 1893, it was possible for a peasant to renew passports *in absentia*, without the trouble of making periodic personal appearances back in one's native *volost*. The record of the correspondence between peasant-workers and their *volost* authorities has in rare cases survived to the present day. Such records have been preserved for more than a single year in only a half dozen *volosti* of Moscow Province; the rest were destroyed or still lie uncatalogued in Russian provincial and regional museums and collections. Reflecting the priorities in the relationship between *volost* offices and local peasant migrants, the files are invariably entitled, "Matters regarding the dispatch of passports to peasants living on [outside] earnings; correspondence regarding the exaction from peasants of various payments, and regarding the sale of property for debts," or, in the event of refusal, "Matters regarding the refusal in the issuing of passports to peasants."[59] Such files focus almost wholly on peasant out-workers.

Consisting largely of correspondence between the *volost* office and the State Exchequer, the files contain vast information on local peasant migrants—extremely detailed reports on their earnings, places of work, and so on. The files also contain correspondence between peasant-workers and their *volost* elders, as well as correspondence with police, various state officials, and even employers.

Three general remarks preface this close investigation of *otkhodnik* correspondence with *volost* authorities. First, it is absolutely clear from these files that the *volost* office and the peasant migrant's native village and family were very well informed about every aspect of an out-worker's earnings, skills, work place, and behavior. At any moment, the vast majority of peasant workers in the Central Industrial Region could be contacted, or summoned back to their villages. The information was collected on the grounds of local self-interest, since the success—personal or professional—of any village official rested on his knowledge of the whereabouts of local peasants who left the region. Upon this knowledge, moreover, rested a *volost* administration's ability to respond to queries from numerous outside agencies, mainly the police, who often tracked criminals through their native villages. (Tsarist police evidently assumed that even criminals would not break all ties with their native villages.) This example, a communication from the justice of the peace in Lefortovo section of Moscow city to the Elmanovskii *volost* office, was typical of the kind of search the tsarist police conducted for a renegade peasant-worker. This particular case involved a certain Petr Grigor'ev, accused of petty theft: "The accused Grigor'ev is hiding from the court, as a consequence of which his case still remains unresolved. . . . I request that you not issue Grigor'ev a new passport [and, moreover that you] notify me of his whereabouts."[60] The documents suggest that *volost* authorities rarely moved to prohibit issuing passports on their own, but rather waited for complaints or instructions from family members, village communes, or outside authorities.

Retention of a peasant official's position rested on his ability to respond to questions from a whole gamut of officials, whose complaints for dereliction of duty could and often did lead to removal from office.[61] Finally, motives of a more personal nature—in a word, greed—also guided such vigilant efforts to monitor the activities of out-workers: in local village administration, it always paid to know from whom a few extra rubles could be extorted in return for services rendered. Peasant-workers, eager to secure passports, without which their outside work would be virtually impossible, were easy prey. The information received came from varying sources: from the peasant-workers themselves, from their kin who remained at home, and most especially from fellow villagers, who frequently traveled back and forth between work place and village.

The potentially lucrative nature of service in the *volost* administration was just one reason why so many local peasant notables sought the job.[62] Another was self-protection: if one did not seize that power for oneself or one's associates, then a local rival might take over who was not so amenable or was even hostile to your interests.

A second notable feature of the *volost* correspondence is the genuine flexibility and understanding often displayed by local officials. Although in their frequent petitions to other organs, peasant-workers often complained of the arbitrariness of *volost* officials, the written record suggests a rather different interpretation: *volost* officials were far more flexible and open to negotiation than tendentious court records suggest.

Third, the record of correspondence showcases the preeminent role of an *otkhodnik*'s personal reputation. In subtle ways, the petitioners constructed letters which intrinsically substantiated the legitimacy of their claims. An illiterate, unmarried Orthodox peasant girl of twenty-two, one Anna Fedorova, who worked as a house servant in Moscow, sent a dictated letter of request on the embossed stationery of her employer, S. V. Vishniak: "On receipt of this letter, I beg you to send me a passport without delay, since I need it for registering at the following address."[63] She received a six-month passport, which she would extend through the local police office for far less than it cost by working through her home *volost*.

The ultimate self-legitimizing act among out-migrants was kowtowing to the *volost* elder. The records are rife with evidence of peasant obsequiousness. Letters to *volost* authorities invariably began with a rite of sycophantic self-subordination: "Most Esteemed Elder!" "Gracious Sovereign!" "I Most Humbly Beg You."[64] This rite was intrinsically an inversion ritual: formally toadying to all-powerful bureaucrats at home, showing a peasant official the excessive display of respect usually reserved for the noble and well-born. The level of supplication seems to have run in direct proportion to a peasant's success outside his or her village, for it was not the destitute who had the most to lose, but rather the better-off peasants who were most vulnerable (and most victimized) by arbitrariness in peasant administration. This letter, dictated by an illiterate, sixty-year-old peasant tradesman with his own family-run shop in Moscow, is typical of the extreme and fawning character of appeals:

Gracious Sovereign,
Lord Elder!

I send You my old passport and two postage stamps at 7 kopecks each, and most humbly beseech You, Lord Elder, would You be so kind as to send me a family annual passport as soon as possible, since in Moscow it is impossible to live for very long without a passport. Stamps for sending the new passport are enclosed herein.

I beg You to send my passport to this address: Moscow, Khamovnicheskaia Borough, Second Section, Tishinskii Lane, Mushchinkov's House, to the tradesman Mikhail Nikonov.

Once again I earnestly beseech You, please send my passport with haste.
Respectfully Yours, Your humble servant,
Mikhail Nikonov
26 July 1897[65]

A metal worker on the Moscow-Iaroslavl railroad was also a vulnerable type, since work in his skill was always plentiful and because it paid well: "Lord Elder Matvei Alekseev! I Most Humbly Beg You to Be so kind and send me an annual Passport and I send you [herein] [my] old Passport, [and] one ruble cash. I Most Humbly Beg You Be ever so kind and do not postpone [but send] my passport as Soon as Possible."[66]

In a "Petition to the Lord Elder of Elmanovskaia *volost*," the fifty-year-old peasant Petr Krylov, an aging factory worker who found it increasingly difficult to find work, emphasized his own good character and long history of reliability:

And as regards . . . the indicated dues and *obrok*, I could not pay even the small quantity of the *obrok* [which I owe] since I have nowhere found work all summer. [The reason is] especially that my years have left me, I have become old, and in the factories nowhere will they hire those of us who have grown old. There was a time when I never failed [to fulfill] fiscal obligations, but now I cannot send even a little for paying *obrok*.
[Signed] *A peasant who is Known to You,* Petr Iakovlev Krylov[67]

In his successful petition for a passport, Krylov based his appeal above all on the argument that he was long known to the "Lord Elder" and that his reputation was good; he reminded the elder that he had always been a good provider and always in the past promptly paid his dues. The implication of this rather common sort of appeal should not be missed: in the absence of any palpable excuse, a peasant's reputation could be called upon as a reliable guarantee for extended departures.

One unique aspect of the correspondence is the clear indication that peasants often found their jobs first and then made appeals for passports, figuring (probably correctly) that a job in hand and an implicit promise of impending payment would melt away any resistance on the part of the *volost* administration. But it is important to remember too that so long as a peasant lacked proper documentation that upheld his legitimate absence from his village, he remained vulnerable to arrest, exploitation, and abuse. It was hard to be a peasant-worker, but far harder to be a peasant-worker without a passport.

A tone of desperation also often comes through the text of the letters, and in the absence of an established reputation a peasant could usually fall back on an appeal for pity. "Lord *Volost* Elder, on receipt of this request, I beg you to send the passport quickly. You leave me without even a crumb of bread!"[68] The forty-six-year-old illiterate stove-repairman Nikolai Ivanov dictated to a barely literate friend this successful appeal:

> Lord Elder Matvei Alekseich! I most humbly beg You to send an annual family passport as soon as you can. I thought I would get back [to the village] when not too long ago my wife was left ill after she gave birth. I will have to come back myself to settle the taxes and check up on the land. But [until then] I humbly beg You to send the passport as soon as possible. You know that it is tough to live here without a passport, and I cannot possibly stop and abandon my big business [here, to come home]. There's just no way![69]

In the discourse of self-subordination characteristic of the letters, 1897 was a pivotal year, because from that year on internal passports were to be issued to peasants without charge. Initially, peasant-workers clearly felt empowered by the new decree, and for a short time the tone of peasant-worker correspondence with *volost* authorities became arrogant, haughty, and didactic, as peasant-workers chose to express feelings earlier left unspoken:

> Lord Elder! Send my Pachport [sic] to Me In the Name of Nikolai Vasilevich, That is, Forward it [through Him].... And besides I beg You Lord Elder Who received money From My Wife For the pachport give it back to Her or count it toward the *obrok* [because] they're issuing pachports for free [now] and my Wife wrote me that you took money From Her for the pachport.[70]

Another letter was more obviously threatening: "Since the passport is [now] issued without charge, I want to warn you not to delay the passports since without a passport I cannot wait for more the two weeks [so] if you delay I will have to deal with this through the Moscow Chief of Police."[71]

There were numerous reports that despite the abolition of fees, *volost* offices continued to use passports as a means of extorting money from peasants. As we have seen, despite changing legal precedents throughout the 1880s and 1890s, the tsarist bureaucracy by and large upheld the rights of *volost* authorities to use their power over passports as a means by which to ensure each peasant household's timely fulfillment of family and fiscal obligations. Not surprisingly, the arrogant tone of peasant correspondence with *volost* authorities which began in mid-1897 ended abruptly soon after.[72]

As a rule, peasant-workers did not appear in person to collect their passports. Instead, the passports were dispatched to responsible agents, either through the local police or through employers, who would then deliver the documents and collect a signature of receipt. These preprinted warrants communicated to all along the line the status of the worker who requested the passport. A sample of the standard document is quite revealing:

Ministry of Internal Affairs
Elmanovskii *Volost* Elder
Mozhaisk District
Moscow Province

To the District Superintendent of Khimovnicheskaia Borough, Second Section
July 15, 1897
No. 154

I humbly request Your Honor to pass on the enclosed passport for No. 1451 to the peasant of Amyska village Mikhail Nikonov living on Tishinskii Lane, Mushnikov's house. Prior to issuing the passport require him to sign with his own hand a signature on the enclosed passport, if he is literate, [or] in the opposite case make note of his features and type of occupation. Along with this, I have the privilege to add to your Honor that the peasant owes 0 rubles in fiscal dues: arrears from previous years of 0 r. 0 k. and a balance of this year of 0 rub. and 0 k. I humbly request that You do all in Your power to recover these [debts] and send them to the *volost* Office for payment to the District Exchequer.
[signed, with *volost* seal affixed]
The *Volost* Elder
[signed]
The *Volost* Clerk[73]

While the record does not show that the State Treasury managed to exact many arrears this way, it is clear that the paper trail had the effect of enlisting the support of police and employers outside the potential scofflaw's native *volost*. Most peasant-workers became known to police in this way since the procedure provided basic elements of the character and reputation of a peasant-worker residing or working in their districts: his home address, his past record, the degree of desperation that drove him away from the village, his reputation for fulfilling (or failing to fulfill) obligations. When police "rounded up usual suspects," these unreliables were always the first to be singled out and squeezed.

Living without a passport was indeed difficult, but living with such a written testament a peasant-worker also fell prey to a whole host of new vulnerabilities and forces. His reputation in his native village created a paper trail that followed him throughout his life, thereby hampering or facilitating his movements. Not surprisingly, the records are rife with letters of peasants defending themselves from scandalous rumors.

Although Boris Tikhonov (with other Soviet historians) emphasized the resentment of employers against these various restrictions, the weight of evidence in Moscow and provincial archives actually falls elsewhere. Nonvillage employers in fact welcomed the restrictions as a means by which to render workers more docile and controllable. Any worker would think twice before risking the intervention of his family, his fellow villagers, and worst of all his *volost* elder in his affairs outside the village. As an employer in Moscow Province wrote rather demonstratively in 1888: "It is impossible . . . to cope with the factory worker without the assistance of the local police."[74] Factories especially coped rather well with the regulations and often handled passport renewal directly, from their own personnel offices. While this removed the complications associated with local obstacles motivated by graft, it did facilitate a considerable degree of rationalization in the complicated process of expropriating a peasant-worker's cash earnings and redirecting them back to the worker's native village for taxes and family support. By the beginning of the twentieth century, such arrangements between factories and *volost* authorities became the rule, not the exception, for the vast majority of industrial workers of peasant origin.[75]

Village Regulation of Demographic Behavior

Village leaders were keenly aware of the importance of family ties as a channel for regulating peasant-workers, which had a telling impact on regional demographic patterns.[76] Drawing from his extensive survey of village life throughout European Russia, D. N. Zhbankov observed that early peasant marriage was universal, regardless of the degree of local labor migration: "In all peasant Russia [it is believed] that every male, upon reaching a certain age, should without fail marry according to purely economic considerations: marriage is thought to be the foundation for family and economy. Without a wife, the peasant economy could not go on. The inhabitants of all the districts of Kostroma Province—who lead a rural economy independent [of outside earnings]—submit to this law. They remain single only when they have no farm at all, or participate only insignificantly in the farm economy of relatives."[77] Zhbankov calculated that 60.7 percent of all marriages in two high-migration districts in northwest Kostroma Province consisted of peasant men who were less than twenty years old. This contrasted to the corresponding rates of 40.9 percent for all of Kostroma Province and 38.57 percent for European Russia.[78]

Certainly, migration for outside labor had an effect on age of marriage. This was true both because family members and dependents remaining at home wanted to retain some hold on departing migrants, but also because marriage was popularly believed to be the necessary prerequisite to good peasant economy. Apparently, Zhbankov adds, "The young wife does not appear as an obstacle for [the husband's] absence, but on the contrary unbinds the hands of the husband, frees him from the land and the village: she remains instead of him as worker in the home, and he—with scarcely a month's honeymoon passed—sets off afresh to 'the side.' For several women, the entire family life is limited to 2–3 months."[79]

To accommodate labor migration, high-migration villages adapted their ritual cycles to facilitate peasant-worker participation. "Having completed his apprenticeship, the young peasant-worker comes home almost every year during the autumn, where he attends evening parties *[vecherinki]* and hunts for a bride."[80] The statistics are telling. For instance, while only 38.1 percent of all peasant marriages throughout European Russia in the 1890s occurred during the winter months, a whopping 86.5 percent of peasant marriages took place during the winter months in the high-migration districts of Kostroma Province.[81] "While the potential groom travels about neighboring villages [in search of a bride], participating in traditional gatherings and meetings, his parents and close relatives, by means of various sources of information and reconnaissance via certain 'good women' *[kumushki]* and matchmakers, try to find out about local maidens, about their character, their income, and the wealth *[dovol'stvo]* of their parents."[82] Numerous sources indicate that having a solid work reputation and a favorable setup in *otkhod* was an essential prerequisite to making a good marriage in high-migration villages:

> *Motives of a higher order* also exert an influence on *otkhod*. *Pitershchiki* are much more sophisticated than those who reside here [in the village]: their speech would often be indistinguishable from city speech, if it were not adorned so with fancy expressions; their manners are copied from the petty bourgeoisie in the capital, they know how to dance, [wear] dandified clothes, etc. The local fair sex

absolutely prefers them, and usually the young men living here permanently get the worst brides, even in spite of the fact that they may sometimes live more prosperously than *pitershchiki*. All the country people are called dullards *[serye]*, and what is strange, they are not at all offended by this appellation and even call themselves such while complaining of parents who did not apprentice them in *Piter*.[83]

Peasants in Liubim District, Iaroslavl Province, complained angrily against "this general opinion, that the person who lives neither in Petersburg nor somewhere else [outside the village] but occupies himself with agriculture or some [local] handicraft, appropriates for the rest of his life the label 'herdsman' *[pastukh]*, and for such a person it's difficult to find himself a bride."[84] Similarly, in a popular *chastushka* or peasant ditty from St. Petersburg Province at the turn of the century, a young peasant-worker courted a future bride with confidence:

> Девки, девки, я вам дядя,
> Вы — племянницы мои;
> Выходите за ворота
> Слушать песенки мои.
>
> Любите, девушки, меня,
> Из Питеру приехал я,
> Тальянку новую привез,
> Играет — слышно за семь верст.
>
> Пойдемте, девушки, купаться,
> Я вас плавать научу,
> А коль плавать не хотите,
> То — на лодке прокачу.
>
> *[Girls, girls, I'm your uncle,*
> *And you are my nieces;*
> *Come out from behind the gates*
> *And listen to my songs.*
>
> *Girls, love me,*
> *I just came from* Piter
> *And brought a new accordion*
> *Which can be heard for seven versts!*

> *Girls, let's go bathing,*
> *I'll teach you to swim,*
> *And if you don't want to swim,*
> *Then I'll take you for a ride in a boat.]*[85]

In high-migration villages, courting rituals were lively celebrations, and young peasant-workers were the guests of honor.

Ultimately, marriage became the link through which households united the village base with earnings from migration. The challenge of integrating the village and nonvillage peasant economies into a relatively stable, single household unit was accomplished through bifurcation, or splitting the peasant family between farm and nonfarm work places. The bifurcated peasant household pooled the resources of the agricultural and wage-income sectors while also creating a bridge that facilitated the integration of subordinate family members into the village community. Paradoxically, bifurcation was the mechanism that sustained and upheld traditional village relations in the face of a crisis of village economy by restoring the capacity of the elder generation to extract the labor products of the young. As one elder put it, the younger generation would abandon the rural world "if there isn't the restraining influence of elders and a wife."[86] Or, as an observer in Tver Province explained, "Peasants regard marriage as a way of attaching a person to the household."[87] A Kostroma schoolteacher of peasant origins added in the late 1890s: "In the peasant's view, marriage ties a person to the family. 'If you don't give him a wife, [they say,] he'll find a stranger. [A young man] goes to Piter—what is his *bat'ka* and his mama to him? But he will remember his wife and children.'"[88] In fact, in most villages, *odinochki*—those without families of their own— were not permitted to leave the village for earnings. In Bronnitsy District, Moscow Province, "Those who migrate for earnings are persons from large *[mnogie rabochie]* families exclusively; *odinochki* all remain in the village."[89] In this way, villages regulated the demographic behavior of individual peasant households.

Moreover, the subtle forces regulating peasant demographic behavior ensured a pattern of endogamy: the choice of a prospective bride almost always fell on a local village girl.

> *Otkhodniki,* both poor and rich, marry village girls exclusively. This is done due to the strength of tradition and on the insistence of the elders, and also in view of [insurance against] the possibility of misfortune. The *otkhodnik* who marries a town girl will not be able to bring her back to the village for the continuation of

the village economy: she will not know how either to work in the fields or keep house in the village, and village life after the town would prove unbearable for her. To continue the village economy . . . is considered necessary: it is consequently necessary to marry a village girl who, in poor as well as rich [families], knows how to work and to manage the fields.[90]

The colorful language of an old woman from Ioakimanskaia *volost,* Shuia District, Vladimir Province, reflects the ways in which nonlocal brides were viewed as threats to family stability: "And the sort of daughter-in-law he's brought [home]! Not only can't you make her do anything, but you yourself [want] to take a breather on the bench, but she's already parked herself there. And when she's managed to eat up all the wedding soup, [she complains] that 'I don't want to live with the family anymore. [I want] to live on my own!' "[91] Such were the notorious problems with daughters-in-law, according to the complaints of old folks living in the village. In this way, a son's choice of a bride carried far more importance than purely economic considerations in a peasant household.

The experience of the peasant-worker from Moscow Province, Semën Kanatchikov, provides us with one last illustration of the power of family ties when combined with passport manipulation. As he became more outspoken in his views, Kanatchikov came into conflict with employers and began to move from factory to factory, first in Moscow then in St. Petersburg, where a distant relative from his region helped him to get settled. Still unable to hold down a job, he received two anxious letters from his father in the village. The first exhorted him to remember the vows he had made on his departure: to attend church, obey his superiors, and above all, honor his family responsibilities. Soon after, another letter arrived.

> The second letter was even more ominous. This time my father categorically demanded that I mend my ways: ". . . and if you don't settle down, you scoundrel, I won't renew your passport. I'll have you brought home by the police, and when they've brought you home, I'll whip you with a birch rod myself, in the district administrative office, in the presence of honest people. . . ." This threatening letter seriously disturbed me, especially because my passport was about to expire. True, I knew that my father would not carry out his threat, although in those days he definitely had the authority to do so, and I remembered several instances of that kind.[92]

Even for a "conscious" worker like Kanatchikov, such overt threats were a source of tremendous anxiety: "I knew my father's hot-tempered yet easily appeased character. So I wrote him a conciliatory letter and sent him ten rubles,

The Social Control of Peasant Labor   75

after which he calmed down somewhat."[93] More often, the family position was presented in the form of a gentle, parental exhortation: "We beg you, our dear son, don't waste money, we have no rich relations, so help no one. Don't play cards, don't smoke tobacco or drink wine, and live virtuously."[94]

The Forced Return of Scofflaws

> *Among petty law-breakers . . . are taken in handcuffs 15–16 year-old boys. . . . We saw three boys crying bitterly from pain, fear and humiliation, who were being sent in chains . . . [to their homes] in Iaroslavl Province.*[95]

In the event that an *otkhodnik* ignored various efforts to exact the payment of taxes and family support, he could be arrested and returned by force to his native village. This return could be accomplished by issuing an order, ordinarily by resolution of the communal assembly, that the "careless member" be brought back to the village under guard *(po etapu, vytrebovanie,* or *vysylka)*. The incurred cost (about twelve rubles in Kostroma Province during the 1880s) was added to the accumulated fiscal debt of the *etapnik* or returnee. Zhbankov summarized the myriad cultural, economic, and legal pressures which came into play.

> Coming home as a prisoner in transit is considered a disgrace in the village. . . . The community indiscriminately looks upon every *etapnik* as a person guilty of drunken behavior, not zealous toward his household, and as such he is usually sentenced by the *volost* court to punishment or arrest or "the birch." All this has a demoralizing effect on young out-migrants. Shame from punishment, the decline of the household, and the impossibility for 1–3 years of going on the side, until payment of the forced-transit fee *[etapnye den'gi]* and arrears, puts the young migrant in an exitless position, the more so as at home he is a poor helper: he doesn't know agricultural work and such workers are not hired. After the light work [of the city or at the factory] he must willingly or unwillingly get accustomed to the heavy field work of the village. Experienced people who have gone through the process before set out anew on a journey without passport or money. Sometimes such a traveler is quickly discovered and again returned home as an *etapnik,* but sometimes he succeeds in finding a place, an occupation, and sends money home for the payment of taxes, his relatives send him a passport, and he again has a legal standing. However, the majority of these "habitual ones" become tramps.[96]

Vytrebovanie was a classic and compelling instrument to uphold the aura of patriarchal authority in the village and to encourage obedience and responsibility among *otkhodniki*. In the context of the village community, it was only the family, injured directly by the delinquent's irresponsibility, that could wield the support of community opinion to such a degree as to warrant so extreme a measure without provoking community defiance against authority. *Etapniki* were not just scofflaws, they were corrupt and immoral individuals who had grossly deviated from community norms. A district tax inspector noted: "They summon for return only those delinquents who are leading a dissolute *[besputnyi]* life."[97] As B. V. Tikhonov observed in his fascinating study of passport manipulation in Moscow Province, the greatest factor in the refusal to renew passports or the arrest and return of *otkhodniki* to the village was "the failure to send to the native village money for the payment of taxes and for the livelihood of disabled or aged parents."[98] In Riazan Province, by far the greatest number of cases of *vytrebovanie* were initiated by such abandoned family members.[99] Likewise, in Smolensk Province, those with high arrears were summoned back to the village "in large part at the desire of the parents or wife."[100] In Moscow Province, there were even cases of the forced return of wives ordered by husbands living in the village.[101]

Vytrebovanie was also used by communities to discourage abandonment by entire households. During the 1890s, the area in Iaroslavl Province with the highest frequency of *vytrebovanie* was Prozorovskaia *volost,* Mologa District. In Sumilskaia village, for instance, thirty of ninety-seven peasant-workers had abandoned their allotments, due to the extreme disproportion of payments to land values. Needless to say, the abandonment of the village by one-third of local households sharply increased already excessive per capita tax rates for the remaining households. The local commune responded by passing a spurious resolution to alienate communal lands "due to the impossibility of fulfilling arrears."[102] In addition, efforts were made to force *pustyrniki*—peasants who had abandoned their land and village obligations—to fulfill their responsibilities. There were throughout Mologa District a total of forty known cases of *vytrebovanie,* due mostly to the intense pressure of *volost* elders. Resistant peasants who had abandoned their allotments were brought back under guard in order to restore solvency to the eroding village tax base.[103]

For obvious reasons, *vytrebovanie* was more a deterrent to inspire obedience and fear among village members, not a procedure that could be used often. The myth of control was more effective for everyone—both those dependents in the village needing money and those away from the village earning it. Such forceful intervention was of necessity an instrument of last resort, used to make a public example of extreme cases. For instance, only 1.8 percent of all passports issued in the two highest migration districts of Kostroma Province during the 1880s actually involved *etapniki*. Ultimately, the community's need for earnings was the overriding concern, setting definite limits on the coercive power of the passport system.

> [*Volost* authorities] do not issue passports to tax delinquents, but this relates only to those adult workers who have accumulated arrears exceeding 1-2 years of apportioned taxes, and [who] lead "on the side" a wild *[razgul'nyi]* life. In general, this measure—not issuing passports to those with arrears—is used by *volost* administrative and higher district authorities with great care, more as a threat to the rest with small arrears accumulated, with the goal of receiving from these some part of the arrears. The strict use of such a measure is positively impossible, which is known well by all. The people have grown accustomed after having, for a long time, used earnings on the side for taxes and their needs; and if a large or small portion of them will be left home, then arrears will grow still more as a consequence of the absence of local earnings.[104]

Corporal Punishment

Efforts to extract taxes, redemption payments, and arrears were designed to coerce, not to destroy. Fines, imprisonment, and revocation or nonrenewal of a passport all represented procedures that were best used rarely, as examples for the rest. The procedure most frequently applied against flagrant delinquents was corporal punishment, limited by law to a maximum of twenty blows with a birch rod. The birch spared the delinquent and his family the hardship of fines, imprisonment or, worst of all, an invalid passport. And the use of such "energetic measures"—the outward appearance of vigorous efforts to collect arrears—regularly spared the community from having to cover the accrued debt from its own coffers under terms of *krugovaia poruka*.

The use of the birch was designed both as a moral lesson for the delinquent and as a public display; both as an effort toward intimidation and as an exercise in public shaming. As a village elder in Kostroma Province noted: "Flogging is little imposed but always feared."[105] In the vast majority of cases, the sentence of corporal punishment was expressed in terms emphasizing the character flaw that had induced the negligent member to deviate from the norm: his drunkenness, profligacy *(durnoe povedenie)*, "blatant stubbornness," or lack of zealousness *(nerachitel'nost)* which had led to his neglect of respon-

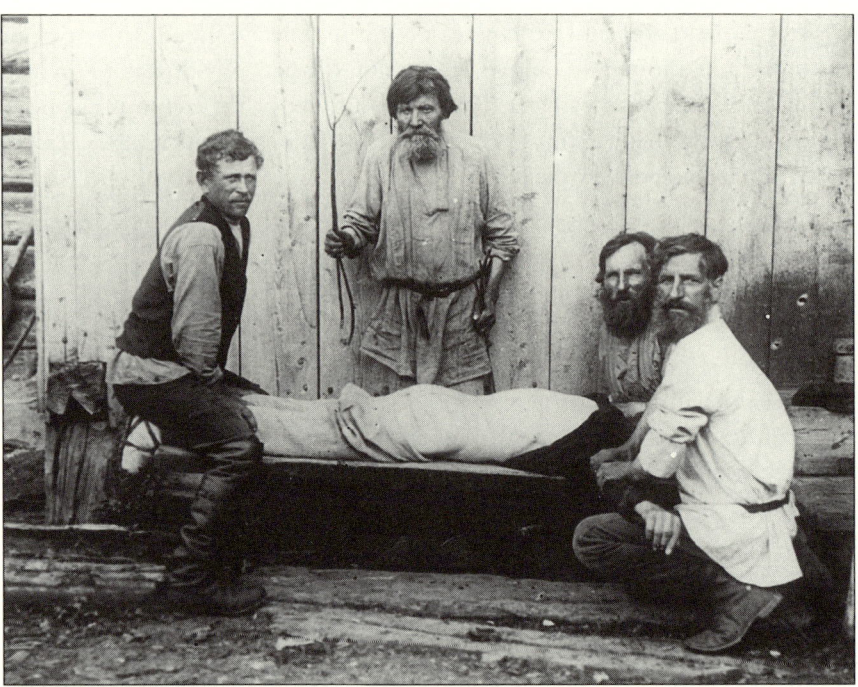

Peasant flogging in a village of Moscow Province, early twentieth century. The birch rod—or "birch noodles" *(berezovye lapshi)*—was commonly used in the Central Industrial Region to coerce peasants to fulfill state dues and obligations. Museum of the Revolution, Moscow.

sibilities to his family and community.[106] Delinquents were held to be in violation of community norms, a violation that had threatened the solvency of the entire community.

Consistent with a standard procedure that prefaced every administrative act with a threat, the rounding up of delinquents was preceded by a public announcement much like this one issued in 1890 by the *volost* elder in Efremov District, Tula Province:

> I instruct the village elder: tomorrow you will convene an assembly and proclaim to the peasants that they are obligated to pay all of the current taxes by Saturday, and if upon my examination there is anyone who has not paid his dues, he will be punished with the birch in the presence of the village assembly.[107]

Such threats gave those peasants with arrears the opportunity to respond by reaching an agreement with the commune, by selling off property, or by turning to local lenders and hiring-agents who—as we shall see—often worked in concert with local authorities to bail out local peasants while also securing labor at favorable rates.

In the event that efforts to coerce peasant compliance were unsuccessful, the threatened public rite of corporal punishment was often carried out. "They are flogged before the eyes of neighbors and even with their help, since frequently the *volost* elder orders the peasants to assist the guard . . . and sometimes even in the presence of one's own and other children, since the school is often situated in line with the *volost* office."[108] Data from districts throughout European Russia suggest that the use of corporal punishment by peasant officials declined during the last quarter of the nineteenth century. Nonetheless, it tended to be applied far more frequently in high-migration districts. According to official statistics on the use of corporal punishment in *volost* court sentences during 1896, flogging was proposed in 2 percent or more of all cases in fourteen of forty-nine provinces of European Russia. Five of these fourteen provinces were located in the Central Industrial Region, and ten were northern, non-black-earth provinces with high rates of migration.[109] In twenty-eight *volosti* of Moscow Province, the birch was the most common form of punishment for tax delinquents, as a means of "beating arrears" *(vykolachivanie nedoimok)* out of scofflaws. As a *volost* elder from Dmitrov District, Moscow Province, declared: "Sometimes in extreme cases one must punish delinquents with the birch for their blatant stubbornness."[110] Typically, however, village officials preferred to intimidate scofflaws into submission. In one *volost* of Kineshma District, Kostroma Province, the birch was used rarely, maybe three times per year, "only to frighten [delinquents] and put them to shame in front of the people." Or, as a *volost* elder from Uglich District in the same province explained: "You don't really always [have to] flog them. Often, it's enough to just strip them and scare them a little."[111] Floggings, like other sanctions, were applied most in areas where the "paternalistic vigilance" of civil authorities was greatest: the "civilizing influence" of authority was imposed with a lurking threat of state-sponsored violence.[112]

The Resistance of Scofflaws

Inevitably, these various controls—passport manipulation, special leave-taxes, forced return, imprisonment, corporal punishment, public shaming, and so on—were applied in the face of considerable resistance from the alleged

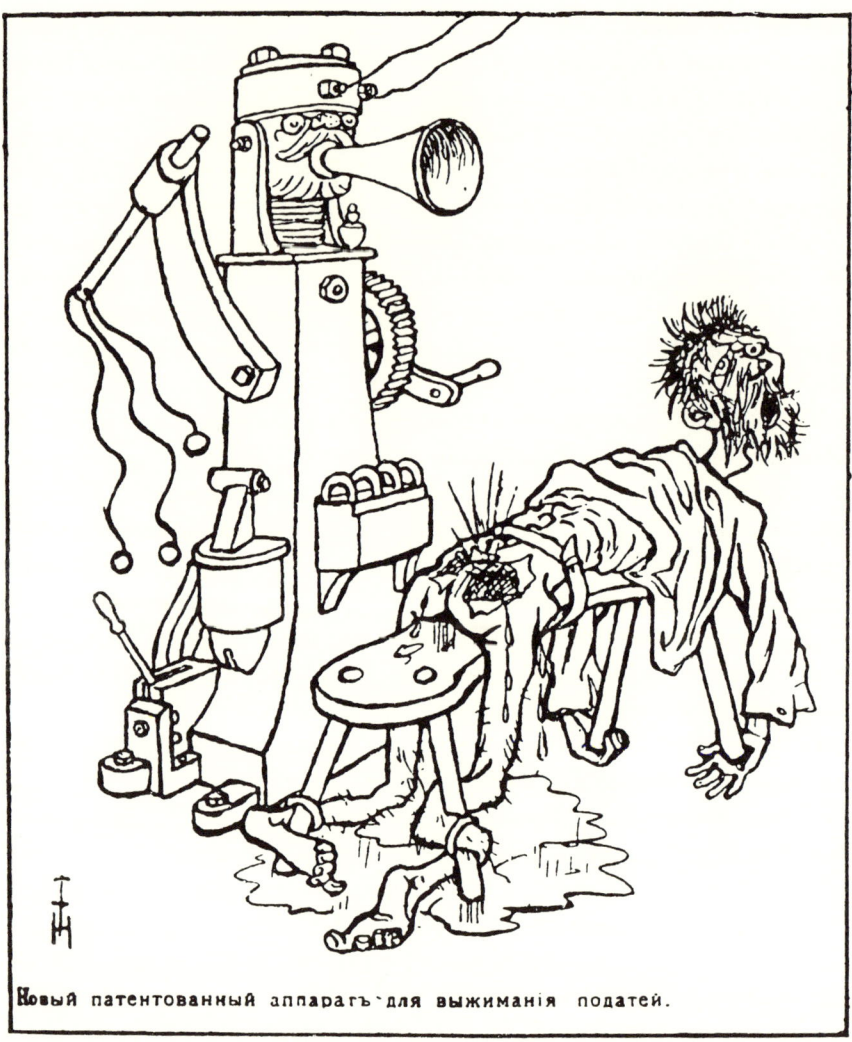

Political cartoon from the journal *Diatel: ezhenedel'nyi organ politicheskoi i obshchestvennoi satiry* (The woodpecker: a weekly organ of political and social satire), no. 1, 1905: "A New Patented Apparatus for Squeezing Taxes [from Peasants]." The apparatus caricatures Tsar Nicolas II.

scofflaws themselves. It is fair to inquire about the nature of peasant-worker opposition to these various restrictions and punishments. On what basis was patriarchal authority challenged?

An especially good illustration of the rhetoric of conflict between communes and accused scofflaws comes from a case tried before the Moscow

Provincial Bureau of Peasant Affairs in May 1895.[113] The well-to-do peasant Vasilii Piskarev, of Podol'ia District, Moscow Province, had prohibited his son Konstantin, as an "inseparable member of the family," from renewing his passport. The justification, which was not required for the parental prohibition, was that the son had failed to provide suitable money and assistance for his father's upkeep in the village. Piskarev's father filed a complaint with the elder of Voronovskaia *volost,* who ordered an injunction for the arrest and forced return of Piskarev junior through the police of the Aleksandr-Nevskii region in St. Petersburg, where the younger Piskarev lived with his wife and children. The forced return was carried out just a few months later, in August 1895.

The case points up the problems associated with unauthorized household divisions. Father and son Piskarev had agreed on the terms of a household division back in 1889, but since the division was never authorized by a two-thirds vote of the village commune (according to strict procedures outlined in the law on household divisions dated 18 March 1886), the division was never recognized by the state. On the one hand, the younger Piskarev felt he could live and work without his father's pretensions. On the other, his father could at any moment, as he eventually did, withdraw his consent and make fresh claims on his son. As head of the "indivisible family unit," Piskarev's father had extensive rights that were intended to enhance his patriarchal authority over the disposition of resources, labor, and income of all members of the household and thereby to strengthen his ability to fulfill state obligations. The matter was further complicated by the fact that the younger Piskarev had signed a written agreement at the time of their division of the household in which he promised to subsidize the cost of an occasional hired laborer on his father's farm for a period of four years, at the rate of twenty-five rubles per year. In this regard, the land captain's report was damning: "To this day, . . . Konstantin Piskarev has not fulfilled the obligation to his father which he voluntarily took upon himself. [Namely,] he has neglected to help his father with the support of the peasant farm and considers himself to be completely free from [the obligation to] pay any sort of duties connected with his father's maintenance of allotment land and a farmstead. Moreover, as a peasant son who has not divided [from his father's household, he has neglected his] family obligations."[114] For local officials, the case was clear: Piskarev's son was a good-for-nothing wastrel.

Throughout the affair, the son, desperate to defend his reputation against such accusations, filed four separate petitions: one with the land captain, two with the Moscow governor, and one with the minister of internal affairs, dated

1 March 1896. The last came almost a year after his native *volost* had failed to renew his passport. Subsequent to that action, twice during the next year the junior Piskarev had been arrested, with serious fines, for living in St. Petersburg without proper travel documents. He was now known to the St. Petersburg police, and without a resolution of the case, it was just a matter of time before he would be forced back to the village under guard. The text of his petition is here reproduced in full:

> *To His Highness the Minister of Internal Affairs*
> *From the peasant . . . Konstantin Vasil'ev Piskarev.*
>
> PETITION
>
> Last year, on May 7, [1895,] I sent the Varonovskaia *Volost* Office [my] passport, which was due to expire on 16 May of that year, and 8 rubles for sending a new passport. But on 31 May, the *Volost* Elder notified me through the police of my father's demand . . . that I send him 25 rubles, otherwise no passport could be issued to me.
>
> I have the honor to explain to Your Highness the following:
>
> My father Vasilii Piskarev already in 1889 cut me off [from his household] in a resolution of the Village Commune and gave [me] land for one soul, which remained in his use, and I have paid 7 to 9 rubles [each year] for this land without any arrears whatsoever. In the same year, my father, a wealthy peasant, according to the rights of a father, demanded from me a written agreement *[rospiska]* [where I promised] him assistance of 100 rubles. Leaving my native village for work in the capital with my wife and four young children, [over the next five years] I sent my father as much as my means allowed, [a sum of] 45 rubles: 25 rubles by postal [cash transfer], and 20 rubles through fellow villagers.
>
> Now . . . my father has instructed the *Volost* Elder not to issue me a passport until I pay him . . . 100 rubles above and beyond what he has already received from me.
>
> Working here in a [St. Petersburg] hat factory, and managing to provide for my wife and four children solely from my own earnings of 25 rubles a month, fearing to lose even this last piece of bread as a result of the inhumanity of my own father, I turned to the Land Captain with an appeal to force the *Volost* to issue me a travel certificate.

That appeal was refused on the basis of the son's failure to fulfill the written agreement and pay the twenty-five rubles per year to his father. Another two appeals to the District Bureau of Peasant Affairs were likewise denied. A final appeal to the Moscow Bureau of Peasant Affairs contained the son's most complete and powerful arguments.

Konstantin Piskarev's defense was based upon the notion that his responsibilities as a son were superseded by his duties as a father: the concept of patriarchal authority remained sacrosanct, but the son was caught in a tragic dilemma in which he impugned his father's motives in order to draw attention to his own fatherly concerns for the livelihood of his children. In his appeal to the rhetoric and values of his village, Piskarev junior presented himself not as a bad son, but rather as a good father. By implication, it was not he who was a prodigal, but rather his father who had betrayed the sacred unwritten covenant between fathers and sons.

The tactic brought the issue to a razor's edge sufficient to get the attention of the Moscow Bureau of Peasant Affairs. In his final petition, the younger Piskarev eloquently threw himself upon the "divine mercy" of the court, charging that his father "arbitrarily" and therefore unjustly withheld his passport.

> I remain subject to this sad decision, living [already] almost a year on extensions *[po ot"srochkam]* issued to me by the Petersburg Town Governor. I have been placed in a critical position, on the basis of which I turn for defense to Your Highness.
>
> That I gave my father a written agreement—this question is undisputed. But as father of a large family of my own I could not tear away from my own children a vital piece of bread just to satisfy the wishes of my father, who does not live in need. . . .
>
> Your Highness, show your just mercy: turn your attention to my exitless position. Put an end to this arbitrariness. Order the *Volost* Office to issue me, a taxpayer without arrears, a travel certificate without hindrance. Intercede before the Eternal God and pray for my four young children who suffer so undeservedly. For seven years my father used me for work. Is it really possible that this gave him no profit?

Next, the younger Piskarev appealed to a notion commonly invoked among Russian peasants: the concept of *trudovoe nachalo*—the "labor principle"—a brand of popular socialism which preached that everyone should work and be rewarded only on the basis of his own labor, and that it was wrong to live off the labor of others. This was a more direct challenge to the tenets of the patriarchal peasant household, since it questioned the unlimited right of a father to expropriate the labor of his son.

> [In contrast to my father], I live only by my own labor, which they want to take away from me by not sending me a travel certificate. At the same time they deprive me of the opportunity to earn my daily subsistence honestly.
>
> My earnings are so limited that I cannot immediately satisfy the pretensions of my father. . . . I have paid out 45 rubles. Moreover, I have [always] reliably sent

the *obrok*. Nonetheless, there is no exit for me, only because of this expense which divides us, these 100 rubles.

What can I do? It is impossible for me to pay everything [I owe] immediately, and it will help no one if I cast aside my factory earnings and go back to my village with my family. My father gave me neither livestock nor a house when he cut me off, and he himself uses my land. Am I supposed to bow to him and his whims, to such obligations? . . . . I have been imprisoned in the commune, left with nothing. . . .

In the last section of his appeal, the younger Piskarev challenged the right of his father and his commune to intrigue against him on the grounds of pure common sense:

So what if I were to cast aside my work, come back to the village and loaf about the commune with my family? What do I have in the village? Nothing. And I think that if they had given me my passport without hindrance, and not impeded me each year, just as they have now, entangling me in their scandalous stories, then I could have long ago fulfilled my obligations. If, in delaying my passport completely against the law, my father thinks he will get from me the required sum even sooner, he's wrong. So long as I do not have the opportunity to live peacefully with my family, but every year must fear loss of my passport, then it stands to reason that I will lose earnings and will be deprived of the chance to satisfy [my father].

Beneath the stormy surface of a civil suit between father and son was an even stormier family relationship. Regardless of his reasons for doing so, the well-to-do peasant Piskarev had every right to impose on his son proper respect due his father. It is notable that in its review of the case following the son's string of petitions, the Moscow Bureau of Peasant Affairs divided the dispute into two issues. First, the court ruled that Piskarev's son had failed to fulfill his obligations to his father regarding his written agreement to subsidize a hired laborer for a period of four years. While this was reprehensible and left the son legally culpable, "it could not serve as an obstacle . . . for the issuing of a passport." As a wholly separate and independent issue, the Bureau nonetheless upheld the peasant father's revocation of his son's passport, solely on the basis of his patriarchal rights: "Issuing to Piskarev a passport . . . without his father's consent cannot be allowed."[115] The patriarchal privileges of the elder-father were sacrosanct, regardless of the father's motivations or style in wielding them, and regardless of any resulting injustice.

Productive Versus Unproductive Members

It would be misleading to overstate the rationality of communal assessment schemes and efforts to regulate out-workers. Obviously, the various forces brought to bear on peasant labor-migrants differed from village to village, and from individual to individual. We need to avoid any hasty, overly rationalized scheme that does not take into account the creative initiatives of communes and individual peasants. Still, one overriding pattern can be observed. As a rule, communes ruthlessly exploited their prerogatives over productive migrant workers, demanding from them as much as they would bear and sometimes more. At the same time, communes resisted having to take on financial burdens for unproductive or infirm members.

Details can be drawn from a review of more than fifty disputes over the rights of migrating peasants vis-à-vis their communes preserved in the records of the Moscow Provincial Bureau of Peasant Affairs.[116] Judging from these cases, there was a widespread practice of squeezing peasant-workers based on their varying abilities to pay. The village's right to assess dues independently of a household's allotment size, or to adjust allotment size to fit a peasant-worker's estimated wealth, gave villagers enormous rights over migrants. An informative illustration of how blatantly this logic was applied was the review of the petition of peasant Mikhail Tukhmanov of Bedovaia village, Klin District, Moscow Province, dated 10 August 1893.[117]

Because Tukhmanov largely ignored his relationship with his village, except when he needed to renew his annual passport, he had developed the reputation for being "well-off" (sostoiatel'nyi). As a result, his commune began in the 1880s to demand from his family of two adults and three young children twice the normal assessment, sixteen rubles per year. Year after year, they raised his assessment still more, so that eventually he was expected to pay out nearly 350 percent of the standard rate for a one-soul allotment! According to the *volost* elder, when interviewed in person by the land captain, "[Tukhmanov]... is well-situated and has [a lot of] money.... The payment of the indicated arrears [of 230 rubles] would be nothing for him."[118] Since Tukhmanov was rich, there was no harm in demanding a little more from him.

The problem was that the commune had been misinformed: Tukhmanov was not rich. In his petition to the Moscow Bureau of Peasant Affairs, Tukhmanov questioned the right of the commune "to assess [taxes] of 26 or 27 rubles a year from a person who does not have and never has had any land" in the village. "When I was in the village, I found out why I in particular have been saddled with such enormous arrears. The communal assembly announced that they had imposed on me an allotment for four souls. I looked that assembly in the eyes and asked them to show me the land for which I owed obligations, and they told me, 'You pay the money, then we'll lead you to it.' It is clear that the Commune has required payment for land which is not available, that all of the land is used by those peasants who live in the village. Meanwhile, living in Moscow with [my wife] and three young children, I am scarcely able to earn enough for their subsistence, and even then, only when I have a valid passport."

In its review of Tukhmanov's case, the Moscow Bureau of Peasant Affairs barely touched upon the charges leveled in Tukhmanov's petition, and no independent investigation was ever conducted; the elder's word, backed by the village commune, was all that was needed as evidence in the Bureau's proceedings. The court also rejected Tukhmanov's claim, arguing that "Tukhmanov's failure to use field lands could not serve as basis for his liberation from the payment of duties, even more so when the village commune does not refuse him land."[119] In other words, the land was his whether he wanted it or not. Either way, he had to pay the arrears.

Tukhmanov's accusation was a common refrain: he was being taxed for land which did not exist, or forced to pay for land from which others (not he) were profiting. Very often, peasants had severed ties with their villages to the degree that their land had for years been permanently taken over for use by neighboring families. The peasant Ermil Kisliakov of Veseleva village, Glydovskaia *volost,* Kolomna District, complained in 1898: "I entered military service on 1 January 1874 and until the end of my military service [some 23 years later] never used my land or other assets *[ugod'ia],* and presently I do not use [them]. I don't even live in the village.... I don't even know where my land allotment is now or who controls and uses it. Moreover, the allotment itself can pay for fiscal dues completely, and even [generate] a surplus."[120] Only later, after his own investigation in the village, did Kisliakov learn the bitter truth: "The arrears have been accumulated by my brother Vasilii.... [He] uses the land and is obligated to pay all dues."[121] This was an all-too-common story. Ermil and Vasilii Kisliakov were regarded as a single household and single taxable unit, holding a two-soul allotment. While Ermil was in military service, his brother Vasilii was responsible for managing their land and had used his brother's absence to drive the family farm into hopeless debt. Despite his long absence for military service, Ermil remained responsible for arrears accumulated by his elder brother.

By 1 January 1897, the two brothers had accumulated arrears of 144 rubles,

2 kopecks on an annual tax obligation of 16 rubles, 80 kopecks. On his return from military service, their village assembly agreed to issue Ermil a passport for side-work in return for a minimum payment of 10 rubles toward arrears each year. This was in accordance with article 60 of the Revised Law on Passports which stipulated that the village commune retained the right to demand payment of all or part of the arrears as a condition for passport renewal. Since Ermil had not divided from his brother's household, he was to be held equally liable for the debts his brother had accumulated in his absence. In fact, through cash transfers Ermil did manage to pay a total of 3 rubles, 35 kopecks in three separate transactions in 1897, but frustrated at Ermil's obvious recalcitrance, his commune ordered that no further passports be issued by the *volost* office and that Ermil be brought back to his village "under guard" and in chains.

The tensions were particularly great with landless peasants forced by their communes to pay exorbitant "leave charges" for the annual right to renew passports and live and work outside their villages. In February 1898, the peasant father Iakov Trofimov filed a complaint against his *volost* authorities that they had wrongfully withheld a passport from his son, Petr. The issue was that he wanted a five-year passport for his son, while the *volost* elder, taking into account Trofimov's household arrears of 126 rubles, 46 kopecks, agreed only to issue a six-month passport. The situation was further aggravated by the fact that even current dues of 20 rubles per year were only partially paid, to the sum of 7 rubles, 15 kopecks. Iakov Trofimov appealed for outside intervention on the basis of the fact that "we have neither land, nor income, nor any privileges whatsoever in our native village."[122] Father and son unsuccessfully requested "liberation from all arrears and fees" and unfettered rights to long-term passports. The implication of the Bureau's refusal to grant the petition was clear: the state would in no way undermine the rights of communes to extract payments from departing laborers.

The same refrain was sounded in case after case. "Neither my father nor I were occupied with arable farming, but always resided in Moscow." Though the family held a four-soul allotment in the commune, "we neither used it nor rented it out. It was used and managed by the peasant commune."[123] And elsewhere: "Neither I nor my father either used the land nor managed it ourselves. Rather it was managed by the Commune, and I don't know who used it."[124] Or, in another case: "I never owned the land and never rented it out to [my] aunt. The land was constantly owned by my uncle Egor Iakovlev and, after his death by [my aunt] Mar'ia Fedorovna and her son Pavel [Egorevich].... It follows that I could never have accumulated such enormous arrears."[125]

Usually, peasant-workers who had been excoriated as scofflaws challenged this affront to their reputations by underlining the senselessness of any decision that restricted their movements. For instance, in July 1893, Aleksandr Golikov—a peasant-worker from Tatishcheva village, Piatnitskaia *volost,* Zvenigorod District, Moscow Province—filed a complaint against his *volost* commune. Living illegally in Moscow and without a valid passport at the time of the petition, Golikov complained bitterly that "the Commune's . . . withholding *[uderzhanie]* of my passport makes no sense whatsoever, and can never achieve the goals [they want], other than to ruin me once and for all and completely deprive [me] of any chance of paying arrears."[126] The issue was that Golikov had divided from his father's multiple-family household years before, without gaining legal sanction for the household division from the village commune. So, when his father died in early 1893 with an accumulated arrears of 92 rubles, 40 kopecks, their commune passed a resolution that attached the debt to Golikov junior's otherwise well-managed affairs. In his petition to the Bureau of Peasant Affairs, Golikov rejected his commune's insistence that he make "the payment of arrears, which had been accumulated by his deceased father." Defending his reputation as a good provider and fellow villager, Golikov pointed out that "I, receiving the paltry earnings of ten rubles per month, [and living] the expensive life in the capital, must [also] help my aged mother and my young sisters. But in spite of my meager means, I have always conscientiously and accurately paid my taxes for two souls."[127] Here as elsewhere, fiscal solvency held priority over family needs: the Bureau of Peasant Affairs denied Golikov's petition and upheld the right of his commune to demand payment of his father's arrears.

These selected cases in the Moscow Bureau of Peasant Affairs are just the tip of the iceberg in the widespread challenges of peasant-workers to the strict controls imposed on them by village communes and family dependents. While various initiatives came and went, one rule dominated: until the very end of the Old Regime, the Russian state continued to grant peasant communes the virtually unrestricted right to extract dues and obligations from migrating peasant-workers. Communal-based coercion schemes grounded in patriarchal authority were time and again upheld by the courts.[128] Inevitably, these schemes to ensure peasant fiscal discipline were wielded with equal measure for collecting private debts, as well as protecting the security of dependent family members who remained in the village, and even proscribing the behavior of peasants who paid their taxes on time, but whose conduct in some important way violated community norms.

4 The Sociology of Class

PEASANT COMMUNES AND MARKET BROKERS

"There was a time, my dear," began [the peasant] Lukyan, who had been a blacksmith [before the Revolution] . . . "there was a time when we were just neighbors in this village. We quarreled, we fooled, we sometimes cheated one another. But we were neighbors. Now we are bedniaks, seredniaks, koolaks. I am a seredniak—a middle peasant. Boris here is a bedniak—a poor peasant. And Nisko is a koolak—a rich peasant. And we are supposed to have a class war—pull each other's hair or tickle each other on the toes, eh? One against the other, you understand? What the devil!" And he shrugged his shoulders as though to emphasize his bewilderment at the fresh social cleavage. To him the launching of the class war in his village was an artificially made affair.

—MAURICE HINDUS, *RED BREAD: COLLECTIVIZATION IN A RUSSIAN VILLAGE* (1931)

IN THEIR EFFORTS to coerce fulfillment of obligations without disabling a delinquent's productive capacity, communes had to find ways to override the strict insistence by the majority of *volost* authorities on the preliminary payment of taxes and arrears prior to the release of passports. There was also need to mitigate against the potentially catastrophic effects posed by distraint and public sale of peasant property, which usually began with the seizure of tax delinquents' property and then moved "to the distraint of the property of the rest of the community in the event that the arrears are not covered by the value of the delinquent's property alone."[1] Two options were commonly used in villages of the Central Industrial Region: credit, and active intervention in the hiring process. Both practices had a far-reaching impact on the evolution of the rural system in the Moscow region, and each will be discussed in turn.

The Social Context of Peasant Credit Transactions

Issuing loans to assist those in arrears with partial and temporary fulfillment of dues was practiced extensively, almost always in place of *krugovaia poruka* —the "mutual responsibility" of all villagers for fiscal obligations—and always coupled with strict passport restrictions. *Krugovaia poruka* and *dopol'nitelnye raskladki* (supplementary apportionments) were used rarely and only in special cases when the solvency of one or a few households was affected, usually following catastrophic destruction by fire, a household chief's death, or a similar inauspicious event.[2]

In 1900, for instance, *krugovaia poruka* was invoked on the initiative of the peasant commune in only 0.22 percent (139 villages) of all communes in European Russia in which the statute applied; in 142 additional instances that year, local tax inspectors ordered compulsory reapportionments.[3] The unifying element in all community affairs was opposition to behavior that would provoke the interference of state agents and the police: for solvent households, loans to delinquent fellow villagers often involved less risk than outsider intervention.[4] And, in most cases, borrowing—even at usurious rates—was a delinquent household's only defense against expropriation by district police and *volost* authorities. This convergence of interests among community members—the need for the collective defense of village autonomy and insulation of local relationships from the interference of unpredictable outsiders—set the context for a rural credit and financial system that developed, in the words of a Vladimir tax inspector, "in order to avoid police intervention."[5] In this sense, the peasant commune served as a buffer to preserve local arrangements and hierarchies against inroads by state agents and other community "outsiders." A corollary to this was the preservation of traditional village hierarchies and power networks against challenges posed by outsiders.

To adapt a phrase from Williams James: there were varieties of exploitative experience. And poorer village members, on their part, showed a marked preference for indebtedness to village insiders rather than running the risk of invoking the intervention of arbitrary and "energetic tax collectors" and nonvillage private lenders.[6] For most peasants, the prevailing challenge was that of finding alternative sources of local credit. A Ministry of Finance study noted in 1894: "There is for the large mass of the population no other means for satisfying their urgent needs, if they do not have any resources on hand, other than turning to the kulaks, lenders *[koshtany]* and various moneylender-benefactors *[rostovshchiki-blagodeteli]*, as they are called now and then according to need. The power of the moneylenders is founded precisely on the fact that except for them poor people frequently have no where else to turn."[7] Any analysis of village exploitation must be interpreted within the context of the paucity of alternatives available to smallholder peasants, who usually lacked the necessary surety for securing a loan from outsiders. The issue is precisely one of marginality, and, in this case, virtual exitlessness. For most peasants, a usurious loan was preferable to the total household failure that often followed outsider intervention. Such loans of expediency were made widely in every province of the Central Industrial Region, carrying interest charges (in cash, goods, or labor) ranging from noninterest loans (in very few cases) to average rates amounting to 20–36 percent interest annually. Usurious rates from private sources often reached as high as 60-100 percent per year.

Before a series of antiusury laws of the mid-1890s, the main source of peasant loans was usually the communal treasury, with the new debt added to the delinquent's accrued household debt, to be repaid before all other arrears.[8] Inevitably, the collection of such loans was much more strictly enforced than efforts expended toward the recovery of tax arrears.[9] In the best cases, communes managed to get low-interest loans through nearby banks and lending cooperatives, at an average of 8 percent per year; then they reloaned the money to communal members, sometimes at higher rates.[10] Just as common were loans from private sources, in particular, from well-to-do fellow villagers and rich peasants, but also from local tavern- and storekeepers, nobles, tradesmen, rural priests and monasteries, and increasingly, local merchant-industrial interests and their agents.[11] In some cases, the lenders were rural officials (village and *volost* elders) who were also owners of small business establishments, especially rural taverns and shops.[12]

Local *zemstvo* studies provide some indication of the scale of peasant private debt in the Central Industrial Region. A study of communal private debt was conducted in Zubtsov District, Tver Province, in 1888.[13] In all, the study included one-third (114) of all villages, and one-fourth (3,802) of all peasant households in the district. As a whole, it was found that local peasants carried a cumulative private debt load of 45,535 rubles, or 399 rubles per village, and almost 12 rubles per household—roughly 75 percent of the annual tax burden for the average peasant household. Fully one-third of all annual peasant expenditures for state and local dues, insurance, and land rental were covered through private loans. Only 1 percent of all loans (based on 189 credit transactions in 1888) were interest free; 57 percent were made at rates of 10–12 percent; 32 percent at rates of 13–20 percent; and 9.5 percent at rates above 20 percent.

Deeply concerned by such high levels of peasant indebtedness, state officials moved to restrict peasant credit transactions. However, state intervention merely aggravated rather than solved the problem, and paradoxically, the net effect was to increase the peasant commune's dependence on wealthy patrons. The primary effect of the antiusury law of 24 May 1893, for instance, was a distinct decline in whole-commune loans: "Formerly, communes borrowed [money] for paying taxes, but now, after the ban [on usury], each person borrows on his own."[14] "Now, loans must be made secretly, since it is prohibited to do so by communal resolution."[15] Or, the basis of the loans merely changed: "This year (1897) since it is prohibited to pawn clothing, everyone has started to pawn livestock" instead.[16] And, the process of certification also changed: "Now, private borrowers obtain money under simple receipts [*rospiski* or *raspiski*] with the signature of the village foreman [*desiatnik*] or elder [*starosta*], since it is easier for the creditor to impose his will through them. [Creditors] avoid concluding such documents in the *volost* office."[17]

The initiatives toward regulation made it much more difficult to study rural loan transactions in general after the mid-1890s. However, it is apparent that while the law was generally ineffective in controlling or limiting usury, isolated local cases where it was effectively imposed led to a dramatic increase in peasant hardship. For instance, a parish priest from Zubtsov District complained quite passionately in a report filed in 1897:

> Peasants most need money and grain in the spring, and from this time the debts begin to grow. In years with favorable harvests, such debts are more or less paid; but in recent years, as a result of poor harvests and lower prices for flax, peasant indebtedness has become almost universal. It has come to the point that peasants sell off their last remaining cows, chickens, even horses in order to pay taxes and arrears and buy grain. At the present time, the peasants are in despair: as a consequence of instructions of the local authorities, pawning [*zaklad*] has been pro-

hibited; and they can't get cash loans without security. With what can they buy grain? How will they pay taxes? These are the questions which are eternally disturbing and which continually demand an urgent resolution.[18]

Another correspondent, also a priest, put the problem in particularly sober terms:

> As a consequence of the prohibition [on certain credit transactions], [creditors] take a high percent, and business is now conducted in secret. But need does not understand interest rates and only begs for money, comprehending nothing— only that [the money] be lent and [the borrower] be trusted.[19]

In 1897, another study was conducted in Zubtsov District, Tver Province, the same district studied back in 1888. An increased overall indebtedness following the new state regulations against usury was reflected in increased interest rates. In 160 cases of known communal credit transactions, only 38.5 percent lay within the legally prescribed rates of 10–12 percent; 49 percent were at rates of 18–35 percent; 14.4 percent were at rates of 40–70 percent; and 17.5 percent of all communal credit transactions were contracted at annual interest rates that exceeded 100 percent of the principal. Besides interest payments in cash or produce, all loans carried varying degrees of additional "natural" obligations in the form of labor or entertainment *(magarych, ugoshchenie)*.

Intended by the debtor to be a short-term expedient during a time of particular need, critics charged that instead such loans formed the basis for a new type of debt servitude among the peasantry: "Once made, the debt is usually passed on year after year," with the principal growing at an enormous rate, eventually dwarfing the size of the initial loan.[20] The scale and impact of such rural credit patterns on the regional peasant economy were enormous, affecting both rural and urban hiring markets, agriculture and land use, and the hierarchy of village relations in general.

Kulaks or Benefactors? Labor/Cash Conversion and the Phenomenology of Village Elites

> *Why does the peasant pay the kulak? The explanation is simple. The peasant has no money, where is he to get it? Knowing this, peasant moneylenders do not demand from the peasants repayment of a given cash loan in cash only. In the majority of cases these debts are paid in labor, in the personal labor of the debtor in the business of the lender.*[21]

Peasant credit transactions rarely involved the exchange of cash for cash. And, in fact, peasants were notorious for their failure to fulfill cash deals. Instead, credit in the village was issued usually as part of a transaction involving the sale of access to communally controlled resources: cash advances *(zadatki)* were given during the peasant's time of greatest need (in fall and winter, when most of the taxes were due, or in spring, for food supplies or new seed) and forward contracts *(zaprodazhi)* were signed that stipulated the transfer of land, labor, and raw materials (usually produce, livestock, and so on) for a fixed period. "The peasant is more willing to pay with labor and products, which he always has at his disposal."[22] Consequently, interest on peasant debt was rarely paid in cash, but usually hidden in the form of entertainment, services, labor, livestock, or products.

Acquaintanceship networks *(znakomstvo)* were so much a part of peasant life that it is difficult to exaggerate the role of informal, personal contacts in village credit networks. In the words of an investigator in Smolensk Province in 1887: "Every peasant has his own 'benefactor' *[blagopriiatel]*, 'merciful'-creditor *[milostivets-kreditor]* with whom he is connected by numerous 'indestructible' bonds. 'Out of friendship' *[po druzhbe]*, 'because of [the borrower's] connections' *[po znakomstvu]*, the creditor does not take a large [cash] percentage in making a loan. In the name of this 'friendship,' the borrower pays with numerous small services, which sometimes amount to a large rate of interest."[23] Living on the margin, without the surety sufficient for official credit, peasants and peasant families survived from season to season only through the patronage and support of more *samostoiatel'nye krest'iane,* solvent peasants with means sufficient to assist fellow villagers and acquaintances in their times of need. The relationship between rich and poor was undoubtedly exploitative, but ultimately must be judged in the context of the dearth of alternative sources. As an unsympathetic observer from Tver Province conceded in 1897: "Without the village kulaks, tavern- and saloonkeepers, who lend money to the peasant until the autumn at high rates of interest, who issue him a debt for each little article, from salt, matches, kerosine, to luxury goods like clothing, tea, and sugar, the peasant could not possibly live even a month in the village. Many correspondents are convinced that without cash loans from kulaks and tavernkeepers, the peasants would live quite poorly."[24] For better or worse, village "kulaks" played an indispensible role in village life: class exploitation was overlaid with a distinct culture of patronage.

In the semiotics of everyday life, the popular Russian myth of "the Good Master" or "Benevolent Benefactor" was both the embodiment of the "peasant dream" and an unwritten blueprint of social expectations. In local jargon, wealthy peasants from one's own native community were often referred to not in the pejorative terms of *kulak* (fist), *miroed* (commune-eater), or *khishchnik* (predator), but rather in the positive expressions *blagodetel* (benefactor), *blagopriiatel* (patron), or *pervostateinik* (first-class citizen). It is in fact extremely hard to find peasants using the pejorative "kulak" to describe any relations with fellow villagers before 1917. These slurs were, as a rule, reserved for exploitative "outsiders."[25] In the Russian countryside, it was not wealth in itself that was corrupt, but rather the ways in which wealth was earned and spent that determined the reputations of local peasant elites.

It is in the close examination of the evolving traditions of peasant patronage that we find the best illustration of the influence of the commodity economy in the subtle transformation of village social relations during the last generations of the Old Regime.

KHLEBOSOL'NYI KHOZIAIN: MYTHS OF "THE GOOD MASTER" IN THE RUSSIAN VILLAGE

The Russian language has numerous terms to describe the hospitality expected of the patron for his employees or neighbors. The *khlebosol'nyi khoziain* —literally, "bread-and-salt patron"—was not only a prominent figure in Russian popular culture, but a necessary prerequisite to expedite social and business transactions in the countryside. Literally nothing would come of a transaction in the countryside that was not sealed (as a sign of good faith) with the requisite *ugoshchenie* (entertainment), *magarych* (as in *postavit magarych,* "to whet a bargain"), *vedro vodky* (pail of vodka), *gostepriimstvo* (hospitality), and often sustained by spiritual and biological kinship ties *(kumovstvo,* or literally: "godparenthood"). Such rituals and institutions reflected a distinct cultural code where the roles were known and generally observed by all the participants. These expectations regulated relations not just between rich and poor peasants, but in numerous small ways demarcated the line between the more fluid and ever-changing notions of fortunate and less fortunate in everyday life, where, say, a peasant-worker who was lucky enough to land a good job was expected to "entertain" *(ugoshchat)* his close circle of friends with a *prival'naia* (entertainment), *vspriski* (sprinkling [with vodka]), or *magarych* (celebration). As always, there were considerable forces at work to ensure compliance with these unwritten rules: "Social pressure was used to pry money from those who were more reluctant . . . in relinquishing . . . cash. Teasing, insults, social ostracism, . . . mocking laughter, verbal threats and social isolation were the most common methods of convincing recalcitrant workers to conform to conventional norms."[26]

In the hierarchy of social relations in the Russian countryside, there were four kinds of favors in the village, each of which—contrary to modern views—carried implicit expectations of reciprocity. The word *odolzhenie,* "favor," was built on the root for "debt" *(dolg)*: there was no word for any favor that might be performed without expectations of some sort of return. The Russian Orthodox virtue of charity (best known through the writings of the Slavophiles) was a building block for idealized social relationships and never held the connotations of Western conceptions of charity as "an act of benevolence of and for its own sake."[27] It is utterly impossible to understand social relations in the Russian village without first recognizing that even freely given favors represented their own form of unwritten debt contract.

First, there were "neighborly favors": lending a measure of sugar or flour, for instance, with the expectation of repayment; helping to place a child in an apprenticeship, with the expectation of gratefulness and support; helping with cash at tax time, in return for the expectation of entertainment, sale of produce, or other small favors (carting, repair, field work, and so on). Second, there were favors performed only by the community as a whole, or by its wealthier members: loans as a rule made in kind (seed, grain) or, less often, in cash. Third, there were the favors performed by all, but especially by the poor for the rich: favors returned in the form of free labor, sale of local produce below market price, and so forth. Finally, for projects involving a greater (though temporary) outlay of collective labor (for tasks impossible or impractical to complete on one's own)—barn- or house-raisings, moving a dwelling, harvesting, etc.—were those which fell under the rubric of *pomoch.*

Pomoch was the tradition of mutual aid among Russian villagers. In the unwritten code that regulated relations between neighbors, "every peasant . . . is obligated to go and help his neighbor in the event of an invitation" to a *pomoch.*[28] A common example of *pomoch* was the *supriaga*—the joint tilling of land—which allowed villagers to pool their labor and livestock for the benefit of all. (Most villagers, even those who were comparatively better-off, lacked the four draft animals necessary for a complete plow team *[tiaglo]*, or for carting a season's supply of wood, for example.) *Pomoch* also included joint, labor-intensive harvest teams, barn- and house-raisings, and so on.[29]

The ostensibly charitable nature of the *pomoch* tradition—free labor freely given to needy fellow villagers, especially to those who were newly married, or to victims of fire—enabled peasants to work on Sundays and holidays with the blessings of the Russian Orthodox Church. A priest in Vladimir Province explained the subtle logic that opened the way for special dispensation from the prohibition of work on Holy Days: "Working on a holiday in the village for one another or in the *volost* center for the priest, the peasant does not take payment [in cash], but works only for 'entertainment' *[ugoshchenie]*, that is for a dinner, tea, and the obligatory rounds of drinks *[vypivka]*. It's a sin to work on a [religious] holiday, particularly for money. But God summons us to assist our neighbors. So [a peasant] can work on a [holiday]—as well as drink and eat, but he cannot take [cash] payment."[30]

A formal procedure was usually followed for invoking assistance from neighbors and fellow villagers.[31] Normally, the peasant notified fellow villagers through the *desiatskii* or village constable of his desire to get the community together in order to render him help of some sort. "Throughout, [the peasant] most strictly watches to ensure that all the household chiefs in the village without exception take part. In the opposite case—that is, when one or a few refuse—the *pomoch* falls apart *[rasstraivaetsia].*"[32] Full participation of the members of the community was a vital ingredient in a successful *pomoch,* since it was in its essence a communitywide, consensus-building ritual.

In her pathbreaking study of traditions of mutual assistance in European Russia, the Russian ethnographer M. M. Gromyko found considerable evidence to support the notion of the resilience of intracommunal *pomoch,* regardless of internal stratification, into the early twentieth century.[33] In my review of her findings and the original evidence from which she drew her conclusions (in the main, published sources plus material from the Tenishev collection at the Russian State Museum of Ethnography), I found considerable support for Gromyko's thesis, at least on the surface.

It is important to note, however, that even Gromyko's own sources show a marked transformation of village traditions of mutual assistance as a result of the development of a cash economy in the countryside. While the surface appearance or shell of those practices had been preserved in the Central Industrial Region, by the end of the nineteenth century, *pomoch* had become a "tradition" reinvented, now affordable only by the rich.[34] While the tradition of *pomoch* apparently continued well into the twentieth century, by the final quarter of the nineteenth century it had already been transformed into something new: not as an act of public charity by which villagers accomplished tasks that exceeded the labor resources of any individual household, but rather as a wealthy peasant's investment in the village ritual cycle, a benefactor's service to his neighbors:

Pomoch always coincides with a [religious] holiday. The principal incentive for *pomoch* is the desire to render a good turn to a neighbor *[blizhnyi]*—[who in turn] is roused to extensive outlays to entertain [the laborers] on completion of the work. In recent years, [however], this expenditure has begun to displace the moral incentive, and the entertainment [itself] now holds first priority. The demands of the helpers regarding the entertainment increase with each passing year, and [the cost of] *pomoch* . . . [now] exceeds the value of the labor.[35]

Why pay inflated prices in the form of entertainment for labor that was supposed to be an act of publicly given charity? The explanation is simple: the marginal cost of labor for nonagricultural work had grown so high in the Central Industrial Region—where average wages bid up by competition with industry were twice as high as in other regions (see table 4.1 below)—that village employers had to compete for scarce labor, meaning that average wages grew substantially for agricultural and village-based work as well. To a certain degree, Russian religious traditions prohibiting "paid labor" on religious holidays, plus the glorification of social charity and charitable work, preserved the vestiges of *pomoch,* but by the end of the nineteenth century fellow villagers' expectations and the sheer cost of the entertainment and food had grown so great that the real cost of *pomoch* far exceeded the value of the labor "purchased." "Only the rich [peasants] host *pomoch*. It is not profitable for the poor peasant to mount a *pomoch* when the [cost] of the entertainment exceeds the value of the labor. But the rich do not stint on the entertainment."[36]

Tradition could not compete with the market, and in the case of *pomoch* tradition was utterly suborned by the market, even as villagers continued to honor the custom. Why then did peasants retain the *pomoch* tradition at all? Theories that reduce culture to nothing more than the garb wrapped around economic relations have no way to explain the historical fact. The anthropology of the personal, on the other hand, where personal relations and reputation are seen as mediating forces in the structure of village economic relations, provides an answer to this apparent conundrum.

The transformation of the tradition of *pomoch* above all demonstrates the importance of recognizing that the relationship between wealthy and poor or middle peasants was not merely exploitative, but contained a degree of reciprocity: every peasant, rich and poor alike, was constrained by community opinion. Once again, we unavoidably return to the importance of a "good name": "The rich [peasant] does not stint on the entertainment, because . . . it brings him honor *[pochet]* and propagates talk *[molva]* about his prosperity."[37] In high-migration villages outside St. Petersburg, "on holidays, well-to-do peasants assemble their neighbors for *pomoch* or *tolk*. . . . *Pomocha*—the participants in a *pomoch*—do not work for free, but for the patron's lunch [*khoziaiskii obed*], snacks [*pauzhin*], and supper, and for a celebration in the evening upon completion of the work."[38] In Vologda, "conducting a *pomoch* is not advantageous [*vygodnyi*] to anyone but the rich."[39]

In high-migration villages, *pomoch* had been transformed into a sort of village inversion ritual: one day (or group of days) each year the master or peasant patron became servant to his less fortunate fellow villagers, and the rich host treated the village to an enormous celebration served by his own hands:

> Upon completion of the work . . . the rich [host] makes arrangements for a sumptuous feast [*pir goroi*], neglecting to mention that during the work he had already brought "breakfast" out to the fields. Helpers are entertained mainly with vodka. They do not stand on ceremony with their hosts and demand not just vodka, but also heaps of some sort of dish, as well as buttered kasha, and so on.[40]

Often, the entertainment was quite lavish:

> How much in the way of spirits they manage to drink on *pomoch* is demonstrated by the following fact: 50 persons—30 of them men and 20 women—mowed rye on *pomoch*. They worked from seven in the morning until three in the afternoon and harvested 4,000 stacks [of rye]. They drank vodka during short intervals [throughout the day], [yet managed] to drink up 15 liters [*vedro s chetvertiiu*]. "Breakfast" consisted of several courses: (1) *shchi* with beef; (2) noodles with beef broth; (3) buckwheat kasha with butter; (4) wheat kasha with butter; (5) fried eggs with white bread. More well-to-do peasants add honey, bergamot, red wine, and beer. The patron himself, or the patron's wife, must serve the food and drink.[41]

Coinciding with religious holidays, *pomoch* gradually became an integral part of the harvest festivals to which so many *otkhodniki* returned for symbolic participation. Performing labor under the aegis of *pomoch*, peasants upheld the image that work was done "not in service, but in friendship [*ne v sluzhbe, a v druzhbe*]."[42] The important thing was to retain at least the appearance of good relations between neighbors, of the personal and interdependent character of local patron-client relations.

There is nothing extraordinary about these relationships, except that Russian contemporaries and Soviet historians generally have repeatedly emphasized the disproportionate influence of nakedly exploitative wealthy villagers—the so-called kulaks—over the less-ominous variety of "neighborly relations," a paradigm more broadly embraced in Western studies. Drawing on his extensive work in nineteenth-century American history, for instance, the noted historian Jack Larkin described the nature and context of village debts in rural America:

> Webs of rural exchange linked neighborhoods together along with "frolics" and habits of visiting. There was not very much cash in circulation in the country[side]; what there was tended to flow quickly back to the cities. Families built up credit or debt balances with each other as they "changed" an enormous variety of labor and commodities—a few days' help at harvest, a young woman to spin, cheese, woven cloth, firewood, meat, the loan of a horse and wagon, a few weeks' pasturing of a cow. Economic life was deeply, inextricably entangled in social life. Visits and economic transactions were usually indistinguishable.[43]

It was precisely this overlay of cultural relations that shaped, defined, and distorted rural class relations—the "idiocy of rural life"—that led Marx to reject the peasantry as a self-sustaining base for social revolution.

A more accurate image of village social relations would integrate the interpretation of economic relations within their local cultural contexts. An observer in Kaluga Province described the complexity of class relations in the Russian village in 1897: "The majority of contractors, knowing the weakness of some workers, send money themselves to the [workers'] families. Contractors display a fatherly concern for their [workers].... No less concerned are the local *kabatchiki*—or tavern keepers—for families with workers on the side.... From paycheck *[prisyla]* to paycheck the majority of such families receive credit from the most intimate spider-*kabatchik,* in whose name the [cash] transfer is sent. Selling cheap goods at higher prices, [they make enormous profits]."[44]

Living away from their villages, peasant labor-migrants could not always cope with the crises and contingencies at home, especially urgent situations demanding large cash outlays: replacing a horse or farm animal, repairing the homestead, obtaining seed for planting, seeking medical help, and so forth. This service was provided by local creditors—again, as a rule, wealthier fellow villagers, the local storekeeper, or tavern keeper. Consequently, numerous observers reported that credit relations were often closer and infinitely more complex in villages situated in the vicinity of factories and commercial settlements: "Peasant [families] with workers on the side take products on credit from shopkeepers, who wait '*do poluchki*'"—"until receipt" of cash sent home by peasant-workers.[45]

Surety consisted in such cases not in the land, dwelling, or livestock of the middle or poor peasant, but rather in the anticipated earnings of absent family members. In such circumstances, the peasant-worker's established reputation as a "good provider" was his best capital for securing a loan from local "benefactors."

The evidence from the Central Industrial Region indicates the need to reinterpret the role of rich peasants or kulaks. While numerous "outside" observers were quick to condemn the exploitative relations that developed as a consequence of the kulak's hegemony in the insulated village community, they failed to note various structural and cultural factors that favored cohesion. The very real influence of traditional conceptions of kinship, social insurance, and mutuality aside, conditions of mutual responsibility for fiscal obligations within each village made it of paramount interest to the wealthier members to promote the well-being of fellow villagers, or face the unsatisfactory alternative of footing the bill themselves. There was, in addition, the genuine role played by "village opinion": investigations of village rituals reveal how much importance the wealthy peasants attached to maintaining the esteem of their fellow villagers. (In contrast, the mitigating role of local-specific factors such as the opinion of fellow villagers would decline as soon as outsiders—such as state agents and market brokers—bypassed local mechanisms in their positions as mere executors of instructions passed down from above.)

In the context of the village "little community," the so-called kulak often received community respect (despite evidence of real exploitation) and earned that respect by performing functions crucial to the economic well-being of the whole community: by acting as brokers for local produce, as sources of credit for village families and departing *otkhodniki*, as mediators with outside agents, as connections with outside employment in certain factories or skills, and so on. In the words of the anthropologist Connor Bailey, wealthy peasants—*blagodeteli* (benefactors) or *pervostateiniki* (first-class citizens)—emerge as leaders not merely because they are exploiters, but because they are also "brokers, mediators, patrons and kinsmen."[46] From this cultural perspective, wealthy peasants—whose own local predominance rested to a great degree on the perpetuation of existing conditions of insularity—may by and large be seen as the staunchest upholders of village traditional relations, not—as is so often asserted in the "kulak mythology" presented by contemporary elite sociologists—as the ruthless and "egoistical" *(slastliubivye)* plunderers of hallowed village traditions. In short, kulak exploitation must be understood within its local cultural context, a context which for rich, middle, and poor peasants alike was characterized by a disproportionate reliance on patronage and personal contacts, or *znakomstvo*.[47]

CREDIT AND LAND TRANSACTIONS

Often, to reduce the burden on community members, the right to use communal lands was sold to outsiders. Usually, such access was granted as part of a credit agreement between communes and local tradesmen or merchant-industrial interests, thereby circumventing the protective communal umbrella which, from 1861, was intended to guarantee "the inalienability of peasant allotments." In Riazan and Kaluga Provinces, for instance, the interest charge on merchant loans to communes was paid heavily, not in cash, but in kind, through concessions for the use of common pastures or arable fields.[48] In addition, some communes rented shares of ceded or confiscated peasant allotments on the open market to interested outside buyers; access to village communal lands or allotments given up or seized by the commune was sold (in single-soul parcels) for one or more seasons at local bazaars. This transformation of restricted peasant allotments into public rental land, usually offered at a bargain price by communes desperate for funds, exerted a powerful downward impact on rental prices in the local land markets throughout the Central Industrial Region.[49] In Vladimir Province, for instance, "Owing to the growth in peasant departures for side-work, rental prices for [arable] land have fallen with each year."[50] Depending on the quality of land resources, official rental prices of individual parcels were three to four times higher than the rate of large parcels rented over long terms by communal resolution to outsiders. In such arrangements, the interests of the commune were met because state obligations on the land were covered, thereby freeing community members to pursue their livelihoods in wage-earning positions elsewhere. The long-term character of such transactions lent a degree of stability to an otherwise unpredictable land market in which the peasantry's fiscal obligations were constant and inexorable, while incomes varied enormously from year to year, depending directly on the strength of the urban and industrial economies. Such rentals of communal and allotment lands to outsiders were particularly common in villages located close to urban and industrial centers.[51]

The Role of the Police

Another local innovation that often went hand-in-hand with efforts to issue loans to delinquent peasant households was the commune's role in the Central Industrial Region as labor broker in the hiring process. Because of local control over passports, villages continued to exert considerable influence on the behavior of their members even after they had departed for side-work. Three official and unofficial elements enhanced this control: the police; group-hiring under the artel principle; and *zemliachestvo,* whereby workers used kinship and fellow villagers' contacts to find work outside the village.

First, there was the role of the Russian police, who could be called upon for assistance in locating, pressuring, and even forcing the return of negligent migrants. Integral with the police role was the requirement that all *otkhodniki* register with local address bureaus (in the towns and industrial settlements) or turn their passports over to employers until the termination of the hiring contract. "All new arrivals in a city, which meant primarily peasants, were required to register with the address office, where they surrendered their peasant passports. In return for their passport and the payment of a fee, they received a permit or ticket *(bilet)* that entitled them to live in the city for a stipulated time period. Since the peasant could not travel beyond the city limits without surrendering his permit and retrieving his passport, the system had the effect of attaching him to the city and accounting for his whereabouts for the duration of his stay."[52] In both urban and nonurban employment, hiring contracts generally stipulated that workers' passports be surrendered until the termination of work; employers held wages and passports in order to exercise control over workers.[53]

Such procedures facilitated the regulation of peasant labor-migrants and greatly enhanced the effectiveness of the internal passport system. For instance, in parts of Tver Province where the cobbler's trade was particularly common, delinquent taxpayers working and living in Moscow or St. Petersburg were personally visited by their village elders during late November or early December, with an additional assessment of thirty to forty kopecks per taxable soul added to their debt for the elders' "traveling expenses."[54]

Aside from keeping tabs on the whereabouts of migrants, the police were also called upon to enforce the payment of arrears, through authorized wage deductions or court-ordered confiscations of property, or even the forced return of negligent *otkhodniki* "under guard" to the village. In parts of Kostroma and Iaroslavl Provinces, for example, on being issued a passport, *otkhodniki* were required to sign a special leave-contract *(podpiska)* that granted village officials explicit rights regarding delinquent migrants. "For those tax delinquents who are absent, [communes] recover [arrears] through the mediation of the police, who lay an injunction on the earnings received by the delinquent workers."[55] In Tver, *volost* authorities throughout the province required that money be sent for the payment of arrears prior to the renewal of passports, "threatening otherwise [the worker's] forced return to the village. Frequently, they communicate with the police . . . about the worker's place of employment, with a request to retain for arrears part of the money earned by them."[56] And in Moscow: "From those peasant workers living on the side, *volost* elders commonly secure payments through the local police."[57] In Vladimir: "From the departing adult worker, arrears are exacted through the police, to whom the *volost* authority turns with the request to coerce the delinquent toward payment or to deduct arrears from his earnings at the factory or shop. If this remains without success, then in Kovrov District, a one-month pass *(bilet)* is issued or, sending a passport, they arrange with the local police that the condition for its issue is the payment of arrears, or they do not send a passport, which is done in all other districts as well, and apply measures against [the delinquent's] property, as specified in article 188 of the General Regulation."[58] In this way, the power of village authorities to impose communal sanctions on members away from the village was considerably enhanced. In effect, the police acted as the community's agents at the work place.

Community vigilance over departing members was further enhanced by *otkhodniki* themselves, who often lived, worked, and socialized together as they engaged in their economic pursuits away from the village. Two principal factors accounted for the high correlation between village origins, skill type, and work place destination: patterns of hiring, and *zemliachestvo*.

The Hiring Market

> *The [Russian] countryside is a land of opportunity for profit-seeking opportunists.*[59]

Patterns of hiring assisted communities in their efforts to control *otkhodniki*. Unlike the Central Agricultural and Southern Steppe Regions, where a labor surplus facilitated the centralization of agricultural hiring in large labor markets, the Central Industrial Region was a net labor importer, forced by rapid industrial development to bring in workers from an increasingly wider radius of surrounding villages. The wage disparity between regions in European Russia was a direct reflection of the competition for labor. In the Central Industrial Region, average annual wages among *otkhodniki* were higher than any other region, and almost twice those of the neighboring Central Agricultural Region. (See table 4.1.) To tap rural labor resources, outside the cities there sprang up *promyshlennyia seleniia*—industrial settlements strategically located to exploit local resources in labor, fuel (as late as the 1890s, primarily wood and

Table 4.1. Average Annual Earnings Among Labor Migrants in European Russia, c. 1900

	Average Annual Earnings of One Otkhodnik (in rubles)	Proportional Relation to Mean Earnings (x/53.5)
1. Northwest Region	46.8	88%
2. Northeast Region	38.8	73%
3. Ural Region	54.5	102%
4. Viatka-Vetluga Region	37.0	69%
5. Middle-Volga Region	37.0	69%
6. Lower-Volga Region	41.6	78%
7. Southwest and Southern Mining Region	44.6	84%
8. Central Industrial Region	**68.3**	**128%**
9. Central Chernozem Region	**34.3**	**64%**
10. Western Region	61.4	115%
11. Kirgiz Region	34.0	64%
12. North Caucasus	48.0	90%
Average for 43 provinces	53.5	100%

Regions
1. Petersburg, Novgorod, Pskov, Olonets
2. Arkhangel, Vologda
3. Ufa, Perm
4. Viatka
5. Kazan, Penza, Samara, Simbirsk
6. Astrakhan, Saratov
7. Khar'kov, Kiev, Poltava, Ekaterinoslav, Chernigov, Volynia, Podol'ia, Kherson, Taurida
8. Moscow, Vladimir, Kaluga, Kostroma, Nizhnii Novgorod, Riazan, Tver, Tula, Iaroslavl
9. Voronezh, Orlov, Kursk, Tambov
10. Vitebsk, Minsk, Mogilev, Smolensk
11. Orenburg
12. Don Region

Source: Adapted from L. E. Mints, *Otkhod krest'ianskogo naseleniia na zarabotki v SSSR* (Moscow, 1925), p. 43.

peat), raw materials, and an intricate network of internal waterways.[60] The comparatively high concentration of industrial development in certain regions of European Russia afforded a hiring process which moved along established networks.

A typical illustration of how such established networks operated in practice was provided by an employer in Bogorodsk District, Moscow Province, at the end of the nineteenth century:

> For more than 20 years, I have hired workers from two *volosti* [in Mikhailov District, Riazan Province], and the hiring was accomplished in the following manner: I write down how many workers I need and a peasant acquaintance [*znakomyi krest'ianin*] sends for them in the village during Fomin's Week (after Easter).... On Sunday of Fomin's Week, one of the workers together with my agent [*sluzhaishchii*] proceeds to Moscow, and at the Khitrovo market they negotiate a price, which—as the peasants say—God has set [*Bog postavit*]. . . . I must mention that in the course of more than 20 years, I have managed [to hire]

workers who are both honorable and not drunkards; there were some lazy ones, but rarely so. Only twice did workers come to me to settle up [before the end of the contract].[61]

Because of the intense competition for scarce labor throughout the Central Industrial Region, employers minimized their own risks by binding their potential laborers to their establishments in several ways. Regionally distinct hiring procedures, as part of a broader entrepreneurial strategy, had developed in the years before the abolition of serfdom.

To reduce the likelihood of a worker's abrogation of the hiring contract (and the employer's loss of the advance), most employers followed a dual strategy. First, increasingly after the mid-1870s, they avoided oral contracts, preferring written agreements, usually accompanied by a resolution from the communal assembly and/or an official seal of approval from the *volost* clerk. "The pay-books *[raschetnye-knizhki]* and contract lists *[dogovornye listy],* for greater reliability, are sometimes submitted to the *volost* office, where the elder witnesses them as a formal contract with his own signature and affixes them with the *volost* seal. In the book is a detailed rendering of the term for which the worker has been hired, the pay rate agreed upon at the completion of the contract, and finally the conditions for work. The latter have sometimes been rendered with very detailed, scrupulous precision."[62]

Contractors—*podriadchiki, khoziaeva, prikazchiki*—by and large were locals, and they restricted their work as hiring agents to distinct regions with which they were intimately familiar and where they had established local networks of personal contacts. Systematic work through the fifty surviving contract books in numerous collections of *volost* administrative archives in Moscow Province has revealed that local hiring was usually monopolized by a single employer, hiring agent, or labor contractor. For instance, in Ignat'evskaia *volost,* Bogorodsk District, during the period 1871–1874, 92 percent of all migrant hiring contracts were signed with a single hiring agent, Ikonnikov. Extant contract books from 1866–1868 reveal that the same contractor also accounted for 54–64 percent of the contracts completed in an adjacent *volost.*[63] Such contracts, deemed "holy and inviolable" by employers and peasant administrators alike, demanded that each peasant-worker agree in writing and under the stamp and seal of *volost* authorities "always to appear for work in a timely fashion; to conduct myself honorably, soberly, and obediently; not to evade responsibilities."[64] Apprenticeship contracts were equally stringent:

> I, Ivanova, will by no means permit my son to depart from the master *[khoziain]* earlier than the end of the period of apprenticeship, nor will I permit family

members to take him from the master earlier than the agreed-upon time and I oblige my son to be considerate to the other workers *[masterstvo]*, never to be absent without the permission of the master and to perform all orders honestly, precisely, and quickly.⁶⁵

Likewise, as much as possible, workers were hired collectively, in large labor artels, and held mutually responsible for each other in order to ensure that all workers would fulfill the terms of the agreement. This description of the typical procedure for hiring unskilled workers was taken from Smolensk Province:

> Contractors usually conclude with indebted-workers *[dolzhniki]* a formal *written contract*, quite detailed and thorough. . . . The main principle in this contract is the grouping together of indebted-workers into an artel [where they are bound under] *krugovaia poruka* and the right [to exact] fines and a forfeiture for breaking a contract. Contractors . . . , in selecting an artel of workers, try always to hire as many as possible from one village or, at least, from one *volost*, in order to make it possible to conclude with them one general contract and obligate them in mutual responsibility of one for another by means of *krugovaia poruka*. In this manner, every large artel . . . in its turn, can be broken up into smaller artels, the members of which are obligated in mutual responsibility; each such artel numbers from 2 to 40 and even 50 members. Contractors almost never hire lone workers into large artels.⁶⁶

The imposition of the principle of *krugovaia poruka* meant in practice that the workers could be held collectively responsible for contract violations of any individual; employers and hiring agents threatened to deduct fines and penalties from the wages of the entire group of workers, who would be issued in exchange a receipt *(udostoverenie)* suitable for recovering damages from the guilty party.⁶⁷ The fact that workers were hired collectively from the same village or *volost* made it easier to enforce such contracts, both because such procedures facilitated informal arrangements between hiring agents and local officials, and because peer pressure discouraged the abrogation of contracts by lone individuals.

Such legal controls were often buttressed with personal contacts between employers or their agents and local authorities. These informal arrangements were the direct consequence of Russia's outmoded tax system, which opened the way for wily labor brokers familiar with the system and often intimately acquainted with village tax and police officials. The prime conditions for their success were provided by aggressive state officials. As a contemporary expert on village credit observed: "Every autumn 'extraordinary measures' are used for collecting taxes and the replenishment of arrears.... Naturally, the peasant tries with all his effort to procure some money for the payment of taxes and arrears."[68] Energetic measures by local officials often coincided with the appearance of ostensible "benefactors" who could step in at the proper moment with a cash advance and a printed labor contract.

> Contractors, ... who treat the hiring of workers as a special profession, come year after year to one and the same place, and are therefore well acquainted with local conditions and local village authorities, who render them a considerable service in the hiring of workers. Contractors are supplied, according to their trustworthiness, a certain sum of money for use as advances to those who are hired, advances which frequently are very large in relation to the total sum of the earnings. They know well the state of affairs in the region of their activity: where there is a particularly strong need for earnings, the time at which peasants experience greatest hardship, [the period] when efforts to collect taxes and arrears will be intensified, etc. Finally, they can be found to be in the very best relations with *volost* authorities, who—in the event of [an employer's] need—can intensify their efforts for the exaction of every type of tax.[69]

Incomplete data from 1899 revealed that there were at least 936 such labor contractors operating in just three districts of Kaluga Province, an average of one contractor for every 50–100 peasant-workers.[70]

Although legally authorized to do so, peasant communities rarely engaged in the forced "hiring-out" of members of delinquent households *(otdat' nedoimshchikov v rabotu)*. The few cases in which this procedure was applied reflect conditions of prior mutual agreement between local officials and employers. For instance, in two *volosti* of Vyshnii Volochëk District, Tver Province, elders hired-out those in arrears for earnings in two factories that bordered the *volosti*, receiving in return money for the payment of taxes directly from factory managers. The two factories only took tax delinquents from their own *volosti*, however, emphasizing that this "is done [only] in order to oblige *volost* elders, whom the factory offices frequently need in their affairs." Reflecting the divergent patterns between localities, however, was the fact that in two other districts in Tver Province, there was no such hiring-out of workers, since no employers in the area would agree to take "forced laborers" *(podnevol'nye rabochie)*, who were generally considered to be both less productive and less reliable than freely hired workers.[71]

More common were prior agreements for deduction of earnings, or the employer's negotiation with *volost* and village authorities for support in the hiring process. Such labor contractors were especially prevalent in areas where a steady supply of labor was needed. For instance, "From Bezsonovo village, Usmerskaia *volost,* [peasant-workers] depart for earnings to the Morozov weaving factory in Nikol'skoe, Vladimir Province, with the assistance of middlemen *(posredniki),* who are compensated an average of 1 ruble per worker. From this village almost a hundred peasants leave for the whole year."[72] Even if one disregards the role of personal motives, local officials benefited directly from such arrangements, since usually "the taxes are paid to the village elder every month directly from the factory office."[73] Such arrangements, which customarily included advances to assist in both the payment of taxes and family needs, were also widespread in the lumber industry.

> Labor contractors are particularly numerous in north Russia. . . . The contractor *(podriadchik)*. . . , usually referred to here as the foreman *(desiatnik),* . . . gives the peasant a loan both for the payment of taxes and for feeding his family through spring, requiring at the same time that the peasant signs a contract, on the strength of which the peasant is obligated at the contractor's discretion to set out with him for gathering and floating timber in Olonets, Petersburg, Novgorod, Pskov, Perm, and other provinces—in a word, anywhere that work is found. . . . Having signed such contracts, peasants at the approach of the spring thaw set out for a hundred kilometers or so to an appointed place—to some river, where timber is stockpiled. Here, the contractor, having arranged for 70–100 workers, resells the right for their labor to a timber merchant or to some other employer, under whose complete command the peasants work.[74]

Peasant-workers hired by labor brokers were contractually obligated not to set out to find new work on completion of individual jobs; this was the sole responsibility of the foreman, who essentially "rented" peasant labor under his control to outside employers.[75] As the typical labor contract stipulated: "Upon completion of the period of work, we peasants must present to our *volost* office a receipt *(kvitantsiia)* of earnings from the factory, and if this is not done we peasants do not have a right to be hired for work at another site."[76] Hiring contractors also protected their interests by maintaining strict hegemony over their specialized information about village labor. The Soviet historian U. A. Shuster found that most of the 19,000 construction workers in St. Petersburg at the beginning of the twentieth century were known to their employers only by skill-classification and the subcontractor's name. For example, a factory record book contained only the following information: "plasterers from Bakhirin, decorators from Sirotkin, stonemasons from Fedorov."[77]

Labor contracts also played a dominant role in arrangements between petty tradesmen and cottage producers. A. N. Karidalin, the *zemstvo* correspondent from Korovaevskaia *volost*, Dmitrov District, Moscow Province, filed this report in 1897:

> The buyers-up *[skupshchiki]* of [a cobbler's] products are usually petty tradesmen or owners of large shops. Receiving the shoes from a petty cobbler, the buyer-up resells them to his own permanent client. At the time of the purchase of the shoes, he assures the cobbler that he is doing him a favor *[blagodeianie]*, deducting 5 kopecks per pair against the market price, which is already reduced, then deducting expenses associated with the transport to market, where they say it will be more profitable to sell. And so the cobbler sells his shoes, getting from his benefactor *[blagodetel]* butter, groats, and other products. Later, [the benefactor] lends him money, having learned all about him beforehand—whether he has heard that the *volost* elder is coming for the taxes, or that a herdsman must be hired [for the communal flock], etc. [In such cases] he lends [money] without fail. . . . Working for such a benefactor, the cobbler sometimes incurs an enormous debt, but it is impossible to refuse the work.[78]

Rural hiring by general contract was especially common among workers in seasonal occupations: sugar-refining in the southwest, stevedores on the Volga and along the internal canal system, navvies and unskilled workers throughout the center, light and heavy carriers who conveyed raw materials and industrial goods between station points and factories, lumber workers, peat cutters, brick makers, railroad workers, miners, and factory workers.[79]

For instance, the work season *(konets)* for peat cutters ran from May to Kazanskaia (July 8) for hand cutters, from May to the first of August for machine cutters. Yet, the hiring was completed long before, during the preceding fall, when peasants were most in need of cash for tax payments. "The hiring of [Vladimir] peat cutters takes place in the fall, usually from among the inhabitants of Kaluga and Riazan Provinces. For this purpose there are sent from the factories hiring-agents *[prikazchiki]* who settle wage rates with the workers; and then the agent issues to the workers an advance *[zadatok]*, and the workers, on their part, [give] to the agent a certificate of guarantee *[poruchitel'stvo]* —[issued] from the *volost* office."[80]

The pattern was the same for Vladimir brick makers. In this sector, too, hiring agents preferred to recruit local workers from the same general area, bound together on the artel principle and guaranteed by their *volost* authorities: at the Troitsko-Aleksandrovsii brickworks, for instance, workers consisted almost exclusively of natives from neighboring *volosti* in Vladimir and Sudogda districts, Vladimir Province.[81]

The extension of community control over departing members was not limited to those in seasonal skills, however. Similar agreements were reached between village and *volost* authorities and factory owners as well. Although there were sometimes complaints among local tax inspectors regarding the difficulty of keeping track of *otkhodniki*,[82] village institutions themselves—under the intense pressure of *volost* authorities, land captains (after 1889) and rural police—managed to exert enormous pressures on migrants to prevent them from relinquishing their village obligations. This was demonstrated by the relatively better position with respect to arrears held by districts in which factory side-earnings represented a high proportion of the incomes of most peasant households. As the chief tax inspector from Vladimir Province observed in the 1890s: "In the majority of districts with factory and shop earnings, punctuality in the receipt of taxes to a significant degree depends on these earnings. They are very great and the collection of taxes is easier in those places where deductions are made from [workers'] earnings by the factories and shops themselves (and also by contractors *[podriadchiki]*)."[83]

Examples abound of agreements between village officials and outside employers for the direct deduction from peasant-workers' earnings for the payment of fiscal obligations. In Nerekhta District, Kostroma Province, where most peasant-workers left for factory work on the side, "In factory areas, in agreement with factory and shop owners, *[volost* and village officials] lay an injunction on part of the wages received by delinquent workers."[84] In northern Riazan Province, where peasants in four districts depended primarily on non-agricultural earnings for the payment of state dues, it was common for deductions to be made by employers, then sent (per instructions) to *volost* officials for payment of fiscal duties, and only then passed on to the village for *mir* dues.[85]

Far from rejecting such arrangements, there is considerable evidence to suggest that *otkhodniki* themselves actively pursued written hiring agreements. N. K. Brzheskii observed at the end of the last century that peasant-workers had begun to demand that contracts be validated by the *volost* clerk, since the *volost* authorities had come to expect that "contractors . . . should be answerable for the punctual payment of taxes" of contracted workers.[86] This gave the peasant-worker a clear line of defense in the event that a contract was abrogated by the hiring agent. In some districts, peasant-workers refused to work altogether without the security a written contract could provide. Communal and *volost* officials likewise favored such agreements, since they could be used, along with corporal punishment, to demonstrate to state officials their own vigilant efforts to collect taxes and arrears.

This pattern of direct deduction from earnings was not unique to the post-

Emancipation world, since *obrok* payments that predominated in non-black-earth districts during the pre-Emancipation era were commonly deducted by factory owners and paid directly to magnate landlord-owners.[87] Before 1861, such concessions reduced the difficulty of extracting estate dues from reluctant serfs and, on the factory owner's part, bought him steady access to a local labor force held in control both by factory authorities and the full coercive apparatus of the estate system. Later in the century, the same logic applied: village communes in the Central Industrial Region gained a partner in meeting high state exactions, while industrialists and other employers found in the village hierarchy an extension of their apparatus for controlling their work force.[88]

Several contemporaries noted the interplay of the rural credit and hiring systems with communal efforts to fulfill state obligations. For instance, G. P. Sazonov of the Russian Free Economic Society argued that a considerable proportion of *otkhodniki* entered the labor force as *kabal'nye rabochie* or *pokruchenniki*—debt- or bonded workers—who were given advances prior to their departure in order to cover the "departure fees" imposed by local authorities. In effect, by prior arrangement between hiring-agents and local authorities, there was a direct transfer of cash advances from employers to local elders, all or part of the peasant's debt was paid, and only what was left over became available for the peasant's household use. In such an arrangement, all the forces for social control came into play: seeking a more reliable and docile labor force, employers imposed written contracts on a collective and mutually responsible group of debt-workers from the same general area. With large advances (or "loans") granted when taxes were due in the fall and winter, local authorities managed to satisfy at least part of the state's demands, thereby reducing the likelihood of intervention by unpredictable outsiders. The legal character of the agreements brought the full power of the state, through its local judicial and executive agents, to support the arrangements.

On the issue of the enforceability of these various schemes, available sources have suggested a distinct pattern. According to N. Dobrotvorskii, the number of cases in which workers were required to pay for their comrades as a consequence of *krugovaia poruka* (excluding death) was very few, despite the fact that one often heard of instances of disgruntled workers' unauthorized departure from work. In the event of strict enforcement of the rules or in cases of mistreatment, all the workers of the artel would threaten to depart at once. In such confrontations, contractors seeking to recover damages would turn either to the *volost* courts or to the local justice of the peace *(mirovoi sud'ia)*, depending on the amount of the suit. Generally, the peace justices were much more severe in penalizing workers. In the *volost* courts, contractors would usually only manage to recover the amount of money actually paid (in advances), minus just compensation to peasant-workers for work performed prior to departure. Requests for forfeiture charges and related penalties associated with breaking the contract were usually declined.[89]

The actual degree of collusion between hiring-agents and local authorities is, by its very nature, difficult to determine and impossible to quantify. Inevitably, such illicit collusion between employers and village authorities varied widely from one area to another, but available evidence suggests that local middlemen exploited local conditions to the utmost. The degree of sophistication that could be attained in such schemes is illustrated by this report on the hiring of lumber workers in the north:

> On an autumn day the timber merchant . . . calls upon the [village] elder and proposes that he convene the peasants for a village meeting. The peasants are assembled; the merchant reminds them that soon the taxes *[sentiabrëvka]* will be expected of them, and asks where they think they will get the money. The peasants scratch the backs of their heads, and are silent. The merchant then offers to hire them to cut and transport logs from his dacha to the pier. For felling and delivering the logs he offers, depending on the amount, from 60 kopecks to 1 ruble 20 kopecks, and an advance of 15 rubles, for a troika with horses. The peasants begin to make a stir, to haggle [over the terms]. The [village] elder, who had earlier been won over by the merchant, begins to curse the peasants, threatening [to take them to] the *volost* office, or to the village constable, etc. The peasants, having in perspective the oppressiveness of the *sentiabrëvka*—the distraint of property, [imprisonment in] the "cooler" and other energetic measures—cause an even greater stir, even shouting, but eventually they accept the merchant's offer. Then they get drunk on vodka served by the merchant and, tipsy, go to the *volost* office "to secure the contract." The merchant then distributes the agreed upon advance, which is immediately used for the payment of state and communal dues. Such a reception is repeated by the merchant in nearly every village of the entire *volost*.[90]

Besides drink, religious rites were often used to further legitimize contracts: "Having negotiated [the agreement], they bow to God and then the boss *[khoziain]* leads him to the tavern. . . . From the moment when they offer a prayer to God, the hiring agreement is considered definitively concluded."[91]

The process—negotiation, contract, advance, prayer, and a drink at the hiring agent's expense—was virtually universal. Violation of these unwritten rules could provoke a powerful reaction among peasant-workers. In Iur'ev District, Vladimir Province, for instance, local workers boycotted a hiring-agent because he refused to buy the customary drinks.[92]

Often, the large advances generally associated with the hiring process would cut into earnings so deeply as to compel peasant-workers to seek further credit, thereby hurling them into a perpetual cycle of debt servitude. The right of employers to impose deductions to repay peasant-workers' debts (to employers and outsiders) was restricted in the general factory law of 3 June 1886.[93] Despite such ineffectual legal initiatives from above, however, tax inspectors' reports and *zemstvo* surveys throughout the 1890s were full of documented violations of such restrictions, leading a disgruntled village correspondent in Bogorodsk District, Moscow Province, to complain: "The written law has no effect here."[94] The links between employers, their hiring-agents, and village and *volost* authorities were real, and certainly they had an enormous impact on Russian labor history.

Zemliachestvo[95]

Just as hiring-agents tried as much as possible to operate along established networks, enlist the support of local authorities, and bind workers together in collective contracts confirmed and enforced by a blend of state and village institutions, the workers themselves—when venturing out in search of employment—relied to a great degree on *zemliak* ties and the contacts they provided. With considerable risk of failure, even in good years, peasant-workers relied as much as possible on the guidance and support of their more fortunate or experienced fellow villagers—*zemliaki* who could supply crucial information and the necessary introductions for finding a job. As the peasant-worker Kanatchikov recalled, "There were, of course, no labor exchanges in those days, but in spite of this we were very well informed about where workers were needed."[96] Particularly among unskilled workers, who often had to "'shuffle along on their own *[bredet rozno]*, on the off-chance *[na avos]*'" of finding employment, the hazards of job-seeking were considerably reduced by relying on the resources of fellow villagers.[97] This was as much a product of the structure of the hiring market in the Central Industrial Region as of the preferences of prospective employers: hiring agents "in selecting an artel of workers, try always to hire as many as possible from one village or, at least, from one *volost*. . . . Contractors almost never hire lone workers into large artels; they are selected only by local contractors, and then more *through acquaintances [po znakomstvu], through connections [po znati]*. Fearing abuse, contractors never hire individual workers who are strangers or newcomers."[98] The typical pattern of hiring and skill acquisition through kinship and *zemliak* networks was observed by a peasant correspondent from Dmitrov District, Moscow Province: "As a rule, peasants of an entire village, or even a whole area [okrug], leave for one and the same occupation, to one and the same destination, which is explained by the fact that persons going for earnings for the first time are more easily able to settle down and find work there where they have an acquaintance [znakomyi]."[99]

Zemliachestvo had a telling impact on patterns of urban settlement, as "urban villages" sprang up in urban and suburban working-class neighborhoods. As an observer in St. Petersburg noted early in the twentieth century: "It's enough just for one villager to come to the city before this pioneer drags along his fellow villagers and helps them get set up. For this reason we have frequently seen apartments inhabited by people of the same village."[100] In the town or settlement, peasant-workers from the same region as a rule socialized together, adopting taverns and saloons as their own. Noting the concentration of peasant-workers from the same village or region in saloons in St. Petersburg, a contemporary observer explained: "Here [the peasant construction worker] finds out all the news from the countryside, . . . who is working for how much, who sent home how much money, who drank how much, who swore at or fought with the contractor—in a word, everything 'interesting' is found here."[101] Observers in Tver Province noted the same high propensity for *zemliak* clustering:

> The population of each district has its own favorite place, where they go for earnings each year. Thus, for example, peasants of Tver District depart only for the large towns of Petersburg, Moscow, and Tver as factory carriers and other types of work. Ves'egonsk, Vyshnii Volochëk, Ostashkov, and Rzhev peasants almost never go to Moscow for earnings, but rather head *en masse* for Petersburg and other towns. In addition to Petersburg, Ves'egonsk boot-makers prefer mainly to leave for neighboring Iaroslavl Province; Vyshnii Volochëk carpenters and factory workers [go] to Kronstadt, and Pskov and Novgorod Provinces.[102]

Throughout Russia, each *volost* was associated with its own special set of skills and professions, which were often passed down through several generations. This pattern of operating within village-based networks was reinforced by annual ritual and pilgrimage routes which, as the historical ethnographer M. M. Gromyko has demonstrated, were closely associated with peasant economic activity.[103] In short, cultural factors played as significant a role as economic ones in the development of more-or-less stable patterns of migration. As a researcher for the Free Economic Society concluded, "Departing *zemliaki* entice others by their example—with their success, with their stories. Successful migrants are themselves transformed into contractors for their own *zemliaki*, who recruit still more [peasant] children from their parents."[104]

Patterns of *zemliak* clustering are clearly evident in migration statistics. For instance, 60.4 percent (98,801) of all peasants with passports from Tver Province went for work in St. Petersburg; more than 30 percent (32,316) went to Moscow. Likewise, almost three-fourths (77,322) of Iaroslavl migrants worked in St. Petersburg.[105] District, *volost*, and village data are even more striking in this regard, with all or almost all local peasant-workers involved in comparable occupations at similar work sites. To take just one of myriad examples common to *zemstvo* reports: "Everyone in Smolinskaia *volost*, Vereia District [Moscow Province] departs for earnings at factories in Moscow city and Borovsk District, Kaluga Province."[106]

Zemliak clustering had two profound effects on the rural system in the Central Industrial Region. First, since workers from the same village tended to concentrate in similar skills and at similar work sites, they were extremely vulnerable to fluctuations in the business cycle. Highly dependent on specific sectors or specific geographical regions, peasant-workers from a particular village collectively developed a pattern of economic behavior comparable to Third World monocultures today: in good years, when their particular skills were in demand, high-migration villages flourished; in bad years, the absence of alternatives forced peasant-workers back to their villages to scrape together whatever living they could. This had the telling effect of generating among peasants and peasant-workers a widespread and deep-seated pathology of distrust in the market and a wariness toward the opportunities it could provide (see chapter 5).

Second, the combined effect of distinct regional patterns of hiring and the reliance on established networks for matching peasant-workers to skills and employers was to generate a powerful instrument for social control. Extending the boundaries of the traditional community to the work place, *zemliak* networks served as conduits for information back to the village, providing details about community members, their state of health, their behavior, even their earnings. In short, *zemliak* networks integrated a peasant-worker's nonvillage experience into his village reputation, that "fund of common knowledge" about each member of the village community which followed them throughout their lives.[107] And information was the vital prerequisite for control. Which is not to say that *zemliak* networks always communicated accurate information. Wherever rumors are concerned, "the process of embellishment and exaggeration is not at all random. As a rumor travels it is altered in a fashion that brings it more closely into line with the hopes, fears, and worldview of those who hear it and retell it.... The rumor is not only an opportunity for anonymous, protected communication, but also serves as a vehicle for anxieties and aspirations that may not be openly acknowledged by its propagators."[108]

Inevitably, *zemliak* networks filtered information in a way that reflected and enhanced the anxieties of village dependents. As the peasant-worker Kanatchikov recalled: "Judging from his letters and from the accounts of fellow villagers, [my] Father was constantly tortured by some kind of dim anxiety about me and about the fate that awaited me."[109] In the few peasant-worker letters of the era which have survived, we get some sense of the degree to which *otkhodniki* fought to defend their reputations from defamatory reports that had filtered back to the village. "I have seen all of my friends and neighbors," wrote a peasant-worker in 1890 in a letter to his wife, "and all seemed in good health. Everyone greets you. I only did not see Petr Petrov, but I heard he had returned to the village for the winter." Defending himself against rumors of his own dissolute lifestyle, he continued: "I am now working as a decorator and have completed twenty days' work and through today have drunk no Petersburg vodka and I hope [to live this way] henceforth."[110]

Zemliaki were the mechanisms by which community norms were projected to urban village life. This included self-policing, to some degree, of village members who deviated from the norms. The overlay of village cultural linkages strengthened the power of institutions that were responsible for regulating the behavior of migrating peasant-workers, so that—as one of the leading contemporary specialists on migration, A. A. Bulgakov, observed: "Even in migration a peasant remains a peasant."[111] Which is just another way of saying that out-workers could not easily forget that they were and would remain peasants working "on the side" with dependent families and neighbors in the village.

5 The Logic of Solidarity

MIGRANTS AND VILLAGERS

> *Carpenters who had gone to work for a while in Moscow would return home laden with presents for their women, old people and children. The warmth and security of life at home had always meant more to them than the bright lights and noisy crowds of the capital.*
>
> VASILII GROSSMAN, *LIFE AND FATE*

The Uncertainty of Earnings

> В Питербурге денег много,
> Только даром не дают.
>
> *[There's a lot of money in Petersburg,
> Only they don't give it away for free.]*
> POPULAR PEASANT SONG, VOLOGDA PROVINCE, 1860s[1]

WHILE COERCIVE MECHANISMS could be called upon to engender a sense of respect and responsibility among *otkhodniki*, and in extreme cases to force the payment of state obligations and family support, they could only be effective during good years, when side-work was steady. In fact, the most powerful component in the arsenals of village communities lay in the shared cultural heritage among migrants and nonmigrants alike, a heritage best expressed as a common sensibility of living on the margin, an overriding concern about subsistence that led peasant households to pursue collective economic strategies to reduce the risks endemic to both the village and the nonvillage economies.

Despite all the Leninist hoopla about class conflict in the countryside, rich and poor peasants lived almost indistinguishably in good times; the differences between their relative situations were only really noticeable in bad times.[2] The distinguishing feature was the question of marginality: wealthy peasants had a reserve that could sustain them during bad times, while poor and middle peasants did not. As we have seen, that vital difference enabled wealthy peasant "patrons" to consolidate their control over fellow-villagers, by offering the only viable form of social security less fortunate peasants and peasant-workers could find.

In contrast to chernozem districts, peasant livelihood in most districts of the Central Industrial Region did not depend on domestic farm harvests or the fortunes of household agriculture. Because most high-migration households purchased a major proportion of their annual food needs on the market, depressed food prices were a boon to most peasant households in the region. In Moscow Province, for instance, the amount harvested from the standard peasant allotment could supply the average peasant household with a mere three to five months' support each year.[3] Vladimir Province was typical. Of thirteen districts, in only two (Iur'ev and Suzdal) did peasant households derive a substantial portion of their annual incomes from agriculture. Two other districts (Pereiaslavl and Aleksandrov) were considered transitional, because there the rate of *otkhod* throughout the 1890s varied directly with the changing fortunes of the local harvests. In these four districts, agriculture represented for most peasants the determining factor in household solvency, and was particularly influential on the timing and magnitude of tax payments. In an overwhelming majority of districts, however, where household agriculture typically played at best only a marginal role in peasant livelihoods, the effects of local harvest failures were usually negligible while the impact of depressed grain prices was overwhelmingly positive.[4]

Instead, it was downturns in the business cycle that wreaked the most havoc on peasant well-being in the non-black-earth regions. For instance, the principal source of peasant side-income in the provinces surrounding Moscow was industrial labor. This included those who actually worked in the manufacturing industry (at home and away) as well as those "dependent" industries such as construction, lumber and peat work, and hauling. During the period 1870–1905, there were five major recessions in Russia which hit the Moscow region particularly severely: 1873–1874, 1882–1886, 1890–1893, 1901–1902, and 1904–1905. At these times, the work force in large factories, towns, and industrial settlements was reduced by at least half, the level of out-work to the cottage industry was drastically curtailed, and overall—for those who were able to find work—wages were reduced while fines and miscellaneous deductions increased, leading to a general reduction in the standard of living among those who were employed as well as the large number unable to find work. The catastrophic impact of industrial recession on peasant well-being in the Moscow region was vividly described in this typical report from Tula Province in 1904:

> With each passing day in the shops and factories of our province production is curtailed . . . [and] the shopowners are dismissing a still greater number of workers as unessential. One even finds those who dismiss the more expensive workers and in their place recruit cheaper ones, who are compelled by extreme need in the current wave of unemployment to take poorly paying work, provided that they will work exclusively "for grub." . . . [This] curtailment of the number of workers . . . exerts a very heavy burden on rural inhabitants. Very many families live almost entirely on the monetary assistance received from their fathers, husbands, brothers, and grown-up sons, who work in factories and shops. . . . The return of such a person [back to the village] is only a heavy burden, because it augments the "number of mouths."
>
> Having been dismissed . . . , workers initially struggle to find themselves work in other industrial establishments. They travel from mill to mill, they go by foot in crowds, they beg and pray [that you] accept them for work, [or] give them a piece of bread, but soon they are persuaded that all the effort has been entirely in vain.[5]

During periods of economic downturn, where were laid-off peasant-workers to turn? Because of the intrinsic unreliability of nonvillage wage labor, few could afford the luxury of a total break with their native villages. In Aleksandrov District, Vladimir Province, in 1897: "For every ten men from our village who left in the fall for outside work, four have returned home without having found on the side any sort of work at all."[6]

Between such tumultuous upheavals as full-scale recessions, there were frequent interruptions in work that abruptly cut off the lifeline between peasant families and the cash economy. One major factor was the Russian ritual cycle. Among all the major European powers, Russia had the highest number of nonworking days due to religious observances. As economic historian Olga Crisp observed, "There was an enormous variety of feast days: major and minor saints, local and national saints, historical and royal anniversaries and occasions." The average length of the working year in Russian factory industry was 264 days in 1900, versus 283.3 days in the United States at that time.[7] This plethora of holidays when factories and shops were closed provided added incentive for peasant-workers to retain ties with their villages. During the Easter and Christmas holidays, for instance, entire plants closed, while many workers returned to their villages. "During these holidays," Semën Kanatchikov remembered, "the factory would close down for almost an entire week. A larger number of workers had ties with their villages. . . . They would await the coming of the holidays with impatience—they saved their money to buy things for themselves and for their village hosts."[8]

Less predictable than annual religious festivals were work stoppages associated with plant shutdowns and supply bottlenecks. Based on data for the years 1901–1912, there were throughout European Russia complete plant closings in 8,590 establishments, forcing more than three hundred thousand workers to look for work elsewhere.[9] Besides permanent shutdowns, temporary supply bottlenecks were common, often leading to an imposition of reduced work hours and unreimbursed idleness.[10] To choose just one example: the extension of the state monopoly on distilled spirits in 1898 and the subsequent closing of numerous private establishments led to the forced return of several thousand inn- and tavernkeepers from St. Petersburg to their native villages, located almost entirely in two southeastern districts of Iaroslavl Province.[11]

Besides the pervasive threat to *otkhodnik* job security due to endemic upheavals in the business cycle, there were also the threats associated with the growing frequency of employer-employee confrontations. In a system where legal regulations played only a minor role mediating the relations between workers and bosses, arbitrariness and abuse were common. Workers often found themselves utterly powerless in the face of a host of loopholes that permitted bosses to dismiss them without explanation or due cause. As Kanatchikov recalled:

> Every year the "Old Bromley" factory would undergo a cleansing of "unsuitable," "unreliable," and generally "undesirable" elements. This operation was carried out rather simply. When the Easter holidays came around, all the workers would be dismissed. Then when the holiday was over the foremen of the various shops would hire their workers anew. In this manner, all the workers whom the foremen found objectionable were left outside the factory gates.[12]

The worst part of it was that "unreliable" workers were dismissed legally and without warning. "The whole situation was so stupid that you could not even learn the reason for your dismissal."[13] V. Dadonov observed that industrialists in Ivanovo-Voznesensk preferred local workers *(mestnye)* over nonlocal ones *(prishlye)*, and systematically purged their ranks of "unruly" or otherwise "unreliable" nonlocals each fall, after the feast of the Protection of the Holy Virgin (October 1).

> With the onset of the autumn season there usually takes place a certain sorting out and selection. All those [workers] who appear too independent and obstinate are asked to leave. And the relinquished spaces are filled by local peasants who have finished field work. . . . [During this time,] the whole unruly element is dismissed.[14]

The files of the Moscow governor's chancellery are filled with workers' complaints against employers for arbitrary mistreatment in this regard.[15] One example will serve to illustrate peasant-workers' vulnerability to abuse by dishonest employers, and the far-reaching consequences even just one bad experience could have on the well-being of the whole peasant household for years to come.

On 19 May 1889, peat boss Daniil Abramov Mirovich, plus an assistant, the reserve underofficer Ovchinnikov, were in Moscow to hire peat workers—fifteen adult men and one boy. They had been subcontracted to hire workers by the merchant's son Ivan Mikhailovich Zaitsev. Consistent with common procedures, the two contractors immediately confiscated the new workers' passports and issued in return a five-ruble advance to each man, two rubles to the boy. The workers arrived at Zaitsev's peat bog on 21 May and began work two days later, when they were given contract books *(ustanovlennyia knizhki)*, where the period of the contract was indicated to run until 20 July. Having worked two days, and having already consumed "grub" worth nearly forty-eight rubles, the workers demanded that Mirovich pay out an additional ten rubles each, in accordance with their agreement back in Moscow. Arguing that pay was due on the first of each month, Mirovich refused the request, "as a consequence of which the workers, leaving work without authorization *[samovol'no]*, departed and submitted a complaint to the justice of the peace of the third district in Vereia," requesting the return of their passports. On 27 May, Mirovich responded with a complaint of his own against the workers' unauthorized departure. As a result of his suit, each worker was sentenced to two weeks in jail during the height of their work season, while their request for a return of their passports was refused.

While still under arrest, on 3 June, the peasant-workers sent a petition to the Moscow Governor-General Prince Golitsyn, signed by two artel chiefs, peasants from two neighboring *volosti* in Tula where all the workers originated. After describing the details of their hiring by Zaitsev via the subcontractor Mirovich, the workers continued: "At the present time, we cannot work, because either the boss Zaitsev or Mirovich (we don't know which) worked improperly, [refused] to give back our pay-books [*raschetnye knigi*], and we have suffered already 11 days, [living] without our passports, and we've had to live off our last reserve, since we paid out the advances for a place to sleep." They unsuccessfully petitioned for the Moscow governor's assistance in getting their passports back, the abolition of the jail sentence rendered by the justice of the peace, and asked that the governor take measures "to defend poor working people according to the law."[16]

Such appeals to the governor's human side and his moral responsibility to intercede on behalf of "poor working people" were commonly reflected in petitions of desperate peasant-workers ruined by the machinations of wily labor brokers: "We have not received our passports for five months, and presently we are unemployed, and our farms have fallen into decline and ruin." In spite of this, "we have not shirked our obligations."[17]

Besides such common but intrinsically unquantifiable breakdowns in the peasant-worker's everyday work routine, there were also strikes, which occurred with far more frequency, duration, and intensity during the last generation preceding 1917. Data from the Columbia University Labor History Project reveal that roughly 5–20 percent (on average) of Russia's industrial labor force were annually involved in strike actions after 1895. In the years of particular crisis—1905–1907 and 1912–1914—35–168 percent of all workers took part in strikes, with millions of wage-earning days lost (see table 5.1).[18]

Strike actions in certain key sectors—raw materials production, for instance, or transport—precipitated mass unemployment in dependent sectors. Frequent railway strikes during the early years of the twentieth century, for example, had a powerful ripple effect on job opportunities for peasants in surrounding regions. This report from Bogordsk District, Moscow Province, in 1905–1906 was typical: "Migrant work has considerably suffered from the railway strikes. Local factory workers have been idle for a long time, in view of the shortage of material, the provisioning of which has been hampered by the railways. Several local factory owners have all but closed their establishments, and one of them has just about been bankrupted altogether."[19]

Peasant-workers coped with strike actions and sporadic layoffs largely by relying on contacts with their families and benefactors living in the country-

Table 5.1. Number of Strikes, Strikers, and Workdays Lost in Russia (1895–1914)

Year	Strikes	Strikers	Days Lost
1895	68	31,195	
1896	118	29,527	
1897	145	59,870	
1898	215	43,150	
1899	189	57,498	
1900	125	29,389	
1901	164	32,218	
1902	123	36,671	
1903	550	86,832	
1904	68	24,904	
1905	13,995	2,863,173	23,609,387
1906	6,114	1,108,406	5,500,652
1907	3,573	740,074	2,431,527
1908	892	176,101	
1909	340	64,166	
1910	222	46,623	
1911	466	105,110	
1912	2,032	725,491	2,378,057
1913	2,404	887,096	3,482,610
1914	3,534	1,337,458	4,691,088

Source: Leopold H. Hamson and Ronald Petrusha, "Two Strike Waves in Imperial Russia, 1905–1907, 1912–1914," in Leopold Haimson, ed., *Strikes, Wars, and Revolutions in an International Perspective* (Cambridge, 1989), pp. 107, 145.

side. Fëdor Samoilov recounted that during the 1905 textile workers' strike in Ivanovo-Voznesensk, "a large portion of the strikers—the main force still had a connection with the countryside—dispersed and went back to their villages for field work, which somewhat relieved the material need."[20] In Murom District, Vladimir Province, "Because of the strike, all the workers . . . are simply loafing about the house, in the village with nothing to do. They arrived here on foot by begging for alms. But on the third of July they again went back."[21]

In this sense, 1905 was a watershed in which there converged numerous elements that directly threatened the security of migrants and their dependent families. The pattern was the same throughout the Central Industrial Region and surrounding districts: the Russo-Japanese war, a recession, and growing unrest in the towns led to a mass exodus of peasant-workers of all types back to the countryside.[22] A peasant house-decorator forced by unemployment to return from Moscow to his village complained: "This year is much worse than last. Wages have dropped from 6 rubles a week . . . to 3 or 3 ½ rubles. I know of three cases in which joiners went for earnings to Moscow by train, but after two weeks they returned home 'on foot,' having left behind their sheepskin coats, which they had to sell in order to eat. During these two weeks, they went around to almost all the contractors, and no one would hire them, even

The Logic of Solidarity 125

just for bread, despite the fact that they are sober and hard-working people."²³ Cyclical economic fluctuations were incomprehensible to peasants and peasant-workers whose main concerns were meeting family needs.

In nonfactory sectors—many of which relied on village consumers who depended on agriculture for their income—there was even greater vulnerability and frequent reversals in the market. A peasant-worker in Kostroma Province, speaking in the late 1880s, summarized the brutal logic imposed on virtually all peasant-workers by the intrinsic insecurity of outside earnings:

> Our side *[piter]* business is not reliable *[ne nadezhnoe]*. [For instance], business is now in a depression, and is always easily bankrupt. Apply the question to our craft: Out there are coopers. They work just as well as before, and yet their business is currently declining. Besides, misfortunes can come in many ways: you get sick, [someone] hires fools who dissipate all your money, they swindle customers. . . . [The danger is] particularly [great] now, when an entire house is built on credit. . . . In the end, where can one take shelter? In the village, [at least,] although you won't have free scope, there will always be your own piece of bread and lump of coal.²⁴

Zhbankov observed that many *pitershchiki* built large houses in the village, usually buying suitable pieces of land to go along with them.²⁵ The reasoning was based on the peasant-workers' fundamental distrust of the market. As Zhbankov explained, "In its main form the uncertainty of an urban profession and even fortune (sometimes from hundreds of thousands [of rubles] and several houses) compels the *pitershchik* to regard the village home and particularly his land as a more solid form of security *[obespechenie]* than any profitable outside *[piter]* profession and wealth."²⁶ Or as a peasant-shoemaker in Vladimir Province put it in 1882: "Today, I'm well-fed and drunk, but tomorrow I may not have even a farthing."²⁷

This deep ambivalence and distrust for the fortunes (and misfortunes) of the market were characteristic of most peasants, regardless of their degree of success away from the village. Indeed, even the so-called permanent peasant emigrants to urban areas usually boarded up their huts and gave strict instructions that they were not to be disturbed.²⁸ In so doing, migrating peasant-worker families were establishing the village as a safety net in the event of misfortune, their right—guaranteed by state statute and their continued payment of dues in the community—to return to the village at their own discretion.

The peasant Ivan Andreev has left a compelling account of the trials and tribulations peasant-workers faced. His substantial handwritten and illustrated unpublished diary offers historians a unique perspective on the preeminent role of pervasive insecurity in the lives of migrant laborers in the Old Regime. At the beginning of the twentieth century, Andreev worked in a shop in the provincial town of Iaroslavl. One day, he badly injured his legs in an accident at work. Without the benefit of doctor's care or any social insurance to fall back upon, Andreev had to keep working: he was the sole breadwinner for his wife and family. Fearing that he might lose his job if detected, Andreev did his best to conceal his injury from his employer. When the pain grew too much to bear, Andreev began to drink. The long hours of working on injured legs drove him to depend more and more on strong spirits, and eventually pushed him into alcoholism. These sections of Andreev's diary are dominated by his self-loathing, as he lamented his hopeless suffering, wallowed in his helplessness, castigated himself for drinking away his family's livelihood. He dreaded that he would some day have to face his wife. Eventually, Andreev suffered a total mental and physical breakdown and was rescued from catastrophe only by the kindly intervention of a local benefactor who advanced him a cash loan and helped him through convalescence and later, to find another job.[29]

The important thing to understand is that Andreev's story was not in the least exceptional. At some point, every migrating worker would find himself in trouble, facing a catastrophic situation with only his family, his neighbors, and village benefactors to fall back upon.

Migration as a Two-Way Street

> *напитриться:* жить в Питербурге столько,
> что тамошная жизнь надоесть
>
> [*napitrit'sia:* to live in Petersburg so long that
> you get sick to death of life there.]
>
> PEASANT SLANG COMMONLY USED IN
> VILLAGES OUTSIDE ST. PETERSBURG, 1870s[30]

As would be expected, the peasant-worker's abrupt separation from the land —his and his ancestors' "benefactress-provider"—his sudden complete reliance on the market and his wage earnings for his livelihood, provoked an uncomfortable feeling in most. The psychic attachment to the village as a form of insurance against the uncertainties of the outside world was graphically expressed by Fëdor Samoilov as he recollected his first days alone at work in Ivanovo-Voznesensk:

> Life wasn't easy, and shortages of all kinds of things were suffered now, sometimes to the point of great need; but the dream of leaving the factory and settling in the village continued to live [inside me]. Its infeasibility was clearly evident to me, but I did not have sufficient strength to part with it, for indeed, it seemed without it one could not have lived. There were no other kinds of hopes for the future. The life of the proletariat appeared as one endlessly difficult, without joy and without a ray of hope.[31]

There is considerable evidence to indicate that village migration was indeed a two-way street. For the Samoilovs—who had three of five family members gainfully employed in Ivanovo-Voznesensk—life in the town just became too difficult. In the spring of 1898, the decision was made to relocate the family back to the village.

> Life in the town made everything onerous to us. Insufficient nourishment and the heavy conditions of factory work cut down our strength; the stifling, dusty, and fetid conditions of the workers' quarter in which we lived drove us to melancholy. Everyone in our family began to think of the village more and more frequently. The bad was forgotten, while the good brightly stood up in our memories. Gradually, my parents came to the decision to return to the village. However, one and one-half years would still pass before they managed to leave the town. Father, mother, and my two younger brothers left to go back to the village. I remained in the town alone.[32]

After this point, Samoilov's stay in the town became most difficult, and his dreams of some day settling back in the village became most intense.

> With what joy would I have set out together with my parents for the village—[that place] about which I had so often reminisced! But I knew well that on our small tuft of land, my family would not be able to survive without my extra earnings on the side. I had to remain in the town. On holidays and every Sunday I went home to the village.[33]

Just as *zemliak* stories of the world outside the village had enticed peasant youths to seek to make their fortunes away from their native homes, once they had experienced the dusty and oppressive conditions common to Russian urban and lower-class life for themselves, peasant-workers would naturally cling to nostalgic images of idealized village life.

The enormous magnitude of the exchange between town and country has been analyzed by Robert Johnson in his comprehensive study of the flow of peasant migrants to and from Moscow City. Of the 113,000 peasant migrants who had moved to Moscow in 1900, more than half were no longer living in the city by 1902.³⁴ Apparently, not all or even most peasant *otkhodniki* could withstand the pressures and challenges of city life. The only choices were to go back to the village or try to find work elsewhere. In his household inventories of four high-migration villages in Kostroma Province, Zhbankov found that the principal factors involved in a former *otkhodnik*'s resettlement in the village were most often sickness, old age, and especially drunkenness.³⁵

Aside from the very real need to maintain economic connections with the village, cultural and kinship ties offered most migrants a source of comfort in the often alienating environment of the town or factory work place. However eager peasant youths were to leave the village, life away from the village often made them look back for moral support from their *zemliaki* in the village and at work.

Socially, peasants in urban or semiurban areas were looked down upon, especially those "hayseeds" freshly arrived from the village—the *novichki* who were the butts of incessant and cruel jokes among their more seasoned peers.³⁶ So too were the tensions associated with the peasant-worker's isolation in a strange and unfamiliar milieu.

Peasant-Worker Insecurity and the Psychology of Nostalgia

Part of the enticement of Moscow or any big city was its very anonymity, one's freedom from the incessant intervention and judgment, the gossip and lack of personal space that characterized village life. On her return to Iaroslavl from Moscow in December, 1892, Elizaveta D'iakonova, the seventeen-year-old daughter of a provincial merchant, recalled in her diary:

> What a stillness here after the noise and animation of Moscow! Arriving here, on the very first day I had heard enough of the sort of gossip which is only possible in the provinces. What a place is Moscow! There a person can disappear unnoticed in the general mass, he can live peacefully, do whatever he wants, dress as he likes, think as he wants—in general, live his own life without being concerned about the opinion of others. And if he is not a celebrity, no one talks about him, they won't even notice him. I have experienced this luxury—it is impossible to be unnoticed in the provinces.³⁷

That very same anonymity in a mass of unfamiliar strangers provoked a mixture of complex feelings. The same village ties that oppressed also supported, and severing those ties provoked a deep sense of anomie and alienation in some. Semën Kanatchikov's memories were particularly vivid:

My [initial] admiration [for the city] began to collapse and [there rose up inside of me] some kind of inexpressible terror before the immensity and cold indifference of my surroundings. I perceived myself as a negligible grain of sand, lost in a sea of surrounding people who were unknown and hostile to me.[38]

Fëdor Samoilov shared this early feeling of agoraphobia, as did so many peasant-workers uprooted from the safe and familiar confines of their villages.[39]

Dr. Vladimir Iakovenko, director of the Pokrov Psychiatric Hospital of the Moscow provincial *zemstvo* at the turn of the century, conducted a comprehensive survey of patients treated for nervous and mental disorders throughout Moscow Province during the latter half of the 1890s. Excluding from his sample those patients whose conditions were congenital or induced by physical causes (such as epilepsy), or those for whom there were insufficient data for the sample, Iakovenko found that by far the greatest single factor accounting for severe mental disorders among Moscow peasants was the experience of nonvillage child and adolescent migrant labor: especially among those peasants who worked in factories, shops, or as apprentices in skilled trades. Of 1,058 peasant patients in the sample, 412 had worked for one or more years before age fifteen: among males, nearly half (46 percent) had worked away from their villages before age fifteen; among females, for whom child labor outside the home was much rarer, about one in four (26 percent) had worked outside the home. The evidence points to a very high correlation between nonvillage work and nervous disorders among young peasant-workers. There was evidently a considerable psychological and emotional strain associated with Russian working-class life, particularly among peasant youths.[40]

In an effort to track down specific cases reflecting the psychic strain of urban living on all peasant-workers, I consulted the files of the Preobrazhenskaia Hospital for the Insane in Moscow. One case will serve to illustrate the overlapping factors of vulnerability, fear, and stress which all peasant-workers knew only too well. Fekla Pavlova, a peasant woman from Kirik village, Novosel'sk District in Tula Province, was an unmarried twenty-two-year-old peasant-worker in Moscow in October 1865 when she was gang-raped and beaten nearly to death. The experience drove her insane, and she was found at night running and screaming through the Moscow streets. After spending a week at the Unskilled Laborers' Hospital to treat her wounds, she was transferred to the Preobrazhenskaia Hospital for the Insane. Her attending physician at Preobrazhenskaia described her as an extremely disturbed patient: "Here she is very quiet, incessantly pensive. She neither says anything nor answers any questions. We've given up on insistently pressing her for answers, since these only make her cry, or start to laugh. She does, however, sleep calmly, eat with a good appetite and occasionally she does needlework." By mid-November, Fekla had lapsed into a deep depression, threatening suicide and repeatedly trying to escape from the hospital. By the end of November, she had begun to speak again intermittently, reporting that she often heard voices, mainly the voice of her mother, recently deceased. By January 1866, she had again lapsed into silence, only overheard whispering to herself at night. Fekla spent the next twenty-eight years of her tragic life in the Preobrazhenskaia Hospital, where she died in May 1893 much as she had lived: hiding crouched beneath a table rocking catatonically.[41]

For most peasant labor migrants, the enthusiasm at the grandeur and wealth of the city decayed not long after their arrival for work. In their souls they yearned for the familiarity and intimacy of the village. Peasant-workers imagined "escaping from the city" into an "idealized rural landscape." As Mark Steinberg observed in his insightful work on Russian workers' literary imagination at the end of the Old Regime: "One cannot escape from the anxiety workers felt in looking at the modern industrial landscape. . . . Apparent nostalgia for a lost rural idyll was a pervasive theme. It was not at all uncommon for worker-writers to portray themselves standing at their machines weeping as they remembered the smells of fields and rivers and springtime in the native village."[42] Fëdor Samoilov recounted just such a nostalgic image in this vivid passage from his memoirs:

> When I was sixteen years old, I—like my father—was passionately drawn to the village. In my sleeping and waking hours, I saw my native fields and forests and the village river with its pellucid, glasslike water and the green carpet of meadows that covered its banks. In dreams I frequently saw a vast field of rye sown with pale blue cornflowers. Vividly, it stirred from a light breeze. In such moments it seemed that I could smell the heady fragrance of grass growing on the green shores of the river. In waking hours, there stood the village with its twenty large and small thatched huts, with kitchen gardens by the stream. Beyond the fields was a pine forest and over everything was a bottomless, clear, pale blue sky. Like a gigantic veil, it was stretched without end or edge, and irresistibly beckoned to its endless azure depths. I dreamed of this picture of my native village—precious since childhood—and wanted then nothing more than to settle there with the rest of my family.[43]

Yearning for the village had a distinct impact on peasant-worker leisure activities. Many spent all their time with fellow villagers—*zemliaki, rodniki*—

The Logic of Solidarity 131

who also worked in the town. They created their own working-class cultures, urbanized and distinct from the countryside but still nonetheless largely structured around and saturated by village ties.⁴⁴ On holidays, nostalgic peasant-workers often returned to their native homes, not for field work—the recurrent theme of contemporary Populist writers—but for rest and relaxation among "their own kind." As Kanatchikov wrote: "Many of my fellow workers had their hearts in the countryside; on holidays they spoke to *zemliaki* about the land, their farms, grain, cattle, etc. Whenever they saved a little money, they took off for the countryside."⁴⁵ The attraction was obvious: migrants left behind the squalid quarters of their dehumanizing urban, suburban, or factory environment and returned to their native villages like heroes. Zhbankov described the customary ritual: "Family members liberate migrants from any kind of village work *(domashniaia rabota)* for the two weeks until their departure [back to side-work]. 'And for those who have exhausted themselves from heavy work for someone else, now let them have a rest.' And indeed, migrant workers do nothing these whole two weeks [except] go about the village with a crowd, sing songs, lead people on the accordion, and—of course—not making do without vodka."⁴⁶ Those peasant-workers employed in occupations nearer to their native villages were more likely to participate actively in the village ritual system: "How near the migrating village cobbler or felt-bootmaker is to his native place and farming is proved by the fact that all of them who are not farther than 100–300 kilometers from home, return home two-three times during the period of their six-month absence for major holidays (Christmas, Festival, Carnival), his name day, and for the weddings of his relatives."⁴⁷

Migration, Social Control, and the Changing Structure of Rural Life, 1861–1914

The principal theme in this study has been the investigation of communal efforts to regulate labor in the Central Industrial Region during the period between the general serf Emancipation of 1861 and the 1905 revolution. The main goal of this regulation was to redistribute the product of wage labor earned by community members working outside their villages. My assertions regarding the strength of the ties between labor migrants and their families can be tested by looking at peasant household budget data.

THE FLOW OF CASH BETWEEN
WORK PLACE AND VILLAGE

Two broad observations can be made about the relative effectiveness of communal schemes to redistribute peasant wage income back to the countryside. First, proximity between village and work place profoundly affected the capacity of villagers to influence out-workers. A number of studies have indicated that an *otkhodnik*'s financial connection to the village declined in direct relation to the distance of the work place from his native village. In one study conducted at the beginning of the twentieth century among 9,500 workers in western Vladimir Province, it was found that one-third (36.7 percent) of all workers lived within seven to eight kilometers of the factory, and two-thirds (65.4 percent) lived within twenty-five kilometers. While 70–72 percent of those workers from villages within forty kilometers of the factory sent money home, only 30 percent of those from villages more than forty kilometers away did so.[48] These data suggest that the police system outside the towns was ultimately less reliable as a means for inducing payment than the coercive mechanisms within the village: as distance grew and direct village pressure dissipated, peasant-workers were more likely to evade fulfillment of their community and family responsibilities. I emphasize that this involved a minority of cases, since this sample, drawn from industrial settlements *(promyshlenniia seleniia)*, was considered by the author to have been more representative of patterns of hiring throughout the Central Industrial Region than the data extrapolated from Moscow City, which do not reflect the genuinely local character of the labor supply. The data from western Vladimir Province showed that 75 percent of all workers came from villages within a twenty-five kilometer radius; 61 percent of all factories and 59 percent of all factory workers were located in such industrial settlements. In the Central Industrial Region, the proportions were higher: two-thirds (65 percent) of all factories and workers were located outside the towns.[49] In the period 1879–1890, 63 of 103 of European Russia's most important industrial settlements were located in rural areas.[50] The Russian labor force by and large originated in villages located in close proximity to work place destinations, suggesting that villages remained in substantial control of peasant-workers settled in nonvillage occupations.

Second, there was a high correlation between the size of the village allotment, as an indicator of peasant household wealth, and the likelihood that peasant-workers would continue to share earnings with their families in the village. Throughout the non-black-earth regions, virtually every peasant

Table 5.2. Proportion of Peasant-Workers Sending Wages Back to Their Native Villages (Shuia District, Vladimir) 1890s (in percent)

Rural Holding	Sent Wages to Their Families	Did Not Send Any Wages to Their Families	Unknown
No sown area	76.0	16.5	7.5
Sown area up to 3 desiatinas	92.4	2.8	4.8
Sown area: 3.1 to 6 desiatinas	92.5	3.1	4.4
Sown area: greater than 6 desiatinas	91.5	5.3	3.2

Source: S. N. Prokopovich, "Krest'ianstvo i poreformennaia fabrika," *Velikaia reforma,* vol. 6 (Moscow, 1911), p. 272. I have corrected a misprint in Prokopovich's table: the data for sown area 3.1 to 6 *desiatiny* read "62.5" in the original text but should be "92.5." The original misprint has unfortunately been repeated in data presented by several historians who did not notice the discrepancies.

household—poor, middle, or wealthy—sent members away for earnings. On this point, a study conducted at the turn of the century in Shuia District, in northern Vladimir Province (see table 5.2), suggests that while most peasant-workers continued to send wages back to their families in the village—a fact which in itself reflects the remarkable persistence of old ways—the proportion of those who did not send wages home was significantly greater among the poorest rural families, that is, those with the least stake in the village economy.[51]

These data indicate that the decision to maintain ties to the village was to a large degree influenced by rational economic choice: wages were sent as an investment in a traditional and generally reliable form of social insurance. But the fact that three-fourths of all *otkhodniki* from landless households continued to send wages reflects the strength of village and household pressures; for the *bedniaki* of the Center, the village connection offered less economic security but nonetheless remained the focal point in the peasant cosmogony. Petr Maslov, a contemporary Marxist observer, agreed: "Usually, such workers send to the village 60–80 rubles and up to 200 rubles per year. Several send money only for the payment of taxes, although they neglect the land. Adolescents who earn in a day 40–50 kopecks send 10–15 rubles in a year 'so that father will not summon [me back] to the village.'"[52] Three case studies will serve to illustrate the overriding significance of these bonds.

Despite the primitive nature of village financial networks, postal data have left us with a rather precise record of the flow of cash between work place and village. Generally, peasant-workers sent money home in specially registered letters *(denezhnye pakety)* by way of the local *volost* office, a local store- or tavernkeeper or, in rare cases, directly to the peasant's home. A study of the flow of such parcels was conducted between 1895 and 1901 in Tver Province. Table

Table 5.3. Official Cash Transfers from Peasant-Workers to Their Villages: Tver Province, 1895–1901

	Parcels	Value (in rubles)	Average Value Each Parcel	Average No. Parcels/ Migrant	Average Value per Migrant
1895	402,524	5,830,305	14.48	1.2	17.96
1896	446,231	6,381,078	14.30	1.3	19.41
1897	453,367	6,259,802	13.81	1.3	17.84
1898	448,148	6,621,860	14.78	1.4	20.04
1899	451,514	6,817,401	15.10	1.3	19.79
1900	417,691	6,477,497	15.51	1.2	17.93

Source: *Statisticheskii ezhegodnik Tverskoi gubernii za 1897 [–1901] god* (Tver, 1898–1902).

5.3 contains a detailed breakdown of wage support between migrants and villagers for the years 1895–1901.[53]

In 1896, Tver *otkhodniki* sent 446,231 cash parcels home, at a gross value of 6,381,078 rubles. This reflected an average of 1.3 parcels per migrant (based on passports issued), with an average value of 14 rubles, 30 kopecks each. Data for the years following reflect a steady, uninterrupted flow of support. The close interrelationship between peasant migrants, their families, local authorities, and local benefactors is powerfully reflected in contemporary accounts: "By virtue of a long-established custom, both the *volost* office and tradesmen, receiving such cash letters addressed to them, first of all deduct from the received sum a certain percentage for commission, and second the money owed by relatives. *Volost* authorities deduct all of the sum or part of the arrears for state and *volost* obligations; tradesmen [deduct] for goods bought on credit in local shops by relatives who have remained at home."[54] Through postal sources alone, peasant-workers transferred receipts which amounted to 100–150 percent of the gross annual burden of all state and local dues imposed on Tver peasants!

Overall, it can be concluded that cultural connections between an *otkhodnik* and his native village remained strongest where there existed tangible economic supports. While it is clear that in the majority of cases village-based pressures dramatically influenced the decision to remain tied to the village community, the economic self-interest of the peasant-workers themselves likewise had a statistically significant effect on the migrants' own efforts to retain ties with their villages.

The central issue was security. Another study of three factories in Pokrov District, Vladimir Province, showed that those peasant-workers who were most likely to break from their villages were the ones in higher skill levels who consequently had higher average incomes and, what is just as important, more security in the wage-based economy.[55] In short, superior skills and greater earnings potential offered sufficient security to enable a total break with the land.[56] But this was the rare exception, not the rule, among peasant-workers, who retained in their hearts a deep distrust for the market.

In this way, we see how migrant wage labor provoked a profound transformation of peasant subsistence strategies in non-black-earth regions. The pattern that developed reflected a strategy of risk reduction through the bifurcation of the peasant household. As in feudal Russia, the *tiaglo,* or conjugal dyad, remained the most basic and viable productive work unit. Conjugality became the nexus that bonded the cash and subsistence economies together in a single household: labor migrants, who persisted in conceiving of themselves as "peasants earning income on the side," essentially "raided" the cash economy in order to sustain the wavering village base, while the village economy served as both a safety net protecting all household members and an anchor that effectively bound migrating peasants to their village. By sending their wages back to their villages (and a large majority of peasant-workers of the Central Industrial Region continued to do so well into the twentieth century), migrants were insuring themselves against the insecurities endemic to a commodity economy and the alienating conditions of their semiurbanized work place.

Iaroslavl Province represents a classic case for illustrating the connection between *otkhod* and wages sent back to the village. Here, 20–21 percent of the entire peasant population (more than 40 percent of all adult peasant males in the province) migrated for earnings in 1901; because of low arrears, more than 90 percent of all passports were long-term (one year or more); and 75 percent of the *otkhodniki* had broken entirely from agriculture, with their allotments and personally owned land left fallow or worked by family members or hired laborers. In some cases, especially in the highest migration districts of Uglich and Rybinsk, fallow land had grown wild with grass or even forests. But even in this case, in which the typical *otkhodnik*'s ties to the land seemed most tenuous, the flow of wages to the village was considerable. According to household inventories conducted in Myshkino District, representing the mean for migration in the province, the average annual earnings of an *otkhodnik* were 155 rubles, even higher in a good year. Typically, 50–65 percent of an *otkhodnik*'s annual earnings were sent home. In the entire province, the *zemstvo* statistician Vorob'ev estimated that 12–16 million rubles were sent each year by *otkhodniki* back to their families, totaling one and one-half to two times the amount taken in from agriculture (which averaged four rubles per *desiatina).* This influx of cash into the ailing village economy enabled Iaroslavl peasants to purchase an additional 628,000 *desiatiny* of land between 1861 and the beginning of 1903, bringing peasant landholding in the province to nearly 2 million *desiatiny*.[57]

Vorob'ev's impressive work in Iaroslavl Province established clear evidence of the substantial support that *otkhodnichestvo* had brought to peasant agriculture. Far from leading to what Lenin called a "divorcement" of the agricultural sector from the industrial one, a symbiotic relationship developed in which peasant households eluded threats from the risks endemic in both the agricultural and the nonagricultural sectors by working simultaneously in both.[58] This remarkable logic was extended throughout the whole of European Russia in a ground-breaking study by A. F. Fortunatov, the foremost expert on Russian agriculture during the last thirty years of the Old Regime.[59] Studying the aggregate annual data of peasant rye and oat harvests in fifty provinces of European Russia for the period 1896–1905, Fortunatov defined a harvest failure for a given year as a year in which harvests were less than 75 percent of the mean level of production for the whole ten-year period. (See table 5.4 and map 2).

Fortunatov's data powerfully demonstrate the crucial role played by peasant migrant earnings in the Central Industrial Region as well as the northern non-black-earth provinces, where *otkhod* income sustained the agricultural economy of high-migration regions. With a maximum frequency of twenty harvest failures in rye and oats for the ten-year period, 1896–1905, map 5.1 demonstrates clearly the clustering of regions with no or just one harvest failure in the highest migration districts of the Central Industrial Region and the industrialized northwest sector of European Russia. Paradoxically, proximity to nonagricultural side-work substantially reduced the likelihood of agricultural failure. In contrast, the areas where the frequency of harvest failures was highest corresponded directly to regions where opportunities for peasant nonagricultural side-labor were lowest: in the Central Agricultural, Volga, and Ural regions, where the rate of harvest failure approached 25-40 percent—or two and one-half to four years of harvest failures in a single ten-year period.

Evidently, even as peasant agriculture was waning in the very regions where peasants most depended on meager returns from their allotments, it boomed in areas of highest peasant labor migration, where outside earnings enabled villages to stave off the irreversible slide that characterized other regions from the 1890s. This unmistakable "return to the land" among peasant-workers in non-black-earth areas—a phenomenon that directly contradicts Lenin's notion of the "divorcement from agriculture"—was cogently evaluated by the nineteenth-century Russian agrarian specialist, P. A. Vikhliaev:

Map 2. Patterns of Harvest Failures (for rye and oats) in European Russia, 1896–1905. Adapted from A. F. Fortunatov, "Chastota neurozhaev na krest'ianskikh nadelakh," *Vestnik sel'skogo khoziaistva,* 1906, no. 29 (16 July 1906), p. 1.

Table 5.4. The Frequency of Harvest Failures in European Russia, 1896–1905

Regions and Provinces	Winter Rye	Oats	Total
I. Nonagricultural/Industrial	13	16	29
North and Northwest	5	2	7
Arkhangel	2	1	3
Vologda	0	0	0
Olonets	1	1	2
St. Petersburg	0	0	0
Novgorod	1	0	1
Pskov	1	0	1
Smolensk	0	0	0
Tver	0	0	0
Central Industrial Region	5	14	19
Iaroslavl	0	0	0
Moscow	0	2	2
Vladimir	0	1	1
Kostroma	0	0	0
Kaluga	0	3	3
Nizhnii Novgorod	0	2	2
Tula	2	3	5
Riazan	3	3	6
Belorussia	3	0	3
Vitebsk	1	0	1
Minsk	1	0	1
Mogilev	1	0	1
II. Southern Agricultural	16	16	32
Ukraine	13	13	26
Poltava	0	1	1
Kharkov	1	2	3
Chernigov	1	1	2
Kiev	2	2	4
Volynia	1	1	2
Podolia	1	1	2
Kherson	2	2	4
Ekaterinoslav	2	1	3
Taurida	3	2	5
North Caucasus	3	3	6
Don Oblast	3	3	6
III. Central Agricultural	28	41	69
Central Chernozem	7	12	19
Voronezh	2	3	5
Kursk	2	1	3
Orel	1	4	5
Tambov	2	4	6
Volga	21	29	50
Astrakhan	3	2	5
Saratov	1	5	6
Samara	4	3	7
Penza	2	4	6
Simbirsk	3	5	8
Kazan	2	3	5
Viatka	3	3	6
Ufa	3	4	7
IV. Eastern Agricultural	4	4	8
Ural	4	4	8
Perm	0	1	1
Orenburg	4	3	7
Total	61	77	138

Source: A. F. Fortunatov, "Rzhanie nedorody na krest'ianskikh nadelakh za 10-tiletie 1896–1905," *Russkie vedomosti*, 1906, no. 177 (12 July); Fortunatov, "Chastota neurozhaev na krest'ianskikh nadelakh," *Vestnik sel'skogo khoziaistva*, 1906, no. 29 (16 July), pp. 1–4.

Note: "Harvest failure" in areas where grain fell below 75 percent of 10-year average.

As a result of a serious depression in industrial life, the middle years of the 1880s coincided with a return to agricultural work of a sizable portion of the population in the non-black-earth region. This ebb tide of workers from nonagricultural occupations [back] to the land was corroborated by a whole series of events, enormously large and massive in character, reflected in the growth in the number of work horses in peasant agriculture and in the reduction of the proportion of horseless households.... This change was stimulated by the vital easing of the tax burden, which consisted of the abolition of the soul tax and the lowering of redemption payments at the beginning of the 1880s. Until these financial reforms, in a considerable number of localities in the non-black-earth region the financial burden on the land exceeded the income that it yielded. Under such conditions, the holder of the allotment, having abandoned agriculture, could not find a renter for his allotment who would pay the entire sum of the duties that lay on the land, and he therefore had to pay for the land from his own nonagricultural earnings or income, and to pay a *"spusta"* [leave-tax], the fee enabling him to return to work on the side. Under such conditions the land was a burden to the population, who strived to free themselves from this burden; the commune imposed these abandoned allotments *[upalyia dushi]* on large families. With the easing of the tax burden [however], the attitude of the population toward the land radically changed: land became more valuable [throughout the non-black-earth regions].[60]

The reduction of the opportunity for outside work, the drastic rise of the cost of living in urban areas, plus the sharp reduction of state duties on peasant allotments in the 1880s blended together to reinvigorate peasant agriculture in Central Industrial and northern non-black-earth regions. Klementii Vorob'ev, the *zemstvo* statistician who evaluated the data in Iaroslavl, came to this conclusion: "Despite all the negative influence on agriculture, migrant-laborers at the same time serve as the main support and sustaining force of the peasant farm. Without the means which *otkhod* gives to the [Iaroslavl] peasants, local farms would have gradually fallen to ruin and withered, and we would have witnessed a stronger impoverishment here than is now being observed in the Central Black Earth Region of Russia."[61]

There is perhaps no better testimony of the degree of resilience of "little community" ties among peasant-workers than the observation made by A. V. Pogozhev, a contemporary Marxist statistician and one of the foremost experts on the Russian factory during the late years of the nineteenth century: "In the majority of cases, Russian workers, when questioned about their professional occupation, tend as a rule to label themselves peasant-farmers, and they consider side-earnings as something occasional and inconstant. In general, this has nearly always been observed, but especially in factory-sanitary investigations in Moscow Province (1880–1902), and even in those cases when *otkhodniki* had been working at the factory for a long time and were accustomed to continual outside work."[62] Most peasant-workers before 1905 persisted in upholding their peasant status. In spite of all the changes that surrounded them, and in spite of their youthful eagerness to flee the village, they nonetheless continued to perceive the world from within the parameters of the village *focos* and according to the norms of the village communal hierarchy.[63]

III

LEGACIES
Otkhod and Russian Popular Culture

Words of a Dying Peasant to His Son:
Let me give you this advice,
Don't set foot in Peter[sburg],
Everyone knows that in the capital
There's enough folk without you;
Furthermore, you are a fool,
And you'll get into quite a scrape.
Stay behind here in our hut,
And stay away from evil people . . .
Don't forget your father's words,
If you go to Peter[sburg],
You will perish.

FROM P. TATARINOV, *FOMUSHKA IN PETER[SBURG],*
OR RICHES WILL NOT HELP THE STUPID SON:
A TALE FROM THE PAST (1852)[1]

HAVING DISCUSSED IN its barest outlines the distinct character of the evolution of the structure and role of the peasant commune in high-migration villages of the Central Industrial Region, I will devote the remaining pages of this study to two specific aspects of the myriad cultural consequences of peasant labor migration for outside earnings. In chapters 6 and 7, I present two case studies intimately connected to the themes previously discussed. Both chapters are devoted to the filters applied by peasants to regulate or control the penetration into the village milieu of outside influences. In its essence, *otkhod* was a conduit between town and country; and the Russian peasantry was by no means its passive recipient.

Chapter 6 addresses the fine line that was crossed in peasant economic strategies during the first forty years after the abolition of serfdom, when the drive for nonvillage cash earnings came to be based less on need and more on a new, rapidly growing, mass obsession with consumer goods. That transition from a culture of need to one of acquisition had a profound impact on the whole regional rural system, in that it generated new formal and informal networks throughout rural and urban Russia and catalyzed the increasingly polarized movement of have-nots versus haves in Russian society which characterized the last generation of the Old Regime.

Chapter 7 is a close study of the language and culture of religious denunciations during the same period. We witness in patterns of peasant religious denunciations a clear effort among fellow villagers to regulate the cultural impact of labor migrants, who returned to their villages laden not just with gifts and money, but also with ideas and attitudes that were perceived to pose profound threats to traditional village society.

6 A Culture of Acquisition

THE GENESIS OF MASS CONSUMER CULTURE IN RURAL RUSSIA

In the "city" [streets of Moscow] it was always lively and noisy: before holidays the buying public crowded the lines. Newcomers, people from the provinces, and indecisive customers lost their heads and bought things which they did not always need, largely owing to the energetic and virtuoso pitches . . . of salesmen who stood by the doors of their shops and in heart-rending voices lavishly elaborated and praised their goods. Salesmen sometimes even dragged timid and overwhelmed customers into their shops by force. . . . The average Moscow resident felt good in such surroundings, loved the "city" and made all his purchases there.[1]

WHILE IT IS CLEAR THAT need drove peasants away from their villages in search of alternative sources of income during the first wave of outmigration, it is just as clear that once the fruits of the outside world were tasted, the "needs" issue became inextricably linked with new consumer preferences and a host of rising expectations spawned by urban culture. The Russian peasants' desire for cash went beyond the need to pay taxes and maintain the farmstead. Peasant passions were also aroused by considerable enticements to consume products available only in the marketplace. The minimum expected standard of living among peasants and peasant-workers in the Central Industrial Region rose in direct proportion to the rise in contacts with the outside world. *Derevenskii,* "of the village," became identified with bumpkin culture, in contrast to the ambivalent glorification of *gorodskoi*—the tastes, styles, and fashions of the town.

In this chapter, I present a survey of the origins and development of a conspicuous consumer culture in the Central Industrial Region during the first generation after the abolition of serfdom. Besides *otkhod,* three additional factors accounted for a fundamental change in patterns of peasant consumption during this period: a distinct shift from home-produced to market-provided products; the centralization and increased efficiency of the market as a purveyor of goods through urban and rural bazaars, itinerant tradesmen, and increasingly supplemented by nearby shops and stores; and the end of wealth concealment as peasants consumed ever more conspicuously.

Initially, suburban villages and regions near trade and transportation routes were transformed by contact with towns. There is evidence that this process began as early as the late eighteenth century. Moreover, numerous observers have noted a rich trade in luxury items—comestibles like tea, coffee, tobacco, and sugar, as well as urban fashions in clothing—by the 1840s.[2] Still, it was not until the last quarter of the nineteenth century that such luxury and consumer goods became a central part of the budget of the typical peasant household in the Moscow and Petersburg regions.

An Unexpected Legacy of the Abolition of Serfdom

The development of commodity relations simultaneously exposed greater numbers of peasants to urban and factory life while also providing new and plentiful varieties of inexpensive consumer goods. While the burden of tax and redemption payments exhausted local sources of income and stimulated a search for cash from nonvillage side-earnings, increased migration was a dominant agent in the fundamental transformation of the cultural life of the Russian countryside in the years following the abolition of serfdom.

In part, this was a direct result of the abolition itself, which allayed fears of possible expropriation of conspicuous peasant wealth. As an observer in Iaroslavl Province reported in the late 1870s: "The elderly attribute the improvement in peasant life entirely to the abolition of serfdom. The peasant, in their opinion, lives better now than formerly—not because the Emancipation gave him more income, but because under serfdom he concealed every ruble, fearing the pretensions of the [noble] landlord. These pretensions quite often prompted even wealthy serfs to live in gray, meager conditions."³ With the end of serfdom came a rapid end to peasant wealth concealment. As a seventy-year-old peasant from Burmakino, a trading village in southeastern Iaroslavl Province, who had accumulated half a million rubles as a peasant-trader in St. Petersburg, recounted in 1880: "I had acquired money already in my youth, but began to live in luxury *[roskoshestvovat]* only after the Emancipation. . . . Nowadays, a *muzhik* with 3,000 rubles lives better than I did then with 30,000."⁴ What was true for the very rich was also true for the rest of the peasantry. Before 1861, peasants, fearing expropriation, often preferred to live in apparent poverty rather than to make a conspicuous public statement of wealth. This was especially true since quitrent payments on manorial estates in the Central Industrial Region were often gauged to the individual peasant's productivity (as measured in earnings) and rarely reflected a general unchanging standard.⁵ It is in this sense perhaps that the abolition of serfdom had its most profound impact on the lives of former serfs.⁶

Several indicators reveal that a mass consumer consciousness emerged among the peasants in the Central Industrial Region some time during the first twenty to forty years after the abolition of serfdom. In the sections below, I will discuss the nature and significance of changes in peasant consumer preferences in diet, clothing, and household furnishings, as well as changing cultural preferences: new attitudes towards leisure, and the changing character of peasant rituals associated with new efforts to use and display wealth.⁷ As we shall see, this mass consumer culture affected village and nonvillage social relations in profound and distinct ways.

A Seduction of the Senses: Enticements in the Russian Cityscape

In his autobiography, the peasant-worker Semën Kanatchikov left us with an invaluable account of his first glimpses of Moscow:

> Moscow, I remember, made a stunning impression on me. My father and I, sitting in our cart, drove through the brightly lit streets at a slow pace. Enormous multi-storied houses, with a multitude of lighted windows, stores, shops, taverns, ale houses, fine carriages, a horse-drawn tramway—and all around us there were crowds of bustling people, rushing to [who knows] where and why. . . . I wasn't

even able to read the signs. Most of all, I was struck by the abundance of stores and shops: that there were no houses, just continuous lines of shops.[8]

Abundance. Coming from the village, that was always the very first, strongest impression of the big city. It was so unlike anything they had ever experienced that peasant-workers fresh in the city found themselves overwhelmed yet intrigued, awestruck but seduced by the obvious wealth and grandiosity. The young Kanatchikov could not help but contrast this overpowering image of Moscow with the village he had left only hours before: "In comparison with our village shacks the Moscow houses struck me with their grandeur, with—it seemed to me—their luxuriousness. 'Will I live in such a house?'—I asked my father, enraptured."[9]

Even in smaller towns and industrial settlements, peasant-workers who sojourned for the first time *von*—"out there"—beyond the borders of their village were struck by the grandiosity of it all. Fëdor Samoilov recalled his first impressions of Ivanovo-Voznesensk:

> At first it seemed to all of us that living in the town was better than in the village. . . . In spite of the tiresome factory work, town life then seemed more interesting and attractive to us.[10]

Exposure to consumers' goods was greatest in cities and market squares. The cityscapes of Old Regime Russia teamed with life, filled with seductive enticements and attractions that were virtually unimaginable for the average peasant. The experience was not restricted to peasants alone, and judging from accounts left by others, we can in some vague way gauge the psychic impact of urban experience on peasant-workers. Recounting his travels in Russia in 1867, the French writer Théophile Gautier vividly recalled the splendor of St. Petersburg:

> If Nevsky Prospekt is beautiful, we should hasten to add that it also profits from its beauty. Both fashionable and commercial, this street has palaces alternating with shops; nowhere else, except perhaps in Bern, are signs done with such splendor. They almost have to be considered as one of the orders of modern architecture. . . . Golden characters, their design traced on blue backgrounds, on black or red panels, or stamped, or cut out and then pasted on glass showcases, are repeated at every door, take advantage of street corners, curve with the arches, stretch along cornices, skip no entrance ledges, go downstairs to basements, and use all possible means to catch the eyes of passers-by. If by chance you don't know Russian and these signs mean nothing more to you than ornamental designs, their French or German translation is right there on the side. You still don't understand? The courteous sign will forgive you for not knowing any of these three

A Culture of Acquisition

The meat market at Apreksin Court, St. Petersburg, early twentieth century. Such shops were part of ubiquitous enticements in Russian cities which drove the development of a village consumer culture. From the private collection of S. Riabov.

languages; it even allows for the possibility that you are completely illiterate by giving a natural representation of the goods for sale. Golden grapes, molded or painted, announce a wine store; farther on, a depiction of ham, sausages, beef tongues, and cans of caviar indicate a grocer. Naively portrayed boots, shoes and galoshes tell the feet what they cannot read: "Come in and get something to wear!" Crossed gloves speak a language understood by everybody. There are also ladies' mantles and dresses topped with hats or bonnets that the artist considered unnecessary to supplement with faces. Pianos invite you to try their painted keys. All this is amusing for a strolling visitor and has a character all its own.[11]

The Russian cityscape was, of necessity, navigable by sight, sound, and smell. And, given that the majority of Russia's urban populations consisted of peasant-workers from the countryside, Russia's cities were places where (even after 1917) one could live and work without the precondition of literacy. The new gospel of consumerism was communicated directly to the senses.

A Russian first-time visitor to St. Petersburg in the 1840s wrote: "With its huge houses and endless numbers of signs, Nevsky Prospekt looked like a kind of picture gallery."[12] And so it was for those accustomed to the riches of city life.

Street scenes of painted shop signs in St. Petersburg, early 1900s. From the private collection of S. Riabov.

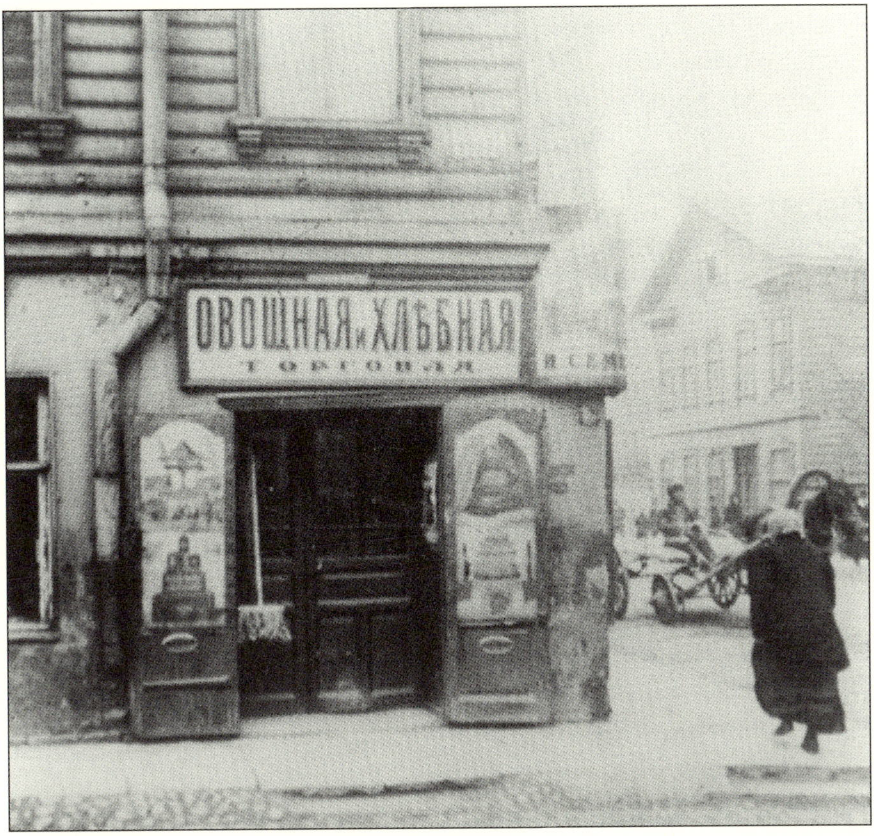
ОВОЩНАЯ и ХЛѢБНАЯ
ТОРГОВЛЯ

ОВОЩНАЯ и ХЛѢБНАЯ
ТОРГОВЛЯ.
МУКА КРУПА

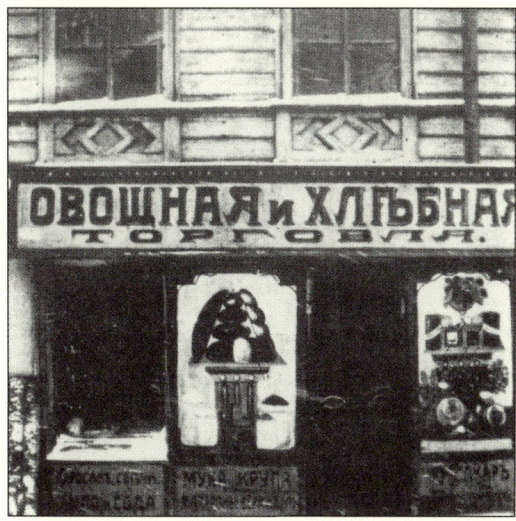

As much as the urban landscape of Russian big-city streets enticed upper-class travelers with their charm, they literally overwhelmed the senses of peasants and peasant-workers who visited the city for the first time. A fifteen-year-old girl from the provinces visiting Moscow for the first time wrote in her diary in 1890: "I am amazed that there are so many signs on the streets [of Moscow]: Where do all the shoppers live for such a multitude of stores? There's almost not a single house without a sign."[13]

Signs and window displays seemed almost to reach out to passersby, stores rich with goods begging to be tasted, and bought. The cityscape overflowed with beguiling attractions: tavern signs depicting robust men feasting on *zakuski* (snacks) and wine; larger-than-life loaves of golden bread, fresh vegetables, meats, confections. Signs of businesses oriented particularly toward the lower classes differed only in their brazen eccentricity. In St. Petersburg, the advertisement for Smekaev's Tobacco Shop was typical. It depicted on one side a gentleman sitting at a small table, holding a glass in his hand, on the other was a beautiful lady handing him a pipe and pulling the glass away. Underneath was this titillating inscription:

> Have a smoke instead of wine,
> A pipe will make you feel so fine,
> I guarantee, you'll get so stewed,
> You'll swear you'd drunk a pint or two.[14]

The message was clear: the surest path to upward mobility was to consume. And, the corollary: conspicuous consumption was the best way to display your success. The Russian author Elena Guro found a voice to describe the full sensual experience of a walk in Petersburg or Moscow in her book *City Songs,* published in 1909: "Painted on the door of a tavern and already darkened by the rain and dirt is a fish on a plate encircled by a necklace of round chunks of crispy golden potatoes fried in oil. How delicious! How very delicious! How unbearably delicious!"[15] Or, as an art critic reviewing the Petrograd street scene in 1915 remarked in more sober terms: "A sign exaggerates the temptingness of things, it invites one to a feast and urges him to buy."[16]

Even in their most rudimentary form, the advertisements of shopowners and tavernkeepers throughout the big cities managed to tug at the strings of elemental peasant passions, to introduce them in a host of ways to a burgeoning culture of acquisition. As a result of their first exposure to mass consumer culture, city life took on for peasants an aura of stupendous grandeur, with hidden opportunities far superior to the relative dullness of village life. "Petersburg possessed a special halo of attractiveness in the peasant imagination," noted a shrewd observer working in villages outside St. Petersburg during the early 1870s. It was already "the cherished dream of all young peasants" to live and work in St. Petersburg. And "when a young [peasant] returns home [to his village] after one or two years' absence [in St. Petersburg], he considers it his duty to display his superiority *[preimushchestvo]* over country folk, so that he criticizes—[in local jargon,] 'talks down' *[khait]*—everything of the village and, heedless of the consequences, curses everything at family meals, to the great horror of his God-fearing relations."[17] A young woman returning to her village from St. Petersburg domestic service "laughs at village girls, calling them 'dull' and 'country bumpkins.' And her former girlfriends meekly and deferentially listen to the abuse, acknowledging her indisputable superiority, even as they may not have such a high opinion of her behavior."[18] In his *"V gorode"* ("In the City"), the Bolshevik worker-poet Mikhail Gerasimov aptly captured the dizzying enticements of city life for the average peasant-worker:

> I fell in love with the flash of bright colors,
> And the noise of street pleasures.
>
> Caught up in the city's swift torrents,
> I became foreign to my own self,
> And the former days among the fields,
> Became to me like a distant dream.[19]

David Burliuk, advocating in 1913 preservation of old shop signs as works of art, also noted their necessity: "Russian signs have no analogies in Western cultures. The total (with no exaggeration) illiteracy of our people made it an essential attribute of the communication between the salesman and the customer."[20] Within this consumer society tailored to serve a largely illiterate mass of consumers, it eventually became so easy to get around sprawling cities like St. Petersburg and Moscow, and shopowners were so successful at luring buyers from all social classes, that there was a burning debate about the wisdom of attracting "illiterate" and "hooligan" undesirables from the lower classes into the better neighborhoods. In 1914, the St. Petersburg mayor even "issued a strict order prohibiting sign artists from painting anything except the name of the company and the type of trade," hoping in this way to mitigate the seductiveness to undesirables in the urban underclass. This prohibition followed a long campaign launched in the contemporary press that lashed out against what they called this "sign bacchanalia," this "orgy of signs" which, they argued, undermined the impression of St. Petersburg as a modern city and enticed "the hooligan rabble" into upper-class neighborhoods where they did not belong. In response, "merchants, artisans, and tradesmen addressed the [St. Petersburg] Senate with a request to cancel the Mayor's decree," insisting that the painted signs displaying enticing pictures were absolutely essential "for the purpose of attracting ordinary people's attention to what was for sale, something especially important for illiterate people, who, after all, constitute the majority in Russia."[21] In the end, commerce won out over the dilettantism and shocked sensibilities of the upper classes.

It was not just the signs and the stores, of course, but the whole urban experience—even just secondhand accounts from neighbors and family members who had experienced the city directly—that stimulated the senses of country folk, luring them in a host of different ways to buy, to consume, to spend money in pursuit of the better life.

New Styles, New Tastes

Contact with cities fundamentally influenced the topography of high-migration villages. The emergence of a new consumer culture corresponded with a dramatic transformation of the appearance of everyday life. Numerous observers noted among peasants the "aspiration 'to live like townspeople' *[stremlenie zhit 'po gorodski']*.... Migration leaves behind a change in peasant notions and habits, introducing into the peasant milieu 'the outward appearance of civilization' *[naruzhnaia tsivilizatsiia]*."[22] While contemporaries critically appraised this decay of traditional Russian folk culture, and often sarcastically scoffed at the mass striving of peasants to adopt urban ways, they usually failed to comprehend the subtle ways in which this new consumer orientation had transformed Russian village life forever.

THE PEASANT DREAM: THE ETHOS OF WEALTH AND POPULAR MYTHS OF UPWARD MOBILITY

> *In the ten years that I have lived with workers, I have rarely met anyone who did not dream of changing his occupation.*
>
> PEASANT-WORKER P. TIMOFEEV,
> WHAT THE FACTORY WORKER LIVES FOR (1906)[23]

There was in the last generation of Old Regime Russia a distinct atmosphere of restlessness, a pervasive impatience, as peasants throughout the more industrialized and urbanized regions each in their own way seized the oppor-

Postcard sent by a peasant-worker to his love in the village of Sereda, Volokolamsk District, Moscow Province, early twentieth century. The caption reads: "I will take a ribbon from my braid / I will buy my dearest one a pocket watch. / This is glory, this is honor / My dear one has a pocket watch." From a private collection.

tunities of the era. By the last quarter of the nineteenth century, migration for side-earnings had become for most Russian peasants of the Central Industrial and northwest regions *the* vehicle for upward social mobility.

Peasant dreams were largely dominated by reigning social myths, permeated with an insatiable yearning, haunted by dreams of someday becoming *tysiachniki*—"thousandaires"—or, better yet, *millionery* who would once and for all escape the endless drudgery and pervasive insecurity of living on the margin. This dream of "making it," of becoming a success in the eyes of fellow villagers and family members, increasingly drove the process in which peasant families dispatched their young into apprenticeships in the cities. "Examples of the accumulation of wealth, sometimes quite quickly, when a poor *pitershchik* manages to become a thousandaire after 10 or 15 years, powerfully entice the village youth, who love to count on our Russian 'luck.'"[24]

Not just the youth, but their parents and loved ones as well, became more and more driven by the desire to succeed: a new, powerful social myth of the patriarchal economy that preached upward mobility for all through the effort and sacrifice of the younger generations. Of course, living on the margin, the preoccupation with security always remained in the backdrop of peasant economic decisions, but numerous sources suggest that the older generations too were enticed by the new culture of acquisition and were prepared to exploit the labor of the young to raise themselves up in the eyes of fellow villagers.

We are talking here about the infectiousness of reigning social myths, the content of which was particularly well expressed by V. O. Mikhnevich, a shrewd observer of St. Petersburg street life during the 1870s and 1880s:

> Among peasants who give their children up to the town—in "apprenticeship" [*v mal'chiki*], in "study" [*v nauku*]—there is the calculation that by this means they themselves will make it "in society" [*vyiti sami v liudi*, i.e., strike it rich] and [thereby] support the family. Peasants are tempted particularly to send their children to commercial establishments, to stores and shops, since through this walk of life they could all the sooner and more reliably make a pile of money and grow rich. In the village, it is of course well known that many "self-made" merchants, capitalist-millionaires who now manage enormous businesses, not to mention merchants of the average sort, began their careers in the wretched role of "apprentices." The founders of the best-known and wealthiest merchant houses in the capital without exception began in their own time as such boy-"apprentices." The story of how they succeeded in making it "in society" is well-known [to every peasant].[25]

The success stories of a few became the stuff of dreams for the many. A peasant correspondent in Iaroslavl Province at the turn of the century expressed it best: "It is the dream of every . . . [peasant] boy to become a salesman *[torgovets]*, contractor *[podriadchik]*—in a word, a businessman *[kommersant]*. To achieve this dream a twelve-year-old boy is sent by his parents to Petersburg, Moscow, Riga—anywhere you like, just so as to set him up [in an apprenticeship in business]. . . . 'Today's millionaires began just this way,' [say the parents], 'and so we will begin the same way they did.'"[26] It was surely no coincidence that Russian popular adaptations of the Cinderella story were normally set in the scenario of *otkhodnik* success. In a host of varied settings, the basic story was always the same: sent away from the village to learn a trade, the young boy or girl strikes it rich, marries well, and comes home a hero to family and neighbors.[27] And peasant popular songs repeatedly emphasized images of peasants striking it rich in the town. In a favored *chastushka* or peasant ditty of the age, "Lukach Kudriavich," a young peasant-worker returns to his village from St. Petersburg and boasts of the high life he found:

> Я во Питери бывал,
> По панели хаживал,
> Я молоденьких куфарочек—
> За ручку важивал.

. . . .
Курил сигару от угару,
Курил я по малешеньку;
Любил я девок для забавы,
Выбирал—хорошеньку.

*[I was in St. Petersburg
(Where) I strolled about the sidewalks.
(And) took liberties with the
Young ladies.*

*I smoked a cigar to intoxication,
I smoked with my pals.
I loved the girls for amusement,
Choosing (only) the best.]*[28]

V. Mel'nikov-Pecherskii, particularly well known for his acute literary depictions of Russian popular life, presented us with a vivid account of the ways in which such popular myths of rags-to-riches infiltrated Russian popular culture. This scene from *In the Forests* (1871–1874) depicts a group of peasant Old Believers from southeastern Kostroma Province as they reminisced about the early days of the Russian cotton industry, focusing in particular on the hero Kuzmich Konovalov, the real-life founder of one of the greatest textile family fortunes in Old Regime Russia:

Take, for example, Vichuga, not too far from these very woods. The soil there is pretty poor. Before the French year (1812) there wasn't a single weaver in those parts, and now in the three districts the only thing the people do is weave napkins and tablecloths. They built big factories too . . . and in some villages there is a loom in every cottage. . . . The old people work at it year-round, and the able-bodied work too, when they aren't in the fields. . . . And how much money those craftsmen make! And how they live! How did this all begin? A clever man came along, who had a little money. His name was Konovalov. . . . he was of our sect, and pious in the old way. He started a small weaving shop, and in his hands the thing grew and grew. The people got rich, and now they live better than those around here. . . . If only there were more Konovalovs around, the people would live better!

— Me too, I've heard of this Konovalov. They have fond memories of him in the region, both near and far. Of such a man one can say: "He sowed good, spread good, harvested good, and distributed good: and his name will be honored from generation to generation."[29]

Honor, glory, fame, reputation—all these concepts are embodied in the Russian value-laden term *slava*. And often, they were inseparably connected in Russian village culture with worldly success.

Through a subtle and complex interweaving of gestures and public rites, everyday life in the countryside by the end of the nineteenth century rapidly came to celebrate and accentuate the intrinsic superiority of wealth: popular culture both reflected and perpetuated an economically inspired rethinking of values and the myths of social mobility. As Father Mikhail Sokolov from Petrovka village in Vladimir Province observed in 1899: "Wealthy peasants enjoy decidedly greater respect from everyone, their words have everywhere greater weight and meaning, than the words of a poor peasant. . . . Peasants always treat influential people with respect. During a conversation with them, they will try to imitate their tone, which turns out rather funny, since peasants try in some words to substitute the letter 'ts' for the letter 'ch'," adopting in this way a peculiar tone of speech they identified with townfolk.[30]

Other observers of Russian popular life concurred: "The well-to-do peasant enjoys great respect among his fellow villagers, who strive to render him every service and in some way or other express their particular attention and respect for him (with a low bow, extolling his graces with name and patronymic, seeking out advice, and so on)."[31]

"The tone of conversations with influential people and the rich is servile, compliant, and deliberately courteous."[32]

"The poor peasant, particularly a neighbor, stands in a subordinate relationship to the rich [fellow villager]. From the first summons he will go [to the wealthy neighbor] to work, and he never contradicts him at communal meetings—[all done] in the hope that he will receive in case of need either cash or grain loans."[33]

In numerous ways, village culture itself became centered on acquisition—not necessarily of and for its own sake, but for the respect and envy it generated among fellow villagers. Sergei Nedeshev, reporting from Vladimir District, Vladimir Province, in 1898, observed the subtle ways in which worldly success was measured and displayed among local peasants:

> If someone [in the village] has good fortune and finds himself with big money, then the increase in prosperity must be made known to all and sundry. Since money contained in bank statements won't be seen by the eyes of others, then [peasants] with newly acquired wealth strive immediately to turn that [money] into a well-appointed *[nariadnoe]* demonstration of wealth: they will buy property—a small parcel of land and woods; they will expand and redecorate their homes and outbuildings; they will obtain better clothes; get a better horse.[34]

In a society where wealth brought status and respect, the important thing was that at least some of that wealth be displayed for other villagers to see. A perceptive observer, Nedeshev described the subtle logic of peasant behavior in Vladimir Province: "Of course, poverty is evident everywhere, but here it is important to strive not to lower oneself in the estimation of others."[35] Even in poor families, this logic dictated a peasant strategy of channeling wealth not into cash savings, but rather into consuming: during good times, peasants would "invest" in consumer goods "so that we won't be so poor." In bad times, these luxury items were unloaded to repay debts, offered as surety to local moneylenders, or sold to more solvent fellow villagers for urgently needed cash.[36] As one observer recounted from Tver Province in the 1890s: local peasant-workers "come home to the village as dandies *[franty]*, but they go back to Peter[sburg] without a penny: for the road they borrow money from local peasants on the security of accordions, shoes, boots, coats, etc."[37]

These impressionistic testimonies are solidly confirmed by peasant household inventories. As illustration, I turn your attention to the comprehensive household inventory of a wealthy peasant: Nikita Alekseevich Kudin was a small-scale peasant manufacturer and contractor involved in silk-weaving who lived in the village of Gorodoka, Ignate'vaskaia *volost*, Bogorodsk District, Moscow Province. His village was located approximately eighty kilometers east of Moscow City, fifteen kilometers from the district town of Bogorodsk, five kilometers from the *volost* capital, and was therefore well situated to take advantage of regional trade in textiles, especially of cotton and silk. In 1852, this village of state peasants consisted of 333 souls (both sexes), in forty-two peasant households. By 1890, Kudin's son Aleksei was manager and owner of a silk manufactory in the village that employed eighteen workers. At this time, the village was still relatively small, with only 161 male souls. By 1913, however, the village was booming: with 171 peasant households, a parish school, and the Kudin Silk Factory, which by then had its own hospital and employed more than a hundred workers.[38]

The elder Kudin died suddenly in 1887, without a valid will. His sons appealed and won the right of guardianship immediately after their father's death; they were awarded all property by right of inheritance almost a year later. The total estimated value of Kudin's estate in 1887 was 7,168 rubles: 6,500 rubles of immovable property—including a large, two-story wooden home on a stone foundation, plus outbuildings—and 668 rubles in movable property, listed in table 6.1.

A survey of the thirty-five items of "movable property" listed in Kudin's household inventory vividly demonstrates the consumer preferences of village

Table 6.1. Inventory of a Wealthy Peasant's Household, 1887

Inventoried Items	Value (in rubles)
1. Icon of the Conception of St. Anne, in an icon case, and silver riza with decorative frame	30
2. Icon of Nikolai the Miracle-worker (no riza)	3
3. Icon of Konstantin (no riza)	4
4. Icon of the Presentation of Sergei (no riza)	2
5. Icon of the Blessed Virgin of Kazan, in an icon case (no riza)	3
6. Weekly clock, in a case, secondhand	10
7. Brass samovar, 30 pounds, new	10
8. Table, made of ash wood, and two chairs, secondhand	5
9. Table, made of ash wood, secondhand	3
10. Table, made of ash wood, and two chairs, secondhand	4
11. Soft divan, filled with woolen material, secondhand	5
12. Two dozen "simple" Warsaw chairs, secondhand	40
13. Mirror, with two partitions of glass, and a dressing-table, secondhand	12
14. Sewing machine, secondhand	30
15. Painted chest of drawers, secondhand	3
16. Wardrobe, unpainted, secondhand	4
17. Four copper candleholders, secondhand	1
18. Copper washstand, secondhand	2
19. Round copper salver, diameter 71 centimeters, secondhand	2
20. Brass samovar, 15 pounds, secondhand	6
21. Tea caddy with a dozen teacups, teapot and slop basin, secondhand	2
22. Sledge, painted in the town style, secondhand	20
23. *Rozvalni* (low, wide sledge), light, secondhand	2
24. Gray stallion	100
25. Eight-year-old gelding	50
26. Brown cow	30
27. Brown cow	30
28. Brown cow, with white head	30
29. Urban-style *tarantass* (springless carriage), reinforced with metal, secondhand	30
30. Fast *droshky*, reinforced with metal, secondhand	10
31. Russian cart (*telega*), reinforced with metal, secondhand	20
32. Harness for two horses, secondhand	10
33. Five hundred kilos of kindling and firewood, worth 2 rubles per meter	120
34. 10 meters of firewood	20
35. Sheepskin coat, secondhand	10
Total value of listed movable property on the Kudin estate	663

Source: TsGIAgM, f. 62, op. 1, d. 139, ll. 12–13.

elites. Note, moreover, that 73 percent (twenty-two of thirty) of the items (excluding icons, which are not bought or sold in the usual sense of the terms)[39] were obtained by the owner secondhand *(poderzhannyi).* If we exclude icons (five items), livestock (five items) and raw materials (firewood, two items), the proportion of secondhand items rises to 96 percent. With the exception of a large brass samovar, all the durable consumer goods *(krasnye tovary)* in Kudin's home were secondhand, a fact that reflects the central significance of debt transactions and debt auctions in the Russian countryside (see chapter 4 above).

Kudin's status as a patron and labor contractor in the village is revealed in his two large samovars and tea set for twelve, plus over two dozen chairs. This was in line with peasant social expectations of a "benefactor" of Kudin's status: "Contractors display a fatherly concern for their [workers]."[40] In Iur'ev District, Vladimir Province, "The small proprietor *[svetelochnik]* is expected to entertain his weavers, or else they won't come to work for him. On religious holidays, the master is expected to entertain weavers and give them tea and wine to drink."[41] Father Vasilii Tabeev in Kaluga Province described the social status—and associated social obligations—of village proprietorship: "Contractors live in a manner entirely different from either other peasants, or gentlemen *[gospoda]*. They supervise the work, decide where to station workers, and drink tea five to eight times per day, and sometimes [—especially during the hiring season—] they spend more in a day [on refreshments] than a large family consumes in a month."[42]

Numerous sources indicate that local proprietors like Kudin functioned not just as market middlemen for local peasants, but as cultural conduits as well, by inculcating and then purveying to newly acquired peasant tastes. This description is taken from petty organizers of the cottage textile industry in northwestern Vladimir Province in the 1880s: "The buyers provisioned [master weavers] with raw materials (for production), cash, and even brought to the village hard-to-get goods (at a 10–15 percent markup): vodka, tobacco, cloth material, clothes, and other items special-ordered by the weavers *[mastera]*. Weavers love to play the dandy: each acquires a silver [pocket] watch and buys a fur coat with a beaver collar costing about 50–60 rubles—this is the cherished dream of many, a dream which is fulfilled at the first opportune moment. In large shops, with ten or more workers, the proprietor never works himself. He supervises and distributes work, goes to bazaars with goods or to purchase raw materials in Moscow or Sergiev Posad."[43]

While the heavy sledges in Kudin's inventory could be marked down as investment items for winter work, the fancy *tarantass,* decorated in "town style," was nothing more than a status symbol, a conspicuous display of the owner's wealth and social standing.

Peasant Pride: The Transformation of Material Culture

Enticed by the new culture of acquisition, peasants in the non-black-earth central and northwestern regions during the last half of the nineteenth century transformed nearly every aspect of the surface appearance of their lives and culture.

THE TRANSFORMATION OF PEASANT COTTAGES

> High-migration districts noticeably excel in their outward appearance: . . . dwellings in their villages are more spacious and [generally] better [constructed], they are kept much cleaner, and only in extremely rare cases are livestock allowed in living quarters. Families of *otkhodniki* live in "white" cottages [with chimneys], their clothes are cleaner, more fashionable, and more hygienic. Almost everyone wears high boots and jerseys *[fufaiki]*.[44]

Numerous studies on the history of Russian village architecture have documented the transformation of peasant cottages after the mid-1860s. The evidence reflects how peasants in the Central Industrial Region (and elsewhere) strived increasingly to live *"po gorodski"*—closer to the standards of Russian city folk. Just as in other ways, the wealthier peasants led the movement for the citification of rural life. As one observer perceptively noted: "With its entire appearance, [the wealthy peasant's cottage] testifies that the owner is a person of substance *[chelovek s dostatkom]*, and that he did not spare any means in order to make his home the most comfortable and beautiful, and in order to demonstrate for all of his neighbors proof of his prosperity, well-being, and his nearness to the styles and tastes of the city."[45]

There were myriad changes in village architecture in this transition to display peasant pride through the emulation of urban styles. More modern huts were covered by wood or metal roofs instead of thatch. Traditionally, peasant cottages had few or no windows. By 1880, however, every peasant cottage, even the poorest, had at least two windows, and the number and size of cottage windows increased steadily until after the Revolution. Small conveniences were added, such as *fortochki*—small hinged panes in the windows used for ventilation; porches *(kryl'sta)* were added to replace entry through the *kalitka*, the traditional wicker gate. It was only after the abolition of serfdom that peasant cottages began to be built with the *chernyi nakat*—black beams running along the ceiling in "town style." And much of the decorative exterior which we normally identify with traditional Russian village architecture—

Table 6.2. Indicators of Peasant Wealth: The Transformation of Peasant Homes

A. Change in Roofs on Peasant Dwellings (in percent)

Year	Thatched (solomennye)	Wooden Shingles (dranochnye)	Metal (zheleznye)
1877 (n=20,440)	85.0	14.5	0.4
1900 (n=4,402)	56.3	38.0	5.7
1917 (n=248)	15.3	71.4	13.3

B. Declining Size of Peasant Dwellings (Living Space in Cubic Meters)

Year	Less than 30 c.m.	30–39 c.m.	40–49 c.m.	Greater than 49 c.m.
Before 1870 (n=19)	42.1	36.8	15.8	5.3
1870–1899 (n=114)	51.8	23.7	9.7	14.9
1900–1916 (n=391)	46.8	16.4	22.3	14.6

C. Increase in Numbers of Windows in Peasant Dwellings

Year	3 windows or less	4 windows	5 windows	6 or more windows
Before 1870 (n=19)	15.8	31.6	26.3	26.3
1870–1899 (n=114)	15.8	32.7	15.8	30.7
1900–1916 (n=391)	12.5	36.3	16.1	35.0

Source: K. A. Solov'ev, *Zhilishche krest'ian Dmitrovskogo kraia (Severnaia chast' Moskovskogo okruga)* (Dmitrov, 1930), pp. 54–56.

ornamental moldings around windows, eaves, and porches—became common only during the last half of the nineteenth century, and in large part to emulate urban styles.[46]

Rural censuses and household inventories conducted at various times during the last forty years of the Old Regime enable historians to confirm the impressionistic evidence provided by firsthand accounts (see table 6.2). In 1877, a census was conducted of peasant dwellings in the Moscow Industrial Region. In an inventory of 20,440 peasant cottages, 85 percent still had roofs thatched with straw, bast, or river reeds *(soloma);* 14.5 percent had roofs of wooden shingles *(dranka);* and a mere 0.44 percent had metal roofs *(zhelezo)*.[47] Less than a generation later, a smaller study of 4,402 peasant dwellings in Dmitrov District (north of Moscow) revealed a considerable change: by 1900, only 56.3 percent of peasant dwellings had thatched roofs, while 38 percent had wooden shingles, and 5.7 percent had metal roofs.[48] By 1917, the contrasts were even more clear: in a study of 248 peasant dwellings in Dmitrov District constructed before 1917, 14.1 percent had thatched roofs, 71 percent had roofs made of wooden shingles, and 14.9 percent had metal roofs.[49]

Interior space of peasant huts in the Central Industrial and northern regions was also radically transformed, particularly in high-migration villages. The traditional peasant hut with just one large room gradually gave way to two- or three-room cottages. Cheap and plentiful alternatives for heating fuel, especially peat and coal, replaced scarce and expensive firewood, so that the traditional Russian *pech* or clay stove was reduced in size, or even supplanted by a cast-iron stove. Likewise, candles and torches, the chief culprits of frequent and destructive fires in the Russian countryside, were gradually replaced by kerosine lamps. "Kerosine is sold to peasants by petty traders, and in stores. In summer, peasants kindle a light at supper-time; in winter, from about five to eight o'clock. By eight or nine o'clock, they are already in bed asleep. They've already begun to use powdered matches, although there are also still [old-style] sulfuric matches."[50]

The most dramatic transformation was in the cottage interior. "Until recently, the only furniture [in peasant cottages] was benches; now everywhere you find wooden chairs, frequently with soft seats."[51] Practical and inexpensive plain furniture of the traditional peasant hut—simple wooden tables and hard wooden benches—was gradually supplanted by furniture purchased for heightened comfort and a more cultured appearance for entertaining visiting relatives and fellow villagers: chairs with cushions, framed beds, bureaus and dressers, mirrors, and so on.

Interior decoration increasingly included lithographs, pictures, and illustrated calendars, which initially depicted religious scenes and well-known historical events. "In the cottages of the Iaroslavl countryside you can find many pictures, some which are quite costly. Alongside five-kopeck pictures you will find drawings worth 75 kopecks to a ruble."[52] Likewise, "In every peasant home are several icons with and without rizas." The icons were treated like holy objects, and they were always kept clean and neat. Before the icons burned lamps or candles. "On major holidays every wealthy and poor peasant is concerned about icons—they order new rizas, or buy new icons or repair old ones, solder holy pictures or repaint them."[53]

Portraits and gifts sent back to the village by *otkhodniki,* especially icons and religious articles, as well as small books, lithographs, and photographs, purchased what Shirley Wajda has called "social currency": they bought good will and provided firm assurances to those at home that all was well. Around the turn of the century, Russian peasant-workers began increasingly to send back portrait photographs of themselves, which as a rule were displayed in peasant huts prominently in the main room of the cottage next to the "red" or icon corner. Such portrait photographs were far more than mere "consumer goods in a status marketplace"; they represented more than just a channel to emulate the upper classes, and something more than merely "staying in touch" with kin and neighbors in the village. According to popular belief, daguerreotypes, and later mounted portraits, reflected a person's character; a successful likeness demonstrated his or her inner spirituality, sincerity, and moral uprightness. Very simply, the portrait was as much an indicator of the subject's social identity as of status and wealth.[54]

Remarkably, and consistent with the psychology of peasant-worker nostalgia discussed in chapter 5, most lower-class portraits (those commissioned by lower-class clientele, and not the portraits of the lower class as studies commissioned by outsiders) consisted not of imitations of the genteel, but replicated village scenes in the urban photographer's studio. The simple peasant-worker, dressed in the garb of his nonvillage occupation, stood before an idealized backdrop of the village, such as birch trees on a summer day or a babbling brook. In contrast, successful peasant contractors preferred portraits of themselves *in situ,* set in the milieu of the new occupation surrounded by objects that characterized their success.[55]

NEW LUXURIES: SAMOVARS, SUGAR, TEA, AND TOBACCO

Contemporaries also observed a profound change in peasant dietary habits. At the time of the abolition of serfdom, white bread was extremely rare, served only on high holidays and only in the homes of the wealthiest peasant families, and even then a lower grade of wheat flour was used to make the bread. "Nowadays [in the early 1880s], every peasant housewife buys wheat flour for holiday meals: the more well-to-do bake bread with *krupchatka*—the finest wheaten flour. When you go into a tavern of a large village, you always find beef and veal as snacks after a glass of vodka. At the weekly bazaar in Burmakino—a trading village with bazaars each Thursday—among other items they deal in meat, selling off a total of 2,400–3,300 kilos each week. The buyers are exclusively peasants who live in surrounding areas."[56]

Observers noted the tendency of consumer preferences in high-migration villages to become urbanized, meaning that less food was produced at home and more was purchased on the market. As a result, peasant diets were more varied: household budgets show that peasants in high-migration villages consumed less rye bread and potatoes, the staples of the traditional Russian peasant diet, and appreciably more meat, lard, wheat flour, tea, and sugar, and even some herring. In short, the proportions of high-migration village incomes spent on consumables approached those of the urban working class.[57]

Portrait of a peasant-worker employed in a St. Petersburg factory, 1910s. Note the village scene in the background. From a private collection.

Portrait of a factory contractor and his assistant in St. Petersburg, 1910s. Both are of peasant origin from the same village. The contractor is shown as a man of means and worldly success. The contract book (on his lap) was a common status symbol denoting the contractor's power and his qualities as a benefactor. From a private collection.

Portrait of the steward of the Dulevo Porcelain Factory in Moscow, with his young assistant, an apprentice from the steward's village. Such portraits upheld the image of wealthy and well-situated peasant-workers as benefactors to fellow villagers. The contract book is prominently displayed. From a private collection.

Portrait of a peasant factory worker and his wife in St. Petersburg, 1910s. The man's fine boots and gold watch chain symbolize his success away from the village. Note the pastoral scene in the background. From a private collection.

A REVOLUTION IN VILLAGE FASHIONS

Perhaps the most obvious symptom of change in the Russian countryside of the non-black-earth north during the last half of the nineteenth century was the revolution in village fashion.[58] "Peasant life has changed. [Local peasants] have begun to dress foppishly, even smartly, [in the manner] which life has taught them while working in Peter[sburg]. Fitting themselves out with the trappings of domestic life has grown more expensive, but incomes have not risen [commensurately]."[59] "Clothing, too, has been transformed. Traditional bast shoes *(lapti)* can be found only in backwoods areas. Instead, all peasants now wear felt boots *(valenki)* in winter, and leather jack (or high) boots *(sapogi)* in summer."[60]

Nowhere was this transformation of clothing more apparent than in village ritual life and the marked disappearance of traditional holiday costumes in favor of new styles a half-step behind reigning town fashions. In her study of Russian peasant women's migration for outside earnings, Barbara Alpern Engel perceptively observed that "migration reinforced women's tastes for urban products and other tangible artifacts of urban culture. Women came home with fashionable clothing, singing the latest songs and dancing city dances."[61] In this way, village women's cultural preferences were dramatically transformed. "The apparel of village girls is becoming more and more refined with each passing day. These days it is not a rarity to meet at village summer festivals *[besedy]* a [peasant] girl dressed in a silk or wool dress sewn in the latest [town] fashion."[62] In her groundbreaking work on the history of Russian fashion, Christine Ruane likewise noted the impact of contact with the city on peasant women: "Rather than spend their money on items deemed more appropriate by the elite, peasant women spent their hard-earned wages on pretty clothes. According to one commentator, in less than a year peasant women who came to the city to work had given up their peasant attire for city fashions. Moreover, the influence of [urban] fashions was so pernicious that it began to reach outside of the city and affect peasant women in the villages close to urban centers."[63] The new demand to keep up with women's fashions carried a commensurate increase in price: "Impoverishment is marked by the splendor of youth and the impossibility of satisfying their new expectations. Ten years ago a young village maiden could dress respectably well for 50 rubles, but now [it costs] not less than 100."[64]

This change was especially apparent at weddings, where peasant families incurred considerable debt to ensure they made the proper impression on fellow villagers: "Nowadays weddings are celebrated more ostentatiously

Village advertisement of fabrics from the Emil Tsindel Manufactory, late nineteenth century. "Buy Tsindel Calico—It's not expensive and it's GOOD to wear!" From a private collection.

[shikarnee]. In our parish there are on average nearly 50 weddings annually, and everyone borrows money, and what is more one must even invite one's creditors."[65] Peasants take out loans "of 10–20 or more rubles for taxes, for weddings, the expenses for which can run up to 30 rubles, for show *[pokaz],* for showing off *[za vykhvalku]* in front of their guests and neighbors."[66] Numerous reports reveal that this yearning to "show off" encompassed not just the richness of the wedding banquet, but even (and especially) the brilliance of the new bride and groom. "The custom has come into being of giving a dowry for [one's] daughters. Without a dowry no young lad would marry an [eligible] maiden. The bride-to-be must have a silk dress, and the lad—a jacket, a thick woolen topcoat, and a [pocket] watch."[67] "For weddings [peasants] borrow up to 100 or 150 rubles. They buy watches, brooches, and other items."[68]

The drive to build respect and a "good name" through conspicuous consumption and "a decent appearance" became a central part of everyday peasant life throughout the Central Industrial Region. Just how much this new commodity fetishism had infiltrated village popular culture was indicated in a letter sent by a peasant woman in Kostroma Province to her husband, an *otkhodnik* in St. Petersburg, in the late 1880s:

> If you decide to come to the village, then bring money for expenses, and if you remain to winter in *Piter,* then send a little more money, and also—presents, about which I wrote earlier, *so that we won't be so poor.* (Two large shawls, a *sarafan,* and printed cotton calico for the children.) . . . If you send money, then I will need to run and fetch some high boots, since [my] leather boots are all in tatters. Also there is need to make some woolens and sew a fur coat, so you had better look after the money.[69]

Buy, "so that we won't be so poor." The irony of that message seemed to escape most peasants, but not the critical outside observer, one of whom noted disapprovingly:

> Having been to the capital, having acquired an ostentatious [quality] of civilization and having tasted of its fruits, the modest country boy returns to the village, but not with a particularly improved material position, so that in spite of the relatively greater earnings of even the simplest workers (up to 200 rubles in a year), the well-being of those family [members] remaining at home is far from splendid. While it's true that almost every *pitershchik* has a [pocket] watch and small chain, that he brings his wife a silk dress, and fits himself out with excellent evening trappings, this beggarly cheap luxuriousness little harmonizes with the extremely meager food and frequently half-starved life. Not infrequently, before

going off for *otkhod*, the ostentatious items are carried off to the moneylender, since the peasant-worker either could not or would not set something aside for the road.⁷⁰

Living on the margin, but trapped by the new consumer culture, peasant families with barely enough to make ends meet made rather unorthodox buying decisions, depriving themselves of virtually everything so as to maximize outlays for a better appearance:

> The influence of the town is most of all reflected in clothing. Not wholly contented with the work of local [village] tailors, young [peasant] lads prefer to buy ready-made jackets *[pidzhaki-gotovye]* of the most varied styles. For warm clothes they prefer overcoats in spring, and sheepskin, lambskin, or fox for winter coats. . . .
>
> If the young lads show off [with their appearance], then the girls have nothing to scoff about. They see their main goal in life, the surest means for a good marriage, in [the acquisition of] smart clothing. The last kopecks in a poor family are spent on outfits for the girls. Rarely [will you find] a peasant girl who does not have three complete outfits of printed calico dresses in the most florid colors, [along with] one or two woolen ones—for going to Church or an outdoor fête. In [village] fashions can be observed the aspiration to mimic town styles.⁷¹

Always just a season or two behind fashions current in the big cities, in the village clothing was nonetheless one of the principal means by which peasant pride was displayed for family, friends, and neighbors. "Since clothing serves as the main indicator of prosperity or poverty among the peasants, each in his own way strives to present himself . . . no worse than the others. Refusing himself vital necessities, depriving himself of the satisfaction of consuming better food, [the peasant] directs every spare kopeck to [the purchase] of clothing. The disproportion between the general well-being of a family and the quality of their clothes . . . sometimes approaches the absurd."⁷²

VILLAGE COSMETICS

A popular song in rural Iaroslavl Province in the 1890s:

> Слободския то девчонки
> Ровно мелконькой горох:
> Щечки клюковкой намажут,
> Брови углем подведут—
> За хороших почтут.

[Village lassies
Just like chalk-colored peas:
Cheeks smeared with cranberries,
Eyebrows raised with coal
So others will think them pretty.]

These lyrics ridiculed peasant women's struggle to be "beautiful." Traditional village-style cosmetics continued to be used in most areas to the beginning of the twentieth century. In pursuit of what we might call the "Anna Karenina look," peasant women went to extreme measures to imitate new, urban standards of beauty.[73] Women and girls from poorer peasant households were by and large limited to mimicking town fashions with rough village imitations. "On holidays hair is greased with butter or wood oil."

> For a clean, healthy face, Russian peasant girls and women traditionally wash themselves in spring water [collected from] a brook or well after the first thunder storm. Instead of rouge the most commonly used [alternative] is scraps of paper dyed with fruit juice. Moistening these papers, they rub them on their cheeks, which then appear flushed with rouge. In addition, river fungus *[kolotik]*, freshwater sponge *[bodiaga]*, and also the root of the herb campanula *[kupely]*, popularly known under the name "God's little hands," are commonly used in some areas. Whitening (makeup) is most frequently of all [substituted] with ordinary white lead. Brushing their hair, [village girls] moisten it with kvass or grease it with butter or lamp (low-grade olive) oil. Eyebrows are colored with antimony.[74]

The cheap and homegrown village imitations of urban products largely accounted for the poor skin quality of young peasant women in the region, whose growing obsession with urban standards of beauty paradoxically (and tragically) decimated women's complexions.

Wealthier peasant women living in the village did manage to obtain rouge and makeup, luxury items much yearned for but rarely obtained by most village girls: "[Store-bought] rouge and makeup are not in use, but perfume has begun to come into fashion among [village girls]."[75] Forced in this way to turn to crude village solutions to imitate the look of society women in the Russian capitals, village girls found great joy from the growing availability of the "scents of the city": "Lately, among peasant girls it is becoming more common to use pomade, perfume, powder, cheap toilet soaps, and even genuine rouge and makeup."[76]

THE REGIMENTATION OF TIME AND
NEW POPULAR CONCEPTIONS OF LEISURE

With the abolition of serfdom came a collective desire to regiment time, a new awareness of the distinctions between work time and leisure time that could not be satisfied by the old means of judging from the sun. Today's peasant "wants to carry time in his pocket or hang it on the wall of his lodgings."[77] And so, pocket watches and wall clocks had become ubiquitous in the Moscow region well before the end of the nineteenth century. As A. A. Isaev noted from his observations in the Iaroslavl countryside in 1880: "From among dozens of peasant homes which I visited in numerous villages, I did not find even one without a wall clock." The poorest families were satisfied with ruble clocks without toners; among the more prosperous were cuckoo or chiming clocks worth up to four to five rubles. "True, these clocks quite often run either very slow or fast; but no peasant household chief misses the opportunity to check it against the watch of the *volost* elder, who visits the provincial capital quite frequently."[78]

Clocks came into such demand precisely because peasants so longed to live in synch with the pulse of the city, to live on urban time. "We need clocks," said one peasant, "so that we won't work too much in summer and sleep too much in winter."[79]

New Social Space: Village Café and Shopping Culture

To satisfy the growing consumer demand of the peasantry, the structure of the rural market in the Moscow region was fundamentally transformed. The periodicity of rural markets and fairs grew rapidly, and by the 1880s, many had become constant shopping areas.[80] The matrix of shopping was increasingly focused on *volost,* district, and provincial capitals, where rural stores began to supplant the previously central role of peddlers, itinerant tradesmen, and home or village produce—or, an annual visit to a nearby town. This development was a direct result of the shifting emphasis on village consumption satisfied through the market, a phenomenon that both reflected and further drove the peasant movement to migrate for side-earnings.

With superior supplies and steady hours, the stores rapidly became the principal purveyors of goods to satisfy increasing peasant demand. In particular, grain and *bakaleinaia torgovlia*—the grocery trade—were central to rural distribution, which accounted for 17.3 percent of all rural trade in Russia by the end of the nineteenth century.[81] Pandering to peasant popular tastes was indeed profitable: markup was up to 200–300 percent higher on such "necessary" luxuries as tea, tobacco, sugar, kerosene, and machine-produced fabrics.[82]

Within the locus of these main supply depots, from the 1860s and 1870s there sprang up two other smaller scale but increasingly more widespread forms of retail trade in the Russian village. The first of these were the *melochnye lavki* or small-goods stores. On this, Tver Province represents an average for rural trade development in provinces of the Central Industrial and northwestern regions of European Russia. By 1899, throughout Tver Province, there were 2,147 rural small-goods stores, one for every five villages in the province. Already by 1899, these stores accounted for 69.7 percent (5,077,435 rubles) in gross retail commercial cash turnover in rural Tver Province.[83]

By far the most lucrative side-deals for supplementing communal income to sustain the waning village tax base were sales of monopoly concessions to agents in this burgeoning village retail trade. The typical agreement granted the tavern- or storekeeper exclusive liquor and/or trading rights in the village, the violation of which could carry stiff financial penalties.[84] The text of the standard agreement is quite revealing:

> I Sapozhnikov will open a tavern *[traktir]*, public house or other like establishment and when I am ready, I Sapozhnikov should pay fifty rubles silver each year to the peasants for land and for permission [to serve] drinks at the site and in the pasture. Neither an outsider nor a peasant in the commune is permitted during the time of my rental to conduct trade in drink and other items—that is, [no one else may] have a tavern or a public house, etc.[85]

For a mere fifty rubles a year, outsiders could purchase exclusive trading rights for an entire village. The standard contract furthermore stipulated rights of the renter in perpetuity, thereby treating commercial concessions agreements like property: those rights could be sold to another party at the will of the renter, and they could be passed on to the renter's descendants in the form of inherited property. If the tavernkeeper chose not to open a tavern on the site, he nonetheless reserved all rights to the property for personal use.

On the face of it, the terms of such agreements were, of course, outrageous. They contained no exit clauses describing procedures for terminating the agreement, nor for arbitration in the event of disputes, nor for upward adjustment of rental fees. Still, as a rule, such concessions were sold (in the 1870s) for fifty to one hundred silver rubles per year in even the smallest villages (much more for larger villages and settlements), payable in cash. That is a rate equivalent at the time to at least four times the average dues per peasant household in the typical Moscow village, and nearly fifteen times the average return on the leased plot of land if it were farmed. Likewise, judging by peasant standards, the land and houses were sold to outsiders at a premium rate: within the commune, complete houses with land went for one hundred silver rubles (in payments usually made over four years).[86]

Such contracts were "holy and inviolable," as a rule legitimized by the mark or signature of every peasant with a voice in the commune, then signed by the renter, witnessed and validated by the village elder, and then again by the *volost* elder and clerk, and sometimes even by the local parish priest.[87]

Village inns, taverns *(traktiri, postoialye dvory,* and *kabaki)* and tea houses *(chainye lavki)* were often indistinguishable in their function and appearance.[88] According to official statistics, there were 679 taverns in the Tver countryside in 1899, one for every fifteen villages. Though fewer in number than the general stores, they did a brisk trade in strong drink: 95.7 percent (4,686,300 rubles) of all retail alcohol trade in Tver Province was sold in rural inns and taverns, about 2 rubles, 80 kopecks for every peasant man, woman, and child in the province. In contrast, in the twelve district capitals and three settlements of Tver Province in 1899, there were 497 officially registered establishments that sold alcoholic spirits, one for every 328 inhabitants; in the countryside, the ratio was one establishment for every 2,345 inhabitants.[89]

Contemporary observers emphasized the difficulty of measuring peasant alcohol consumption in general, because of the constant influx of peasant consumers to the towns and market centers on bazaar days, when drinking was heaviest. Such measurements are also hampered by the flow of migrants (reputed to have been the heaviest drinkers) back and forth between town and country, as well as the immeasurable role of blackmarket or moonshine establishments, which became particularly common after the establishment of the state vodka monopoly in 1894.[90]

According to a study conducted in Vladimir Province in 1911, there were considerably more unauthorized "speakeasies" and illegal taverns *(shinki)* than state-run stores trading in spirits and beer. From 670 correspondents in Vladimir Province in 1910, only 13 percent reported the absence of illegal taverns in their locales. The correspondent from Dmitrievo-Gorskaia *volost,* Melenki District, reported with some exaggeration: "While there are three state liquor stores in this county, there are [in the villages] 3,000 bootlegging saloons and taverns."[91] Or, as the correspondent from a neighboring *volost* added: "There's one state [liquor] store in the village, but there are saloons *[shinki]* in nearly every house."[92] In a different study conducted by the Russian Ministry of Finance, it was estimated that the number of beer bars in rural Russia increased tenfold between 1902 and 1907.[93]

Contemporary critics focused their attention on the skyrocketing growth of speakeasies, saloons, and tea rooms in rural Russia as clear evidence of increasing peasant drunkenness.[94] Dominated by activists in the Russian temperance movement, contemporary discussions were marked by a myopic preoccupation with popular alcoholism. As a result, contemporary observers often missed the far more profound implications of this phenomenon: a fundamental transformation of the social and cultural centers of village life throughout Russia.[95] The critical point was not that peasants were drinking more—and there were numerous indicators to suggest they were not—but rather that they were associating with one another in new ways. Judging from his observations of peasant tavern life in Petrovka village in Shuia District, Vladimir Province, Father Mikhail Sokolov summarized the far-reaching social impact of the growth of tavern culture in rural Russia (1899): "In our villages . . . one can meet [in the village saloon] the most respected people, such as for instance: the church elder, or the *volost* elder, etc. . . . People go to the saloon not to drink or to get drunk. Many people sit in the saloon without drinking spirits at all. The village saloon attracts [people] because it is a place where one can hear all sorts of news, or get needed information."[96] Information like the price of oats at the last bazaar, where to find work, news heard from loved ones working outside the village. For visitors to the village, the local saloon was the ideal setting for conducting business regarding rental, property division, hiring, and so on.[97]

A less idealized but equally provocative picture of the social culture of the village saloon was provided by A. Lebedev, from Kaluga District, who argued that the central preoccupations were nothing more than gossip and scandal.

> In the majority of cases local peasants free from work pass their time in the saloon, which they fill with useless and at times even harmful conversations, which soon are transformed into squabbles and end in fights. This relates mainly to the men. Peasant women are another thing altogether. They assemble in circles *(kruzhki)* in favored homes and there pass the time, if one cannot say exclusively, then mainly exchanging gossip.
>
> When free from work, peasants fill the tavern from early morning. [Judging] from conversations [one overhears,] most noticeable are the complaints of locals against their nemeses.[98]

Offering a third perspective, I. Shchelgov in Melenki District, Vladimir Province, compared the village saloon to a kind of social club for peasants:

The village saloon is its own type of club in Liakhi. In winter, it is packed with people. The atmosphere is flavored with an almost unbearable steam of spirits, tobacco, the smell of sheepskin and dampness. It is the sort of tavern common in our age—an enormous place for gathering together, where one can have a chat, or just listen, pass one's free time, in a word, just like the *zavalinka* in front of one's home in summer, or the square in front of the general store.[99]

F. Lashmanov, *volost* clerk from Volosovo village in Kaluga Province, concurred in depicting village saloons as social clubs for local peasants:

> For the peasants village saloons play the role of a club, where they get together evenings to while away the time. [Local] peasants are rarely in the saloon during the day, but in the evening it's hard to get inside. They gather here not just to be here, but in order to get together with other villagers and to exchange a few words. Wealthy [peasants] drink vodka, while poor [peasants] look on. There are all sorts of conversations: scabrous, narrative, or agricultural, and sometimes in the saloon a resolution of the next meeting of the communal assembly is prepared.[100]

For better or for worse, in good dealings and in bad, the village saloon had by the last quarter of the nineteenth century become the center of village social life.[101] As V. D. Krestov, Bronnitsy District (Moscow), confirmed: "In the evenings of holidays or free days, peasants assemble in the local 'club'—the [village] tea room."[102]

There was nothing particularly remarkable about the physical appearance of village saloons. As a rule, they were one- to two-story wooden huts virtually indistinguishable from neighboring peasant cottages. The main floor generally opened into a large common hall where there were usually five to six tables, each table surrounded by benches. There was always a bar *(prilavok)* along one wall, where the proprietor or his wife poured spirits for those who were drinking alcohol, scalding hot tea brought to a third boil from a samovar for those who were not. Behind the bar were shelves where bottles of vodka, *samogon* (moonshine), and snacks or desserts were arranged, and on the floor next to the bar there was usually a barrel filled with wine, beer, or kvass. In the corner by the bar, there was almost always a traditional Russian stove, used for heating and cooking. In two-story saloons, the upper floor was usually divided into two or more rooms, each furnished with tables covered with red cloths, and used for smaller parties.[103]

THE EMERGENCE OF A NEW INFORMATION CULTURE

Contact with the market had a powerful transforming effect on sources of peasant information. Writing in 1880, Andrei Isaev observed in rural southeastern Iaroslavl Province that peasant "inquisitiveness" was growing: "If fairly literate, a peasant subscribes to an inexpensive newspaper; if not so literate, he buys a religious calendar *[krestnyi kalendar]*, spending 15 kopecks just to have the opportunity to read through two or three big events in Russian history syllable-by-syllable."[104] Less than a generation later, fueled by the development of a commodity economy, the expansion of parish schools, and new village cultural centers focused on the saloons and tea houses, this inquisitiveness had been transformed into nothing short of passion.

The growing predominance of rural saloons and tea shops as the centers of village social life corresponded with a sort of "information revolution" in the Central Industrial Region, and a rocketing growth of popular interest in national issues. As peasant correspondent P. P. Shelagin (Ploskovskaia *volost*, Volokolamsk District, Moscow Province) wrote: "In our village, a newspaper is received almost three times each week. Every mail day, peasants gather at the saloon, waiting to listen to the reading of the newspaper. At work time, [they] will even abandon field work and run to find out what's new in the newspapers."[105] M. N. Davydov of Vereia District, Moscow Province, added: "In the tea room, usually one reads the newspaper, while the others come to listen. Near their homes peasant neighbors will sometimes crowd together for the reading of the newspapers."[106]

In 1905, a comprehensive survey of peasant newspaper reading was conducted in Moscow Province. A total of 296 of 363 correspondents to the Moscow *zemstvo* responded, reporting on conditions in 142 of 167 *volosti* in Moscow Province.[107] The results of this invaluable survey were startling and did much to shatter well-worn presumptions about the allegedly ignorant and backward Russian peasant. Despite staunch police efforts to interdict newspapers with a nonofficial slant, 564 villages in Moscow Province subscribed to 1,395 newspapers and journals, an average of 2.5 per village. Besides this, still more newspapers were subscribed to by tea shops and taverns: 164 tea shops for which information was available subscribed to 283 newspapers and journals. And, of course, many peasants acquired newspapers irregularly through retail shops *(v roznitsu)* and itinerant traders. Once in the countryside, the newspapers passed through countless hands, and read aloud, reached the ears of countless more peasants, both literate and illiterate: "Newspapers in the countryside rarely remain the property of just one person. Peasants love to read the newspaper aloud and often almost an entire village will gather to listen. . . . The favorite places for gathering to find out the latest news and to hold political discussions and arguments are the tea rooms."[108] It was in rural saloons and village tea rooms that peasants co-opted modern forms of information culture to sustain and enhance traditional perspectives on Russia's burning social issues. Peasant correspondent A. A. Kurochkin of Bronnitsy District, Moscow Province, recalled: "Each day the [village] tea room is transformed into an auditorium. Reading and discussion have become the favorite activity" of local peasants.[109] Besides the saloon, the village store *(lavka)* also became a social center: "Usually peasants get together at the village store, where one peasant who likes to read will read aloud" to the rest.[110]

The evidence of peasant newspaper reading and of the growth of village taverns and tea rooms as new social centers provides ample material to resolve a conundrum that has haunted Russian social historians for decades: by what conduits did news in the cities reach the Russian countryside overnight? The question is all the more baffling given the predominance of mass illiteracy in the Russian countryside before the Revolution, an illiteracy which in itself would have presented a powerful obstacle to modern, self-sustaining forms of organized resistance. Russian police authorities were so baffled by this seemingly inexplicable phenomenon that they persisted to the very end of the Old Regime in the belief in *agents provocateurs,* fully convinced that simple peasants were incapable of constructing and sustaining effective information networks of their own, or that they were prone to manipulation by cunning operators or unsubstantiated rumors.[111]

Available data from Moscow Province suggest that rates of peasant newspaper subscriptions were highest in the outlying regions (Mozhaisk, Volokolamsk, Klin Districts), and in areas most cut off from railway and communications routes (where mail was delivered perhaps once a week). They were lowest in areas closest to such routes: Moscow District, for instance, where retail purchase was easiest, and where timely access to less formal networks of information was greater.

The overwhelming majority of correspondents in the Moscow study (212 of 226) noted that reading was almost always followed by heated discussion among the peasants. A peasant from Moscow District, S. Ia. Makhonin, observed: the peasants "passionately discuss what was read, usually divided into two parties: the Progressives and the Black Hundreds."[112]

Most observers likewise noted that far from uncritical and passive acquisition of printed information, peasants nurtured a deep, stubborn suspicion of everything they read, and often self-consciously recognized their own lack of political sophistication. Far from discouraging them, this seems to have driven peasants even more passionately toward the acquisition of the requisite understanding that could be obtained through newspapers. As a peasant correspondent from Volokolamsk District complained:

> The foreign words and mass of scientific terms in the newspapers are incomprehensible. In the news of the day, we [peasants] don't understand what is meant by a "constitution," "representative government," "three-tiered elections," a "petition," "amnesty." We don't know the responsibilities of the *zemstvo* [or] how it will fulfill them, and what this will do for the peasants. We know nothing about the ministries. Particularly hazy for us are the reports of the Ministry of Finance: where does it get its income and how does it spend it? We're hazy about the agrarian question, and we don't understand how they want to resolve it. And why have they have foisted the rural constables *[strazhniki]* on us? We don't understand why the gentlemen *[gospoda]* can receive education, but the *muzhik* nothing, nor why in the schools they don't teach our children [how] to interpret the newspaper.[113]

Working to reach a new sector of the mass reading public, publishers from 1905 on began to develop a press specifically tailored to the interests and reading level of the peasantry. *Sel'skii vestnik (Village Herald)* was the traditional mainstay for officials in rural Russia, but its official slant undermined its popularity, despite its broad availability and low cost.[114] In 1905, by far the most popular paper in the countryside was *Russkoe slovo (Russian Word)*, mainly because of its accessibility. *Syn Otechestva (Son of the Fatherland)* was perhaps the first left-of-center newspaper deliberately written in a style comprehensible to the peasants, and it was therefore eagerly sought after by the peasant reading public, even though the police worked particularly to interdict its delivery in the countryside.

All of this sudden interest in reading among the peasantry did not escape the attention of the tsarist authorities, who in report after report grew quite justifiably concerned about the Russian peasantry's new eagerness to be informed. For instance, in a secret report to the governor of Vladimir Province, the police superintendent of Iur'ev-Pol'skii District wrote on 3 June 1906:

> I report to your Excellency that owing to the mass of newspapers which have been received by the peasants, in which the peasants have very great interest, they know everything that is happening in Petersburg, and among them the firm belief has been generated that "they have been begrudging the Duma and that it is

necessary to stand up for it." All conversations revolve around this, and if the State Duma passes a resolution with an appeal for support, then—profoundly persuaded—all the peasants and factory workers forthwith respond, stopping at nothing. . . .

The peasants know how the Duma relates to the ministers, and this acquires enormous meaning and strength, since it is done openly, written in all the newspapers, while editorials explain still more the sense of what is happening, standing completely on the side of the most impertinent deputies. Owing to this, the peasants' respect for authority is falling with startling rapidity. [State]-circulated leaflets of the response of the Council of Ministers addressed to the Duma have produced on the peasants an unfavorable impression and have contributed to the worsening mood.

If by the end of June the agrarian question does not take some definite direction, agrarian disorders will inevitably begin in the district.[115]

Appraising the upheavals of 1905–1907 for the Free Economic Society in 1908, the respected analyst D. I. Rikhter focused his own observations on the Central Industrial Region where, he concluded, "a not insignificant role was played by the intellectual ferment *[umstvennoe brozhenie]* that has seized all of Russia in recent years. This ferment could not but have affected the region in which industry is developed like nowhere else and in which a considerable part of the [peasant] population has come into contact with the larger industrial and cultural centers of the country."[116]

The political catalysis of the countryside was directly associated with the consumer revolution, just one of many side effects in the honeycomb of shocks that spread through the regional rural system following the development of out-migration and the subsequent peasant passion to acquire urban culture. Ironically, in their efforts to embrace urban culture, Russian peasants likewise acquired inchoate forms of horizontal political organization. In this way, taverns and tea rooms in rural Russia came to serve the same role as saloons in eighteenth-century America, cafés in revolutionary Paris, or beer halls in working-class Germany. As James S. Roberts observed in an essay on the critical role of taverns in the German labor movement, taverns were "primary social centers" and a "crucial institution" for members of the German working class, the places where "traditional forms of popular leisure activity fused with modern forms of political organization."[117]

The new social atmosphere in the Russian countryside associated with village taverns, tea rooms, markets, and stores enabled a traditional culture largely dependent on oral traditions to tap into the modern nexus of information normally restricted to literate, urbanized societies. As later events would show, the conduit of that information was just as explosive and important as its content.[118]

Epiphany: Rising Expectations and Consumer-Inspired Protests

The argument in this chapter fundamentally alters our own view of the Russian rural crisis, in which nearly all historians who have participated in the discussion have treated peasant consumption as a more-or-less constant and stable quantity, and have failed to recognize that peasant consumer expectations had themselves been radically transformed by the transition to a commodity economy. Implicitly, most historians have assumed that the minimum standard which would satisfy peasant needs at mid-century was the same as the one for 1900. As we have seen, that simply was not the case. The growth of peasant labor migration had transformed peasant consumer expectations. Increasingly, the minimum "break-even point" for village life approached that of the minimums expected for town dwellers, not of the traditional Russian peasants. The presumption that peasant consumer preferences were constant has led to rather misguided attempts to resolve issues, such as the rural impoverization debate, with little relevance to the actual situation.[119]

As a theoretical construct, this discussion of the transition from a "culture of need" to a "culture of acquisition" has considerable pertinence to the burning academic debate regarding the social and economic behavior of marginalized groups. James Scott, among others, has argued that risk aversion is the chief feature of the "moral economy" of peasants living close to the margin. Driven by a subsistence ethic, peasants operate from a "risk-averse," "safety-first" perspective. Scott's argument has found substantial support in the work of economic historian Donald McCloskey, who has studied peasant scattering of agricultural plots (twenty separate one-acre plots instead of one large twenty-acre consolidated holding) as a response to risk in Early Modern England. In contrast, Samuel Popkin has been most closely identified with the so-called "rational peasant hypothesis," wherein the behavior of marginal groups has been depicted as intrinsically similar to the "rational" and "self-interested" tactics of nonmarginal actors in the modern world. For Popkin, there is no intrinsic difference between the "risk-averse" peasant and the "profit-maximizing" capitalist: marginal groups are not characterized by any essential, distinct, or peculiar mode of economic behavior.[120]

In my own research, the evidence clearly points to the overriding role of defense against risk which guided peasant behavior. On the other hand, contact with urban culture led to a transformation of peasants' own varying definitions of their "break-even point"—the acceptable standard below which living became hardship. The culture of acquisition preached concerns not just about securing basic subsistence needs for the worker and his family, but also about having (or not having) basic luxuries that only the market could provide. The sensibility was founded on a collective awareness of social differentiation: why do I work so hard and have nothing, while the man who lives off my labor has so much? Indeed, the mythicization of rags-to-riches through *otkhod* intrinsically contained the heady message of social justice. The dialectic of everyday experience was the greatest dynamic of enticement in the "culture of acquisition," breeding desire and passion, but also their corollaries: envy and resentment.

The resentment of have-nots against haves in Russian urban society was a powerful catalyzing force in social actions outside the village that preceded the Revolution. As a workers' proclamation angrily complained in 1900: "We detest an order where by the dire need and inordinate work of millions a small group of shit-eating spongers lives in happiness and luxury."[121] Another workers' proclamation from the cataclysmic upheavals of 1905 voiced the same concern:

> Our life is dark, hard-working, oppressive, and is passed in a continuous [cycle] of excruciating, uninterrupted work. Is this any kind of life? Is it possible in our cramped and dirty box-size rooms or within the noisy walls of the factory, where the din of the machines keeps us even from comprehending our own thoughts, is it possible really to have any joy in life? We are born, we marry, we die, leaving as a legacy to our children the very same eternal hard labor, which we ourselves inherited from our fathers and grandfathers, and the very same eternal agonizing brooding over a piece of bread.
>
> While right next to us there pass the joyous, light and easy lives of well-fed and contented people—our bosses. When we, sullen, sick, and embittered, pass by them and see their contented life. . . . All joy of this life [of theirs] is founded on our labor, steeped in the blood and tears of our grandfathers, fathers, and sons.
>
> Our life, filled with work, worry, lacking even in anger, lies like a heavy weight on our souls and presses us down. And only now and then our hearts, tired from suffering, become hardened and a sharp burning hatred toward these well-fed and contented people starts to blaze in them. This hatred, comrades,—is an awakening. It is the human part of every one of us beginning to speak! Because of this awakening . . . we can no longer submissively bear this slave's yoke as before.
>
> We must defend our hard-earned crumbs, which the hands of our enemies-bosses are trying to take away.

Everyone who has for so long remained silent, obeying like slaves, everyone is rising for the struggle.¹²²

A popular *chastushka* sung in the voice of a peasant-worker in St. Petersburg in the early 1900s struck the same chord:

Я гуляю по ночам,
Не поддаюсь богачам;
Я любому богачу
Рыло на бок сворочу.

[I walk (the streets) at night
(Refusing) to yield to rich folks;
I will twist the snout
Of any rich person.]¹²³

In his very perceptive recent study of the strike at Kreenholm in 1872, Reginald Zelnik has considered the dynamic application of popular conceptions of justice in Russian and Estonian factory actions. Zelnik's original translation of a leading labor activist's memoirs is especially pertinent here for a better understanding of worker activists' motivations. The worker Vasilli Gerasimov wrote: "I quickly absorbed the ideas of the socialists and passionately devoted myself to their cause. Their ideas did not seem alien to me. Abandoned by my family, compelled from earliest childhood to wander among strangers, to endure every possible misfortune, I was conscious of the complete inadequacy of the existing order. I had seen how my brothers and sisters at the Kreenholm factory perished, and I could not remain a passive witness to their destruction." After recounting the death of a young, apparently healthy woman within weeks of their arrival together at the factory, Gerasimov continued: "So there's one fact for you, though I could easily have recounted a hundred more. *During my leisure hours I would often ponder these facts, drawing a line between the conditions that surrounded us and the conditions that obtained for our employers—the manufacturers who drank our blood, who devoured our lives in the literal sense of the word. I became aware of the insanity, the injustice of this order of things.* The only thing I did not know was how to get out of this condition, what to replace it with."¹²⁴ However vague the feeling, however uncertain the response, peasant-workers were increasingly driven to act out against perceived violations of intrinsic social justice. This deep-seated resentment subtly affected a whole series of social relations between workers and bosses. Zelnik describes "some inventive new modes of defiance that workers had begun to deploy. . . . Some workers were displaying open if prudently conveyed disrespect for [the factory manager] Andrée and his aide. When walking past a manager they no longer doffed their caps as a token of deference, as had been their wont; instead, in a thinly veiled gesture of disdain, they lightly raised the peaks of their caps while expressing 'ill will' *(nedobrozhelatel'stvo)* by their grimaces. At times," Zelnik adds, "their conduct was more openly aggressive, even violent."[125]

Inevitably, the resentments that seethed under the surface and shaped the contours of worker-employer relations did periodically burst forth into more open and violent demonstrations of dissatisfaction. Rites of violence in the Russian workers' movement often included ritualized destruction of upper-class symbols of conspicuous consumption. A powerful illustration of how the seething anger of the have-nots translated into action took place during the strike in 1897 at the Guseva textile factory of Vikula Morozov in Vladimir Province. The highlight of the action was a workers' raid on the home of the shop director, Chernak. Workers ransacked his cellar, then broke into his home, where they lived like the bosses for the evening. They lit the gas fire and drank up all three hundred bottles of Chernak's expensive imported Scotch whiskey, while they snacked on his food, smoked his imported cigars, played his piano and sang songs. When a guard had the gas turned off, the occupying workers lit candles and continued their revelry late into the night. When they had finished ransacking the home, the workers set it afire. Dragging into the streets whatever they could carry away with them, they tore various symbols of the director's wealth to pieces and strewed them about the streets, stomping on them in a public demonstration of dissatisfaction. They wanted to burn down the warehouse of cotton stores as well, in order to close down the factory altogether. In all, the angry crowd of workers broke more than twelve thousand panes of glass in a single night. The riots ended long before troops appeared at the scene, and only as a result of the workers' organization of a committee of representatives, elected to present grievances directly to the factory owners.[126]

Such violent, consumer-oriented riots, which by and large typified Russian workers' actions before the Revolution, have been generally ignored by successive generations of Soviet historians, who have been preoccupied with demonstrating above all a working-class movement characterized by organization and self-restraint, not spontaneous, violent, and short-lived outbursts. Largely ignored in most studies of Russian workers was the fact that in nearly every working-class action, "shops were sacked and many goods, mainly foodstuffs, were taken by the angry rioters."[127]

To focus on the preeminent role of a new consumer consciousness as a catalyst for lower-class protest of such open and violent form is not to suggest by any means that these were the most prevalent forms of social conflict during the last generation of Old Regime Russia. On the contrary, short of open riot or rebellion, Russian social life in urban and semiurban areas was filled with innumerable channels where have-nots expressed discontent, most of which fell, when they became serious enough as to disturb the public peace, under the heading of "hooliganism." As Joan Neueberger has observed in her study of hooliganism in St. Petersburg: "In the years after 1905, hooliganism was associated with two issues that were very likely to trouble society: violence and open displays of the 'uncultured' behavior associated with the raw, unassimilated masses. Even people who remained optimistic about cultural development . . . discovered the cultural chasm dividing them from their poor subjects to be much wider than they expected."[128]

Behind the terrifying veil of consumer-driven protest lurked a far more powerful and threatening feeling, usually unspoken: deep-seated social envy among the have-nots. It is of course very difficult for modern historians to unearth that pervasive "feeling" for closer study, let alone define its role in the context of Russian society at the turn of the century. For some hint of how social envy influenced behavior, we might turn to the real-life Cinderella story of Masha Shustova, a "clever and mischievous" young woman from the provinces, an archetypal social climber of her era. Shustova went to Moscow in 1870 at age twenty-three and spent the next eight years in domestic service while she (by her own admission) connived, double-dealed, back-bit, and whored, searching for a rich husband. Fortunately for us, she chronicled that successful search in a five-volume diary of nearly a thousand handwritten pages preserved in the Manuscript Section of the Russian State Library in Moscow. Writing with surprising candor and articulateness about her engagement in 1878 to a wealthy but rather aged tobacco merchant, Shustova left us with invaluable insight into the psyche of a poor woman from the provinces yearning above all for success in the big city:

> This evening, MS was quite coarse with me. I know the reason. He doesn't like the fact that I am going to marry SI. While such a slut [as I] was living with him on his charity, I suddenly and on my own have found a husband. Yes, he is quite a good person, lonely, intelligent . . . and [he] is someone who wants to take me without a dowry. But the main thing is that I will be wealthier than [MS]!
>
> Will this really be? Everything is alright; it's just that [SI] is so old. However, it is good he is old; I will seem even prettier if I go with him. I am still young, and I will grow even younger. He loves to go to the theater and I will be so merry, and I will always be well-dressed (and this for me is the main thing).[129]

With all the lofty aspirations often attributed to the lower classes in Marxist and post-Marxist discourse, it might come as some surprise to discover that the peasant dream probably consisted of no more than the banal realization of material comfort. No wonder that Lev Tolstoi, who took part in a survey of urban working-class neighborhoods in St. Petersburg in 1884, was forced to the unhappy conclusion that any connection between the genteel classes and the Russian poor in the cities had already utterly broken down: "They all looked at me not as a *person,* but as a *means.*"[130]

In contrast to the growing strains between have-nots and haves outside the village in the Central Industrial Region, there is the nagging anomaly that, contrary to Lenin's stratification thesis which pits poor and middle peasants against the kulaks, social differentiation in the village did *not* tend to generate much social discord unless it was also sustained by other social and cultural factors: ethnic differentiation, religious heterogeneity, or long-standing feuds between rival clans. As we have seen, their peculiar status as village insiders meant wealthy peasants were largely perceived not as class enemies, but as potential benefactors; not as market agents, but as influential neighbors.

The explanation of this anomaly lies in the distinct way in which peasants managed to transform market relations with fellow villagers into a "natural economy" dominated by personal relations. Very simply, peasants resisted forces that allowed the market to mediate social relationships with fellow villagers. Those relationships were first and foremost personal, not structural or objective. Russian peasants treated the vast social forces that transformed their era not as "phantomly objective" and thereby impossible to control, but rather as the products of individual decisions by individual persons who were to be held accountable to deep-seated, popularly shared forms of social justice.

7 A Culture of Denunciation

PATTERNS OF RELIGIOUS ANATHEMATIZATION IN RURAL RUSSIA

Deciphering Peasant Denunciations

IN EARLY OCTOBER 1872 the peasant-worker Iakov Poliakov from Kolomna District in southeastern Moscow Province was working at the machine construction mill of the Struve brothers in Moscow City. In horror at a scene he had witnessed in the factory, he wrote a denunciation to the Moscow District superintendent of police against two other peasants from his district, the metalworkers Vasilii Iakushev and Vasilii Kukushkin. On 7 October, Poliakov later testified in Moscow circuit court, he witnessed these two commit an abhorrent act of blasphemy before the icon of the Mother of God and in plain sight of other workers.

Upon investigation, the Moscow police learned that Iakushev, a thirty-five-year-old skilled craftsman, and Kukushkin, a twenty-one-year-old timekeeper, were on their lunch break when they happened upon a discarded axle box from a railway car in the skilled workmen's shed. For reasons which are never made clear in the report—either drunkenness, or boredom, or simple tomfoolery (intentions were never considered relevant by either the police or the Church authorities)—the two workers decided to conduct a "funeral service" *(otpevanie)* for the dear, departed axle box. "In plain view of the holy image," as the report emphasized repeatedly, the two blasphemers took their unholy charade to greater and greater lengths. They dressed themselves in mock priests' clothes, wrapping their torsos in bast mats to create the impression of vestments. A cross was made from iron bars. A teapot was transformed into a makeshift incense burner. Tallow candles that had been placed before the "casket" burned ever brightly throughout the blasphemous ritual as Iakushev "the priest" and Kukushkin "the deacon" sang bawdy street songs in mock bereavement. At the end of the service, Iakushev, removing his trousers and baring his naked rear, bowed to several workers and proclaimed: "The mass is ended."[1]

For this blatant act of hooliganism, the two unfortunate peasants were exiled from the capital and escorted in chains and leg shackles under police guard to their native villages. There they were probably imprisoned for a few days, publicly whipped, fined, and anathematized by the local priest and fellow villagers alike. Three factors in particular influenced the severity of their sentence. First, the key witness of the events was considered an unimpeachable source: Iakov Poliakov was the *starosta* or elder of his own artel of *zemliaki*—neighboring peasants from his district—and was so offended by the display that he appealed to the police to bring the miscreants to justice. Second, the entire blasphemy was far more serious because it was carried out in the presence of the icon of the Mother of God, which hung on the wall of the room where the sacrilege took place and before which workers had placed an icon lamp. Third, the public nature of the offense, the "pernicious moral influence" it exerted on the other workers, was clearly a factor: by their sacrilege, Iakushev and Kukushkin not only damned themselves but also threatened to ensnare fellow workers.

Anthropomorphizing Threats of Change

Historians can amass all the statistics, lists, and examples in the world, but none will give us a contextualized picture of the integrated role of the various weapons in the arsenals of communes, households, and families. The challenge for historians is the reconstruction of a totality: how to visualize these various disparate elements introduced from a host of sources in order to conceive of their operation together in practice. How are we to decipher events like Poliakov's denunciation of his fellow workers?

It should not be surprising that it was through the prism of their religious beliefs that Russian peasants handled the tensions of their daily lives. In practice, the religious dimension was pervasive, defining every aspect of the everyday life of the community, overlaying and forming the language of rivalry between clans or socioeconomic groups. In this context, peasant denunciations nearly always took the form of impugning the reputations of fellow villagers by dynamically constructing an image of scofflaws as morally reprehensible.

This chapter traces the development of a distinct culture of denunciation in village parishes as the growth in peasant migration for side-earnings threatened to destroy the ties which bound rural Russia together. Evidently, Russian villagers did not treat threats of urbanization, modernization, and commoditization like "abstract phantoms" against which struggle was impossible. Rather, threats were anthropomorphized, brought down to earth, and individual peasants considered to embody those threats were subjected to a wide variety of traditional weapons in the village community arsenal: shaming, insults, social ostracism, banishment, ridicule, verbal threats, social isolation, even violence. Most remarkable from an anthropological point of view, peasants made use of outside agents—state authorities, police, the Church—to proscribe the behavior of fellow villagers.

The discussion below is drawn from over three hundred cases of religious denunciations in village parishes that were recorded in the archives of the Moscow Spiritual Consistory throughout the nineteenth and early twentieth centuries.[2] I have devoted particular attention to cases of religious deviation involving the rejection *(uklonenie)* of Russian Orthodoxy for the Old Belief or for sectarian faiths.[3] The most remarkable feature of this material, and the factor that unifies nearly all of the cases, is that over 90 percent of the three hundred cases of religious denunciations reviewed were directed against peasant-workers who migrated for side earnings: evidently, the most vivid agents of change were also the primary targets of denunciation.

"The Slippery Path of Evil": Otkhodniki and Parish Priests

Ostensibly, the extension of moral controls over peasant labor-migrants began in the village parish, and in particular, with the village priests. As the official arbiters of morality in Russian Orthodox villages, all priests were encouraged to denounce to Church authorities or the police anyone who was deemed a threat to the spiritual or civil order. The notorious *Ecclesiastical Regulation,* promulgated at Peter the Great's initiative in the spring of 1722, explicitly required Orthodox priests to honor a "higher moral code" in fulfillment of their Christian duty, and even to violate the sanctity of confession when information thereby obtained threatened the interests of the state.[4] Until the very end of the Old Regime, all new parish priests—as a prerequisite of appointment—were required to make an oral and written oath *(prisiaga)* of loyalty to the reigning tsar which explicitly placed civil authority on a higher plane than that of the Church and which made a virtue of denunciations against parishioners.[5]

The question of whether parish priests actually fulfilled their oaths is extremely controversial. The dual roles of parish priests as agents of state authority and spiritual pastors certainly generated confusion and considerable conjecture. To be sure, until the very end of the Old Regime official edicts were announced from the priestly pulpit, lending a distinct aura of officialdom to even the most recalcitrant parish priest. The important issue here, however, is not whether priests actually fulfilled their oaths in practice but, rather, that they were perceived to do so: priests were widely seen as channels to higher authorities. As we shall see, this perception set the stage for a popular culture of denunciation in rural Russia: imparting information against a fellow villager to a parish priest was the primary channel for denouncing neighbors.

The Church hierarchy's position on the threat to parish life posed by labor migration was unequivocal: in numerous ways village priests were called upon to battle vigorously against the disintegration of religious belief that was engendered by migration. In official correspondence and in the ecclesiastical press, priests received a barrage of communications and reminders about their social and spiritual roles. A particularly comprehensive and articulate program appeared in 1894 in *The Helmsman (Kormchii)* and was subsequently reprinted in religious journals throughout Russia under the rather innocuous title "One Subject Deserving the Particular Attention of Village Pastors."[6] The article was a manifesto against the nefarious influence of the outside world on the social and spiritual life of the village parish: "Our task consists above all . . . in turning the attention of village pastors to the *necessity* of struggling against the corrupting influence on the simple people of those who live outside of their parishes: in the towns, at the factories, [among workers] in the mills, hired agricultural labor, and various forms of outside employment."[7] A particular threat to village spirituality and cohesion was perceived in the growing prevalence of peasant out-work, especially among unmarried men and women:

A long way from their families and homes, free from any restraining moral authority and, not infrequently, deprived for a more or less prolonged period . . . of an opportunity to satisfy their religious needs, these people naturally display insecurity and irresolution in their moral conceptions. Moreover, the temptations —particularly in the towns—are too great for them; and the comradeship in which they are thrown by chance, in which they will always find evil and corrupted elements, set an infectious example and not infrequently push them along the same slippery path of evil. . . . Drunkenness, moral dissoluteness, disrespect toward elders, the absence of religious piety, the inclination toward various kinds of luxury, wild living and revelry, and many other undesirable habits and tastes are introduced into the healthy peasant environment by this means.[8]

In response to this challenge, the author proposed an ambitious social program that promoted greater spiritual regulation of peasant labor migrants. Pastors were exhorted to pay special attention to the salvation of those "lost souls" who had been particularly corrupted by outside life.[9] Rehabilitation and reintegration of *otkhodniki* were closely tied to village rituals—the collective worship and celebration of births, weddings, deaths, saints' days, and numerous religious holidays, as well as religious processions and annual pilgrimages.[10] Noting that "regular annual performance of the Christian duty of Confession and Holy Communion has a great importance for each person and is a wholesome influence on his spiritual life," *The Helmsman* commended the practice observed in several villages whereby "some of the parishioners who are away from the parish for several years unfailingly send their priest every year written statements about their attendance at Confession and Holy Communion" and sometimes even "appear in person in their parish during the Lenten season for fasting. . . . Under these conditions this practice serves as a clear and persuasive demonstration of the living moral-religious bond between members of the parish—those present and those away—and testifies to their unchanging faith in the Orthodox Church."[11]

At least once each year, often more than once, priests would visit each household individually to bless the home and farmstead, pray with the family, test the children's knowledge of basic prayers, and in general affirm the relationship between priest and parishioner. These visits were not just celebrations of spiritual renewal but also the primary means by which a vigilant parish priest tested the faith of parishioners and discovered if any of them had grown reluctant to take part in sacred rituals of the Church. As in Catholic Medieval Europe, the "refusal to take communion was tantamount . . . to an admission of guilt."[12] A typical case was reported in mid-July 1872 in Klin District, northwest of Moscow. The parish priest in Selinskoe village, Father Dmitrii

A Culture of Denunciation 191

Religious procession in a high-migration parish, Simbukhovo village, Vereia District Moscow Province, late nineteenth century. Note how the men—peasant labor-migrants who have returned to share in village holiday rituals—tend to congregate together, while the crowd is made up mostly of women, who stand separately. From A. I. Kovalevskii, *Selo Simbukohovo: Istoricheskii ocherk* (Moscow, 1901), between pp. 10–11.

Sokolov, was going from house to house in an annual visit, blessing peasants' homes and praying with the families. The recurring ritual went ahead without interruption until the priest reached the home of one peasant-worker, Fëdor Petrov, who happened to be home from his usual work in Moscow City. The priest, "having finished prayers in [Petrov's] home, bid [Petrov] to bow down before the Icon, the cross, and the Evangelist," but Petrov refused. The refusal caused a scandal, and the parish priest convened a meeting of the communal assembly where he vehemently denounced Petrov for religious apostasy. A heated public discussion followed in which "the entire community of peasants began to reproach" Petrov for "deviating from the Orthodox faith." The tension grew, but when threatened with physical punishment, Petrov refused to conform: "You can cut me to pieces," he cried in a dramatic confrontation with fellow villagers, "but I will not renounce my faith."

In the police inquiry that followed, at least twelve witnesses were interviewed. All of the signs of a fall from faith were discovered: Petrov had not partaken of the Blessed Sacraments for two years; he had frequently been absent for long periods working in Moscow. When interrogated, the recusant peasant Petrov revealed that he had lived in Moscow City each winter for five consecutive years, working at the factory of the peasant Timofei Ermolov Sergeev, who belonged to the Old Believer sect at the Rogozhskii cemetery. "At this factory there lived many workers, natives of Kaluga Province, schismatics, from whom I learned to read and obtained Holy books. Having read [these books] and having listened to the workers' discussions about church matters, I came to the conviction that one should not bow before icons or priests." Even worse, several parishioners testified that Petrov had openly defied the true faith in the fateful communal assembly where he had been summoned to explain his blasphemy. In open defiance of the community, he had ardently proclaimed: "You have been baptized with an accursed cross! You bow down to accursed icons, made with your own accursed hands!" One fellow villager, Lev Ivanov, testified that when he had visited the blasphemer's home Petrov had read to him from a book that proved that Orthodox Christians do not make the sign of the cross as they should." Even more damning was evidence that Petrov had actually succeeded in converting a fellow villager, the peasant woman Dar'ia Fedorova.

Petrov was found guilty on three counts of criminal conspiracy. First, he was proved to be a recusant religious dissenter who had fallen away from the true faith and had cursed holy images. Second, and much more seriously, he was deemed to be a danger to his community, as demonstrated by his efforts to attract others to his renunciation of faith. For this he was found guilty of violating articles 72 and 134 of the Russian criminal code, which prohibited missionary efforts to convert others to the schismatic faith and to deny Orthodoxy. Third, Petrov was likewise found guilty of open slander *(khula)* against the Orthodox faith. His case was transferred from the ecclesiastical court to the jurisdiction of the civil authorities, and Petrov was ordered to stand trial before the prosecutor of the Moscow circuit court.[13]

Elsewhere the same pattern was followed: a peasant's refusal to take part in local religious rituals drew the attention of the parish priest and fellow villagers alike. In another typical case, the parish priest, Father Viktor Gur'ev, denounced a negligent peasant woman to his local superintendent in December 1886: "The widow Florova does not permit discussions [with the priest] about faith at home with her children. Likewise she [resists] prayer services [at home] on Holy Days.... She always avoids discussions about faith."[14]

The imposition of ritual obligations was the chief means by which priests, acting on their own, could root out religious nonconformists. The annual duty was considered so important that all parish priests were required to file annual reports—confession and communion registers *(ispovednye vedomosti)*—in which religious attendance was discussed and deviants were singled out. These reports were one of the only means by which the Holy Synod could monitor parish religious life, and they were treated with the utmost seriousness. Repeated failure to submit an annual report led to severe reprimands and even loss of one's parish. Reports that revealed declines in religious attendance in one's parish provoked investigations, usually performed by representatives of the central Church administration—the local superintendents *(blagochinnye)*.[15]

The authority of priests in a village community was not generally limited, however, to the powers granted them by law. In traditional society, as in Third World villages today, outsiders seeking information often worked through references provided by local priests, which lent priests enormous authority and influence. Finding work outside the village often depended on a good relationship with one's parish priest, as did obtaining or renewing a passport; securing a loan or a cash deal; and receipt of packages, letters, and cash transfers. When the police intervened, they often followed the lead of the parish priest to establish the reputation and reliability (or unreliability) of locals.[16] In short, priests played an essential role in sustaining a good reputation with local peasant officials, as well as with outsiders.

Besides reporting a parishioner's failure to fulfill ritual obligations, priests also actively denounced peasants for immoral behavior in two other types of cases: noncanonical marriages and the failure of families to baptize newborn infants. The parish priest wielded enormous power to regulate marriages. At the end of January 1887, for instance, the parish priest Aleksei Zhuravlev of Nativity Church in Dmitrov District filed a denunciation against the Old Believers who had led astray the nineteen-year-old son of one of his parishioners. The young peasant-worker, Vasilii Nikolaev, had been a faithful servant of Orthodoxy: "Every Sunday and Holiday he attended matins and the Liturgy without omission." Then, charged the priest, he was lured away by false promises of personal gain to follow from his blasphemous marriage to a young girl of the priestly sect: "I am convinced that the . . . peasant [son] went astray to the *raskol* [schism, or sectarianism] not according to the desire of his heart, but from [the seduction of] worldly personal advantages, fearing he might let this notorious [wealthy] bride-*raskol'nitsa* slip away. I consider the behavior of the young bachelor to be brazen blasphemy and insulting to the Orthodox Christian Church."[17] Father Zhuravlev turned to the police, and with their help he presented the young recusant with an ultimatum: he must either marry the girl in the Church or leave her. The Church considered such noncanonical marriages as illegal or adulterous cohabitation *(nezakonnoe* or *liubodeian-noe sozhitel'stvo),* and priests were instructed to do everything in their power to restore the deviant to proper Orthodox rites.

And that power was considerable. If the priest or local ecclesiastical superintendent could demonstrate (1) that the case involved the "falling away" of a former Orthodox Christian and (2) that "undo influence" was used to delude the peasant or to force him to act against his "true will," then priests could call upon the police to separate the married couple. This was true even in cases where the couple had lived together as husband and wife for several years, and even when they had children. To prevent reunification of the pair, local police, officials, and even neighbors were required to sign sworn oaths promising they would help to keep the couple apart.

Because the parish priests maintained the parish registers, upon which all future documentation rested—everything from military service to passports, loans, arrests, and state tax obligations—every peasant, Orthodox or Old Believer, had to reach some sort of understanding with the local parish priest.

The effectiveness of religious controls was dependent largely, but not exclusively, on their vigilance. But several factors severely undermined their ability to monitor the moral activities of their parishioners. First, most parishes were far too large. The number of parishioners in Russia as a whole expanded far more rapidly than the number of available priests: by 1904, the ratio of parish priests to parishioners was 1:1,844, and even if all clerical staff are included, the ratio would still be a discouraging 1:826.[18] Second, Orthodox parish priests were overburdened by a surfeit of rituals and practices. As the leading historian of Russian parish priests, Gregory L. Freeze has observed, "The Russian parish priest had to perform a plethora of rites and sacraments, often in the parishioner's home, and it was just physically impossible to minister to the ritual needs of overly large parishes. . . . And the task in Russia was further complicated by the low population density; often a parish consisted of many hamlets scattered all over the surrounding countryside."[19] Third, the turnover of priests was too high to allow them to develop intimate acquaintances with members of their parishes. Far more than in the West, Russian Orthodox parish priests depended directly upon parishioners' contributions and on the fees they collected for performance of rites in order to make ends meet. The high rate of parish turnovers was directly associated with the extreme disparities between parishes and parish incomes, as well as the career patterns of the clergy, who competed to win and retain berths in wealthier parishes.[20]

The priest's task was particularly difficult in parishes with high rates of out-migration for side earnings. It was in fact quite easy for a recusant to avoid the parish priest for long stretches. Out-migration presented a very special set of circumstances that undermined the parish priest's ability to supervise parishioners and facilitated tactical escape by wily apostates. The peasant recusant Iakov Grigor'ev, for instance, managed to use his migrant status as a means by which to escape detection for several years. It was only when he was denounced to the Moscow police—probably by his own father—that Grigor'ev was brought to justice. As the local superintendent's report indicated,

> This falling away *[otpadenie]* was completed in secret, so that Grigor'ev's father did not immediately notice it. But it was also never discovered either by the parish priest at St. Sergei's Church [in Moscow City], nor by the parish priest in Domodedovo village, the parish to which [Iakov] belonged [from birth]. The former did not notice Grigor'ev's turning away *[uklonenie]* because he [the recusant] lived at St. Sergei's parish only temporarily and could have gone to church at a nearby monastery . . . where many parishioners of St. Sergei's Church confess and partake of the Blessed Sacraments. Nor did the latter notice because he [Grigor'ev] lived constantly in Moscow.[21]

Each act of concealment or resistance increased the missionary task faced by the parish priest. Father Aleksei Omviiskii complained with exasperation that a recusant peasant woman in his parish "stubbornly continued to remain with her false opinions, and once even ran away from me into the garden. Moreover, several times I did not find her at home. And to my question, 'Where is Matrona?' her family usually said that she had gone out somewhere, or that she had gone to a neighboring village."[22] Father Viktor Blagolev complained that a husband simply lied to him when he promised to baptize a newborn son. But he could not manage to track the peasant down, "since Ivanov himself lives constantly at work in Moscow, and in spite of my exhortations his wife Evdokiia Kirillova remains unmoved. Following several such exhortations, whenever I appeared in her village, . . . she . . . tried either to hide from me, or to remain concealed at home."[23]

To guard against such lying and evasion, more vigilant priests increasingly demanded that peasant-workers unable to fulfill religious obligations in their native parishes would be required to bring certificates *(svidetel'stva)* signed by the priest in the parish near their workplaces verifying their religious attendance.[24] In one case, three peasant women of the same family from Moscow District lived and worked not far from their native village sewing gloves at a local workshop. After a fellow villager denounced them, their parish priest invited them to fulfill their religious obligations, to which they responded "that they had fasted while on religious pilgrimage." On his insistence, the women promised to present the proper documentation. "But in spite of their promises and my requests," Father Smirnov later wrote in his formal denunciation to the ecclesiastical superintendent, "the Skundova women have hitherto presented no evidence either of their attendance at Confession or Holy Communion or of their preparation for Communion at [another] church. Moreover, it was rumored in the parish that [they] had turned away from Orthodoxy." In order to verify the rumors, Smirnov confronted the women, who eventually admitted that they had left the Church.[25]

As long as there was no denunciation, a peasant's lapse from Orthodoxy might go undetected for quite some time. For instance, the peasant Boris Martynov was fifty-six years old before his long-standing Old Believer status was discovered and investigated. Born in a village in Kolomna District, Moscow Province, in 1839, Martynov was baptized the day after his birth into the Orthodox Church. In the confession registers for 1848, the eight-year-old Martynov attended confession and communion—the one and only time in his life. In 1849, Martynov's father died, and with him ended his young son's only tie to the Orthodox Church. Martynov was raised by his mother, who immediately lapsed back into Old Belief. Upon questioning in 1895, the elder Martynov claimed, probably truthfully, that he did not even know he was Orthodox—a credible remark given the forty-eight years that separated him from his last affirmation of Orthodoxy. In the confession registers for 1849, Martynov was cited as not attending confession out of spiritual negligence *(neradenie)*. But this was the only year of his life in which this Orthodox Christian turned Old Believer was identified as recusant. Between 1850 and 1860, and for the rest of his life as a peasant-worker in Moscow, he was listed in confession registers as a nonparticipant due to his absence *(za otluchku)* from his native parish. In this case, the parish priests in Martynov's native village had for the greater part of his life turned a blind eye to his apostasy. In the end, a disgruntled fellow worker denounced him—but to the police, not to the ecclesiastical authorities.[26]

The sheer overload of cases discouraged even the most vigilant and conscientious parish priests.[27] As the Duma's clerical deputies complained in 1915: "The authority of spiritual pastors is steadily falling, so that even the best, most energetic of them sometimes are powerless and, as if in despair, give up."[28] The inevitable vacuum in the regulation of spiritual life was filled by the development of a distinct culture of denunciation in rural parishes: unable to perform the duty of moral vigilance on their own, priests depended enormously on denunciations from within their parish communities to root out deviants. This was especially true in parishes marked by high rates of out-migration for side earnings. Ultimately, the extensive powers wielded by parish priests to regulate the behavior of fellow villagers were increasingly co-opted by the village community. The crucial issue was the transformation of religious controls into secularized, community-based norms—not village mores founded on Church law, but, rather, Church law whose enforcement depended on village norms. This is more than just a semantic transformation: what it meant was that peasants could utilize the power of the Church to root out "deviants" of their own. As we shall see, this gave villagers a powerful weapon in the effort to regulate the behavior of *otkhodniki*.

A Culture of Denunciation: The Community's Role in Rooting Out Deviants

Rites of denunciation, like all culturally embedded codes, follow distinct procedures and patterns.[29] Historical research in the West has repeatedly demonstrated that heretics themselves—the victims of denunciations—were rarely guilty of heresy; or, at the very least, it was not usually for heretical acts alone that they were singled out for anathematization by members of their own communities. A corollary of this notion is that even when heretics were heretical, special local conditions beyond the act of heresy alone accounted for the singling out of some, while other "heretics" often were not only tolerated, but even allowed to flourish. Numerous studies in Western Europe have emphasized "the crucial role of the village community in regulating the identification and persecution of . . . deviants."[30]

A spoken denunciation, delivered in secret to the parish priest, was usually the trigger for proceedings against deviants. Family members, concerned neighbors, or even the police would inform a parish priest, who would proceed according to the law. The seriousness with which family members perceived a turning away from Orthodoxy was revealed in the high frequency of denunciations of recusants by members of their own families—representing nearly 60 percent of the three hundred cases studied. An example will illustrate the usual pattern. Grigorii Fedorov's adolescent son Iakov left his father's farm in Podol'sk District to work in Moscow during the first half of the 1860s. Raised in Orthodoxy, he upheld his faith during his first years in the city. However, not long after he began to work for an Old Believer merchant named Karasev in 1866, Iakov threw aside both Orthodoxy and his family. Without notifying his parents he married Karasev's niece Arafima Rylova, in July 1869, "and through her help became completely lost in the delusion of the Old Belief."[31] Having exhausted himself in various schemes to reclaim his son, the elder Fedorov petitioned the Moscow Metropolitan for help in 1873, in the process denouncing both his son and the "evil-doers" who had led him astray:

> My son Iakov . . . already for seven years has not partaken of the Blessed Sacraments. He has, moreover, married a girl of the priestless sect, which has still more deeply rooted [him in the *raskol*]. [Unable to break] my son of his fanatical conviction, I turn to Your Excellency as to the Father and Head of the Church to heed me, an aged and old man, [and to] return him to the Christian Faith. I hope that as an adherent and Head of the Church You will direct Your Gracious attention to a 67-year-old man for whom it is painful to see his own son living in such delusions.[32]

The degree of the breakdown in relations between Iakov and his family was soberly evaluated by the superintendent's report: "Contrary to the will of his parents, [the younger] Fedorov took his share from his parents' home in the village and settled in Moscow, probably depending on the help of a rich relative of his boss, the merchant Karasev. He does not conceal his enmity toward his father and brothers."[33]

Following a police investigation, and on the basis of his father's grief-stricken petition, Iakov Fedorov was subjected to a forced separation *(razluchenie)* from his "illegal wife" Arafima: Iakov and his wife were bound by their signatures on a written oath to separate, with compulsory relocation to different residences. Arafima Rylova was issued a separate passport by the Moscow authorities and moved in with her mother. Iakov remained in their former home. Their infant son Mikhail was transferred to Fedorov's passport alone, and was registered in his native village in Podol'sk District, where he was raised by members of Fedorov's extended family.[34] In addition to forced separation, the recalcitrant Iakov was charged in his *volost* court with "marrying without the consent of his father."[35]

Peasant heads of households often used denunciations to Church or secular authorities as a means of exercising control over subordinate household members. Wives often employed the same method to free themselves from the repressed and often arbitrary atmosphere of the peasant patriarchal household, denouncing the immoral characters of their spouses in petitions for annulment or for separate passports, which were typically dictated for a fee to scribes who specialized in this service at village markets and annual fairs. As the peasant woman Marfa Iartseva from Volokolamsk District, Moscow Province, complained in 1905: "From the day of our wedding, my husband drank and lived a depraved way of life. Having endured for three years all possible torments and suffering, I am not strong enough to live with him any longer."³⁶ Likewise, from Ekaterina Sablina, a peasant woman from Bronnitsy District, living in dire poverty on the streets of Moscow in 1896: "My husband, Stepan Andreev Sablin, for several years now has led an impossibly drunken life, and for the past five years he has completely abandoned me with three young children. He shows up only to beat me, and then takes away any valuables I have, only to drink them away in the nearest saloon. . . . A week ago he made off with my last pair of shoes. . . . In the recent past, the children and I have frequently been left hungry, and now he has driven us from our apartment."³⁷

Similarly, Luker'ia Guseva, a peasant woman from Riazan Province, was forced to live and work on her own in Moscow because of her husband's abandonment. Despite her anguish, Guseva waited almost eleven years before she filed for an annulment on the grounds of her husband's adulterous behavior. Adultery seemed the least of her worries. "My husband Aleksei Gusev showed no concern for me from the first day of our marriage. He abandoned me to the whim of fate. I have been deprived of my last piece of bread since he has no base in the village *(net krest'ianskoi osedlosti)* and he takes away from me side earnings with which I might support myself." Guseva was desperately afraid of being stalked by her husband and begged the Moscow Spiritual Consistory for an annulment.

> My husband . . . leads an extremely debauched way of life. He wanders everywhere around Khitrovo market and does not have a constant place of residence. Nothing can be done to correct either his nasty behavior or his unruly character in general. For almost two years we have not lived together, since he lives only God knows where. I live here [in Moscow] and earn a piece of daily bread for myself with my own personal labor. If my husband finds out that I am living here, then he will come to this house and make all sorts of trouble: he will revile me with insulting words and deeds, and [he will] also make threats that if the owners keep me he will commit murder or write anonymous letters.

Such had already been the case more than once, when Guseva was forced to move by her husband's harassment and threats. Even though she filed for and won restraining orders from the police, and even though her husband had been condemned for his abusiveness by both the village assembly and the *volost* court, he refused to heed the orders and often had appeared at her residence, issuing every kind of threat and swearing he would kill her.³⁸

Morals charges were also an effective means by which husbands could regulate wives. A particularly detailed written denunciation was filed by the peasant-worker Ivan Lavrov against his wife Evdokeia in the spring of 1905: "I accuse my wife," wrote the disaffected Lavrov to their parish priest, "of drunkenness and infidelity. . . . I . . . do not desire to live with [her] . . . in Christian wedlock, and want . . . a divorce."[39] Lavrov was a peasant-worker from Pokrov District, Vladimir Province, who married a peasant girl from Dmitrov District, Moscow Province, whom he had met in factory work. The couple was married at the end of June 1898. The newlyweds then moved to a large industrial settlement in Bogorodsk District, east of Moscow, so that Lavrov could work at a local textile factory. But, as the unhappy husband reported, "I did not enjoy marital happiness for long. Shortly after our marriage, my wife said that she was not accustomed to such a monotonous life as they live [in the village], but that she loved 'society' and 'amusement'." Only after the wedding did Lavrov learn that

> before marrying me, she had lived four years in a Moscow brothel. You can be completely sure that after such a debauched and wild life . . . this [worker's] life for her really would be torture. There were many times when, after I left for work, my wife brought young men into my own apartment in my absence and remained alone with them until my return from work. And there were times that upon my return from work, I did not find her at home in the apartment. She appeared after such absences the next day, or the day after, always smelling of vodka. All my [attempts] to make her understand, all my exhortations, she stubbornly answered with silence, and at the present time she has renounced married life.

What made this case particularly striking were the identities of witnesses whom Lavrov named as persons able to verify his story: four of five of these witnesses were fellow peasant-workers from his factory who had themselves had "adulterous relations" with his wife.[40]

Beyond the family circle, fellow villagers also exerted considerable influence on the social behavior of their neighbors. In comparative studies of village life, historians have consistently noted "the tyranny of local opinion and the lack of tolerance displayed toward nonconformity and social deviation," the "high value set on social conformity by this tightly-knit, intolerant world."[41] In this, Russia was no exception. The noted historian of the Russian peasantry Boris Mironov has described how the peasant commune exercised "the strictest social control" over the behavior of locals, "a censorship of morals, from which in practice it was impossible to escape."[42] "Attendance at church and appropriate performance of all religious prescriptions played a major role in the formation of individual reputations," the Russian historical ethnographer M. M.

A Culture of Denunciation   201

Gromyko has observed. "Not only the elders in a family but the entire community would watch to see that youngsters did not miss especially important church services. The neighbors would tell a mother if her son was 'lazy' in going to mass."[43]

Usually, such information was passed on informally, anonymously, or as hearsay—in the third person, "I heard that your son . . ." format. Such oblique denunciations were part of the rich oral tradition of the Russian village, where "reputation [among Russian peasants] was attributed to families and could be passed on from generation to generation."[44] The village's "little community" had numerous ways of censuring the behavior of nonconformist fellow villagers: "Slander, character assassination, gossip, rumor, public gestures of contempt, shunning, cursing, backbiting, outcasting" were all sanctions that could be wielded effectively.[45] Almost a third of the cases of deviancy reviewed from the records of the Moscow Spiritual Consistory became known to parish priests through rumors: essentially, angry fellow villagers "let it be known" that a certain peasant was living improperly.[46]

Rumors served a distinct function within village communities. The anthropologist Max Gluckman, among others, has identified "the pervasive role of gossip in community life": "Gossip does not have isolated roles in community life, but is part of the very blood and tissue of that life."[47] A fundamental part of village life is that

> struggles between villagers are not fought openly . . . until crises are reached. Instead, differences of opinion are fought out in behind-the-back tattle, gossip, and scandal, so that many villagers, who are actually at loggerheads, can outwardly maintain the show of harmony and friendship. They remain a community, despite the verbal cut-and-thrust in the dark, where they try to advance their separate causes against their ostensible friends who are their enemies. Some accommodation is thus reached. In this gossip they evaluate people as leaders, as good villagers, and the like, so that gossip also serves to bring conformity with village values and objectives.[48]

By spreading rumors, villagers could criticize the behavior of their neighbors without actually taking it upon themselves to effect a breach—for to begin a feud within one's commune was to invite disaster. As the parish priest Father Mikhail Sokolov observed in village Petrovka, Vladimir Province, in 1899: "Peasants in general are a people who are very self-respecting and proud. Endeavor to offend a peasant . . . with a word, [expressing] some unflattering opinion about him—and he will remember it until he is presented with the chance to avenge [the offense]."⁴⁹ Open denunciations by a lone fellow villager against a neighbor were extremely rare; covert, behind-the-back attacks were far safer than open breaches.

Nevertheless, open condemnation of behavior that violated general norms was tolerated when backed up by support from other community members. Community opinion often acted as a force unto itself, restraining and—to a certain degree—directing the initiative of village priests. A powerful illustration of a community-based denunciation is the case of the literate, thirty-four-year-old peasant tradesman Vasilii Skvortsov, who had converted to a priestless sect of the Old Belief some ten years before his confrontation with his community. Although Skvortsov refused to reveal the agent of his conversion, "it was rumored that he had been seduced" by the ex-*volost* clerk, who had been removed from his official position for his nonconformist religious beliefs. As the local superintendent reported, Skvortsov had been subjected frequently to concerted entreaties by his parish priest, several fellow villagers, and even some monks who were brought in from a nearby monastery. Despite the imprecations, Skvortsov remained stubborn in his faith, declaring before witnesses to the parish priest: "I do not want to speak with you, nor hear your words and attempts to persuade me. I do not wish to be a follower of your faith, [since] I recognize it to be unjust. Think what you want of me, and report me to your authorities [if you must]."⁵⁰

Throughout the discussions and meetings that followed—"educational discussions" that civil and religious authorities forced Skvortsov to attend—Skvortsov met with the parish priest Mikhail Parusnikov as members of his family and community looked on. The community was duly mesmerized and scandalized as Skvortsov laid before them in intricate detail the content of his beliefs: his admission that he had in fact for some time "stood aloof from the Orthodox Church and [now] belonged to another community [*obshchina*]"; his Sunday services without priests, instead run by so-called Elders or spiritual advisers *(Startsy)*; his two-fingered sign of the cross (versus the post-Nikonian Orthodox three-fingered sign). After the first few meetings, where Skvortsov's family sat silently and listened, they stopped coming altogether. On the evening of 14 June 1877, Skvortsov's wife was notably absent. The next day, "despite his promise" to the parish priest, Skvortsov himself failed to show up for the meeting, leaving word simply that he had gone to Moscow. Outraged, the parish priest summoned Skvortsov officially through the *volost* administration, "in order to advise him again to return to Orthodoxy." On 18 June 1877, his commune passed a condemning resolution, which anathematized him for his defiance of local norms:

> We . . . the peasants of Serpukhov District, . . . Belopesotskii settlement . . . respectfully submit: Our neighbor the peasant Vasilii Filipov Skvortsov really did convert from Orthodoxy to the *raskol* some ten years ago. We have confirmed this directly. It is demonstrated by the fact that all this time Skvortsov has neither confessed nor taken part [in the spiritual life of the community.]. . . . The wife of Vasilii Skvortsov . . . has also converted to the *raskol*. This is demonstrated by the fact that she too began to go to Church rarely. Their children, as a result, will undoubtedly convert to the *raskol*. There have never been *raskol'niki* in our village, and if [Skvortsov] does not return to Orthodoxy, then we with all the peasants will try to throw him out of the commune. We will not tolerate the *raskol*.[51]

Against his will, Skvortsov was returned to his village on 5 July, when he had another long exchange with Father Parusnikov. At this time, Parusnikov demanded a written and signed account of Skvortsov's beliefs, and Skvortsov put him off by saying that "perhaps I will again start going to Church." From that time on, Skvortsov refused to meet with any priests, and he continued to defy the community's attempts to force him to desist. Eventually, his fellow villagers were true to their promise: Skvortsov was expelled from the commune altogether.

Such sober, openly defiant confrontations, though common, occurred far less frequently than the insidious, everyday forms of antagonism between Orthodox and Old Believer peasants. Such confrontations, denunciations, and counterdenunciations often led to violent skirmishes during the holiday season, when peasant labor-migrants were home for winter holidays, and when alcohol exacerbated the tensions and led to eruptions above the surface of official calm and toleration.[52]

Inevitably, the interests of priests and parishioners did not always coincide in the social regulation of morals. Sometimes, frustrated or disappointed with the inactivity of overburdened or negligent priests, communities would take matters into their own hands. This was especially facilitated by the fact that the Church hierarchy, always driven by the imperative of keeping its priests in line, readily took heed of the opinions of parishioners communicated outside official channels. In 1871, for instance, the peasant Nikofor Matveev—parish elder of the Church of Our Savior in the village of Arkhangel, Vereia District, Moscow Province—sent a petition of concern to the Moscow Spiritual Consistory on behalf of his fellow parishioners. The gist of Matveev's complaint was the alarming incidence of religious nonparticipation in his parish, where, owing to high rates of out-migration for side earnings, "up to 400 persons have not attended Confession in the past year." Matveev charged that the negligence of the parish priest, Matvei Vinogradov, had allowed more than half the parish to fall away from Orthodoxy. Upon investigation, the negligent priest was removed from his post.[53]

Numerous sources indicate that vigilante justice was often applied in cases where the parish priest either neglected or refused to heed denunciations. One particularly vivid case powerfully illustrates the role of *samosud*—peasant self-justice—in community control over peasant-workers who blatantly violated community norms.[54] In the village of Gridkina—a few kilometers from Shuiia (Vladimir Province)—in 1897, a young female peasant factory worker named Elena had begun to flout community norms: at the age of sixteen, she began to take lovers openly. As the recusant's parish priest reported: "Working at the factory, living on her own without any sort of family supervision, this girl began 'to roam about' *[shatat'sia]*—that is, to have lovers, of which she had several." Frustrated at the failure of the local priest to take the decadent woman in hand despite numerous denunciations of her immoral behavior, fellow workers gossiped bitterly. Eventually, some lads from her village instigated a plot to humiliate the recusant for her misdeeds. "They lay in waiting for Elena . . . while she walked from her factory in the town to her home in the village. As soon as she came alongside a cemetery along her route, the plotters seized her, raised her dress [above her waist], and tied the ends over her head with a noose and secured her in this way to one of the crosses [in the cemetery]. Here she hung until she was seen by others coming from the factory, who freed her from the ignominy" of her position.[55]

Police and People

As skyrocketing rates of peasant labor migration seriously challenged the skills of even vigilant parish priests, disgruntled peasant-workers and fellow villagers increasingly turned to state agents outside the village as channels for denunciations. Urban police archives are filled with written denunciations (usually anonymous) of fellow-workers accused of religious profligacy or of interfering in the religious life of the other workers.[56] For instance, a peasant-worker from Vladimir District, Grigorii Tarasov, had come to Moscow in 1867, when he was twenty-seven. He lived and worked in Moscow for almost six years. For the entire period he had identified himself as Orthodox on his passport. On his return from a two-month visit to his native village in August 1873, Tarasov presented a one-year passport in which he and his wife and young daughter were all listed as Old Believers of the Rogozhskii sect. A suspicious Moscow policeman—apparently tipped off by a denunciation from an unidentified source—noted the discrepancy and filed a secret report, which eventually made its way through the office of the chief of police to the Moscow Spiritual Consistory. The chief of police sent an inquiry to the Vladimir District police chief, asking whether Tarasov had in fact thrown aside Orthodoxy. The answer was expected, and conformed to a pattern of police experience: "Having lived without interruption for seven or eight years in Moscow, where he married, [his] creed was Orthodoxy." His family, consisting of a father and four brothers, were likewise Orthodox. It was clear, therefore, that Tarasov's "seduction *(sovrashchenie)* to the *raskol* had occurred in Moscow."[57]

The Moscow police moved quickly on the case, working jointly with the Moscow Consistory, which reconstructed Tarasov's life before and after his apostasy. They painted the following scenario: "Seventeen years from birth, arriving in Moscow, [Tarasov] started working for a schismatic, a furniture dealer, the Moscow petty merchant Aleksei Akimov (now deceased). After six years of living in the home of the schismatic Akimov, persuaded by his boss and with the blessing of his parents, who were themselves not steadfast Orthodox [believers, but were] inclined toward the *raskol*, he turned aside to the *raskol*."[58] In 1862, the twenty-three-year-old Tarasov married Praskov'ia Fedorova, a girl from a priestly sect.

Following the decree of the Holy Synod of 14 August 1808 regarding marriages of persons who had deviated to the *raskol*, the Consistory ruled the marriage invalid and the couple's marital state "adulterous." The husband and wife were forced to separate after almost twelve years together; this ruling was carried out on 24 December 1874, almost sixteen months from the time Tarasov's profligacy was first discovered. Tarasov remained in his Moscow apartment, while his wife Praskov'ia was forced to relocate to her former residence. Local officials were instructed to be vigilant and were made to sign oaths in which they swore to observe the couple's activities and to prevent a renewal of adulterous relations.[59]

It was standard operating procedure in city police stations to investigate cases of religious deviation and to report the results to Church officials.[60] The sheer effort expended in this and other cases illustrates the degree to which recusants and their apostasy were taken seriously. The documents reflect a close, friendly relationship between priests and police—although they were not as close as generations of Soviet historians have suggested by treating clerics and police as a reactionary monolith. Nonetheless, the style and language of police denunciations make it clear that priests often wielded considerable authority. It is as if the policemen, by upholding Orthodoxy, were paving their own paths to salvation. Typical were these reminiscences of Ivan Golyshev, a peasant lithographer from Vladimir Province. His father, a *volost* elder, was "a zealous upholder of Orthodoxy, persecutor of the *raskol*, who lived in great numbers in [our village]. He at every moment of his official service was concerned about the defense of Orthodoxy, and about the persecution of the *raskol*."[61]

One of the most complex associations in the Russian countryside was the relationship between village or parish opinion, the priest, and the local police. It would be hasty, as many Soviet historians have done, to lump priests and police together in the reactionary forces of Black Hundreds activity, pitted against the "progressive" and allegedly anticlerical and antireligious tendencies of the popular movement. As studies of this phenomenon in other areas of the world have shown, the real situation was far more complex. Just as Ku Klux Klan activity in the American South during the nineteenth century was aimed not just at terrorizing blacks, but also at intimidating whites who appeared "soft" on black issues, so too was Russian *samosud* or vigilante activity aimed not just at the deviant, but also at the potential deviants and nonconformists lurking within the community at large.[62] Though actual interventions were rare, every case of communal censuring of nonconformity was also a warning to the rest.

Preliminary research suggests the preeminent role in popular moral policing of Klan-style parish brotherhoods throughout Russia, founded on the rooting out and annihilation of religious dissenters and enemies of Orthodoxy. The brotherhoods, formed by militant and self-styled defenders of the faith, represented a conjoining of forces of local vigilantes with the rural police. The true precursors of the better-known Black Hundreds organizations which emerged in reaction to social crisis throughout Russia after 1905 (the Union of Russian People, the Society of the Archangel Michael) were the highly decentralized fraternal organizations like the Brotherhood of the Holy Cross, the Brotherhood of St. Nikolai, and the one which was largest and best known, the Brotherhood of Saint Peter Mitropolit. Founded in 1872 by members of the Russian Orthodox leadership, the Brotherhood of Saint Peter Mitropolit professed its intention to stamp out the Schism, "the deadly enemy of [Russia] and the [Russian Orthodox] Church."[63] It is no coincidence that such brotherhoods grew more common as the efforts of tsarist authority to regulate moral behavior diminished. During the last generations of Old Regime Russia, popular vigilantism grew to fill the vacuum left by waning institutional controls.

Regardless of the widespread role of militant parish brotherhoods for the defense of Orthodoxy, it is also clear that priests were not always pleased with policemen taking on the initiative as brutal saviors of souls, and it is my impression that the Black Hundreds more often than not came into conflict with "soft, overly indulgent" priests.[64] A prime illustration was a denunciation filed by the parish priest Father Mikhail Sareevskii against the local constable Kamenskii in the industrial village of Ivanovskoe, Moscow District, in the Church of Predtechevskaia in early December 1886.

> On the 26th of November, on the feast day of the Great Martyr Saint George in our Predtechevskaia Church, at the time of the Sacred Liturgy, the following event took place: the cossack's wife, Evdokia Pestova, who lives at the factory of the Reutovskaia Manufacturing Company, attended mass together with her friend, a peasant woman from Tver Province, Staritsa District, Blaginna village, Evdokeia Semenova, who also lives there [at the factory]. During the submersion of the Cross in holy water, before the Liturgy, Pestova suffered a fit: she cried out and fell lifelessly to the ground. In that condition she lay for some time, cared for by her friend throughout the service, at the end of which the local constable Kamenskii entered the Church. He stood near the prostrate Pestova and as soon as he saw her . . . lying there, he took her for a drunk and began to shake her, during which he uttered indecent and insulting words, summoned the deputy . . . , threatened to send her to the Iusupov [mental hospital], pounded her about the head and face and kicked her in the side; but Pestova still lay there without moving, lifeless.

Pestova's friend Semenova and others standing near the woman pleaded with Kamenskii not to disturb her, since they knew that she was a woman subject to seizures. But Kamenskii, cursing Pestova with words like "you pig" and other more indecent and insulting expressions, said that she was only pretending to be ill and that he would cure her.

All this Kamenskii said so loudly that it could be heard not only in the refectory but even at the altar, so that Kamenskii "with his conduct drew glances and the attention of everyone in the Church." Hearing the noise, Father Sareevskii had to send two ushers, one after another—the unfortunate Piatnitskii and Zaitsev—in order to get the constable to stop interrupting the service. But Kamenskii only answered that he knew well enough what to do without their advice, and continued with his disturbance. Angered by the notice he had drawn, he took violent reprisals on the poor woman's lifeless body with renewed vigor.

The priest, only halfway through the reading of the prayer for the tsar, had to stop and wait until the noise in the church subsided in order to proceed. Not wishing to interrupt the mass, Father Sareevskii again set about reading the prayer. Beside himself with rage, Kamenskii made another peasant, a certain Kolobov, aided by the hapless usher Zaitsev, carry the still-unconscious Pestova outside of the church. Kamenskii accompanied the pair, pushing Pestova all the way to the church porch.

> And when they had brought her to the jail and laid her down there, Kamenskii again began to stomp on the unconscious woman with his feet, screaming all the while in a rage expressions like: "You drunken bitch!" *[pianuiu stervoiu].* Later, when Pestova had come to, Kamenskii ordered her to go home and refused to admit her into the Church, even when she fell before him on her knees and begged forgiveness, [asking] for his permission to reenter the Church in order to pray. The usher Zaitsev, returning from the jail to the Church, grew afraid that Kamenskii might do something horrible to the poor woman, so he soon started back to the jail. Along the way, he met with Kamenskii, who told him: "I healed her and took her home." Having taken her home, Kamenskii again appeared in Church after the cherubic song.

Turning to the Church elder, Kamenskii was overheard to say: "I have the power to heal and to resurrect the dead," but was restrained from further conversation during the mass by the ever more vigilant Zaitsev. Father Sareevskii concluded his denunciation with a strong indictment: "I consider this transgression of the constable Kamenskii to have been an offense against the spiritual atmosphere and an insult to the moral sensibility of everyone present in the Church."[65]

REPUTATION, COMMUNITY OPINION, AND MORAL TYPING

> *I greatly fear something in him. After such apostasy, is it possible to believe in his friendship and honor? To a man who has changed his religion, what am I worth?*[66]

In these reflections of the Moscow-based Orthodox peasant-merchant Petr Medvedev from his unpublished diary in 1854, we find some indication of the degree to which religious deviation could disturb a complex web of social relationships. To ignore the powerful role of religion as a mediating force in social relationships is to miss one of the chief factors that defined, shaped, and largely explained Russian social behavior before the Revolution.

Peasant communities often applied subtle distinctions in the social control of out-workers. The sources suggest that some professions were deemed more reliable than others, and that some individuals, regardless of profession, were deemed trustworthy while others were more suspect and therefore subjected to the full line of pressures discussed throughout this study. This point is very important: while the intricate web of community-induced controls was universal for all, an ever-present reminder against straying too far from the path, explicit controls and, in particular, the assistance of community outsiders (especially state agents and the police) were as a rule restricted to those who, either because of individual shortcomings or by virtue of their professions, had acquired reputations for unreliability, untrustworthiness, or a propensity toward deviancy. Norms applied to all, but controls were imposed individually, *gliadia po cheloveku*, "depending on the person." Fellow villagers often distinguished patterns of behavior which could be attributed to certain professions, the distance between village and work place, frequency of home visits, preservation of religious belief, and a host of shared norms specific to each community. In ways in which written texts leave few hints, a locally derived, highly contextualized sensibility interpreted *otkhodnik* behavior.

A particularly insightful local perspective on the relationship between villagers and *otkhodniki* was presented in a report by A. A. Kurochkin, peasant correspondent to the Moscow *zemstvo* in 1899, whose village lay to the north of Moscow City, in Bronnitsy District. Kurochkin's account is valuable for the distinctions he draws between the wide variety of migrant occupations.

> Unfortunately, I must say that the majority of workmen living on the side (box-makers, blacksmiths, . . .), despite their seemingly tolerable earnings, abandon their village families to such misery, [leaving them with,] as they say, a "sexton's lot" *[ponamareva dolia]*—that is, an absolute trifle, with the larger part of [the migrants'] earnings usually dissipated in Moscow taverns either at billiards or drinking bouts.
>
> In contrast, from waiters there is incomparably more profit, although many admittedly view this profession with disdain. We have many [waiters] who work in sizable Moscow inns and most of them have not been so morally corrupted as the "skilled workers" *[masterovshchina]* mentioned above. They are considered in the village to be good providers and good heads of household. More often than not, they send to the village 200–250 rubles annually, and some even send 400–500 rubles in a year, which is clearly reflected in the healthy farmstead, decent clothes, good metal-roofed homes, and so forth. . . . In recent years it has become very popular for [local] peasants to try to settle their children in apprenticeships in Moscow clubs and restaurants.[67]

For Kurochkin, as for most of those who remained in the village, the main criterion for evaluating a worker was the degree of his support for his family in the village. What is most striking is the realization that in village popular opinion, the occupations themselves, regardless of the level of earnings, followed patterns of comparative support or abandonment of village responsibilities.

In the Russian countryside, the question of support was integrally tied to a peasant's reputation. For abandonment or neglect was not merely an economic issue, but a moral concern as well: those who abandoned their families in the village were believed to have been enticed by the temptations of urban life, morally corrupted by alcohol, billiards, and a surfeit of worldly goods. Reputation was the totality of the community's memory regarding any individual, and it was through the prism of the individual's reputation or perceived character that his social behavior was understood and social constraints applied or withheld.

Besides occupation, the distance of the work place from the village was also popularly believed to have exerted a powerful "moral" influence on peasant out-workers. This corresponds to my conclusions in chapter 5: the large majority of peasant migrants who worked within forty kilometers of their native villages sent substantial support back to their families. Among peasants who remained in the village, proximity became a principal factor determining the level of trust to be extended to departing workers. In Kurochkin's village, for instance, factory work was the most common side-occupation: all the female and more than half the male labor migrants were employed in factory labor. Kurochkin noted, however, that members of his community drew a sharp distinction between *domashnye fabrichnye,* those working year-round at the neighboring Shlikhterman factory only six kilometers from the village, and *fabrichnye na storone,* Moscow factory workers. Even though members of both groups lived full-time at the factory, the forty-nine "local" factory workers were considered to be far more conscientious of their responsibilities. "In the first place, never having moved away from the home, they see well all the vital needs and requirements of the household, as a consequence of which they are naturally more thrifty and close-fisted; they waste very little money. In contrast, '*Moskvichi,*' who rarely live with their families and have only the dimmest understanding of their needs, in the majority of cases eagerly give themselves up to every sort of temptation, as a result of which they drive their households into impossible decline."[68]

Kurochkin's village had an easy solution: to ensure fulfillment of dues and obligations by the high-risk *fabrichnye na storone* (fifteen men and six women from ten families), his commune had negotiated an arrangement with hiring contractors representing two factories in Moscow—the Zueva and Bogorodtsy works—whereby dues were deducted from earnings and sent directly to the village by factory administrators: "The land allotments [of the Moscow factory workers] are turned over for use by family members 'without charge,' and duties in full are sent by factory offices."[69]

This imposition of strict restraints was a common method by which to ensure fulfillment of obligations. Out of "fatherly concern," in the words of the peasant correspondent Ianov in Kaluga Province, local contractors or employers always made sure that stonemasons were left with little money of their own: "Such a bridle compels even a person with bad inclinations to behave properly. Knowing the weakness of some workers, the majority of contractors themselves send wages to the workers' families." In such circumstances, "Few [stonemasons] turn out to be profligates *[zabuldygi]*." Ianov expressed the consensus opinion of local peasants when he noted that, in contrast to these "bridled" stonemasons, scutchers *(trepachi)* from his village who worked in the flax industry were considered notoriously unreliable: they usually went "on the side" only in order "to free themselves of the control and supervision of their wives, fathers, and mothers, and in freedom to drink hard and to carry on disgracefully as much as they please." Although a common occupation in the village, at least one in ten of the scutchers was forced home under guard each year for immoral behavior.[70]

This general disdain and mistrust for certain types of *otkhodniki* was a characteristic element in village popular culture. "In our area," observed a peasant correspondent in Glumovskaia *volost,* Iur'ev-Pol'skii District, Vladimir Province, "there are two trades: carpentry and factory work. Carpentry is held in great respect, while factory work—although more make their living this way—is not, because among the people it is identified with a loss of morality, manifested as insolence [expressed] in various unseemly forms."[71]

Occupation and character were closely associated. For instance, sometimes industrial workers would leave factory work and open up their own businesses nearer their villages. As S. T. Semenov, a peasant correspondent from Volokolamsk District, Moscow Province, observed: "Such artisans are more 'restrained' *[vozderzhenno]* than factory workers, drink less, soon acquire a certain intellectual development, and are very thoughtful toward the agricultural economy: the 'portion sent home' from their side is more considerable."[72]

Heresy and Labor Migration: Deciphering Patterns of Denunciations

In this chapter, I have surveyed religious denunciations in the Russian countryside in the Moscow region during the last half of the nineteenth century. But it is quite clear that many of these denunciations were not motivated by religious issues alone: the language of the confrontations suggests that the denunciations were often a kind of popular theater that overlay tensions that were far more profound. For example, in one dispute a peasant migrant husband denounced his estranged wife in the terms of religious anathematization. But he also mentioned a host of other factors: "I am suffering enormous deprivation from my schismatic wife Matrena Nikolaeva, who with the help of her brothers—[also] schismatics—are taking all my property away from me. [She] says that it is all hers and not mine. I have turned to the police with a petition, but received no help."[73] For this peasant, religious denunciation against his wife and her family was a last desperate attempt to block his own economic marginalization. He was like a drowning man clutching at a straw, using a religious denunciation only when other more direct tactics had failed.

Similarly, when Orthodox parishioners in the village of Ignatovo, Bogorodsk District, Moscow Province, collectively signed a resolution denouncing their village elder in July 1884, they did so using the language of religious anathematization to argue for a resolution in their favor of a dispute about economic exploitation.

> The elder—the schismatic Ivan Arkhipov—is himself also a long-standing malevolent enemy of the Church. In order to get revenge on us . . . , he tries to hurt us in every possible way. He, both as a rich man and as a factory owner who has on his side rather many accomplices-schismatics among his fellow villagers, makes things up and accuses us of crimes that we never committed. Some of us he drags into court. Others—using his wealth—he puts under arrest. Still others he threatens with banishment from the commune and exile to some distant province. Others he threatens with the most horrible misfortunes. And others he entices with money—so that from our elder there is neither a life nor a livelihood for us Orthodox peasants of Ignatovo village.[74]

The villagers in this case appealed for the "heretic"-elder's removal on the basis of a law of 9 March 1839 that prohibited election of non-Orthodox officials in areas where a large number of Orthodox Christians resided.[75] This tactic could sometimes be relied upon to upset the normal order of communal self-management through appeal to an outside agency that could settle local feuds and vendettas in favor of the weaker party. In short, where direct challenges failed, religious anathematization could often be relied upon to confuse issues and possibly tilt ongoing disputes toward a more favorable resolution.[76]

The anthropologist Basil Sanson identified such accusations as a tactical strategy, as a means of modifying the relationship between the perpetrator and his denouncer. Religious denunciations often served as a convenient method to degrade the status of the accused, to profoundly alter the nature of social relationships in the village, to radically invert village hierarchies.[77] Understood in this way, acts of building or impugning reputations—distribution of acclamation and defamation, praise and denunciation, approbation and disapprobation, patronage and ostracization, blackballing or exclusion in village gossip networks—were assuredly an integral part of the language of rural power and control, where kinship and religious factors were equally if not more important than economic and social stratification. In everyday village life, it was not only structural forces such as wealth, class, and power that determined status but, rather, popular conceptions of reputation and popular, locally grounded definitions of morality. In village society, an individual's "good name" was his "most vital social possession," yet—paradoxically—also his most vulnerable one, since a good name was not held but conferred by other members of the community.[78] As the anthropologist J. G. Peristiany observed: "Honour and shame are the constant preoccupations of individuals in small-scale, exclusive societies where face-to-face personal, as opposed to anonymous, relations are of paramount importance."[79] In this lay the vital premise for establishing a central and fluid role for reputation as a mediator of all social relationships of peasants inside and outside their native villages.

Given the central importance of a peasant's reputation in village relations, it was precisely the channel of building or impugning social reputations that best defined the various formal and informal networks of social control which developed as peasant labor migration challenged traditional forms of regulating community members. An outsider—such as a state agent, a policeman, employer, or creditor—through complex and subtle ways tapped into the fund of common knowledge about locals that made up each peasant's social reputation.

As we have seen, a peasant's reputation in village society carried considerably more weight than the mere question of tolerance or intolerance by fellow villagers. As James Scott has argued, "Reputation in any small, closely knit community has very practical consequences. A peasant household held in contempt by their fellow villagers will find it impossible to exchange harvest labor, to borrow a draft animal, to raise a small loan, to marry their children off, to prevent petty thefts of their grain or livestock, or even to bury their dead with any dignity."[80] In Russia as elsewhere, to flout community norms was to risk not just one's reputation but also, inevitably, one's livelihood. Conversely, to impugn a peasant's reputation was to challenge directly his or her ability to make ends meet, for the social milieu of the Russian peasantry before the Revolution was indeed a context fraught with need and a disproportionate reliance on patronage and personal contacts, or *znakomstvo,* in order to survive from one season to the next.⁸¹ In the universe of the Russian peasant, reputation and opportunity were inextricably fused.

One example will illustrate the brutal realities of this fundamental relationship between reputation and opportunity. The peasant commune could be ruthless against members who ignored their village obligations and then found themselves rendered unproductive by bad health or accidents. The only exceptions were those peasant-workers with other productive kin in the village who were willing to take on extra mouths to feed. One peasant-worker, Stepan Burylin of Troitskaia settlement, Morodovskaia *volost,* Dmitrov District, Moscow Province, had flagrantly neglected his village responsibilities all his life, but having no family in the commune, somehow managed to evade punishment with minimal payments sent to his village irregularly. In 1893, his health ruined at age forty-five by heavy factory labor, Burylin was forced to retire to his village.

Almost immediately, Burylin's commune began to apply inexorable sanctions. Branded an "irredeemable scofflaw" for his lifetime neglect of village responsibilities, Burylin was soon after ostracized from his community. To cover his accumulated arrears, Burylin's commune seized everything, "and I have neither a home, nor any kind of peasant life *[osedlost]*, and have received . . . no allotment." Adding insult to injury, the commune also demanded exorbitant payments—a "wanderer's tax" of two rubles per month to cover current dues on his seized allotment, plus accumulated arrears. That rate was equivalent to nearly 400 percent the average assessment on the standard peasant allotment. As Burylin described his dire circumstances in a petition written in his own hand to the Moscow governor in September 1893:

> [I write] . . . regarding the imposition on me by the commune at Troitskaia settlement of a landless or wanderer's tax and the failure to issue to me a written [travel] certificate for industrial work, without which I not only cannot pay the Commune arrears *[guliadskie nedoimki]*, but cannot even support my young family of eight persons. Without [this passport] I myself and even my children must of necessity seek subsistence, clothes, and shoes by begging alms.

Without any means of subsisting in the village, and deprived of the right of a passport until he paid past obligations, Burylin could do nothing but live in penury, wandering with his wife and six children like a beggar: "I am able [to live] only like a tramp deported under guard from one place to another."⁸² Burylin appealed unsuccessfully for "a written passport, without which I cannot legally be absent anywhere [away from the village], constantly exposing [myself] to deportation for lacking proper travel documents, and the accumulation of more and more arrears."[83]

Denunciation as an act of impugning reputations was not exclusively the weapon of peasants against fellow peasants. Other social groups also seized on reputation as a means of social control. It is common, for instance, to find reports that village officials had willfully and arbitrarily *(proizvol'no)* abused their authority by compromising the reputation of a successful local: insiders who threatened local hierarchies by their very success (measured by the attention they received from outsiders) were denounced as politically and morally suspect. As the peasant-lithographer in Vladimir Province, Ivan Golyshev, recalled with indignation, it was not uncommon for suspicious, envious, or resentful local elites to order through the *volost* courts "punish[ment] with lashes, in order to completely discredit and besmirch a person."[84] Local village officials had their own way of dealing with upstarts: they were secretly denounced; they were harassed, jailed, even whipped; they were exiled, or sent off for military service. Here too, acts of denunciation or repression were not ends in themselves but, rather, they became part of the paper trail that followed (and haunted) suspected "political unreliables" in the tsarist system.[85]

Employers also tried to impugn the moral characters of peasant-workers in order to subordinate them and to isolate troublemakers. In 1888, to take just one of myriad examples, Vladimir N. Suvirov, a merchant of the first guild and owner of a cloth factory in Moscow District, withheld wages due a peasant-worker, Osipov, because Osipov had left for field work prior to the end of his contracted period (1 September 1888). Osipov filed a countercomplaint against his employer with the local police in an attempt to recover the unpaid wages. Eventually, both Osipov and his wife (who worked together at the factory for a mere eighteen rubles per month) were deprived of passports and exiled to their village because Osipov allegedly posed "a most evil *[durnoi]* example . . . for the rest of those working at the factory." The "nefarious influence" was their "willful disrespect" *(svoevolnoe bezobrazie)* and, alleged Suvirov (probably slanderously), Osipov's drunken behavior.[86]

In the three hundred cases of denunciation reviewed here, I have found that the overwhelming majority of village "heretics"—by my reckoning nearly 90 percent of those whose occupations were recorded—were peasant-workers who migrated for earnings outside the village. Why did peasant-workers constitute the vast majority of persons denounced on religious and moral grounds? Ultimately, the answer lies in the popular culture of denunciation: the peasants' use of religious denunciations to settle personal scores. Local squabbles between feuding clans were fought within peasant "little communities" by drawing on the language and rhetoric of the official struggle against religious sectarianism which the Russian Orthodox Church had waged since the mid-seventeenth century. Essentially, rival local forces used the language of religious anathematization as a means to isolate, undermine, or destroy opponents. To adapt a phrase from Evans-Pritchard's work on witchcraft, it is in the idiom of religious denunciations that Russian peasants expressed moral rules that lay mostly outside of criminal and civil law.[87]

The evidence from the Moscow Consistory supports the notion that the distinguishing characteristic of the overwhelming majority of "heretics" was their link to migration for side-earnings. Village communities worked to protect themselves from the nefarious influence of nonconformity conveyed by the stories, habits, and style of peasants who had experienced life outside their villages. Even when peasant-workers wandered far beyond the village boundaries they remained subject to village norms. A typical case was that of fifty-five-year-old peasant-worker Spiridonov, who was denounced as a heretic collectively by fellow villagers in a communal resolution addressed to the district chief of police.[88] The report of the police constable in Veria made it very clear that Spiridonov's principal "moral" offense lay in his refusal to abide by his community's rules: "Spiridonov's family is not well provided for materially and has accumulated nearly 170 rubles in unpaid fiscal dues. Members of the family receive a means of subsistence from day work, but in view of the limited [availability of such work] they suffer extreme hardship. . . . Spiridonov, as his fellow villagers explained, roams *[skitaetsia]* in Moscow without any fixed occupation or residence. . . . No earnings are sent to his family. No one can say anything definite about Spiridonov's behavior and morals, since for quite some time he has not appeared for work and no one keeps up a correspondence with him."[89] In this case, the mere absence of reliable information regarding Spiridonov's behavior, combined with the relatively low standard of living of his dependents in the village, were sufficient grounds to excoriate him. Subsequently banished from his commune in 1895 "because he cannot be a wholesome member of the commune," Spiridonov learned the hard way the fruitlessness of flagrantly ignoring communal opinion: judged to be a "grave threat" *(ves'ma vrednyi)* to his commune, he was prohibited from living or working in Moscow Province.[90]

None of this discussion is intended to deny, however, that those branded "heretics" may in fact have been nonconformists. Indeed, there is considerable evidence to support the argument that peasant labor-migrants as a social group showed a higher propensity to rebel against village traditions and to challenge village norms. The real question here is why peasant labor-migrants in particular were singled out for their heresy, even as others were not. We must recognize that the declining insularity of communal life reflected in the staggering growth of peasant labor migration did pose a serious threat to traditional village hierarchies. A powerful illustration is the way in which peasant-workers who had become "politically conscious" through contact with "reds" or labor organizers were anathematized as religious heretics. Fëdor Samoilov, who grew up to become a Bolshevik peasant-worker from northeast Vladimir Province, described an event that took place following a major strike among textile workers in Ivanovo-Voznesensk in 1905:

> In the beginning of September in my village, with which I then still had a connection, a characteristic event took place that vividly illustrated the attitude of the clergy of that time toward the strike and revolutionary movement. My father came to the town and, in an agitated manner, told my brother and me that our parish priest Dmitrii from the village of Lezhnevo, after a religious procession that took place in the village every year at this time, had at the end of the service delivered before the peasants a reactionary sermon [*pogromnaia propoved*] in which he unequivocally summoned them to deal with all strikers and revolutionaries, mentioning my brother and me by name, which—so it seemed to my father—made the peasants very hostile to us.[91]

It was inevitable that the scapegoats in the popular culture of denunciation would be selected representatives from the very channel through which change had been introduced into the village: the peasant labor migrants.

What is perhaps most fascinating is that the migrants themselves often refused to accept anathematization at face value but, instead, counterposed an alternative social vision that was itself deeply rooted in the language and traditions of the Schism: consciously or unconsciously, many peasant-workers found in the Old Belief a support for their own rebellion against the binding ties of their villages. For instance, battling the powerful forces favoring endogamy that would anchor the peasant laborer to his native community by forcing him to marry a local village girl, a peasant-worker "fell away" from the Church by simply taking a wife of his own choosing. The language and practice of religious dissent became the pool from which opponents to traditional forms of social control drew their strength. They refused to bow down to authority, because "according to the sacred books, one should not bow down before icons or priests." They became indifferent to the rites of the Church, but retained their Christian and religious identities by insisting on their own right to stand before God alone, "without your damned icons, without your accursed priests, without your bloody Evangelists!"[92]

As dramatic and forceful as were these cases of religious anathematization of peasant labor-migrants under the Old Regime, they paled in comparison to the attacks that marked the Soviet era, most notably during the early years of collectivization. Peasant denunciations from the period 1927–1932 substantiate that peasant labor-migrants were often singled out by nonmigrating fellow villagers as pernicious enemies of Soviet power and active opponents to socialized agriculture. Provoking widespread envy among less fortunate fellow villagers, and self-marginalized by their very absence from village meetings, *otkhodniki* were often ruthlessly attacked in dekulakization campaigns.[93] For instance, the peasant Pavel Vasil'evich Belov in Tver District—a self-styled spokesman for the real, 'pure-blooded peasants' *(chistokrovnye krest'iane)*— passionately denounced all peasant labor migrants as vicious enemies of collectivization: "The *otkhodnik* . . . , having earned decent money 'on the side,' comes home with quite a purse, and copes well with taxes, [while] he clothes and provides for his family and even has enough left over for drinking. This is an indisputable fact, and no decrees or other incentives will persuade him to join the collective."[94] In Belov's village, any peasant-worker who had labored more than a year outside the village was stripped of his land, largely to protect the collective from so-called *kulaki-otkhodniki,* rich and greedy peasant labor-migrants.[95]

This apparent continuity illustrates one very important and remarkable point: while the language and content of peasant denunciations in Russia changed according to context and opportunity, the pool of "heretics" seems to have remained more or less the same. The primary victims of village religious denunciation during the last generations of the Old Regime, the peasant labor migrants were likewise prime candidates for the label "enemies of the people" in villages during the early years of Soviet power.[96]

APPENDIX

ABBREVIATIONS

NOTES

GLOSSARY

BIBLIOGRAPHY

INDEX

APPENDIX

Appendix 1. Reduction in Redemption Payments, 1881 (37 Provinces of European Russia)

Regions and Provinces	Total Households	Manorial Households	Proportion Manorial	Vykup Before Reductions	General Sum Reduction	Percent Reduction
I. Nonagricultural	**2,744,086**	**1,452,979**	**52.95%**	**24,411,178**	**7,341,591**	**30.07%**
North and Northwest	1,010,679	501,494	49.62	8,141,374	3,146,195	38.64
[Arkhangel]	n.a.	n.a.	n.a.	n.a.	n.a.	n.a.
Vologda	157,023	42,287	26.93	639,245	142,579	22.30
Olonets	46,306	2,018	4.36	25,704	23,705	92.22
St. Petersburg	88,668	55,983	63.14	946,503	424,515	44.85
Novgorod	176,365	79,551	45.11	1,206,266	510,717	42.34
Pskov	124,603	72,141	57.90	1,066,771	411,694	38.59
Smolensk	163,912	118,108	72.06	2,096,633	870,704	41.53
Tver	253,802	131,406	51.78	2,160,252	762,281	35.29
Central Industrial	**1,474,834**	**913,638**	**61.95**	**15,742,933**	**4,082,084**	**25.93**
Iaroslavl	160,688	96,467	60.03	1,693,118	318,807	18.83
Moscow	181,907	103,858	57.09	1,979,036	729,867	36.88
Vladimir	192,580	119,810	62.21	2,026,788	420,067	20.73
Kostroma	199,504	114,548	57.42	1,790,959	538,851	30.09
Kaluga	145,114	102,432	70.59	1,844,457	578,783	31.38
Nizhnii Novgorod	208,160	125,070	60.08	1,958,102	506,271	25.86
Tula	163,103	120,390	73.81	2,258,719	422,215	18.69
Riazan	223,778	131,063	58.57	2,191,754	567,223	25.88
Belorussia	**258,573**	**37,847**	**14.64**	**526,871**	**113,312**	**21.51**
Vitebsk	116,757	4,740	4.06	65,570	12,983	19.80
[Minsk]	174,232	n.a.	n.a.	n.a.	n.a.	n.a.
Mogilev	141,816	33,107	23.35	461,301	100,329	21.75
II. Southern Agricultural	**1,360,557**	**415,251**	**30.52**	**4,437,421**	**1,001,174**	**22.56**
Ukraine	1,360,557	415,251	30.52	4,437,421	1,001,174	22.56
Poltava	331,153	120,666	36.44	1,024,493	182,455	17.81
Kharkov	275,960	78,122	28.31	963,940	196,153	20.35
Chernigov	270,352	107,707	39.84	1,148,635	396,023	34.48
[Kiev]	337,162	n.a.	n.a.	n.a.	n.a.	n.a.
[Volynia]	245,626	n.a.	n.a.	n.a.	n.a.	n.a.
[Podolia]	330,559	n.a.	n.a.	n.a.	n.a.	n.a.
Kherson	187,293	57,725	30.82	682,964	111,678	16.35

Appendix 1. (continued)

Regions and Provinces	Total Households	Manorial Households	Proportion Manorial	Vykup Before Reductions	General Sum Reduction	Percent Reduction
Ekaterinoslav	200,145	45,663	22.81	546,324	97,177	17.79
Taurida	95,654	5,368	5.61	71,065	17,688	24.89
[North Caucasus]	n.a.	48,406	n.a.	580,514	151,476	26.09
[Don Oblast]	n.a.	48,406	n.a.	580,514	151,476	26.09
III. Central Agricultural	**3,038,042**	**692,178**	**22.78**	**10,820,237**	**2,233,022**	**20.64**
Central Chernozem	1,115,090	398,679	35.75	6,383,879	1,337,164	20.95
Voronezh	300,545	61,487	20.46	1,048,390	224,908	21.45
Kursk	277,159	99,506	35.90	1,560,051	301,911	19.35
Orlov	233,506	119,662	51.25	2,009,281	423,315	21.07
Tambov	303,880	118,024	38.84	1,766,157	387,030	21.91
Volga	1,922,952	293,499	15.26	4,436,358	895,858	20.19
Astrakhan	45,325	2,903	6.40	30,715	9,093	29.60
Saratov	265,839	77,712	29.23	1,159,501	211,432	18.23
Samara	291,352	20,793	7.14	328,750	61,834	18.81
Penza	191,978	82,706	43.08	1,218,064	256,366	21.05
Simbirsk	190,059	60,855	32.02	974,225	176,601	18.13
Kazan	296,618	26,105	8.80	399,409	97,366	24.38
Viatka	397,479	6,466	1.63	88,053	29,573	33.59
Ufa	244,302	15,959	6.53	237,641	53,593	22.55
IV. Eastern Agricultural	**313,222**	**73,657**	**23.52**	**814,404**	**234,671**	**28.82**
Ural	313,222	73,657	23.52	814,404	234,671	28.82
Perm	199,406	69,995	35.10	764,372	225,476	29.50
Orenburg	113,816	3,662	3.22	50,032	9,195	18.38
Total	**7,455,907**	**2,634,065**	**35.33**	**40,483,240**	**10,810,458**	**26.70**

Source: Household data from Russia, Ministerstvo Vnutrennykh Del, Tsentral'nyi statisticheskii komitet, *Konskaia perepis' 1882 goda* (St. Petersburg, 1884), pp. 69–96. Data on reductions from *Ponizhenie vykupnogo platezha* (St. Petersburg, 1885), pp. 82–111.

Note: Bracketed provinces are excluded from aggregate numbers.

ABBREVIATIONS

d.: *delo,* archival or manuscript file

ed. khr.: *edinitsa khraneniia,* archival unit of preservation, generally but not always the same as *delo*

f.: *fond,* archival collection

g.: *god,* year

GAIaO: Gosudarstvennyi Arkhiv Iaroslavskoi Oblasti (State Archive of Iaroslavl Oblast, Iaroslavl)

GARF: Gosudarstvennyi Arkhiv Rossiiskoi Federatsii (State Archive of the Russian Federation, Moscow)

GME: Gosudarstvennyi Muzei Etnografii (State Museum of Ethnography, St. Petersburg)

l.: *list,* manuscript sheet or page in an archival file (pl. ll.: *listy*)

ob.: *obratnaia storona,* the reverse side of a manuscript page

op.: *opis,* inventory number of an archival file

PSZ: Polnoe sobranie zakonov (Complete Collection of Russian State Laws)

RGAE: Rossiiskii Gosudarstvennyi Arkhiv Ekonomiki (Russian State Archive of the Economy, Moscow)

RGALI: Rossiiskii Gosudarstvennyi Arkhiv Literatury i Iskusstva (Russian State Archive of Literature and Art, Moscow; formerly, TsGALI)

RGB: Rossiiskaia Gosudarstvennaia Biblioteka (Russian State Library, Moscow)

RGIA: Rossiiskii Gosudarstvennyi Istoricheskii Arkhiv (Russian State Historical Archive, St. Petersburg; formerly, TsGIA SSSR)

SP: Sushchestvuiushchii poriadok vzimaniia okladnykh sborov s krest'ian. Po svedeniiam, dostavlennym podatnymi inspektorami za 1887–1893 gg. (Materialy dlia peresmotra uzakonenii o vzimanii okladnykh sborov), 2 vols. (St. Petersburg, 1894–1895)

t.: *tom,* volume number in multivolume archival file or published collection

TsGIAgM: Tsentral'nyi Gosudarstvennyi Istoricheskii Arkhiv goroda Moskvy (Central State Historical Archive for Moscow City)

NOTES

The Politics of Reputation

1. This operational definition of the peasant commune *(mir, obshchina, obshchestvo)* may be contrasted to the more detailed exposition in the excellent article by Boris N. Mironov, "The Russian Peasant Commune After the Reforms of the 1860s," *Slavic Review* 44, no. 3 (Fall 1985): 441–42.

2. From an unpublished report of a *zemstvo* correspondent cited in V. V. Petrov, "Promysly i vne-zemledel'cheskie zarabotki v zimy 1893–94 goda," *Sel'skokhoziaistvennyi obzor Tverskoi gubernii za 1894-i god* (Tver', 1895), 2: 7.

3. Georg Lukacs, "Reification and the Consciousness of the Proletariat," in *History and Class Consciousness: Studies in Marxist Dialectics* (Cambridge, 1971), pp. 83–84.

4. In recent years, an enormous body of research has developed in Western historiography regarding peasants' everyday forms of resistance. Peasant communities, confronted with a superior force, appeared to comply, even as they "fought" from within to destroy the system to its core. The accumulation of small deeds—everything from petty pilfering to foot-dragging, grain hoarding to machine-breaking—was a potent force in peasant resistance before and after the Revolution. See especially: James C. Scott, *Weapons of the Weak: Everyday Forms of Peasant Resistance* (New Haven, 1985), *Domination and the Arts of Resistance: Hidden Transcripts* (New Haven, 1990), and "Resistance Without Protest and Without Organization: Peasant Opposition to the Islamic *Zakat* and the Christian Tithe," *Comparative Studies in Society and History* 29, no. 3 (July 1987): 417–52. In Russian/Soviet historiography, see Rodney Bohac, "Everyday Forms of Resistance: Serf Opposition to Gentry Exactions, 1800–1861," in Esther Kingston-Mann and Timothy Mixter, eds., *Peasant Economy, Culture, and Politics of European Russia, 1800–1921* (Princeton, 1991), pp. 236–60; Daniel Field, *Rebels in the Name of the Tsar* (Boston, 1976), pp. 208–15; and Tat'iana Mironova, "Bytovye formy soprotivleniia protiv kollektivizatsiia," paper presented at the first World Agrarian Conference, Moscow, June 1990.

5. James C. Scott, "Protest and Profanation: Agrarian Revolt and the Little Tradition," *Theory and Society* 4 (1977): 5.

6. Under the heading of an analysis of the role and significance of ideology in peasant protest, this very issue became a matter of heated debate among Soviet students of the Russian peasantry in the 1970s and 1980s. See a summary of the main positions in a work by V. A. Fedorov, *Krest'ianskoe dvizhenie v tsentral'noi Rossii, 1800–1860 (Po materialam tsentral'no-*

promyshlennykh gubernii) (Moscow, 1980), pp. 12–14. In addition, see Fedorov's *Pomeshchich'i krest'iane tsentral'no-promyshlennogo raiona Rossii (kontsa XVIII–pervoi poloviny XIX v.)* (Moscow, 1974).

7. V. I. Lenin, *Collected Works* (Moscow, 1964), 3: 40.

8. Classic and recent works containing this brand of Soviet historiography are: A. G. Rashin, *Formirovanie rabochego klassa Rossii* (Moscow, 1958); A. M. Pankratova, "Proletarizatsiia krest'ianstva i ee rol' v formirovanii promyshlennogo proletariata Rossii (60–90e gg. XIX v.)," *Istoricheskie zapiski* 54 (1955): 194–220; M. K. Rozhkova, "Fabrichnaia promyshlennost' i promysly krest'ian v 60–70-kh godakh XIX veka," in L. M. Ivanov, ed., *Problemy sotsial'no-ekonomicheskoi istorii Rossii* (Moscow, 1971), pp. 195–217, and *Formirovanie kadrov promyshlennykh rabochikh v 60-kh–nachale 80-kh godov XIX v.* (Moscow, 1974); P. G. Ryndziunskii, *Utverzhdenie kapitalizma v Rossii* (Moscow, 1978), and *Krest'iane i gorod v kapitalisticheskoi Rossii vtoroi poloviny XIX veka (Vzaimootnoshenie goroda i derevni v sotsial'no-ekonomicheskom stroe Rossii)* (Moscow, 1983).

9. Olga Crisp, "Labour and Industrialization in Russia," in *The Cambridge Economic History of Europe*, vol. 7, pt. 2 (Cambridge, 1978), pp. 362–63. Emphasis added.

10. Classic works in English on the role of peasant side-work in the village economy are: G. T. Robinson, *Rural Russia Under the Old Regime* (London, 1932); Teodor Shanin, *The Awkward Class* (Oxford, 1972), and *Russia as a Developing Society: The Roots of Otherness*, vol.2, *Russia 1905–1907: Revolution as a Moment of Truth* (London, 1986); Richard Robbins, *Famine in Russia, 1891–1892* (New York, 1975); Anita B. Baker, "Deterioration or Development? The Peasant Economy of Moscow Province Prior to 1914," *Russian History/Histoire Russe* 5, no. 1 (1978): 1–23; R. Munting, "Outside Earnings in the Russian Peasant Farm: The Case of Tula Province, 1900 to 1917," *Journal of Peasant Studies* 3 (1976): 428–46. For an insightful analysis of the transition from peasant origins to working-class consciousness, see Reginald Zelnik, "Russian Bebels: An Introduction to the Memoirs of Semen Kanatchikov and Matvei Fisher," *Russian Review* 35 (1976): 249–89, 417–47.

11. Representative works in English are: Theodore Von Laue, "Russian Labor between Field and Factory," *California Slavic Studies* 3 (1964): 33–66, and "Russian Peasants in the Factory," *Journal of Economic History* 23 (1961): 61–80; Leopold Haimson, "The Problem of Social Stability in Urban Russia, 1905–1914," in Wayne Vucinich, ed., *The Peasant in Nineteenth-Century Russia* (Stanford, 1968), pp. 158–90; Robert Eugene Johnson, *Peasant and Proletarian: The Working Class of Moscow in the Late Nineteenth Century* (New Brunswick, 1979).

The "peasantization" hypothesis originally appeared in the work of Moshe Lewin, *Russian Peasants and Soviet Power: A Study of Collectivization* (Evanston, 1968), and has since been adapted in various ways and contexts by several historians. Most representative are: John Bushnell, "Peasants in Uniform: The Tsarist Army as a Peasant Society," *Journal of Social History* 13 (1980): 563–74; Ben Eklof, "Peasant Sloth Reconsidered: Strategies of Education and Learning in Rural Russia Before the Revolution," *Journal of Social History* 14 (1981): 355–85; and Anne Louise Bobroff, "Working Women, Bonding Patterns, and the Politics of Daily Life: Russia at the End of the Old Regime" (Ph.D. diss., University of Michigan, 1982).

12. Von Laue, "Russian Peasants in the Factory," p. 74. On the peasant versus proletarian controversy, see Jerzy G. Gliksman, "The Russian Urban Worker: From Serf to Proletarian,"

in *The Tranformation of Russian Society: Aspects of Social Change Since 1861*, ed. Cyril F. Black (Cambridge, 1960); David Pretty, "Neither Peasant nor Proletarian: The Workers of the Ivanovo- Voznesensk Region, 1885–905" (Ph.D. dissertation, Brown University, 1997); and Diane Koenker and William G. Rosenberg, "Skilled Workers and the Strike Movement in Revolutionary Russia," *Journal of Social History* 19, no. 4 (1986): 605–29.

13. See Johnson, *Peasant and Proletarian*, passim. For arguments for the early Soviet era, see William Chase, *Workers, Society, and the Soviet State: Labor and Life in Moscow, 1918–1929* (Urbana, 1987); and more recently, David Hoffman, *Peasant Metropolis: Social Identities in Moscow, 1929–1941* (Ithaca, 1994).

14. One notable exception is the recent study of Russian peasant women workers by Barbara Alpern Engel, *Between the Fields and the City: Women, Work, and Family in Russia, 1861–1914* (Cambridge, 1994). Also see the work of Robert J. Brym and Evel Economakis, who correlate peasant origins with working-class militancy in individual factories. Brym and Economakis, "Peasant or Proletarian? Militant Pskov Workers in Petersburg, 1913," *Slavic Review* 53, no. 1 (Spring 1994): 120–39; Evel G. Economakis, "Patterns of Migration and Settlement in Prerevolutionary Petersburg: Peasants from Iaroslavl and Tver Provinces," *Russian Review* 56, no. 1 (1997): 8–24; and Economakis, "Patterns of Peasant Recruitment and the Making of the St. Petersburg Industrial Working Class" (Ph.D. dissertation, Columbia University, 1994).

15. Boris N. Mironov, "Traditsionnoe demograficheskoe povedenie krest'ian v XIX–nachale XX v.," in A. G. Vishnevskii, ed. *Brachnost', rozhdaemost', smertnost' v Rossii i v SSSR. (Sbornik statei)* (Moscow, 1977), p. 84. For a similar notion, see A. F. Kistiakovskii, "K voprosu o tsenzure nravov u naroda," *Zapiski Imperatorskogo Russkogo Geograficheskogo Obshchestva po otdeleniiu etnografii*, vol. 8 (St. Petersburg, 1878).

16. Keith Thomas, *Religion and the Decline of Magic* (New York, 1971), p. 527.

17. F. G. Bailey, "Gifts and Poison," in *Gifts and Poison: The Politics of Reputation* (Oxford, 1971), pp. 2, 4.

18. Ibid., p. 2.

Part I. Emancipation, Interregnum, and Rural Crisis

1. S. I. Kanatchikov, *Iz istorii moego bytiia* (Moscow-Leningrad, 1929), 1: 9. His father repeated the warnings when he left him at the factory. The memoir has been translated by Reginald E. Zelnik as *A Radical Worker in Tsarist Russia: The Autobiography of Semën Ivanovich Kanatchikov* (Stanford, 1986). There is also a partial translation of this and other workers' memoirs in Victoria E. Bonnell, ed., *The Russian Worker: Life and Labor Under the Tsarist Regime* (Berkeley, 1983). For a useful psychological study of the peasant-worker struggle for consciousness, see Zelnik, "Russian Bebels."

2. Kanatchikov grew up in Lezhnevo village, Volokolamsk District, Moscow Province.

3. Kanatchikov, *Iz istorii moego bytiia*, 1: 6.

4. Ibid., p. 4.

5. Kanatchikov quotes this proverb with a certain sense of sorrow and anxiety upon his father's death. See ibid., pp. 130–31: "With my father's death the last thread that had tied me to

my home, to my village, was torn away. . . . While my father was alive, dimly, unconsciously, but stirring within me nonetheless had been some kind of vague feeling of 'obligation,' 'responsibility.' Now all that was torn away and vanished forever." His sense of loss was palpable: "Of all the feelings I experienced, the most painful was the sense that I was now alone, with myself, with my thoughts, feelings, and doubts."

6. Ibid., 1: 7–9.

7. Mary Matossian, "The Peasant Way of Life," in *The Peasant in Nineteenth-Century Russia,* ed. Wayne S. Vucinich (Stanford, 1968), p. 31: "When a young peasant is drafted, the whole village mourns him. He is expected to go on a drunken debauch until the date he is to report for duty. The village holds a *pechal'nyi pir* (sorrowful repast) for him, at which professional wailers bewail his loss in the name of his mother, wife, sister, and other dear ones. After being blessed by his parents, the recruit is accompanied by a great crowd of peasants to the outskirts of the village."

8. F. N. Samoilov, *Po sledam minuvshego* (Moscow, 1934), p. 21.

9. F. N. Samoilov, *Vospominaniia ob Ivanovo-Voznesenskom rabochem dvizhenii,* vol. 1, *1903–1905 gg.* (Moscow, 1921), p. 9. *Po sledam minuvshego* is a less reliable abridged version; I use it only for the newly added sections where Samoilov recounted his childhood years. Some biographical details of this Bolshevik peasant-worker *cum* Duma representative have been confirmed in the official biography by L. K. Vinogradov, *Fedor Samoilov* (Moscow, 1961).

10. Samoilov, *Po sledam minuvshego,* p. 24; Samoilov, *Vospominaniia,* 1: 9.

11. Samoilov, *Po sledam minuvshego,* p. 24.

12. Ibid., pp. 24–25.

13. Samoilov, *Vospominaniia,* 1: 10–11; Samoilov, *Po sledam minuvshego,* p. 37.

14. See B. V. Tikhonov, *Pereseleniia v Rossii vo vtoroi polovine XIX v. (po materialam perepisi 1897 g. i pasportnoi statistiki)* (Moscow, 1978); A. A. Kaufman, *Sibirskoe pereselenie na iskhode XIX veka* (St. Petersburg, 1901); K. R. Kachorovskii, "Krest'ianskoe khoziaistvo i pereselenie (Itogi razmerov i rezul'tatov pereselencheskogo dvizheniia za istekshee tridtsatiletie)," *Russkaia mysl'* 1894, no. 6.

Chapter 1. The Roots of Ambivalence

1. For a fascinating interpretation of the social, economic, and demographic significance of the patriarchal multiple-family household in serf Russia, see V. A. Aleksandrov, *Sel'skaia obshchina v Rossii (XVII–nachala XIX v.)* (Moscow, 1976), p. 304; Peter Czap, Jr., "Marriage and Peasant Joint Family in the Era of Serfdom," in David Ransel, ed., *The Family in Imperial Russia: New Lines of Historical Research* (Bloomington, 1978), pp. 103–123; Steven L. Hoch, "Serfs in Imperial Russia: Demographic Insights," *Journal of Interdisciplinary History* 13, no. 2 (Autumn 1982): 221–246, and *Serfdom and Social Control in Russia: Petrovskoe, a Village in Tambov* (Chicago, 1986).

2. P. G. Ryndziunskii, *Krest'ianskaia promyshlennost' v poreformennoi Rossii (60–80e gody XIX v.)* (Moscow, 1966), p. 68.

3. S. V. Pakhman, *Obychnoe grazhdanskoe pravo v Rossii* (St. Petersburg, 1879), 2: 140.

4. Ibid., p. 142.

5. A. A. Leont'ev, *Volostnoi sud i iuridicheskie obychai krest'ian* (St. Petersburg, 1895), p. 115.
6. Ibid.
7. For the evolution of *krugovaia poruka*, see S. A. Shchepot'ev, "Krugovaia poruka v bytovom i fiskal'nom otnoshenii," *Severnyi vestnik*, 1886, no. 7, sec. 2 (July), pp. 1–19; 1886, no. 8, sec. 2 (August), pp. 1–24. Mutual responsibility for peasant dues and obligations was abolished on 26 February 1903.
8. Peter Czap, Jr., "The Perennial Multiple Family Household, Mishino, Russia 1782–1858," *Journal of Family History* 7, no. 1 (Spring 1982): 25.
9. There are several fine works on the logic of household and estate organization in Russia under serfdom. A selection of the best among these are: Hoch, "Serfs in Imperial Russia," and *Serfdom and Social Control*; Czap, "Marriage and Peasant Joint Family," and "The Perennial Multiple Family Household." See also V. A. Aleksandrov, *Obychnoe pravo krepostnoi derevni Rossii XVIII–nachalo XIX v.* (Moscow, 1984), and "Tipy sel'skoi obshchiny v pozdne feodal'noi Rossii (XVII–XX vv.)," in *Problemy tipologii v etnografii* (Moscow, 1979), pp. 92–104.
10. For a classic account, see M. I. Tugan-Baranovsky, *The Russian Factory in the Nineteenth Century* (New York, 1970), pp. 363–412. There are several informative Soviet works on the sources of industrial wage labor in the Central Industrial Region. See E. V. Matveeva, "Formirovanie proleteriata v tekstil'noi promyshlennosti Kostromskoi gubernii (80–90-e gg. XIX v.)," *Uchenye Zapiski Kostromskogo Gosudarstvennogo Pedagogicheskogo Instituta*, no. 24, *Istoriia* (Kostroma, 1971), pp. 70–88; M. G. Meierovich, "Fabrichno-zavodskaia promyshlennost' Iaroslavskoi gubernii v nachale XX v.," *Vestnik Iaroslavskogo Universiteta*, no. 1, (Iaroslavl', 1972), pp. 62–70; idem, "O proiskhozhdenii promyshlennykh rabochikh Iaroslavskoi gubernii (kontsa XIX–nachala XX v.)," *Vestnik Moskovskogo Universiteta*, series 9, 1969, no. 6, pp. 26–42; idem, "Ob istochnikakh popolneniia fabrichno-zavodskogo proletariata v epokhu imperializma (na materialakh Iaroslavskoi gubernii)," *Istoriia SSSR*, 1980, no. 5, pp. 151–168; idem, "On the Sources from Which Factory and Plant Workers Were Recruited in the Imperialist Era (Based on Data from Iaroslavl Guberniia)," *Soviet Studies in History* 19, no. 4 (Spring 1981): 43–77; Pankratova, "Proletarizatsiia krest'ianstva"; A. G. Rashin, *Formirovanie promyshlennogo proletariata v Rossii. Statistiko-ekonomichesikie ocherki* (Moscow, 1940); Rozhkova, *Formirovanie kadrov*; B. N. Vasil'ev, "Formirovanie promyshlennogo proletariata Ivanovskoi oblasti," *Voprosy Istorii*, 1952, no. 6, pp. 99–117; idem, "K kharakeristike formirovaniia proletariata v Rossii (po materialam Vladimirskoi, Kostromskoi i Iaroslavskoi gubernii)," *Uchenye Zapiski Shakhtinskogo Pedagogicheskogo Instituta*, vol. 2, pt. 2 (Shakhta, 1957).
11. Russia, Ministerstvo finansov, Departament okladnykh sborov, *Sushchestvuiushchii poriadok vzimaniia okladnykh sborov s krest'ian. Po svedeniiam, dostavlennym podatnymi inspektorami za 1887–1893 gg. (Materialy dlia peresmotra uzakonenii o vzimanii okladnykh sborov)*, 2 vols. (St. Petersburg, 1894, 1895), hereafter *SP*, 2: 48. These largely untapped reports did not in most cases present a rigorous statistical accounting, but rather a general overview of patterns of peasant economy and tax collection in the years 1887–1893 in each of the fifty provinces of European Russia. Viewed in their entirety, they give us a much better picture of the actual institutional forces at work in the countryside than do the legal guidelines alone.

Each report consisted of a detailed summary of information on eight main subjects:

(1) the procedures for distributing tax burdens—state, land, and communal obligations; (2) the extent of tax relief within the commune to counteract the temporary decline of the economic position of some households (the viability of mutual responsibility *(krugovaia poruka)* and so-called supplementary apportionments *(dopol'nitelnye raskladki))*; (3) the use of coercive measures against individual peasant households for the payment of taxes and exaction of arrears—the relative roles of the rural commune, rural officials, and the police; (4) the measures used to guarantee payment of assessed dues by heads of peasant households living on the side (away from the village); (5) the procedures used by police to recover arrears from individual households bound together by mutual responsibility; (6) the procedures of tax collection in villages with less than forty households (where *krugovaia poruka* was not in force) and also in areas where land was privately owned; (7) the main causes of the accumulation of arrears in different areas; (8) the degree of cooperation between members of the police and tax inspectors relative to this survey. For the comprehensive study of the mechanisms used to control *otkhodniki,* section four is of particular interest.

For comparison, the best short study of taxation in villages of the Central Agricultural Region is A. S. Ermolov, *Neurozhai i narodnoe bedstvie* (St. Petersburg, 1892), pp. 154–93. Also, V. Trirogov, *Obshchina i podat' (sobranie issledovaniia)* (St. Petersburg, 1882).

In fact, in Vladimir Province, there was only one case in which apportionment of dues was not based on landholding: this was in Melenki District, where ironworkers assessed every adult worker individually, without regard for communal land use: a whole *tiaglo* or share for adult males aged eighteen to fifty-five, and a half-share for males aged fifteen to eighteen and fifty-five to sixty.

12. For detailed statistics on the regionalization of methods used to extract dues from peasants, see S. Arkhangel'skii, "Krest'iane krepostnoi derevni Moskovskogo promyshlennogo raiona vo vtoroi polovine 18 veka (po dannym votchinnykh instruktsii)," *Arkhiv istorii truda v Rossii* (Petrograd, 1923), bk. 8, pp. 135–47; I. D. Koval'chenko, "Rassloenie obrochnykh krest'ian Tsentral'no-promyshlennogo raiona vo vtoroi chetverti XIX v.," *Materialy po istorii sel'skogo khoziaistva i krest'ianstva SSSR* 4 (1966): 140–95; idem, *Russkoe krepostnoe krest'ianstvo v pervoi polovine XIX v.* (Moscow, 1967); N. M. Shepukova, "K voprosu o chislennosti barshchinnykh i obrochnykh pomeshchikh krest'ian Evropeiskoi Rossii vo vtoroi polovine XVIII v.," *Ezhegodnik po agrarnoi istorii vostochnoi evropy 1964 god* (Kishinev, 1966), p. 408; V. A. Fedorov, "Barshchina i obrok v tsentral'no-promyshlennykh guberniiakh Rossii v pervoi polovine XIX v.," ibid., p. 323; V. I. Semevskii, *Krest'iane v tsarstvovanie Ekateriny II,* vol. 1 (St. Petersburg, 1881), pp. 492–93; A. Skrebitskii, *Krest'ianskoe delo v tsarstvovanie imperatora Aleksandra II,* vol. 3 (Bonn-on-the-Rhine, 1865–66), pp. 1265–67.

13. See E. L. Mints, *Otkhod krest'ianskogo naseleniia na zarabotki v SSSR* (Moscow, 1925), pp. 10–11. Also see the perceptive analysis by Alexander Gerschenkron, "Russia: Agrarian Policies and Industrialization, 1861–1917," in *Continuity in History and Other Essays* (Cambridge, Mass., 1968), pp. 174–85.

14. The classic work on the abolition of serfdom contrasts agricultural areas, where allotments were reduced so as to ensure a continued supply of peasant labor for demesne agriculture, with nonagricultural areas, where noble landlords were reimbursed for lost quitrent income by redeeming land at inflated prices. See P. A. Zaionchkovskii, *Otmena krepostnogo prava v Rossii,* 3d ed. (Moscow, 1968), pp. 301–02. In his excellent article on the impact of the

1861 reforms on landlord-peasant relations in chernozem areas, N. M. Druzhinin evaluated the varying degrees to which these designs were realized: "The Liquidation of the Feudal System in the Russian Manorial Village (1862–1882)," *Soviet Studies in History* 21, no. 3 (Winter 1982–83): 14–67.

15. For detailed gross and regional statistics on the growth of peasant labor migration in European Russia, see tables 1.2 and 1.3. In the same way, the Soviet collective farm system under Leonid Brezhnev operated on the presumption that subsistence-oriented peasants would manage to survive through self-exploitation on private plots. For a provocative account, see the work by the Soviet agronomist Lev Timofeev, *Soviet Peasants (Or, The Peasants' Art of Starving)* (New York, 1985).

16. *SP*, 2: 48.

17. *SP*, 2: 49.

18. To avoid confusion with migrant labor as it is more popularly understood in the West, I will retain the Russian terms. *Otkhod* or *otkhodnichestvo* refers to the departure of a peasant worker *(otkhodnik)* for outside earnings.

19. Except where otherwise indicated, all the data on migration in the next four paragraphs is taken directly from P. A. Vikhliaev, "Ob ustoichivosti vnezemledel'cheskikh otkhozhepromyslovykh zarabotkov sel'skogo naseleniia," *Narodnoe khoziaistvo*, 1900, no. 3, pp. 74–76. Also see Mints, *Otkhod krest'ianskogo naseleniia*, pp. 10–11, 16–18, 22–24.

20. Statistics on peasant labor migration were taken from the multivolume series *Rossiia: Polnoe geograficheskoe opisanie nashego otechestva*, edited by V. P. Semenov (Tian'-Shanskii). Data for Moscow, Vladimir, Tver', Iaroslavl', Kostroma, Nizhnii Novgorod, and Kaluga Provinces from V. V. Morochevskii, "Promysly i zaniatiia naseleniia," in vol. 1, *Moskovskaia promyshlennaia oblast' i verkhnee povol'zhe* (St. Petersburg, 1899), pp. 184–86. Data for Tula and Riazan' from V. P. Semenov, "Promysly i zaniatiia naseleniia," in vol. 2, *Srednerusskaia chernozemnaia oblast'* (St. Petersburg, 1902), pp. 260–64. Data were also drawn from Vikhliaev, "Ob ustoichivosti," pp. 73–90; V. Kolpenskii, "Otkhozhie promysly krest'ian po ofitsial'nym dannym 90-kh godov 19-go veka," *Arkhiv istorii truda v Rossii*, bk. 11/12 (1924), pp. 220–228; Z. M. and N. A. Svavitskii, *Zemskie podvornye perepisi, 1880–1913: pouezdnye itogi* (Moscow, 1926), pp. 45–54. More recently, P. G. Ryndziunskii, *Krest'iane i gorod*, p. 106, drawing upon data for the seven central industrial provinces—Moscow, Vladimir, Kaluga, Kostroma, Nizhnii Novgorod, Tver', and Iaroslavl'—showed that 1.8 million annual passports were issued in 1897.

21. The aggregate data are confirmed by myriad local studies. For instance, in Vladimir around 1900, as much as 60 percent of all adult peasant males worked on the side. A. V. Smirnov, "Chto chitaiut v derevne," *Russkaia mysl'*, 1903, no. 7, p. 113. In Moscow, in 1885, fifteen passports were issued for every ten peasant families: eleven for men, four for women. "Vidy na zhitel'stve, vydannye krest'ianskomu naseleniiu Moskovsk. gub. v 1880–1885 g.g.," *Statisticheskii ezhegodnik Moskovskogo gubernskogo zemstva 1886 g.* (Moscow, 1886), pt. 6, p. 7.

22. K. I. Vorob'ev, *Otkhozhie promysly krest'ianskogo naseleniia Iaroslavskoi gubernii. Statisticheskii ocherk* (Iaroslavl', 1903), p. 3.

23. N. N. Vladimirskii, *Otkhod krest'ianstva Kostromskoi gubernii na zarabotki* (Kostroma, 1927), p. 73.

24. D. N. Zhbankov, *Otkhozhie promysly v Smolenskoi gubernii v 1892–95 gg.* (Smolensk,

1896). See the summary in N. A. Karyshev, "Narodno-khoziaistvennye nabroski: Otkhozhie promysly Smolenskoi gubernii," *Russkoe bogatstvo,* 1897, no. 6, pp. 180–85.

25. S. N. Prokopovich, "Krest'ianstvo i poreformennaia fabrika," *Velikaia Reforma: Russkoe obshchestvo i krest'ianskii vopros v proshlom i nastoiashchem* (Moscow, 1911), 6: 270. Peasant women's migration for side-earnings has received considerable attention in recent years. See Bobroff, "Working Women"; Rose L. Glickman, *Russian Factory Women: Workplace and Society, 1880–1914* (Berkeley and Los Angeles, 1984); Engel, *Between the Fields and the City;* and Mandakini Arora, "Boundaries, Transgressions, Limits: Peasant Gender Roles in Tver' Province, 1861–1914" (Ph.D. dissertation, Duke University, 1995).

26. Prokopovich, "Krest'ianstvo i poreformennaia fabrika," p. 271.

27. D. N. Zhbankov, "Vliianie otkhozhikh promyslov na dvizheniia naseleniia za 1866–1890 gg." *Vrach* 16, no. 24 (1895): 637.

28. Compiled from inventories in D. N. Zhbankov, *Bab'ia storona: statistiko-etnograficheskii ocherk (Materialy dlia statistiki Kostromskoi gubernii,* no. 8) (Kostroma, 1891), pp. 103–10.

29. From an unpublished report of a *zemstvo* correspondent cited in A. V. Smirnov, "Sostoianie mestnykh i otkhozhikh promyslov naseleniia Vladimirskoi gubernii vesnoi i letom 1899 goda," *Obzor Vladimirskoi gubernii v sel'skokhoziaistvennom otnoshenii za 1899 god,* no. 3 (Vladimir, 1900), p. 33. (The original peasant correspondents' reports have, unfortunately, been destroyed.) On the impact of migration in northwestern Kostroma, see Barbara Alpern Engel, "The Woman's Side: Male Out-Migration and the Family Economy in Kostroma Province," *Slavic Review* 45, no. 2 (Summer 1986): 257–71. For a useful comparative perspective, see Gay L. Gullickson, "The Sexual Division of Labor in Cottage Industry and Agriculture in the Pays de Caux: Auffay, 1750–1850," *French Historical Studies* 12, no. 2 (Fall 1981): 177–99.

30. A. V. Smirnov, "Zemledelie i zemledelets tsentral'noi promyshlennoi gubernii," *Russkaia mysl',* 1901, no. 7, p. 174. Based on a study of 100,000 households in Murom, Melenki, Vladimir, Suzdal, and Viazniki Districts, Vladimir Province. On the relative ignorance of male *otkhodniki* about agricultural work in general, see Zhbankov, *Bab'ia storona.*

31. On traditional life-cycle patterns, see the insightful demographic analysis by Hoch, "Serfs in Imperial Russia," pp. 221–46. The age of return varied with economic conditions, but did show an upward tendency after 1890.

32. "Vliianie otkhozhikh promyslov," p. 636.

33. Referring to the high-migration Chukloma District, Kostroma Province, in the 1870s. Adapted from a passage cited in James I. Mandel, "Paternalistic Authority in the Russian Countryside, 1856–1906" (Ph.D. diss., Columbia University, 1978), pp. 113–14.

34. *SP,* 2: 100. For similar complaints in Vladimir and Iaroslavl', see pp. 55, 71.

35. Smirnov, "Sostoianie mestnykh," p. 34. Also, Smirnov, "Zemledelie i zemledelets," p. 183. For an informative comparative anthropological analysis of the effects of wage labor on traditional peasant family organization, see Eric Wolf, *Peasants* (New York, 1966), pp. 70–72.

36. From an unpublished report of a *zemstvo* correspondent cited in Smirnov, "Zemledelie i zemledelets," p. 184.

37. From an unpublished report of a *zemstvo* correspondent cited in Smirnov, "Sostoianie mestnykh," pp. 33–34.

38. See especially V. Dadonov, "'Russkii Manchestr" (Pis'ma ob Ivanovo-Voznesenske),"

Russkoe Bogatstvo, 1900, no. 12, p. 58. For comparable evidence from other areas, see Tugan-Baranovsky, *The Russian Factory,* p. 410; Zhbankov, *Bab'ia storona,* pp. 25–27.

39. From an unpublished report of a *zemstvo* correspondent cited in Smirnov, "Sostoianie mestnykh," p. 33.

40. Z. N., "O krest'ianskikh semeinykh razdelakh," *Pravo,* 1901, no. 12, p. 638. In 1874, Russia adopted a universal military draft and reduced the period of service from twenty-five to six years, with further reductions in the period of service depending on the conscript's level of formal education. As a result of this change, the proportion of young men serving in the military increased to one-third among eligible peasant males. While formerly, draftees rarely returned, or returned only when they had been been disabled by injury, sickness, or old age, many of the new draftees after the 1874 reform returned to their native villages while they were still vigorous and strong young men who had experienced the ways of the world. While Z. N., the author of the cited passage, identified the universal draft as a significant factor in peasant life (an interpretation I am inclined to accept), an American historian has provocatively challenged this accepted view of military service as a mechanism of change in the Russian village. See Bushnell, "Peasants in Uniform."

41. From the report of the peasant *zemstvo* correspondent Avdeev, in Kozel'sk District, Kaluga Province, "Sostoianie promyslov," *Statisticheskii obzor Kaluzhskoi gubernii za 1896 god* (Kaluga, 1897), pt. 2, p. 49.

42. From an unpublished report of a *zemstvo* correspondent, ibid., p. 38.

43. T. S. Stepanov, peasant correspondent from Molodinskaia *volost',* Podol'sk District, Moscow Province. "Promysly i vne-zemledel'cheskie zarabotki v zimu 1888–89 gg.," *Statisticheskii ezhegodnik Moskovskoi gubernii za 1889 g.* (Moscow, 1889), sec. 3, pp. 21–22. On this issue, see the study of village youth culture by Stephen Frank, "Simple Folk, Savage Customs?" See also the works by Engel: "Peasant Morality and Pre-Marital Relations in Late Nineteenth-Century Russia," *Journal of Social History* 23, no. 4 (1990): 695–714; Engel, "St. Petersburg Prostitutes in the Late Nineteenth Century: A Personal and Social Profile," *Russian Review* 48, no. 1 (January 1989): 21–44; Engel, "The Woman's Side"; and Engel, *Between the Fields and the City.* And finally, Christine D. Worobec, *Peasant Russia: Family and Community in the Post-Emancipation Period* (Princeton, 1991), p. 145.

44. Stepanov, "Promysly i vne-zemledel'cheskie zarabotki v zimu 1888–89 gg.," p. 37. It is important to emphasize that we are dealing here with perceptions, not hard facts. I would argue that this general consensus of a rising trend of peasant immorality was less a reflection of reality than a symptom of insecurity among dependent peasants who remained in the countryside. That perception dictated strict control over migrant behavior, which resolves the apparent paradox between the assertion of abandonment and vulnerability on the one hand (discussed here in chapter 1), and the widespread evidence of migrant support for village dependents (discussed in chapter 5), on the other.

45. From an unpublished report of a *zemstvo* correspondent cited in Smirnov, "Sostoianie mestnykh," pp. 34–35.

46. Ibid., p. 34.

47. See the tendentious summary in F. V. Livanov, *Raskol'niki i ostorozhniki. Ocherki i rasskazy,* 4th ed., vol. 1 (St. Petersburg, 1872), pp. 356–57. For research that confirms popularly perceived ties between labor migration, urban life, and immorality, see Laurie Bernstein,

Sonia's Daughters: Prostitutes and their Regulation in Imperial Russia (Berkeley and Los Angeles, 1995), pp. 91–93; Engel, *Between the Fields and the City,* pp. 81–83; and Worobec, *Peasant Russia,* pp. 145–50.

48. Reginald E. Zelnik, "'To the Unaccustomed Eye': Religion and Irreligion in the Experience of St. Petersburg Workers in the 1870s," *Russian History/Histoire Russe* 16, nos. 2–4 (1989): 302.

49. Diutkova village, Kubinskaia *volost',* Vereia District, Moscow Province. "Promysly i nezemledel'cheskie zarabotki krest'ian Moskovskoi gub. v 1899–1900 g.," *Statisticheskii ezhegodnik Moskovskoi gubernii za 1900 god* (Moscow, 1900), sec. 2, p. 22.

50. From an unpublished report of a *zemstvo* correspondent cited in G. I. Baskin, "Mestnye i otkhozhie promysly," *Obzor Vladimirskoi gubernii v sel'skokhoziaistvennom otnoshenii za 1897 god* (Vladimir, 1898), p. 499.

51. Tritskaia *volost',* Klin District, Moscow Province. "Promysly i vne-zemledel'cheskie zarabotki v zimu 1888–89 gg.," *Statisticheskii ezhegodnik Moskovskoi gubernii za 1889 god* (Moscow, 1889), sec. 3, p. 17.

52. Russia, Komissiia dlia issledovaniia polozheniia sel'skogo khoziaistva v Rossii, *Doklad vysochaishe uchrezhdennoi komissii dlia issledovaniia nyneshnego polozheniia sel'skogo khoziaistva i sel'skoi proizvoditel'nosti v Rossii* (St. Petersburg, 1873), cited by N. K. Brzheskii, *Ocherki iuridicheskogo byta krest'ian* (St. Petersburg, 1902), p. 112. P. A. Valuev was the president of the commission. Also see I. N. Milogolova, "Semeinye razdely v Russkoi poreformennoi derevne (na materialakh tsentral'nykh gubernii)," *Vestnik Moskovskogo Universiteta,* series 8, *Istoriia,* 1987, no. 6, pp. 37–47; and idem, "Sem'ia i semeinyi byt russkoi poreformennoi derevni, 1861–1900 gg. (na materialakh tsentral'nykh gubernii)," Kand. ist. nauk., Moscow State University, 1988.

53. Brzheskii, *Ocherki iuridicheskogo byta krest'ian,* p. 156; V. A. Fedorov, "Semeinye razdely v Russkoi poreformennoi derevne," in *Sel'skoe khoziaistvo i krest'ianstvo severo-zapada RSFSR v dorevoliutsionnyi period* (Mezhvuzovskii sbornik nauchnykh trudov) (Smolensk, 1979), p. 30. For contemporary accounts, see Smirnov, "Zemledelie i zemledelets," p. 183.

54. Brzheskii, *Ocherki iuridicheskogo byta krest'ian,* p. 112.

55. A correspondent to the Tenishev survey, cited in Fedorov, "Semeinye razdely," p. 33.

56. From an unpublished report of a *zemstvo* correspondent cited in Smirnov, "Sostoianie mestnykh," p. 33.

57. "Razdely semeinye," *Entsiklopedicheskii slovar',* F. A. Brokgauz and I. A. Efron, eds., 82 vols. (St. Petersburg, 1890–1904). See also A. A. Isaev, "Znachenie semeinykh razdelov krest'ian," *Vestnik Evropy,* 1883, no. 7, pp. 333–49; V. P. Vorontsov, "Semeinye razdely i krest'ianskoe khoziaistvo," *Otechestvennie zapiski,* 3d ser., vol. 266 (1883), no. 1, pp. 1–23; no. 2, pp. 137–61. More recently, Cathy A. Frierson has downplayed the impact of family divisions on village life. See "*Razdel:* The Peasant Family Divided," *Russian Review* 46 (1987): 35–52.

58. Isaev, "Znachenie semeinykh razdelov krest'ian," p. 337.

59. For a good summary of the effects of migration on family and demographic ratios, and the comparative regional development of peasant household structures in European Russia, see the articles by B. N. Mironov and A. G. Vishnevskii, in A. G. Vishnevskii, ed., *Brachnost', rozhdaemost', smertnost' v Rossii i v SSSR (Sbornik statei)* (Moscow, 1977). More recently, see

R. E. Johnson, "Family Relations and the Rural-Urban Nexus: Patterns in the Hinterland of Moscow, 1880–1900," in D. L. Ransel, ed., *The Family in Imperial Russia: New Lines of Historical Research* (Illinois, 1978), pp. 263–79.

60. I. M. Liadov, "Iuridicheskie obychai krest'ian Shuiskogo uezda," *Ezhegodnik Vladimirskogo gubernskogo statisticheskogo komiteta*, vol. 1, no. 2 (Vladimir, 1877), p. 81. Also see Brzheskii, *Ocherki iuridicheskogo byta krest'ian*, p. 112.

61. See Frierson, *"Razdel,"* for a summary of nineteenth-century opinion. Also see C. A. Frierson, *Peasant Icons: Representations of Rural People in Late Nineteenth-Century Russia* (Oxford, 1992). Z. N. has argued that the unexpected positive effect of the ineffective state law promulgated in 1886 to restrict unauthorized divisions *(samovol'nye razdely)* was to regularize the process of division and to formalize the definitions of *dvor* and *domokhoziain*—household and head-of-household, two key components in communal assessment schemes. Most dividing families found it advantageous to secure the prior approval of the communal assembly: "Ultimately, the role of the village commune is [merely] to sanction the division which has in fact already been completed. But although in such cases the confirmation by the village commune of family divisions by means of its resolution often appears to be only a formal act, the newly divided family tries quickly to confirm its division by a verdict of the commune. This is explained by the fact that legal division gives the newly separated member of the family several fairly important rights: he is recognized in everything as possessing equal legal rights *[ravnopravnost']* with other *domokhoziaeva* and receives the right of personal voice in the commune. During repartition of the land, as a representative of an individual household he has the right to demand an allotment for himself.... Moreover, the recognized *domokhoziain*, according to the resolution, pays taxes and arrears only for himself and is not bound to pay such [duties] for the former family, from which he has formally divided. In this there exists a practical, real meaning of the formality" (p. 636). For a similar expression, see F. G. Terner, "Krest'ianskie platezhi i sposoby ikh vzyskaniia," *Vestnik Evropy* 1895, no. 10, p. 450.

62. Z. N., *Pravo*, 1901, no. 12, p. 639. A similar interpretation was presented by A. D. Pedashenko and I. N. Syrnev in Semenov, *Rossiia*, 1: 105–06. Pedashenko and Syrnev likewise cited *otkhodnichestvo* and wage-earning among junior household members as key factors in promoting family divisions. See also: Smirnov, "Zemledelie i zemledelets," p. 183; Brzheskii, *Ocherki iuridicheskogo byta krest'ian*, p. 112.

63. V. Dadonov, "'Russkii Manchestr'," p. 58.

64. Ibid.

65. For examples, see Zhbankov, *Bab'ia storona*, pp. 24–25; Tugan-Baranovsky, *Russian Factory*, pp. 407–12.

66. Zhbankov, *Bab'ia storona*, pp. 25–27. This translation was adapted from an abridged passage in Tugan-Baranovsky, *Russian Factory*, p. 410.

67. See Zhbankov, *Bab'ia storona*, pp. 24–25; Tugan-Baranovsky, pp. 406–08. Prior to 1861, forced labor away from the village was also a way of punishing tax delinquents. See Fedorov, *Pomeshchich'i krest'iane*.

68. Kanatchikov, *Iz istorii moego bytiia*, 1: 9. For a vivid description of his father's violent rampages, see p. 7. Cf. Samoilov, *Po sledam minuvshego*, p. 13.

69. F. F. Erisman, comp., *Sbornik statisticheskikh svedenii po Moskovskoi gubernii, Otdel sanitarnoi statistiki* (Moscow, 1882), vol. 3, pt. 4, p. 124.

70. For a chronology of the rate of divestment and reinvestment into peasant agriculture in the Central Industrial Region, see Vikhliaev, "Ob ustoichivosti," pp. 89–90. For similar recent Soviet statements, see Ryndziunskii, *Krest'iane i gorod,* pp. 112–13; and V. A. Fedorov, "Krest'ianin-otkhodnik v Moskve (vtoraia polovina XIX v.)," *Russkii gorod (issledovaniia i materialy),* vol. 6, (Moscow, 1983), pp. 191–203. On reductions of land obligations, see Russia, Ministerstvo Vnutrennykh Del, Tsentral'nyi Statisticheskii Komitet, *Ponizhenie vykupnogo platezhi* (St. Petersburg, 1885), appendix, pp. 82–111. The relevant data have been reproduced in the appendix of this book.

71. I. M. Krasnoperov, "Otkhozhie promysly," *Statisticheskii ezhegodnik Tverskoi gubernii za 1897 god* (Tver', 1898), pt. 2, p. 28.

72. A. A. Bulgakov, *Sovremennyia peredvizheniia krest'ianstva. Napravleniia, razmery i usloviia krest'ianskikh dvizhenii Moskovskoi gubernii po novym tsifrovym dannym za desiatiletie 1894–1903 gg.* (St. Petersburg, 1905), pp. 15–16. Also on *zabroshennaia zemlia* (deserted or neglected allotment lands), see the detailed study of Iaroslavl' Province: A. P. Svirshchevskii, ed., *Otkhozhie promysly krest'ian Iaroslavskoi gubernii (Obzor Iaroslavskoi gubernii,* no. 2), (Iaroslavl', 1896). Local tax reports contain several examples of the ubiquitous horror stories of imprudent communes which had permitted unrestricted departures in the early years after Emancipation. See, for examples, *SP,* 2: 69, 100.

Part II. In Defense of Peasant Patriarchalism

1. On Stolypin's reforms, see David A. Maccy, *Government and Peasant in Russia, 1861–1906* (Dekalb, 1987), and Mandel, "Paternalistic Authority."

2. There are several excellent studies which demonstrate the administrative and policing roles of the manorial system before 1861. Most notably, see Fedorov, *Krest'ianskoe dvizhenie,* and *Pomeshchich'i krest'iane;* Koval'chenko, *Russkoe krepostnoe krest'ianstvo;* and Hoch, *Serfdom and Social Control.*

3. A review of the decisions of the general assembly of the Governing Senate *(Resheniia Obshchego Sobraniia Pravitel'stvuiushchego Senata)* for the first fifteen years following the abolition of serfdom reveals that the main focus of cases was jurisdictional: to define the proper procedures and jurisdiction of the newly created government agencies. It is clear that legal chaos reigned well into the 1870s. For all intents and purposes, there was an interregnum of state power in the countryside. The first substantive issue on peasant affairs to reach the highest court concerned the nature of property inheritance and the rules for succession to the deceased *domokhoziain.* This case, dated 15 December 1880 (No. 63), conceded that no clear guidelines had been presented in the original Emancipation edict and that there were, therefore, considerable divergencies in local procedures. That the principles to be discussed below were upheld in the Central Court is clear from four decisions in 1892: (No. 41) 23 November; (No. 42) 23 November; (No. 22) 18 May; and (No. 33) 26 October. On jurisdictional disputes in the central apparatus, see the discussion in A. M. Guliaev, "Krest'ianskii dvor," *Zhurnal Ministerstva Iustitsii,* 1899, no. 4, pp. 53–99; S. P. Nikonov, "Domokhoziain i ego sem'ia," *Pravo,* 1899, no. 29 (18 July), pp. 1427–33; M. A. Lozina-Lozinskii, "Nechto o zakono-

datel'nom poriadke i krest'ianskom dvore," *Pravo*, 1899, no. 46 (14 November), pp. 2197–201.

All three articles discuss the peasant household as a legal category, describing as well as reflecting the immense confusion that existed among jurists regarding the peasant household even as late as 1899. For a superb intellectual history of the debates between those who saw in peasant customary law sufficient consistency and universality to establish the foundation for general statutory law and those statists who denied the viability of such claims, see Leont'ev, *Volostnoi sud*.

4. Neil B. Weissman, *Reform in Tsarist Russia: The State Bureaucracy and Local Government, 1900–1914* (New Brunswick, 1981); M. S. Simonova, *Krizis agrarnoi politiki tsarizma nakanune pervoi rossiiskoi revoliutsii* (Moscow, 1987); P. A. Zaionchkovskii, *Rossiiskoe samoderzhavie v kontse XIX stoletiia (Politicheskaia reaktsiia 80kh–nachala 90kh godov)* (Moscow, 1970); and Thomas S. Pearson, *Russian Officialdom in Crisis: Autocracy and Local Self-Government, 1861–1900* (Cambridge, 1989).

Chapter 2. Autocratic Authority and the Peasant "Little Community"

1. Quoted in Pakhman, *Obychnoe grazhdanskoe pravo*, 2: 142–43. For an excellent survey of state efforts to uphold peasant patriarchal authority in the Russian countryside, see Mandel, "Paternalistic Authority."

2. For an account of the difficulties of imposing such regulations on peasants outside the Central Industrial Region, see the discussion in M. N. R., "Sud v derevne (Iz dnevnika byvshego mirovogo sud'i)," *Nabliudatel'*, 1882, no. 2, pp. 95–124, no. 3, pp. 45–62.

3. Typical was the experience in Nizhnii Novgorod Province: "Measures of coercion of individual *domokhoziaeva* toward payment of assessed dues are only very rarely taken by rural communes by their own personal initiative." *SP*, 2: 59. See also pp. 44–45, 98, 104.

4. *SP*, 2: 41, 46–47, 63, 94, 100, 111. On graft, embezzlement, and favoritism for the rich, see pp. 41, 44, 65, 84, 87, 94, 101. On excessive leniency, see pp. 47, 63.

5. See the example in A. I. Novikov, *Zametki zemskogo nachal'nika* (St. Petersburg, 1899), p. 48.

6. E., "Spekulatsiia krest'ianskim lesom (Pis'mo iz Viatskoi gubernii)," *Severnyi Vestnik*, 1886, no. 12, pp. 87–100.

7. *SP*, 2: 95, 100 (Podol'sk District). Cf. "Krest'ianskie vybory v Kostromskoi gubernii," *Moskovskiia vedomosti*, 1864, no. 134 (18 June), p. 2.

8. *SP*, 2: 53, 99.

9. "Krest'ianskie vybory v Kostromskoi gubernii," p. 2.

10. N. A. Blagoveshchenskii, "Sborshchiki podatei," *Ekonomicheskii zhurnal* 1889, no. 10–11, pp. 33–52.

11. Arrears had accumulated among well-to-do *domokhoziaeva* in almost all districts of Nizhnii Novgorod Province, "owing to their fear of *krugovaia poruka*, and the indulgence [*potvorstvo*] of the village authorities." Arrears among village officials were also considerable. No assessments whatsoever were made of Nizhnii Novgorod peasants in 1891 and the first half of 1892. *SP*, 2: 63. Likewise, in Moscow (*SP*, 2: 101), and in Tula (*SP*, 2: 41).

12. Lashmanov's remarks about tsarist procedures were so critical that large parts of his reports to the Tenishev Commission were destroyed for fear of charges of possessing seditious materials. GME, f. 7 Materialy "Etnograficheskogo Biuro" V. N. Tenisheva, 1897–1901, op. 1, d. 541, ll. 9–9 ob. Also, on the weight of demands placed on local officials, see these relatively complete collections of *volost'* records from Moscow Province: TsGIAgM, f. 378 (Tsaritsinskoe, Moscow District); f. 581 (Elmanovskoe, Mozhaisk District); f. 683 (Boronovskoe, Dmitrov District); f. 705 (Bogorodsk District); f. 795 (Timonovskoe, Dmitrov District).

On the "peasant problem" in Russia and the profound factors that affected perspectives, see Andrzej Walicki, *The Slavophile Controversy: History of a Conservative Utopia in Nineteenth-Century Russian Thought* (Oxford, 1975); Richard Wortman, *The Crisis of Russian Populism* (Cambridge, 1967); and Frierson, *Peasant Icons.*

13. *SP,* 2: 37, 66.

14. See V. V. Tenishev, *Administrativnoe polozhenie Russkogo krest'ianstva* (St. Petersburg, 1908), pp. 99–100.

15. For cases of arrest, fines, and other pressures against village officials, see *SP,* 2: 37, 44, 59–61, 66, 78, 86, 98–99. On the use of fines and arrest to motivate local officials, see Tenishev, *Administrativnoe polozhenie,* pp. 99–101.

16. "Krest'ianskie vybory v Kostromskoi gubernii," p. 2.

17. *SP,* 2: 44. Such reports led opponents to attack *krugovaia poruka* as a powerful weapon in the hands of the rich to enslave their less well-off fellow-villagers. Count Vorontsov-Dashkov's view was typical among those who favored the abolition of communal members' mutual responsibility for dues and obligations: "*[Krugovaia poruka]* is a terrifying weapon in the hands of the wealthy against the poor. Until now, government efforts have been directed only towards guaranteeing that peasants will not be ruined by civil suits brought by private individuals—in that respect what may be sold to pay a private debt may be specified. But, with respect to the commune's claims, there are no such limitations. The commune is always the least charitable, the most cruel collector of taxes. Collective responsibility forces each to remember that if he does not squeeze the poor peasant then he must pay for him and it is this which makes the commune pitiless. . . . [T]he accumulation of arrears in essence varies only with the degree of administrative leniency." Quoted in Mandel, "Paternalistic Authority," p. 333.

Also, see Terner, "Krest'ianskie platezhi," p. 463; N. K. Brzheskii, *Obshchinnyi byt i khoziaistvennaia neobespechennost' krest'ian (Po povodu predstoiashchego peresmotra krest'ianskikh polozheniia)* (St. Petersburg, 1899), pp. 44–48; M. S. Simonova, "Otmena krugovoi poruki," *Istoricheskie zapiski* 83 (1969): 175–77.

N. K. Brzheskii, the leading expert on peasant taxation in Old Regime Russia, concluded that "the collective responsibility of the rural commune poses a serious danger in social relations: it gives to the rich members of the commune a strong weapon against the poor villagers and intensifies the struggle of property interests, the outcome of which in the majority of cases is to the detriment of the poorest elements of the peasantry." *Nedoimochnost' i krugovaia poruka sel'skikh obshchestv. Istoriko-kriticheskii obzor deistvuiushchego zakonodatel'stva, v sviazi s praktikoiu krest'ianskogo podatnogo dela* (St. Petersburg, 1897), p. 412.

18. From a memorandum in the state revenue office of Tver' Province, 13 July 1896, cited in *Statisticheskii ezhegodnik Tverskoi gubernii za 1897 god* (Tver, 1898), 2: 106.

19. *SP,* 2: 86. See also the cases in Nizhnii Novgorod, p. 63. For every province of the Cen-

tral Industrial Region, section 3 of each tax inspector's report began with a discussion of initiatives aimed at coercing the commune to play a greater role in tax collection.

20. Summary of paragraph 188 in the Emancipation decree, dated 19 February 1861, *PSZ*, 2d ser., no. 36,657. *SP,* 2: 51. The rights and responsibilities of the *volost'* courts were defined in article 102: "The *volost'* court is empowered, when dealing with such offenses, to sentence the guilty: to public labor—up to six days; or to a monetary fine—up to three rubles; or to arrest—up to seven days; or, finally, with persons not exempted from corporal punishment, to punishment with rods, up to twenty blows."

21. N. K. Brzheskii, *Nedoimochnost' i krugovaia poruk,* p. 411.

Chapter 3. The Social Control of Peasant Labor

1. Quoted in Mandel, "Patriarchal Authority," p. 333.

2. This view of communal-based coercive schemes, which emphasizes the entire community's self-interest vis-à-vis the state, differs from the mainstream position which has emphasized the dominant role of village kulaks.

3. For a typical case demonstrating that solutions were derived from communal—not state—initiatives, see *SP,* 2: 50–51 (Vladimir). The best recent analysis of migration and the peasant commune in Russia is Tikhonov, *Pereseleniia v Rossii,* p. 114. In the nineteenth century, the logic of communal organization in non-black-earth areas was best elucidated by three authors: Terner, "Krest'ianskie platezhi," pp. 474–75; V. Vorontsov, *Progressivnyia techeniia v krest'ianskom khoziaistve* (St. Petersburg, 1892); and V. Orlov, *Krest'ianskoe khoziaistvo,* no. 1, *Formy krest'ianskogo zemlevladeniia v Moskovskoi gubernii* (Moscow, 1879).

4. Based on a report in V. I. Barykov, A. V. Polovstev and P. A. Sokolovskii, eds., *Sbornik materialov dlia izucheniia sel'skoi pozemel'noi obshchiny* (St. Petersburg, 1880), Volume I, p. 236. (Hereafter, cited as *SMISPO).* In fact, *otkhodniki* seem to have received the very worst allotments, a practice *(skidka-nakhidka,* "stripping off and piling up") which seems to have been greeted with indifference by migrants. "To *shaltai*"—a local term for absent members—"are assigned allotments of poor quality, and often these are given only when they return [to live in the village] and sometimes only after complaints to authorities." Bulgakov, *Sovremennyia peredvizheniia,* p. 7.

5. E.g., Torkhovskaia obshchina, Tula province. *SMISPO,* p. 192. Later in the century, communes in the Central Agricultural Region were also threatened by excessive abandonment of allotments (as families of *pereselentsy* headed to Siberia), since this could deplete the local force available to work the land. See the case in Saratov described in Terner, "Krest'ianskie platezhi," p. 475.

6. Quoted in Tikhonov, *Pereseleniia v Rossii,* p. 115. V. Sudeikin has shown that only 1 percent of all peasant allotments had been redeemed by 1886, the preliminary condition for a household's right to break permanently from the commune as an independent proprietor (according to paragraph 165 of the Emancipation statute). Early redemption of allotments was concentrated in nine northern non-black-earth provinces. Eight of nine provinces in the Central Industrial Region accounted for almost four-fifths of all redeemed peasant lands. See "Dosrochnyi vykup krest'ianskikh zemel," *Ekonomicheskoe obozrenie,* 1886, no. 7, pp. 35–36.

7. Passage cited in Tikhonov, *Pereseleniia v Rossii,* p. 134. For comparable cases, see Svirshchevskii, *Otkhozhie promysly,* p. 23; Iaroslavl', Statisticheskoe Biuro Iaroslavskogo Gubernskogo Zemstva, *Otkhozhie promysly krest'ianskogo naseleniia Iaroslavskoi gubernii (po dannym o pasportakh za 1896–1902 g. g.), Statisticheskii sbornik po Iaroslavskoi gubernii,* no. 19, (Iaroslavl', 1907), pp. 23, 38, 75.

8. Terner, "Krest'ianskie platezhi," p. 474. Also see Vorontsov, *Progressivnyia techeniia.*

9. Smirnov, "Sostoianie mestnykh," p. 34. See also Smirnov, "Zemledelie i zemledelets," pp. 177–79; and A. V. Smirnov, "Iz nabliudenii zemskogo statistika," *Russkoe bogatstvo,* 1904, no. 4, pp. 8, 10–11.

10. On the conditions for a household's complete withdrawal from the commune and registration as a private landholder, see *PSZ,* 2d ser., no. 36,657, chap. 5, para. 130.

11. Smirnov, "Zemledelie i zemledelets," p. 178. For evidence of the support among state officials for such exactions, see *SP,* 2: 95.

12. Smirnov, "Sostoianie mestnykh," p. 34. On deliberate coercion of *otkhodniki,* see B. V. Tikhonov, "Migratsii fabrichno-zavodskikh rabochikh v Shuiskom uezde Vladimirskoi gubernii (po materialam zemskoi podvornoi perepisi 1899 g.), in *Istoricheskaia geografiia Rossii XII–nachalo XX v.* (Moscow, 1975), p. 109.

13. Dadonov, "'Russkii Manchestr'," p. 58. A *desiatina* was generally equivalent to 2.7 acres.

14. Ibid.

15. Smirnov, "Zemledelie i zemledelets," p. 178.

16. *SP,* 2: 96.

17. *SP,* 2: 57. The data are based on eighty-seven villages in Nizhnii Novgorod Province.

18. Cited in Zaionchkovskii, *Otmena,* pp. 301–02. On the requirement of preliminary signed contracts from migrants with tax arrears, see *SP,* 2: 77. For a content analysis of 640 peasant land rental contracts in Moscow Province which substantiates this argument, see T. I. Selina, "Krest'ianskie arendnye dogovory epokhi kapitalizma kak istochnik dlia izucheniia krest'ianskogo khoziaistva," *Istoriia SSSR,* 1987, no. 3, pp. 118–31.

19. *SP,* 2: 96.

20. On the enormous number of legal battles surrounding such claims to the land during the years 1908–1910, see the fascinating discussion in "Nishchenstvo," *Statisticheskii ezhegodnik Moskovskoi gubernii za 1910 god* (Moscow, 1911), pp. 89–91. See also the discussion on the sales that followed privatization of allotment lands after 9 December 1906 in the now-classic article by L. M. Ivanov, "Preemstvennost' fabrichno-zavodskogo truda i formirovanie proletariata v Rossii," in *Rabochii klass i rabochee dvizhenie v Rossii, 1861–1917* (Moscow, 1966), pp. 117–19. While land claims among peasant-workers who had maintained their dues were sacrosanct under the law, the reality was that cash-poor communes had, since the abolition of serfdom, paradoxically charged far more dues than there were corresponding allotments in the communal fund of arable land. This widespread communal-based land fraud was an inevitable result of local efforts to adjust land fees to a peasant-worker's ability to pay. Particularly in villages where migration for outside earnings had occurred for more than one generation, a considerable proportion of peasant-workers who returned to claim their allotments after 1906 found themselves empty-handed. As real allotments were gradually con-

sumed by natural population increases, migrating workers increasingly paid dues for spurious allotments. See the discussion in P. N. Zyrianov, *Krest'ianskaia obshchina Evropeiskoi Rossii v 1907–1914 gg.* (Moscow, 1992). Also see Corinne Gaudin, "Governing the Village: Peasant Culture and the Problem of Social Transformation in Russia, 1906–1914" (Ph.D. diss., University of Michigan, 1993).

21. *SP,* 2: 110.

22. Smirnov, "Sostoianie mestnykh," p. 34.

23. *SP,* 2: 109.

24. For the history of internal passport law from its beginnings under Peter I to its abolition in 1906, see B. V. Anan'ich, "Iz istorii zakonodatel'stva o krest'ianakh (vtoroi poloviny XIX veka)," in *Voprosy istorii Rossii XIX–nachala XX veka (Mezhvuzovskii sbornik)* (Leningrad, 1983), pp. 34–45. See also the summary on passports in the *Entsiklopedicheskii slovar'.* The best summary of the magnitude of passport manipulation by *volost'* authorities is in Tikhonov, *Pereselenie v Rossii,* pp. 117–24. In English, see Von Laue, "Russian Peasants in the Factory," and "Russian Labor Between Field and Factory."

25. Passage cited in Tikhonov, *Pereseleniia v Rossii,* p. 119.

26. Resheniia Pravitel'stvuiushchego Senata, no. 1392. Cited in I. L. Goremykin, *Svod uzakonenii i rasporiazhenii pravitel'stva ob ustroistve sel'skogo sostoianiia i uchrezhdenii po krest'ianskim delam,* vol. 1, pt. 1 (St. Petersburg, 1903), p. 344.

27. *PSZ,* 3d ser., no. 10,709, 3 June 1894.

28. Summary and passage are adapted from M. S. Simonova, *Krizis agrarnoi politiki tsarizma nakanune pervoi rossiiskoi revoliutsii* (Moscow, 1987), pp. 117–18.

29. The law that officially abolished parental control over peasant passports appeared as part of the Stolypin reform initiative, dated 5 October 1906. In practice, though, village officials were as a rule unwilling to contravene parental wishes.

30. E. I. Iakushkin, with S. P. Nikonov, *Grazhdanskoe pravo po resheniiam Krestobogorodskogo volostnogo suda Iaroslavskoi gubernii i uezda* (Iaroslavl', 1902), p. 179.

31. Text from 1888 case cited in Tikhonov, *Pereseleniia v Rossii,* p. 122.

32. The following list identifies regions specifically cited where passport restrictions of one form or another were applied: *SP,* 2: 38, 44–45, 52, 60, 67–68, 77–78, 88–89, 98, 105 110.

33. *SP,* 2: 38, 60, 67–68, 88–89, 98, 105, 110.

34. For examples, see *SP,* 2: 77–78, 67.

35. *SP,* II, pp. 67–68.

36. *SP,* II, pp. 88, 60.

37. *SP,* II, pp. 53, 67–68, 88, 98. In Kostroma District, authorities issued passports freely to family members, regardless of the level of arrears. SP, II, p. 77. In Kovrov District, Vladimir Province, authorities summoned home only the peasant heads of household, not household members. *SP,* 2: 53.

38. On short-term *(kratkosrochnye)* passports, see *SP,* II, pp. 44, 67–68. On the procedures for renewal *(vozobnovlenie),* see *SP,* II, pp. 44, 68, 88–89, 105, 110.

39. Ibid., p. 77.

40. Ibid., p. 60.

41. Ibid., pp. 67–68.

42. Passage quoted in Tikhonov, *Pereseleniia v Rossii,* p. 118. (Emphasis added.)

43. From Vikhliaev, "Ob ustoichivosti," p. 81. For a regional breakdown of duration of out-work, see Karyshev, "Narodno-khoziaistvennye nabroski," pp. 13–14.

44. Vladimirskii, *Otkhod krest'ianstva,* p. 84. For a comparative summary of the data on passport duration between 1861 and 1910, see Mints, *Otkhod krest'ianskogo naseleniia,* p. 29. On the rising duration of absence among *otkhodniki* in the Central Industrial Region, see the data in Erisman, *Sbornik statisticheskikh svedenii po Moskovskoi gubernii,* vol. 3, pt. 4, p. 147.

45. As a result, studies of migration based on the number of passports alone (as a proportion of the general population) have overestimated the rate of *otkhod,* since each household could have received several passports in the course of a year. Pending a comprehensive investigation of sources such as the land inventories conducted in most provinces of European Russia, a more detailed calculation of the real rate of migration is difficult. Preliminary surveys suggest that the figures for passports far exceeded real rates of migration, while an enormous amount of qualitative evidence based on firsthand observation suggests that the rates were actually higher than those calculated on the basis of passports. Contrast the figures in Ryndziunskii, *Krest'iane i gorod,* pp. 108–09, with the analysis of passports in "Vidy na zhitel'stvo."

46. *SP,* 2: 105.

47. Ibid., p. 38.

48. Ibid., p. 110. Also see pp. 44, 88.

49. Ibid., p. 68.

50. Ibid., pp. 38, 44, 53, 60–61, 66, 75, 78, 87, 89, 99, 104. Not surprisingly, published tax inspectors' reports contain very little information about the use of flogging to coerce tax payments.

51. On the sale of luxury items first, see ibid., pp. 66, 77, 98. On the distraint of more essential items, see p. 66. Certain items, such as icons, were generally excluded from distraint. See Tenishev, *Administrativnoe polozhenie,* pp. 100–01.

52. *SP,* 2: 89.

53. For similar data in other provinces, see ibid., pp. 38, 44, 60–61, 66, 75, 99, 104. In Nizhnii Novgorod Province, distraint had been conducted in virtually every village of the province during the six-year period 1887–1893; no actual sale of property occurred in any year except in 1893, and then only rarely. Ibid., p. 60. For comparable figures in other provinces (Tula and Tambov), see A. M. Anfimov, *Ekonomicheskoe polozhenie i klassovaia bor'ba krest'ian Evropeiskoi Rossii, 1881–1904* (Moscow, 1984), pp. 98–99.

54. *SP,* 2: 53. Distraint and sale were widespread in Suzdal, Iur'ev, and Aleksandrov Districts. Debt sales were prohibited by a resolution of the land captains in Shuia District. Both distraint and sale were insignificant in all remaining districts of Vladimir Province.

For other cases of public boycott of debt sales, see ibid., p. 99. Also see Brzheskii, *Nedoimochnost',* pp. 289–93. On the common use of distraint, and the rarity of auctions in general, see Tenishev, *Administrativnoe polozhenie,* p. 101. Tenishev describes some of the strategies used by villagers to undermine the effectiveness of public auctions of confiscated property.

55. Written by his own hand. Preserved by Zhbankov, *Bab'ia storona,* pp. 113–14. *Ot"srochka* referred to the price of obtaining a residence permit in the city while the peasant

awaited a new passport from home. Often, this permit enabled a peasant to avoid (for a short time) complications with the passport. Having a residence permit did not, however, protect a peasant without a passport from fines and forced return if arrested by the police.

56. Ibid., pp. 114–15.

57. *Otkhozhie promysly krest'ianskogo naseleniia Iaroslavskoi gubernii*, p. 54.

58. See Vorob'ev, *Otkhozhie*, pp. 5–7.

59. "Delo o vysylke passportov krest'ianam, prozhivavshie na zarabtokakh; perepiska o vzyskanii s krest'ian raznykh platezhei i o prodazhe imushchestva za dolgi," and "Delo ob otkaze krest'ianam v vydache pasportov." A statistical compilation of the correspondence would not be all that revealing, since even the more extensive files are evidently not complete: cases appear and disappear, frequent cross-references are made to missing items, and much of the relevant correspondence between out-workers and village officials seems not to have been preserved.

60. TsGIAgM, f. 581, op. 1, d. 78 "Delo ob otkaze krest'ianam v vydache pasportov" (1897–1900), l. 2 (2 September 1897). The request was filed on a preprinted form, suggesting that searches in the native village played a central role in police methods. In pencil, the cantonal clerk had scribbled the last-known address of the suspect: "Nizhnaia street, Mafonametochnaia factory, in the 14th section of Lefortovo borough." For other examples, see TsGIAgM, f. 581, d. 78, ll. 3–25. After 1889, the land captains became responsible for expediting such requests.

61. For reprimands *(vygovory)*, see TsGIAgM, f. 581, op. 1, d. 78, l. 1.

62. This is amply demonstrated in numerous reports in the Tenishev archive. See GME, f. 7, op. 1, d. 5, l. 9; d. 11, ll. 7–7 ob.

63. TsGIAgM, f. 581, op. 1, d. 76, ll. 7–8 (1 July 1897).

64. See examples in TsGIAgM, f. 581, op. 1, d. 76, ll. 16, 27, 30, 36, 41, 63.

65. Ibid., ll. 16, 19. Nikonov sought a passport for himself and his thirty-eight-year-old wife, with several children.

66. Ibid., l. 140 (26 July 1897).

67. Ibid., l. 63–63 ob., 65 (20 July 1897). Krylov was married and literate; he sent his own handwritten letter from Bogorodsk, at the Shibaev Factory. Emphasis added.

68. Ibid., l. 41 (2 June 1897). Letter of Ivan Pavlich Medvedev.

69. TsGIAgM, f. 581, op. 1, d. 76, l. 66 (27 July 1897).

70. Ibid., l. 85 (1897, but letter undated).

71. Ibid., l. 152.

72. Such transitional moments, when the private transcript of peasant resentment against the arbitrary willfulness and abuse *(proizvol)* of local peasant officials was publicly expressed, provide us with a classic example of James Scott's arguments on the underlying and often untraceable continuums of social conflict that connected moments of upheaval, open social conflict, or rebellion. In this case, momentarily challenged by a new state decree, local peasant officials rather rapidly reasserted their hegemony in communal fiscal and passport affairs. See Scott's provocative argument in *Domination and the Arts of Resistance*.

73. See the typical accompanying letter in TsGIAgM, f. 581, op. 1, d. 76, l. 98.

74. TsGIAgM, f. 17, "Kantseliariia Moskovskogo Gubernatora," op. 66, d. 12, l. 12 (14 October 1888).

75. See samples in TsGIAgM, f. 581, op. 1, d. 76 (1897), ll. 86, 145. Using preprinted forms, the factory office sent any necessary fees, pre-addressed envelopes, stamps (for return postage of the renewed passport), and even fiscal obligations, when appropriate. On direct deductions from salaries for payments to villages, see TsGIAgM, f. 710 , op. 1 (1902), d. 111, passim, "Svedenie o sbore nedoimok s krest'ian rabotaiushchikh na fabrikakh po volostiam 1 uch. Bogorodskogo uezda."

76. See Engel, "The Woman's Side,"; and Mironov, "Traditsionnoe demograficheskoe povedenie."

77. Zhbankov, "Vliianie otkhozhikh promyslov," p. 638. Redemption payments were abolished in a manifesto of 3 November 1905. Under the terms of the manifesto, redemption payments were reduced for all peasants by 50 percent in 1906, and abolished altogether as of 1 January 1907.

78. Zhbankov, *Bab'ia storona*, p. 82.

79. Ibid., p. 82.

80. G. Gertsenshtein, "K voprosu ob otkhozhikh promyslakh," *Russkaia mysl'*, 1897, no. 9, p. 153.

81. Ibid., p. 155. Less than half the peasant marriages in Kostroma Province's agricultural districts occurred in winter months, versus 60.5 percent for districts in Kostroma's eastern forest region, and 65.6 percent in factory districts of the south and southwest.

82. A. Balov, "Ocherki Peshekon'ia," *Etnograficheskoe obozrenie*, 1897, no. 4, p. 60. On regional variations in the village ritual cycles, see Frank, "'Simple Folk'," and A. F. Nekrylova, ed., *Kruglyi god: russkii zemledel'cheskii kalendar'* (Moscow, 1991). Note that *kumushka* was village slang synonymous with *kuma*—the godmother of one's child. In its diminuitive as *kumushka* or "little godmother," it can be translated either in a positive sense as "a good woman" or in the derogatory sense of "a gossip" or "a scandal-monger." Either way, the characteristic of slyness is implied.

83. Zhbankov, *Bab'ia storona*, pp. 26–27.

84. Cited from an unpublished *zemstvo* correspodent's report in Vorob'ev, *Otkhozhie*, p. 118.

85. V. Kniazev, *Zhizn' molodoi derevni: chastushki-korotushki S.-Peterburgskoi gubernii* (St. Peterburg, 1913), p. 21.

86. Cited by Zhbankov, *Bab'ia storona*, p. 63. The logic of bifurcation from the migrant's perspective was explicated by Johnson, *Peasants and Proletarians*.

87. Cited in Engel, "The Woman's Side," p. 262.

88. Quoted in Rose L. Glickman, "'Unusual Circumstances' in the Peasant Village," *Russian History/Histoire Russe* 23, nos. 1-4 (1996): 221–22.

89. "Promysly i vne-zemledel'cheskie zarabotki v zimu 1888–89 gg.," *Statisticheskii ezhegodnik Moskovskoi gubernii za 1889 g.* (Moscow, 1889), sec. 3, p. 7.

90. Zhbankov, *Bab'ia storona*, p. 63; Zhbankov, "Vliianie otkhozhikh promyslov," p. 638. Emphasis in the original. For comparable observations, see *Otkhozhie promysly krest'ianskogo naseleniia Iaroslavskoi gubernii*, pp. 26–27, 73.

91. GME, f. 7, op. 1, d. 58, l. 7.

92. Kanatchikov, *A Radical Worker*, p. 94.

93. Ibid., p. 94.

94. From the appendix of migrant family letters preserved by Zhbankov, *Bab'ia storona*, p. 116.

95. V. N. Nikitin, *Zhizn' zakliuchennykh. Obzor peterburgskikh tiurem i otnosiashchikhsia do nikh uzakonenii i administrativnykh rasporiazhenii* (St. Petersburg, 1871), p. 157.

96. Zhbankov, *Bab'ia storona*, p. 55. On the escalation of such procedures, see *SP,* 2: 60.

97. Shuia District, Vladimir Province. *SP,* 2: 53.

98. Tikhonov, *Pereseleniia v Rossii*, pp. 122–23.

99. *SP,* 2: 44.

100. Ibid., p. 23. Also see p. 88.

101. Tikhonov, *Pereseleniia v Rossii*, pp. 119, 123.

102. *SP,* 2: 69.

103. Ibid., 68. Returning workers *po etapu* was also part of the autocratic exile system. For cases of strikers exiled "under guard" to their villages, see V. Sokolov, ed., "Stachka tkachei Ivanovo-Voznesenskoi manufaktury v 1895 g.," *Krasnyi Arkhiv* 72 (1935): 118.

104. Zhbankov, *Bab'ia storona*, p. 34. It was inevitable that with stakes so high, potential *etapniki* would be encouraged toward noncompliance. See the discussion about the black market for counterfeit passports among peasant *etapniki* in *Nabliudatel'*, 1885, no. 7, pp. 21–24. Also, *SP,* 2: 98. On the flow of beggars who had lost their jobs and were roaming the countryside without passports, see "Nishchenstvo," pp. 78–91. On the peasant trade in false documents, see the section on Zaponoroskaia *volost'*, Bogorodsk District, Moscow, in "Promysly i nezemledel'cheskie zarabotki krest'ian Moskovskoi gub. v 1899–1900 g.," *Statisticheskii ezhegodnik Moskovskoi gubernii za 1900 god* (Moscow, 1900), sec. 2, p. 23.

105. Cited in V. I. Semevskii, "Neobkhodimost' otmeny telesnykh nakazanii," *Russkaia mysl'*, 1896, no. 2, pt. 2, p. 20.

106. Ibid., pp. 15, 19–20. See also M. I. Zarudnyi, *Zakony i zhizn': itogi issledovaniia krest'ianskikh sudov* (St. Petersburg, 1874), pp. 176–77, 131, 133.

107. Cited in "Vnutrenee obozrenie," *Vestnik Evropy,* 1890, no. 11, p. 388.

108. D. N. Zhbankov and V. I. Iakovenko, *Telesnyia nakazaniia v Rossii v nastoiashchee vremia* (Moscow, 1899), p. 115. For similar cases, see V. V. Tenishev, *Pravosudie v Russkom krestianskom bytu (dobytykh etnograficheskimi materialami Kniazia V. N. Tenisheva)* (Briansk, 1907), pp. 45, 188–92.

109. Zhbankov and Iakovenko, *Telesnyia nakazaniia v Rossii v nastoiashchee vremia*, p. 77.

110. Semevskii, "Neobkhodimost'," p. 15.

111. Cited in ibid., pp. 12, 16. Compare an extract from a report to the Tenishev Commission: "Peasants themselves are terribly frightened of the birch, not [because] of the physical pain (peasants endure it with astonishing stoicism), but most of all [because] of the insult to their human dignity and the disgrace of public punishment." Quoted in Tenishev, *Pravosudie*, p. 189. The general argument on shaming is upheld in the provocative recent study by William Ian Miller, *Humiliation and Other Essays on Honor, Social Discomfort, and Violence* (Ithaca, 1993), pp. 131–202.

112. On the direct correlation of bureacratic intervention with rising rates of the use of corporal punishment, see the fascinating discussion in Semevskii, "Neobkhodimost'," p. 18. With a clever analysis of statistics, Semevskii demonstrates that village officials imposed such "energetic measures" to impress state officials. The point is that while village authorities

themselves were generally reluctant to use the knout, they were convinced that state officials were impressed by public beatings. Contrary to tsarist denials (based on the presumption of a "civilizing influence" of an educated elite), greater state intervention meant greater use of authorized violence.

113. TsGIAgM, f. 62, "Moskovskoe gubernskoe prisutstvie," op. 1, d. 708 (November 1895).

114. The case material is located in ibid., ll. 2–9 (November 1895–April 1896). The land captain's report, dated 11 November 1895, is located at ll. 2–3.

115. Ibid., l. 9 ob. (24 April 1896).

116. TsGIAgM, f. 62, "Moskovskoe gubernskoe prisutstvie." For an introduction to the material, see Tikhonov, *Pereseleniia v Rossii,* pp. 114–24. From 1861 to 1889, see TsgIAgM, f. 66, "Gubernskoe po krest'ianskim delam prisutstvie."

117. TsGIAgM, f. 62, op. 1, d. 553 (27 September 1893).

118. Ibid., l. 1.

119. Ibid., l. 4.

120. TsGIAgM, f. 62, op. 1, d. 1051, ll. 1–2 (28 February 1898).

121. Ibid., l. 2.

122. TsGIAgM, f. 62, op. 1, d. 1069, l. 2 (February–June 1898).

123. Petition of Efim Zernov, Reserve Junior Under-Officer, residing in Moscow, but attached to village Dubneva, Malinskaia *volost',* Kolomna District, Moscow Province. Zernov had accumulated arrears of 79 rubles, 70 kopecks while performing military service, 1885–1890. TsGIAgM, f. 62, op. 1, d. 117, l. 2 (December 1891).

124. From Zernov's petition to his local land captain. Ibid., l. 3. Zernov's appeal was ultimately successful, on the basis of a precedent established by a circular of the Ministry of Internal Affairs, dated 28 October 1877, no. 4: "Payments for those persons in military service should not be levied from their families, but rather should be apportioned in supplementary shares among the remaining members of the village commune by communal resolution." (Ibid., l. 4 ob.)

125. Petition of peasant Gavril Alekseev, native of village Ivleva, Gul'nevskaia *volost',* Dmitrov District, Moscow Province, deprived of his passport for arrears of 60 rubles, 91 kopecks. TsGIAgM, f. 62, op. 1, t. 1, d. 52, ll. 4-5. (December 1890). In this case, the commune only cracked down on Alekseev when he submitted a petition for transfer to another commune. Until that time, Alekseev had regularly received passports for side-work. Cf., TsGIAgM, f. 62, op. 1, t. 1, d. 72.

126. TsGIAgM, f. 62, op. 1, d. 469, l. 2 (July 1893).

127. Ibid., ll. 1–2.

128. For other important precedents where patriarchal rights were upheld, see TsGIAgM, f. 62, op. 1, d. 565; d. 623; and d. 476. Ostensibly, peasants were granted rights to receive passports without the consent of heads of household or the village commune in a decree dated 5 October 1906 (PSZ, Series III, no. 28,392). However, communes and family members continued to exert enormous influence. See Zyrianov, *Krest'ianskaia obshchina Evropeiskoi Rossii v 1907–1914 gg.;* Gaudin, "Governing the Village."

Chapter 4. The Sociology of Class

1. *SP,* 2: 53.

2. The practice of *krugovaia poruka* was rare or nonexistent in all provinces of the Central Industrial Region. For exceptions, see: *SP,* 2: 36, 43, 49–50, 73, 97. The emergent pattern suggests that aside from obvious cases of isolated catastrophe, *krugovaia poruka* was applied most frequently in Old Believer villages and in wealthy, highly stratified villages where community members perceived a direct threat to local interests if outsider intervention were provoked by nonpayment of taxes.

Typical on the nonuse of "mutual responsibility" guidelines are: *SP,* 2: 37, 43, 50, 58, 65, 73, 84, 102, 107. Also see Terner, "Krest'ianskie platezhi," p. 454; *SMISPO,* p. 236.

In rare cases when it was used, *krugovaia poruka* does not seem to have been entirely effective. A. Vesnin observed in Bogorodsk District, Moscow Province, that *krugovaia poruka* had rarely been applied. However, following the appointment of a new land captain, "When it was made known that this measure would be carried out, many peasants rushed to sell off their property at bargain prices, or at least they intended to do this, preferring to convert their property to cash, which is easier to hide." "Ob otmene krugovoi poruki sel'skikh obshchestv," *Narodnoe khoziaistvo: Nauchnoe obshchestvennyi zhurnal,* 1901, no. 8, pp. 7–8.

3. See Anfimov, *Ekonomicheskoe polozhenie,* pp. 100–03. The terms of mutual responsibility for state dues were abolished by Imperial Manifesto on 12 March 1903 (PSZ, Series 3, No. 22,629), when direct taxes and arrears became the obligation of each individual peasant household. Regardless, many of the practices identified continued until the end of the Old Regime.

4. On village insecurity in dealing with tax agents and other outside authorities, see Terner, "Krest'ianskie platezhi," pp. 454–59.

5. *SP,* 2: 50 (Vladimir District, Vladimir Province). In Nizhnii Novgorod Province, police intervention often led to the reassessment of arrears among solvent households. Ibid., p. 58. In Egor'ev District, Riazan' Province, the persistent pressure of the police forced wealthier peasants to pay for delinquent households. Ibid., p. 43. (See related cases in Tula, p. 37; and Kostroma, p. 74.) In Tver' Province, "usually the village and *volost'* authority or the police forces the commune to take these [harsher] measures, threatening otherwise to recover arrears through *krugovaia poruka.*" Ibid., p. 86. *Volost'* authorities and the police in Tver' relied almost exclusively on distraint and sale to recover arrears. Ibid., p. 87. State officials rarely considered peasant well-being when imposing obligations. In only one case, in Moscow Province, was it reported that "neither the police nor the *volost'* elder would not proceed with sale from fear of ruining the remaining peasants." State officials were generally considered insensitive to peasant needs. Ibid., p. 99.

6. On the harmful impact of energetic state officials on peasant livelihood, see the survey in M. E. Kadek, "Sel'skoe khoziaistvo Iaroslavskoi gubernii v nachale XX veka," *Trudy Iaroslavskogo Pedagogicheskogo Instituta,* 1, no. 2 (Iaroslavl', 1926), pp. 1–39. For a discussion of governmental conceptions of the kulak problem, see Mandel, "Paternalistic Authority," pp. 329–52; and Simonova, "Otmena krugovoi poruki," pp. 173–77. Also see A. Eropkin, "Pervyi god podatnoi reformy," *Narodnoe khoziaistvo,* 1901, no. 2, pp. 67–68.

7. Quoted by M. Ia. Gertsenshtein, "Melkii kredit," in *Nuzhdy derevni po rabotam komitetov o nuzhdakh sel'skokhoziaistvennoi promyshlennosti* (St. Petersburg, 1904), 2: 405.

8. The village commune was the main lender to assist peasants in the payment of dues (as separate from other uses of credit) in all but three provinces of the Central Industrial Region. See *SP*, 2: 37, 42, 65, 73, 84, 102, 109. Such communal loans were rare in three provinces: Moscow, Nizhnii Novgorod, and Vladimir. A study of 1,247 communal loans in Moscow Province during the period 1876–1878 revealed, in contrast, that the communes had been the main source of loans to households at this time. See N. N. Chernenkov, "Nekotoryia svedeniia o krest'ianskikh obshchestvennykh zaimakh v Moskovskoi gubernii (po issledovaniiam 1876–1878 gg.)," *Statisticheskii ezhegodnik po Moskovskoi gubernii za 1889 g.* (Moscow, 1889), sec. 4, pp. 54–75. For additional information, see in the same volume N. N. Chernenkov, "Krest'ianskii kredit v Moskovskoi gub. po soobshcheniiam gg. korrespondentov," sec. 4, pp. 1–53.

9. *SP*, 2: 37, 43, 50, 58, 65, 73, 84. In Riazan', communal loans were "enforced vigorously." Ibid., p. 43. For a description of the use of *samosud* or "unofficial" and usually coercive peasant methods for debt collection, see the example in Tenishev, *Pravosudie*, pp. 45–46.

10. *SP*, 2: 65.

11. Ibid., pp. 43, 50, 58, 65, 73, 84, 97, 102, 109. V. M. Kolobov, comp., and P. A. Vikhliaev, ed., *Sel'skii kredit v Moskovskoi gubernii* (Moscow, 1914), appendix, p. 23. For a not uncommon case in which the local parish priest came to the rescue of delinquents, see the example from Kozlov District in Smolensk Province in an article entitled "Denezhnaia pomoshch' sviashchennika svoim prikhozhanam," *Kostromskiia eparkhial'nyia vedomosti*, 15 March 1889, pp. 143–44.

12. *SP*, 2: 65, 41.

13. I emphasize that these figures refer to the sum of money borrowed by whole communes only, and not to separate debt transactions incurred by individual peasant families. I. M. Krasnoperov, "Krest'ianskii kredit," *Sel'skokhoziaistvennyi obzor Tverskoi gubernii za 1897 god* (Tver', 1898), pp. 66–68. The best survey of peasant credit and indebtedness in the Central Industrial Region is Kolobov and Vikhliaev, *Sel'skii kredit*.

14. Unpublished correspondent's report, cited in Krasnoperov, "Krest'ianskii kredit," pp. 73–74. On the general limits of the law, see pp. 70–75.

15. From Nikolosozinskaia and Fedorovskaia *volosti*, Korcheva District, Tver' Province. Unpublished correspondent's report, cited in ibid., p. 73.

16. Ibid., p. 73.

17. Ibid., p. 74.

18. Ibid., p. 74.

19. Ibid., p. 74.

20. *SP*, 2: 58. Communal and peasant debts through private sources were so great in Nizhnii Novgorod Province by the 1890s that local land captains intervened and refused to confirm resolutions in which village and *volost'* communes tried to secure loans. Ibid.

21. "Krest'ianskii kredit," *Novoe vremia*, 8 September 1898, pp. 1–2.

22. I. N. Kharlamov, *Sbornik statisticheskikh svedenii po Smolenskoi gubernii*, vol. 1, no. 2, *Viazemskii uezd* (Moscow, 1886), p. 159.

23. Ibid., p. 161.

24. Krasnoperov, "Krest'ianskii kredit," p. 57.

25. Typical was the result of a comprehensive search by *zemstvo* investigators in Tver' Province in the 1890s. Setting out to generate a list of the province's "village kulaks," a team of several hundred *zemstvo* correspondents could only manage to come up with a list of twenty-five, only six of whom were peasants! See Krasnoperov, "Krest'ianskii kredit," pp. 36–75.

For additional peasant appellations for exploiters, and varying definitions of what peasants meant by these terms, see the rich list of local jargon in Vladimir Dal', *Tolkovyi slovar' zhivogo velikorusskogo iazyka* 4 vols. (St. Petersburg-Moscow, 1881), 2: 215.

26. Laura Lynne Phillips, "Everyday Life in Revolutionary Russia: Working-Class Drinking and Taverns in St. Petersburg, 1900–1929" (Ph.D. diss., University of Illinois at Champaign-Urbana, 1993), pp. 35–36, and the broader discussion on pp. 32–43; Patricia Herlihy, "Joy of the Rus': Rites and Rituals of Russian Drinking," *Russian Review* 50, no. 2 (March 1991): 131–47. Also see the description in Samoilov, *Po sledam minuvshego.*

27. Jack Larkin has suggested that early modern American popular conceptions of "favors" likewise denoted forms of indebtedness. The conception of a favor as an act of benevolent and unrequited charity seems to be a modern invention. See Larkin, *The Reshaping of Everyday Life, 1790–1840* (New York, 1988). On Russian Orthodox and Slavophile notions of charity, see Walicki, *The Slavophile Controversy.*

28. *Zhurnal Ministerstva Gosudarstvennykh Imushchestv,* 1852, no. 12, p. 192; GME, f. 7, op. 1, d. 5, l. 15. This section is largely based on extremely detailed and valuable material from the Tenishev Collection: GME, f. 7, op. 1, dd. 5, 9 (Vladimir District, Vladimir Province); dd. 14, 28, 39 (Viazniki District, Vladimir Province); d. 511 (Kaluga District, Kaluga Province); d. 546 (Meshchovsk District, Kaluga Province); d. 570 (Vetluga District, Kostroma Province); dd. 1736, 1740 (Odoev District, Tula Province).

29. See V. I. Lenin, *The Development of Capitalism in Russia,* in *Collected Works,* 3: 56. The standard study of *pomoch',* based on observations of peasant life in the Vladimir-Kostroma region, is I———. Kh———., "Pomoch'," *Russkoe bogatstvo,* 1879, no. 1, pp. 66–74. See also a dissertation by S. V. Kuznetsov, "Khoziaistvennye traditsii v zemledelii russkikh krest'ian nechernozemnogo tsentra vtoroi poloviny XIX v.," Kand. ist. nauk, Moscow State University, 1992.

30. GME, f. 7, op. 1, d. 72, l. 10.

31. GME, f. 7, op. 1, d. 5, ll. 13–15.

32. Ibid., ll. 13, 15.

33. M. M. Gromyko, "Obychai pomochei u russkikh krest'ian v XIX v. (K probleme kompleksnogo issledovaniia trudovykh traditsii)," *Sovetskaia etnografiia,* 1981, no. 4, pp. 26–38; no. 5, pp. 32–46. The article also appears in her monograph, *Traditsionnye normy povedeniia i formy obshcheniia russkikh krest'ian XIX v.* (Moscow, 1986).

34. For the fascinating discussion of "inventing" and "re-inventing" traditions, see Eric Hobsbawm, "Introduction: Inventing Traditions," and "Mass-Producing Traditions: Europe, 1870–1914," in Eric Hobsbawm and Terence Ranger, eds. *The Invention of Tradition* (Cambridge, 1983), pp. 1–14, 263–307.

35. GME, f. 7, op. 1, d. 5, l. 14.

36. Ibid.

37. Ibid.

38. Vladimir Vil'er de-Lil'-Adam, "Derevnia Kniazhaia gora i ee okrestnosti," *Zapiski Rossiiskogo Geograficheskogo Obshchestva po otd. etnografii* (St. Petersburg, 1871), 4: 243–44.

39. *Vologodskie gubernskie vedomosti*, 1886, no. 34. See also Dubenskii, "O krest'ianskom gospodstvom khoziaistve v Opol'shine Vladimirskoi gubernii," *Sovremennaia letopis'*, 1871, no. 5.

40. GME, f. 7, op. 1, d. 5, l. 14.

41. Ibid., ll. 14–15.

42. I———. Kh———., "Pomoch'," p. 69.

43. Larkin, *The Reshaping of Everyday Life*, pp. 36–37.

44. K. M. Ostrovyi, "Promysly," *Statisticheskii obzor Kaluzhskoi gubernii za 1897 god* (Kaluga, 1898), p. 47.

45. Kolobov and Vikhliaev, *Sel'skii kredit*, pp. 9, X–XI. On the interrelationship between village credit and migrant earnings, see *Sel'skokhoziaistvennyi obzor Tverskoi gubernii za 1897 god*, 2: 56–57.

46. Connor Bailey, *Broker, Mediator, Patron, and Kinsman: An Historical Analysis of Key Leadership Roles in a Rural Malaysian District* (Ohio, 1976).

47. This cultural indictment of Lenin's stratification theory supplements a rich and growing literature. Largely ignored in Western discussions has been the scathing attack on Leninist-style kulak theories by A. M. Anfimov (1916–1995), in an untitled discussion which appears in *Voprosy istorii sel'skogo khoziaistva, krest'ianstva i revoliutsionnogo dvizheniia v Rossii. Sbornik statei k 75 letiiu Akademika Nikolaia Mikhailovicha Druzhinina* (Moscow, 1961), pp. 218–35. Arguing that the material conditions for a socialist revolution did not exist in the Russian countryside in 1917, Anfimov took the alternative standards for evaluating kulak status—land wealth, hired labor, or harvest size—and showed that the 9 percent of peasants claimed by Lenin were actually three distinct, nonoverlapping groups, each with its own distinct identity and interests. Anfimov drew the inevitable and shattering conclusion: the material conditions for a "socialist" revolution did not exist in the Russian countryside in 1917. In response to Anfimov's open challenge of Lenin's stratification theory, a commentator at the conference where the paper was presented angrily noted that there were "political implications" to his findings (328). Just three years later, Khrushchev's removal corresponded to reprisals against "Thaw historians" like Anfimov; he was stripped of much of his authority and forced to relocate to a minor post in the Siberian Section of the Soviet Academy of Sciences. Meanwhile, Anfimov's own volume on 1905–1907 in the multivolume documentary collection *Peasant Movement in Russia (Krest'ianskoe dvizhenie v Rossii)* was suppressed. Sources in the Institute of History indicate that Anfimov's crime was his failure to document antikulak activity in the Russian countryside during the 1905 revolution. For Anfimov's own version of the events, published posthumously, see "Neokonchennye spory," *Voprosy istorii*, no. 5 (1997): 49–72. In Anfimov's own words, his challenge to Lenin's theory led to "almost universal condemnation" from among other Soviet historians (53).

The question is: where did Lenin come up with a theory that not only contradicted traditional Marxism's rejection of the peasantry as a class incapable of self-conscious and self-sustained class warfare, but likewise contradicted the evidence available even then? That issue awaits further research. A preliminary investigation of Lenin's sources reveals he relied primarily on research that focused on the Ukrainian peasantry, for whose investigators *"kulatskoe delo"*—the "kulak question"—was synonymous with *"zhidskoe delo"*—the "Yid" or

"Jewish question." Lenin's intellectual inspiration came from Roman Tsimmerman (Gvozdev), *Kulachestvo-rostovshchichestvo: Ego obshchestvenno-ekonomicheskoe znachenie* (St. Petersburg, 1899); and the Free Economic Society's G. P. Sazonov, *Rostovshchichestvo-kulachestvo: nabliudeniia i issledovaniia* (St. Peterburg, 1894). In their work grounded in anti-Semitism, "kulak" was a euphemism for "Jew"; in Lenin's work, the overt references to Jews were removed, while the intrinsic point of exploitative wealthy peasants remained intact.

For other perspectives on the artificiality of Bolshevik notions of kulak, see the discussions in M. Lewin, "Who Was the Soviet Kulak?" in M. Lewin, ed., *The Making of the Soviet System: Essays in the Social History of Interwar Russia* (New York, 1985); Lynne Viola, "The Campaign to Eliminate the Kulak as a Class, Winter 1929–1930: A Reevaluation of the Legislation," *Slavic Review* 45, no. 3 (Autumn 1986): 503–24.

48. *SP,* 2: 43, 104.

49. See the discussion in Terner, "Krest'ianskie platezhi," pp. 480–81. Also, Trirogov, *Obshchina i podat'.*

50. Smirnov, "Zemledelie i zemledelets," p. 176. For statistical confirmation, see the data on rental prices in *Sbornik statisticheskikh i spravochnykh svedenii po Vladimirskoi gubernii,* no. 1 (Vladimir, 1898). Also see *Otkhozhie promysly krest'ianskogo naseleniia Iaroslavskoi gubernii,* p. 25.

51. See L. V. Make-ov, "Arendnaia sdacha nadel'noi zemli," *Ekonomicheskii zhurnal,* 1889, no. 4, pp. 27–28, 33. Also see Bulgakov, *Sovremennyia peredvizheniia,* p. 10.

52. Reginald E. Zelnik, *Labor and Society in Tsarist Russia: The Factory Workers of St. Petersburg, 1855–1870* (Stanford, 1971), pp. 20–21. On the role of address bureaus under serfdom, see P. G. Ryndziunskii, *Gorodskoe grazhdanstvo doreformennoi Rossii* (Moscow, 1958), pp. 93–95, 449–52. Kanatchikov used the address bureau upon first arriving in St. Petersburg to enlist the help of a distant relative who was residing there. Kanatchikov, *A Radical Worker,* p. 83.

53. The collection of workers' passports *(pasporty, bilety,* or *vidy)* was required by law in the factory regulations of 3 June 1886. The practice of confiscating passports by employers was widespread in both factory and nonfactory labor. See G. P. Sazonov, "Kabala v otkhozhem promysle," *Nabliudatel',* 1889, no. 3, pp. 28–56; P. A. Peskov, *Fabrichnyi byt Vladimirskoi gubernii. Otchet za 1882–1883 g.g.* (St. Petersburg, 1884), p. 67; A. A. Titov, *Iuridicheskie obychai sela Nikola-Perevoz, Sulostskoi volosti, Rostovskogo uezda* (Iaroslavl', 1888), p. 87.

54. *SP,* 2: 88–89.

55. Ibid., pp. 77–78. On the use of leave contracts in eight districts of Iaroslavl' Province, see p. 67.

56. Ibid., p. 88.

57. Ibid., p. 98.

58. Ibid., pp. 52–53.

59. Krasnoperov, "Krest'ianskii kredit," p. 57.

60. The industrial settlements, like the procedures for securing an obedient local labor force, developed in most cases in the years prior to the abolition of serfdom in 1861. The best single work on the growth of industrial settlements in Russia is Ia. E. Vodarskii, *Promyshlennye seleniia tsentral'noi Rossii v period genesiza i razvitiia kapitalizma* (Moscow, 1972). On the critical role of waterways in Russian economic development, see E. G. Istomina, *Vodnye puti Rossii vo vtoroi polovine XVIII–nachale XIX veka* (Moscow, 1982).

61. Correspondent's report cited by S. A. Korolenko, comp., *Vol'nonaemnyi trud v khoziaistvakh vladel'cheskikh i peredvizhenie rabochikh, v sviazi s statistiko-ekonomicheskim obzorom Evropeiskoi Rossii v sel'sko-khoziaistvennom i promyshlennikh otnosheniiakh,* no. 5, in Russia, Departament zemledeliia i sel'skoi promyshlennosti, *Sel'skokhoziaistvennyia i statisticheskiia svedeniia po materialam, poluchennym ot khoziaiev* (St. Petersburg, 1892), p. 268. Hereafter, cited as *Volnonaemnyi trud*.

In contrast, Timothy Mixter has shown how peasant agricultural laborers in the Central Agricultural and Steppe regions of European Russia resisted employers' efforts to rationalize and control the hiring process. See "The Hiring Market as Workers' Turf: Migrant Agricultural Laborers and the Mobilization of Collective Action in the Steppe Grainbelt of European Russia, 1853–1913," in *Peasant Economy, Culture, and Politics in European Russia, 1800–1921,* ed. Esther Kingston-Mann and Timothy R. Mixter (Princeton, 1991), pp. 294–340; and "Migrant Agricultural Laborers in the Steppe Grainbelt of European Russia, 1830–1913" (Ph.D. diss., University of Michigan, 1992).

62. N. Dobrotvorskii, "Iukhnovskie zemlekopy," *Severnyi vestnik,* 1887, no. 6, sec. 2, pp. 54–77. See also Sazonov, "Kabala v otkhozhem promysle," p. 45.

63. Data for Ignat'evskaia *volost'* are based on two contract books for 1871–1873 and 1874. TsGIAgM, f. 705, op. 1, d. 257 (1871–1873 gg.) and d. 284 (1874 g.), passim. Data from neighboring Stepanovskaia *volost'* revealed that Ikonnikov accounted for 54 percent of the contracts in 1866–1867, and 64 percent in 1868. See ibid., d. 829 (1866–1868 gg.).

64. From a standard, handwritten hiring contract with Ikonnikov in ibid., d. 257. For a similar discussion based on hiring contracts in Smolensk archives, see D. I. Budaev, "Polozhenie sel'skokhoziaistvennykh rabochikh Smolenskoi gubernii po dogovoram o naime," *Sotsial'no-politicheskoe i pravovoe polozhenie krest'ianstva v dorevoliutsionnoi Rossii* (Voronezh, 1983), pp. 226–34.

65. The full texts of this and other contracts are reproduced in Zhbankov, *Bab'ia storona,* appendix 2, p. 111.

66. Dobrotvorskii, "Iukhnovskie zemlekopy," pp. 72–73. See also Sazonov, "Kabala v otkhozhem promysle," p. 37. For other examples of the use of "mutual responsibility" in written contracts, see *Vol'nonaemnyi trud,* pp. 323, 325.

67. Sazonov, "Kabala v otkhozhem promysle," p. 37.

68. Ia. Abramov, "Krest'ianskii kredit," *Otechestvennye zapiski,* 1884, no. 1, sec. 2, p. 7.

69. P. Chervinskii, "Ekonomicheskiia skitaniia," *Otechestvennye zapiski,* 1880, no. 7, pp. 71–116. See also, Sazonov, "Kabala v otkhozhem promysle," pp. 31–32.

70. *Statisticheskii obzor Kaluzhskoi gubernii za 1899 god* (Kaluga, 1900), appendix, p. 86–87; Iu. Kharitonova and D. Shcherbakov, *Krest'ianskoe dvizhenie v Kaluzhskoi gubernii (1861–1917 gg.)* (Kaluga, 1961), p. 69.

71. *SP,* 2: 87. For other examples, see pp. 51, 59.

72. "Promysly i nezemledel'cheskie zarabotki krest'ian Moskovskoi gub. v 1898–99 g.," *Statisticheskii ezhegodnik Moskovskoi gubernii za 1899 god* (Moscow, 1900), sec. 2, p. 26.

73. A. A. Kurochkin (Rozhdestvennaia *volost',* Bronnitsy District), in "Promysly i vnezemledel'cheskii zarabotki krest'ianskogo naseleniia za 1896–97 godu," *Statisticheskii ezhegodnik Moskovskoi gubernii za 1897 god* (Moscow, 1897), sec. 2, p. 22.

74. Abramov, "Krest'ianskii kredit," pp. 20–21.

75. Ibid., p. 21.

76. Passage cited from an unpublished labor contract in Sazonov, "Kabala v otkhozhem promysle," pp. 42–43.

77. U. A. Shuster, *Peterburgskie rabochie v 1905–1907 gg.* (Leningrad, 1976), p. 41.

78. "Promysly i vnezemledel'cheskie zarabotki krest'ianskogo naseleniia za 1896–97 godu," *Statisticheskii ezhegodnik Moskovskoi gubernii za 1897 god,* p. 14. Cunning operators protected their investments in labor from encroachments by would-be competitors. During a period of economic downturn, local employers protected their exclusive control over laborers by encouraging village officials not to issue passports. See, for a typical example, the case of cottage weavers from Bronnitsy District, Moscow Province in 1892. V. V. Petrov, "Promysly i vnezemledel'cheskie zarabotki v zimu 1891–1892 g.," *Statisticheskii ezhegodnik Moskovskoi gubernii za 1892 g.* (Moscow, 1892), sec. 2, p. 9. On Russia's lasting relationship between cottage production and large-scale industry, see Jonathan Mogul, "In the Shadow of the Factory: Peasant Manufacturing and Russian Industrialization, 1861–1914" (Ph.D. dissertation, University of Michigan, 1996).

79. Sazonov, "Kabala v otkhozhem promysle," pp. 28–56.

80. Peskov, *Fabrichnyi byt,* p. 66.

81. Ibid., p. 66.

82. See the complaint of the tax inspector in Gorokhovets District, Vladimir Province. *SP,* 2: 55–56.

83. Ibid., p. 56.

84. Ibid., p. 77.

85. Ibid., p. 46. For other examples, see pp. 47, 98, 100, 38, 52, 77–78, 88. Also, see the Moscow police report summarizing such arrangements quoted by Johnson, *Peasant and Proletarian,* p. 179.

86. Brzheskii, *Nedoimochnost',* p. 191.

87. For the typical pattern, see the descriptions of such direct deductions by employers (paid directly to gentry serf-holders) in the following selection from a much larger literature: N. V. Kozlova, "Krepostnoi trud na Serpukhovskoi manufakture Kiskinykh v 30–40-e gody XVIII veka," *Voprosy istorii,* 1983, no. 3, p. 179; I. S. Kuritsyn, "Formirovanie rabochei sily na tekstil'nykh manufakturakh v XVIII v.," *Istoricheskie zapiski* 5 (1939): 170–72; "Selo Teikovo," *Zhurnal Ministerstva Vnutrennykh Del,* 1855, 9, sec. 5, p. 37; Vasil'ev, "Formirovanie promyshlennogo proletariata," p. 102; A. Stepanov, "Krest'iane-fabrikanty Grachevy," *Zapiski istoriko-bytovogo otdela Gosudarstvennogo russkogo muzeia,* vol. 3 (Leningrad, 1928), pp. 221–22; L. B. Genkin, *Pomeshchich'i krest'iane Iaroslavskoi i Kostromskoi gubernii pered reformoi i vo vremia reformy 1861 g. (k voprosu o razlozhenii feodal'no-krepostnicheskoi sistemy i genizise kapitalizma v Rossii),* vol. 1 (Iaroslavl', 1947); Zelnik, *Labor and Society,* pp. 36–37. On the sale of state-peasant labor to surrounding textile manufacturers in the first half of the nineteenth century, see the summary in N. M. Druzhinin, *Gosudarstvennye krest'iane i reforma P. D. Kiseleva* (Moscow-Leningrad, 1946–1958), 2: 320–42.

88. Dadonov observed that industrialists in Ivanovo-Voznesensk preferred local workers *(mestnye)* over nonlocal ones *(prishlie)* for the core of year-round laborers, but—when hiring for seasonal labor during summer months—preferred peasant-workers from distant provinces, who could be deported from the area during autumn layoffs and cyclical downturns. Each au-

tumn, after the feast of the Protection of the Holy Virgin (Pokrov day, 1 October), industrialists systematically purged their ranks of unruly nonlocals. "Russkii Manchestr'," pp. 60–61, 66.

89. Dobrotvorskii, "Iukhnovskie zemlekopy," p. 73. Sazonov, "Kabala v otkhozhem promysle," p. 38. Sazonov observed a similar pattern of enforcement in village debt collections: the *volost'* courts, applying popular notions of fairness, often permitted the rescheduling of payments (rather than the expropriation of property and foreclosure). *Volost'* courts were also generally unwilling to reimburse lenders or employers for court fees, travel fees, or other damages. As a result, wealthy villagers and outsiders generally avoided these courts in favor of the more strict *mirovoi sud'ia*. See Sazonov's *Krest'ianskaia zemel'naia sobstvennost' v Porkhovskom uezde [Pskovskoi gubernii]* (St. Petersburg, 1890), appendix, p. 89.

The critical role of infrastructure in the enforceability of employers' claims is upheld by the contrast with the Central Agricultural Region, where M. N. R.—a justice of the peace—noted the interminable frustration of landlords seeking legal redress against indebted *batraki* who accepted advances and then disappeared. See M. N. R., "Sud v derevne," *Nabliudatel'*, 1882, no. 2, p. 110.

90. Passage cited in Sazonov, "Kabala v otkhozhem promysle," p. 47.

91. Titov, *Iuridicheskie obychai*, p. 86.

92. A. V. Smirnov, "Ruchnoi tkach ili fabrika," *Russkaia mysl'*, 1903, no. 9, p. 204. Cf. Laura Phillips, "Everyday Life in Revolutionary Russia," p. 40: "Relationships between workers and superiors were more complicated. . . . Ritual treating by the boss was designed to reinforce relationships of mutual respect, but constant testing of acceptable boundaries of behavior by both parties meant that there was a good deal of ambiguity inherent in this ritual."

93. See *PSZ*, 3d ser., no. 3,769, sec. 1, para. 15, 3 June 1886. The demands for annual taxes, local duties, redemption, arrears, family upkeep, plus "special charges" became so great as to threaten peasant livelihood itself: in a statute dated 4 February 1894, Minister of Finance Sergei Witte pushed a new law through the State Council which sought to restrict the collection of arrears to the sum of the tax assessed for any single year, so that no peasant household could—in theory—be assessed more than twice the annual rate. *PSZ*, 3d ser., no. 10,328. See the discussion in Mandel, "Patriarchal Authority," pp. 342–43. The following year, the State Council passed a resolution (dated 22 May 1895) limiting wage deductions to 33 percent if the worker were unmarried, and 25 percent if he were married or a widower with children. See a draft of the resolution in Goremykin, *Svod uzakonenii*, vol. 1, pt. 1, p. 344.

94. "Promysly i nezemledel'cheskie zarabotki krest'ian Moskovskoi gub. v 1899–1900 g.," *Statisticheskii ezhegodnik Moskovskoi gubernii za 1900 god*, sec. 2, p. 24.

95. A *zemliak* was a person from one's native village or region. *Zemliachestvo* referred to the friendly "insider" relations typical among peasants from a particular area, as contrasted with the notorious distrust of "outsiders." *Zemliachestvo* may be identified with that characteristic distinctiveness which the anthropologist Robert Redfield has suggested is an integral part of the "little community" culture in all peasant societies: "The distinctiveness is apparent to the outsider and is expressed in the group-consciousness of the people of the community." *The Little Community and Peasant Society and Culture* (Chicago, 1965), p. 4.

96. Kanatchikov, *A Radical Worker*, p. 64. On the function of *zemliak* networks as an unofficial information bureau for unemployed workers, see Shuster, *Peterburskie rabochie*, pp. 40–41. Also, see *Stanovlenie revoliutsionnykh traditsii piterskogo proletariata. Poreformennoi period, 1861–1883 gg.* (Leningrad, 1987), p. 211.

97. I. M. Krasnoperov, "Mestnye i otkhozhie promysly i zaniatiia naseleniia v 1900–1901 g.," *Statisticheskii ezhegodnik Tverskoi gubernii za 1901 god* (Tver, 1902), pt. 2, sec. 2, p. 10.

98. Dobrotvorskii, "Iukhnovskie zemlekopy," p. 72.

99. Sinkovskaia *volost'*. "Promysly i nezemledel'cheskie zarabotki krest'ian Moskovskoi gub. v 1902–1903 g.," *Statisticheskii ezhegodnik Moskovskoi gubernii za 1903 god* (Moscow, 1904), sec.2a, p. 11. For similar evidence on the role of *zemliachestvo* in labor migration, see Johnson, *Peasant and Proletarian;* Diane Koenker, *Moscow Workers and the 1917 Revolution* (Princeton, 1981); Glickman, *Russian Factory Women*, pp. 3–7, 120–21; Henry Reichman, *Railway and Revolution: Russia, 1905* (Berkeley and Los Angeles, 1987), pp. 44–47; Laura Engelstein, *Moscow 1905: Working-Class Organization and Political Conflict* (Stanford, 1982); Joseph Bradley, *Muzhik and Muscovite: Urbanization in Late Imperial Russia* (Berkeley and Los Angeles, 1985), pp. 103–41.

100. The passage refers to St. Petersburg in 1902, and was cited by Bradley, *Muzhik and Muscovite*, p. 116. B. N. Vasil'ev observed *zemliak* clustering in the migration patterns of textile workers in the North Volga region. "K kharakteristike," pp. 202–54; and his brilliant but largely neglected dissertation, "Formirovanie tekstil'nogo proletariata v Shuiskom raione," Dokt. ist. nauk, Moscow State University, 1949.

101. Cited in Laura Phillips, "Everyday Life in Revolutionary Russia," p. 119.

102. Krasnoperov, "Mestnye i otkhozhie promysly krest'ianskogo naseleniia," *Sel'skokhoziaistvennyi obzor Tverskoi gubernii za 1894-i god*, sec. 2, p. 11.

103. For a discussion of annual pilgrimages and religious processions, see Gromyko, *Traditsionnye normy*, pp. 99–105. On the close relationship of markets and religious festivals, see also G. K. Zavoiko, "Verovaniia, obriady i obychai velikorussov Vladimirskoi gubernii," *Etnograficheskoe obozrenie*, bks. 103–04, nos. 3–4 (1914): 158.

104. L. A. Kirillov, "K voprosu o vnezemledel'cheskom otkhode krest'ianskogo naseleniia," *Trudy Imperatorskogo Vol'nogo Ekonomicheskogo Obshchestva*, vol. 1, bk. 3 (1899): 292.

105. Krasnoperov, "Mestnye i otkhozhie promysly krest'ianskogo naseleniia," *Sel'skokhoziaistvennyi obzor . . . za 1894-i god*, sec. 2, p. 15. The data on St. Petersburg are based on the 1890 census. Moscow data are based on the 1882 census.

106. "Promysly i nezemledel'cheskie zarabotki krest'ian Moskovskoi gub. v 1902–1903 godu," *Statisticheskii ezhegodnik Moskovskoi gubernii za 1903 god* (Moscow, 1904), sec. 1, p. 11. The best published study of *zemliachestvo* vis-à-vis the high correlation of village origin with skill type and work place destination is Vorob'ev, *Otkhozhie*. Also see the comprehensive review of *otkhodnichestvo* for most villages in Moscow Province in "Svedeniia o vnezemledel'nykh zaniatiiakh krest'ian uezdov Moskovskoi gubernii," TsGIAgM, f. 184, op. 10, d. 2699, ll. 1–71. Cf., Economakis, "Patterns of Migration and Settlement in Prerevolutionary Petersburg: Peasant from Iaroslavl and Tver Provinces."

107. F. G. Bailey, "Gifts and Poison," pp. 2, 4.

108. Scott, *Domination and the Arts of Resistance*, p. 145. On rumors among the Russian peasantry, see V. A. Vinogradov, "Istochniki dlia izucheniia mirovozzreniia poreformennogo krest'ianstva," *Istochnikovedenie otechestvennoi istorii. Sbornik statei, 1979* (Moscow, 1980), pp. 157–76.

109. Kanatchikov, *A Radical Worker*, p. 73.

110. Zhbankov, *Bab'ia storona*, pp. 112–13. Cf., "Opisanie prakticheskoi zhizni Liubeznova Efima Petrovicha," [Scenes from the Everyday Life of [Peasant-Worker] Efim Petrovich Li-

ubeznov, from village Usta, Smolensk Province], an autobiographical letter sent to the editors of *Krest'ianskaia gazeta* in 1938. Rossiiskii Gosudarstvennyi Arkhiv Ekonomiki [hereafter, RGAE], f. 396, "Redaktsiia 'Krest'ianskoi gazety' izdaniia TsK RKP(b)," op. 10, d. 133, ll. 21–24. Liubeznov provides a detailed description of his 61 years of exemplary work as a skilled worker (from August 1874), defending his reputation from charges he was a "prodigal son."

111. Bulgakov was the first to apply the concept of "peasantization" *(krest'ianstvovat')*. See his *Sovremennyia peredvizheniia*, pp. 3–4.

Chapter 5. The Logic of Solidarity

1. V. Aleksandrov, "Derevenskoe vesel'e v Vologodskom uezde," *Sovremennik*, 1864, no. 7, pp. 172–74.

2. For the typical observation, see Ostrovyi, "Promysly," p. 39.

3. In 1897, 3.5 months; in 1898, 5 months; in 1899, 4.5 months. See "Promysly i nezemledel'cheskie zarabotki krest'ian Moskovskoi gub. v 1899–1900 g.," *Statisticheskii ezhegodnik Moskovskoi gubernii za 1900 god* (Moscow, 1900), sec. 2, p. 1.

4. A. A. Iablonskii, "Vliianie urozhaia 1896 g. na blagosostoianie naseleniia," *Obzor Vladimirskoi gubernii v sel'skokhoziaistvennom otnoshenii za 1896 god* (Vladimir, 1897), pp. 131–43.

5. "Krizis v Tul'skoi gubernii." Reprinted from *S.-Peterburgskiia Vedomosti* in *Sovremennyi mir (Mir Bozhii)*, 1904, no. 9, pp. 36–37. The best studies of the impact of industrial recession on the Russian village are: A. F. Iakovlev, *Ekonomicheskie krizisy v Rossii* (Moscow, 1955); S. G. Strumilin, "K voprosu o promyshlennom perevote v Rossii," *Voprosy ekonomiki*, 1952, no. 12; and N. A. Egiazarova, *Agrarnyi krizis kontsa XIX veka v Rossii* (Moscow, 1959).

6. From an unpublished report of a *zemstvo* correspondent cited in Baskin, "Mestnye i otkhozhie promysly," p. 496.

7. On the religious calendar and work days, see Crisp, "Labour and Industrialization in Russia," pp. 380–81.

8. Kanatchikov, p. 51 *A Radical Worker*. On the exodus from Moscow, see Bradley, *Muzhik and Muzcovite*, pp. 113–14.

9. On plant closings, see "Kharakteristika iavleniia vremennoi priostanovki i zakrytiia predpriiatii v russkoi promyshlennosti," *Vestnik finansov, promyshlennosti i torgovli*, 1914, no. 24, p. 522. Based on data in the *Svod otchetov fabrichnykh inspektorov za 1901–1912 gg*. In the years 1901–1912, this number approaches the same increment of growth as the number of industrial workers for the period: 404,541. Note that these figures represent conservative data. They do not include establishments with less than fifty workers, which were far more vulnerable to sudden changes in the market.

10. On bottlenecks, see the example in "Prom. Kost. 1913," *Vestnik finansov, promyshlennosti i torgovli*, 1914, no. 19, p. 295. In this case, a labor shortage in spinning factories had interrupted the supply of thread to weaving factories, leading to a reduction of the work week from six to four days for almost two months.

11. See Vorob'ev, *Otkhozhie promysly*, p. 5.

12. Kanatchikov, *A Radical Worker*, p. 63.

13. Ibid., p. 63.

14. Dadonov, "'Russkii Manchestr'," p. 66. Clothing and appearance were telling factors for selecting out "unreliable" peasant workers. Citing the Bolshevik newspaper *Iskra*, No. 9 [October 1901] David Pretty noted: "By 1901, good grooming had become so identified with worker activism in Ivanovo that there was 'a persecution of all workers who, being decently dressed, do not look completely stupid. Each owner has secretly ordered his directors to take on workers only after looking them over from head to toe. And if someone is well dressed, he is thrown out of the factory on his ear. Against one's will it has become necessary to dress in bums' clothing.'" David Pretty, "The Saints of the Revolution: Political Activists in Ivanovo-Voznesensk and the Path of Most Resistance," *Slavic Review* 54, no. 2 (Summer 1995): 276–304.

15. See TsGIAgM, f. 17, especially op. 66, dd. 10, 62, 63, 79, 102, 104, 167, 409, 472, 489.

16. From the police chief's report from Epifan District, Tula Province. TsGIAgM, f. 17, op. 66, d. 63, ll. 3–4.

17. "Most humble" petition to the Moscow governor, prepared and presented by the artel elder Ivan Egorovich Fomin, dated 3 June 1889. TsGIAgM, f. 62, op. 1, d. 62, ll. 3–4.

18. The main patterns of Russian strike activity are analyzed in Leopold H. Haimson and Ronald Petrusha, "Two Strike Waves in Imperial Russia, 1905–1907, 1912–1914," in Leopold Haimson, ed., *Strikes, Wars, and Revolutions in an International Perspective* (Cambridge, 1989), pp. 101–66; Diane P. Koenker and William G. Rosenberg, *Strikes and Revolution in Russia, 1917* (Princeton, 1989), pp. 23–60, 347–50; and Ivanov, "Preemstvennost' fabrichno-zavodskogo truda."

19. Unpublished correspondent's report cited in "Promysly i nezemledel'cheskie zarabotki krest'ian v 1905–1906 gg.," *Statisticheskii ezhegodnik Moskovskoi gubernii za 1906 god*, pt. 1, no. 2 (Moscow, 1907), p. 23.

20. Samoilov, *Vospominaniia*, 1: 60. Those who remained barely survived on assistance from the Soviet of Workers' Deputies and from contributions made by sympathetic owners of food and grocery stores. On mass departures to the village for "field work" during the strikes, see N. I. Vorob'ev, "Iz zhizni Ivanovo-Voznesenskikh rabochikh," *Obrazovanie*, 1906, no. 3, sec. 2, p. 70.

21. "Sostoianie promyslov za pervuiu i vtoruiu polovinu 1905 g. (tekst)," *Obzor Vladimirskoi gubernii v sel'skokhoziaistvennom otnoshenii za 1905 god* (Vladimir, 1906), p. 316.

22. Typical is the account in ibid., pp. 315–37. See page 316 for a detailed report on the movement of strikers between factories and villages. Also see accounts of the leading role played by unemployed peasant-workers in village actions during 1905–1907. Maureen Perrie, *The Agrarian Policy of the Russian Socialist-Revolutionary Party from Its Origins Through the Revolution of 1905–1907* (Cambridge, 1976).

23. "Sostoianie promyslov," p. 316. From Pokrov District, Vladimir Province. For a similar case among weavers in Iur'ev District, see p. 317.

24. Quoted by Zhbankov, *Bab'ia storona*, p. 60.

25. Ibid., pp. 60, 159.

26. Ibid., p. 60.

27. S. I. Kharizomenov, *Promysly Vladimirskoi gubernii*, no. 2, *Aleksandrovskii uzed* (Moscow, 1882), p. 4.

28. Ibid., pp. 58, 60. For the Samoilov case, see *Vospominaniia*, 1: 9, and *Po sledam minuvshego*, p. 24.

29. GAIaO, *Kollektsiia rukopisei*. "Dnevniki [Iaroslavskogo krest'ianina-otkhodnika] I. G. Andreeva, 1905–1914 gg*," ed. khr. 527, 670, 1065, 1071, 1135, 1161–71, 1394.

30. Vil'er de-Lil'-Adam, "Derevnia Kniazhaia gora," 4: 260.

31. Samoilov, *Vospominaniia*, 1: 11.

32. Samoilov, *Po sledam minuvshego*, p. 37; *Vospominaniia*, 1: 10.

33. Samoilov, *Vospominaniia*, 1: 10.

34. Robert Eugene Johnson, "Peasant Migration and the Russian Working Class: Moscow at the End of the Nineteenth Century," *Slavic Review* 35, no. 4 (December 1976), p. 659. In addition, see the detailed breakdown of census material from 1882 and 1902 in Bradley, *Muzhik and Muscovite*, p. 137.

35. Zhbankov, *Bab'ia storona*, pp. 103–10.

36. See Samoilov, *Po sledam minuvshego*, pp. 24–40.

37. *Dnevnik Elizavety D'iakonovoi*, vol. 1 *(1886–1895 g.) Literaturnye etiudy-stat'i* (St. Petersburg, 1905), p. 95.

38. Kanatchikov, *Iz istorii moego bytiia*, 1: 9.

39. Samoilov, *Po sledam minuvshego*, pp. 24–30.

40. Vladimir Iakovenko, *Dushevno-bol'nye Moskovskoi gubernii* (Moscow, 1900), pp. 243–44. Also see the fascinating account on psychic disorders associated with the social upheavals during the 1905 events in Moscow: F. E. Rybakov, *Dushevnyia rasstroistva v sviazi s poslednymi politicheskimi sobytiiami* (Moscow, 1906).

41. TsGIAgM, f. 217, "Preobrazhenskaia bol'nitsa dlia dushevnobol'nykh" (1791–1917 gg.), op. 1, d. 53, ll. 2, 5, 36. Unfortunately, the 2,892 files of the Preobrazhenskii Hospital are indexed by last name of patients only, rendering the collection extremely difficult to use if one is seeking specific types of case files. Pavlova's case was found wholly by accident, by sifting through a random sampling of several dozen files. Significantly, all cases reviewed were of peasant origin. Also of interest is the fact that the costs of Fekla's term in Preobrazhenskii Hospital (about 1 ruble, 25 kopecks per month) were paid by her native *volost* administration.

42. Mark D. Steinberg, "The Urban Landscape in Workers' Imagination," *Russian History/Histoire Russe* 23, nos. 1–4 (1996), p. 57.

43. Samoilov, *Vospominaniia*, 1: 10.

44. For details on the social conditions and informal associations of peasants in the cities, see Bradley, *Muzhik and Muscovite*; and Iu. I. Kirianov, *Zhiznennyi uroven' rabochikh Rossii (konets XIX–nachalo XX v.)* (Moscow, 1979). On working-class taverns, see Phillips, "Everyday Life in Revolutionary Russia." On women's communities, see Bobroff, "Working Women." On other social activities of Russian workers, see Mark D. Steinberg, *The Culture of Class Relations in the Russian Printing Industry, 1867–1907* (Berkeley and Los Angeles, 1992).

45. Kanatchikov, *Iz istorii moego bytiia*, 1: 18.

46. Zhbankov, *Bab'ia storona*, p. 15. For a similar report, see Smirnov, "Zemledelie i zemledelets," p. 174.

47. Zhbankov, *Bab'ia storona*, p. 15.

48. Smirnov, "Iz nabliudenii," pp. 2, 6.

49. Bradley, *Muzhik and Muscovite*, p. 16.

50. A. S. Nagaev, "Iz istorii sel'skikh promyshlennykh tsentrov podmoskov'ia (vtoraia polovina XIX veka), in *Voprosy obshchestvennogo i sotstial'no-ekonomicheskogo razvitiia Rossii v XVIII–XIX vekakh (po materialam tsentral'nykh gubernii). Sbornik* (Riazan', 1974), p. 155.

51. See the informative discussion in Petr Maslov, *Agrarnyi vopros v Rossii: Uslovie razvitiia sel'skogo khoziaistva v Rossii*, 2 vols. (St. Petersburg, 1905–1908), 2: 370–73.

52. Ibid., p. 372.

53. Krasnoperov, "Otkhozhie promysly," pp. 33–35. Also by I. M. Krasnoperov: "Mestnye i otkhozhie promysly krest'ianskogo naseleniia," *Statisticheskii ezhegodnik Tverskoi gubernii za 1898 god* (Tver', 1899), pt. 2, p. 23; "Mestnye i otkhozhie promysly i zaniatiia krest'ianskogo naseleniia," *Statisticheskii ezhegodnik Tverskoi gubernii za 1899 god* (Tver', 1900), pt. 2, pp. 47–49; "Mestnye i otkhozhie promysly i zaniatiia naseleniia," *Statisticheskii ezhegodnik Tverskoi gubernii za 1900 god* (Tver', 1901), pt. 2, pp. 86–87; "Mestnye i otkhozhie promysly i zaniatiia naseleniia v 1900–1901 g.," *Statisticheskii ezhegodnik Tverskoi gubernii za 1901 god* (Tver', 1902), pt. 2, sec. 2, pp. 12–13. The numbers indicated are based on data from all seventy-four postal–telegraph stations in rural Tver' Province, each of which served in 1901 an average area of 740.6 square versts, or 784.4 square kilometers.

54. Krasnoperov, *Statisticheskii ezhegodnik Tverskoi gubernii za 1897 god*, pt. 2, p. 34. On cash transfers elsewhere in the Central Industrial Region, see N. Anoso, "Platezhy," *Sbornik statisticheskikh svedenii po Smolenskoi gubernii*, vol. 2, Sychevksii uezd (Moscow, 1885), p. 59; and TsGIAgM, f. 795, op. 1, d. 51 (comparable data on cash transfers to Timonovskaia *volost'*, Dmitrov District, 1883–1885).

55. A. V. Smirnov, "Fabrika i fabrichnyi rabochii," *Russkaia mysl'*, 1902, no. 5, pp. 164–67.

56. Shestakov's oft-quoted study of Tsindel's textile factory in Moscow lends support to these conclusions: "A worker's profession exerts influence on his connection with the village, on his fate as a cultivator. The more the worker is experienced with factory work, the less he is a cultivator." P. M. Shestakov, *Rabochie na manufakture tovarishchestva "Emil' Tsindel'" v Moskve: statisticheskoe issledovanie* (Moscow, 1900), p. 41. See also Shestakov's supporting data on p. 39.

57. Vorob'ev, *Otkhozhie*, pp. 23–24.

58. The model of peasant behavior this suggests is very close to the one put forth by A. V. Chayanov in his classic work *The Theory of Peasant Economy* (Manchester, 1986).

59. See A. F. Fortunatov, "Chastota neurozhaev na krest'ianskikh nadelakh," *Vestnik sel'skogo khoziaistva*, 1906, no. 29 (16 July 1906), pp. 1–4, and on rye crop failures, see A. F. Fortunatov, "Rzhanie nedorody na krest'ianskikh nadelakh za 10-tiletie 1896–1905," *Russkiia vedomosti*, 1906, no. 177 (12 July 1906), p. 3.

60. Vikhliaev, "Ob ustoichivosti," pp. 88–90.

61. Vorob'ev, *Otkhozhie*, pp. 23–24. For further discussion on the reinvestment in agriculture in the non-black-earth north, see Vikhliaev, "Ob ustoichivosti," pp. 88–90; and V. V. Petrov, "Promysly i vnezemledel'cheskie zarabotki v zimu 1893–94 goda," *Statisticheskii ezhegodnik Moskovskoi gubernii za 1894 g.* (Moscow, 1895), sec. 2, p. 13. And most recently, see the observations of Ryndziunskii, *Krest'iane i gorod*, pp. 112–13. See also the data in appendix 1 below.

62. A. V. Pogozhev, *Uchet chislennosti i sostava rabochikh v Rossii* (St. Petersburg, 1906), p. xiv.

63. There is ample evidence to suggest that such strategies continued long after 1905, even into the Soviet period. See S. I. Antonova, *Vliianie Stolypinskoi agrarnoi reformy na izmeniia v sostave rabochego klassa (po materialam Moskovskoi gubernii 1906–1913 godov)* (Moscow, 1951); Koenker, *Moscow Workers*, pp. 48–50; Chase, *Workers, Society, and the Soviet State*, pp. 73–135; B. N. Vasil'ev, "Sotsial'naia kharakteristika fabrichnykh rabochikh," in *Rabochii klass i rabochee dvizhenie Rossii (1861–1917)* (Moscow, 1966), pp. 141–51.

Part III. Legacies

1. Cited in James Von Geldern, "Life in Between: Migration and Popular Culture in Late Imperial Russia," *Russian Review* 55, no. 3 (April 1996): 365–83.

Chapter 6. A Culture of Acquisition

1. N. V. Davidov, as cited in I. N. Paltusovo, "[Introduction]," *Torgovaia reklama i upakovka v Rossii XIX–XX vv.: Iz fondov Gosudarstvennogo Istoricheskogo Muzeia* (Moscow, 1993), p. 3.

2. On the impact of urban contact on the peasantry in high-migration villages before the abolition of serfdom, see L. V. Vyskochkov, "Vliianie Peterburga na khoziaistvo i byt gosudarstvennykh krest'ian Peterburgskoi gubernii v pervoi polovine XIX v.," in *Staryi Peterburg: istoriko-etnograficheskie issledovaniia* (Leningrad, 1982), pp. 129–46, and "Gosudarstvennye krest'iane S.Peterburgskoi gubernii v doreformennoi period (1836–1866)," Kand. ist. nauk, Leningrad State University, 1980; B. G. Pliushchevskii, "Vozdeistvie otkhozhikh promyslov na sotsial'no-psikhologicheskii sklad russkogo krest'ianstva," in *Sotsial'no-politicheskoe i pravovoe polozhenie krest'ianstva v dorevoliutsionnoi Rossii* (Voronezh, 1983), pp. 173–77, and "Krest'ianskii otkhod na territorii Evropeiskoi Rossii v poslednie doreformennye desiatiletiia (1830–1850 gg)." Kand. ist. nauk, Leningrad State University, 1974. On the psychological addiction of serf peasant-workers to urban life, see V. A. Fedorov, "Krest'ianin-otkhodnik v Moskve (konets XVIII–pervaia polovina XIX v.)," *Russkii gorod (Istoriko-metodologicheskii sbornik)* (Moscow, 1976), pp. 165–80, and "Krest'ianin-otkhodnik v Moskve," pp. 191–203.

3. A. A. Isaev, "V Iaroslavskoi gubernii (iz putevykh zametok)," *Otechestvenye zapiski*, 3d ser., vol. 251, no. 8 (August 1880), p. 177. Besides published reports, this chapter relies heavily on the work of the Tenishev Commission in the 1890s and early 1900s. For a general overview of the collection, see B. M. Firsov, I. G. Kiselev, eds., *Byt velikorusskikh krest'ian-zemlepashtsev. Opisanie materialov etnograficheskogo biuro Kniazia V. N. Tenisheva (na primere Vladimirskoi gubernii)* (St. Petersburg, 1993), pp. 365–469.

4. Isaev, "V Iaroslavskoi gubernii," p. 178. Rumors abounded of clever peasants having swindled their "trusting" and "hapless" masters. "I had a rich peasant," M. was quoted as saying, "he wanted to buy his freedom. We haggled *[potorgovalis']*, and agreed on 16,000 rubles. But the muzhik—that rascal!—outwitted me: he turned out afterward to have had 200,000 rubles. I could have taken at least fifty thousand from him! But here my sister was more clever! She let one of her peasants go, and took 30,000 rubles from him. And she took well, because his capital turned out to be only 45,000 rubles. . . . What difference does it make to

the peasant if he pays a third or even half of his capital when he is receiving his freedom for this; he'll get it back in one or two good years!" Cited by A. P. Zablotskii-Desiatovskii in an 1841 article entitled "O krepostnom sostoianii v Rossii." Reprinted in the author's *P. D. Kiselev i ego vremia* (St. Petersburg, 1882), 4: 290. For a fascinating account of serf wealth-concealment, see the cases in P. A. Berlin, *Russkaia burzhuaziia v staroe i novoe vremia*, 2d ed, rev. (Moscow, 1922–1925), pp. 84–96.

5. In his review of L. B. Genkin's masterful study of the abolition of serfdom in Iaroslavl' and Kostroma Provinces, V. K. Iatsunskii surveyed the growth of quitrent payments *(obrok)* from the end of the eighteenth to the mid-nineteenth century. His description of the logic of Russian seigneurial strategies can be extended generally to include the entire Central Industrial Region: "Having a well-defined sense of the limits of peasant earnings, *pomeshchiki* individualized *obrok* payments. [Thus] the *obrok* system of exploitation reinforced the peasants' connections with the market and in this way undermined the very foundations of landlord-serf relations." Review of *Pomeshchich'i krest'iane Iaroslavskoi i Kostromskoi gubernii pered reformoi i vo vremia reformy 1861 g.,* by L. B. Genkin, *Voprosy istorii,* 1948, no. 2, p. 124. On the regionally distinct character of feudal expropriation that generated a more complicated village communal structure in the Central Industrial Region, see Arkhangel'skii, "Krest'iane krepostnoi derevni," pp. 135–47; Koval'chenko, "Rassloenie obrochnykh krest'ian," pp. 140–95, and *Russkoe krepostnoe krest'ianstva;* L. S. Prokof'eva, *Krest'ianskaia obshchina v Rossii vo vtoroi polovine XVIII–pervoi polovine XIX v. (na materialakh votchin Sheremetevykh)* (Leningrad, 1981); V. A. Fedorov, "Barshchina i obrok v tsentral'no-promyshlennykh guberniiakh Rossii v pervoi polovine XIX v.," *Ezhegodnik po agrarnoi istorii vostochnoi evropy 1964 god* (Kishinev, 1966); idem, *Krest'ianskoe dvizhenie; Pomeshchich'i krest'iane;* and *Verkhnee povol'zhe v period razlozheniia feodalizma. Mezhvuzovskii tematicheskii sbornik* (Iaroslavl, 1978).

6. Isaev, "V Iaroslavskoi gubernii," p. 179.

7. In the course of my work, I have drawn enormously from the insights of historians of consumerism in the West. Most notably, see Colin Campbell, *The Romantic Ethic and the Spirit of Modern Consumerism* (Oxford, 1989). See also John Brewer and Roy Porter, eds. *Consumption and the World of Goods* (London, 1993); Simon J. Bonner, ed., *Consuming Visions: Accumulation and Display of Goods in America, 1880–1920* (New York, 1989); James Laver, *Taste and Fashion from the French Revolution to the Present Day* (London, 1945); Neil McKendrick, Colin Brewer, and J. A. Plumb, *The Birth of a Consumer Society: The Commercialization of Eighteenth-Century England* (Bloomington, 1982); Rosalind H. Williams, *Dream Worlds: Mass Consumption in Nineteenth-Century France* (Berkeley and Los Angeles, 1982); and Michael B. Miller, *The Bon Marche: Bourgeois Culture and the Department Store, 1869–1920* (Princeton, 1981).

8. Kanatchikov, *Iz istorii moego bytiia,* 1: 8.; cf. *A Radical Worker,* p. 7.

9. Ibid., p. 7.

10. Samoilov, *Vospominaniia,* 1: 9.

11. Théophile Gautier, *Voyage en Russie* (1867). See Alla Povelikhina and Yevgeny Kovtun, *Russian Painted Shop Signs and Avant-garde Artists* (Leningrad, 1991), p. 1.

12. A. Antonov, "Vyveski," *Neva,* 1986, no. 4, p. 188. (Cited in Povelikhina and Kovtun, *Russian Painted Shop Signs,* p. 22.)

13. *Dnevnik Elizavety D'iakonovoi*, 1: 68.

14. "Peterburgskie vyveski," *Illiustratsiia*, 1848, no. 30, p. 81; Povelikhina and Kovtun, *Russian Painted Shop Signs*, p. 28.

15. E. Guro, *Sharmanka. Rasskazy* (St.Petersburg, 1909), p. 27. Quoted in Povelikhina and Kovtun, *Russian Painted Shop Signs*, p. 113.

16. Ia. Tugendkhold, *Problemy i kharakteristiki. Sbornik khudozhestvenno-kriticheskikh statei* (Petrograd, 1915), p. 17. Quoted in Povelikhina and Kovtun, *Russian Painted Shop Signs*, p. 113.

17. Vil'er de-Lil'-Adam, "Derevnia Kniazhaia gora," 4: 25.

18. Ibid., 25.

19. Poem published in 1914, as quoted in Steinberg, "The Urban Landscape in Workers' Imagination," p. 49. Since Steinberg's sources are drawn overwhelmingly from literary depictions written by the so-called "conscious" worker elements, his findings reflect a far more negative and critical popular perception of the city than my own, which emphasizes popular ambivalence. Steinberg writes: "In essays, stories, and poems, workers repeatedly denounced the city's 'licentiousness' *(raspushennost')* and 'vulgarity' *(poshlost')*, portrayed it as a 'vampire' *(vampir)* and a 'monster' *(chudovishche)*, and condemned it as a 'pool of debauchery and ambition' *(omut razvrata i chestoliubiia)*, where amidst 'complacent, vulgar laughter / The boulevard with a serpent's head / Calls you to terrible sin'" (p. 51). It is indeed remarkable the degree to which Bolshevik perceptions of the city corresponded less with the peasant-workers' own views, and more with those of dependent family members and patriarchs living in the village. Compare Barbara Alpern Engel, "Russian Peasant Views of City Life," *Slavic Review* 52, no. 3 (1993), pp. 446–59.

20. David Burliuk, *Moscow Gazette*, 25 February 1913, as cited in Povelikhina and Kovtun, *Russian Painted Shop Signs*, p. 185.

21. Povelikhina and Kovtun, *Russian Painted Shop Signs*, pp. 114, 117. The text of the appeal taken from *Peterburgskii listok*, 1914, no. 42. On the general problem of hooliganism in the early twentieth century, see Joan Neuberger, *Hooliganism: Crime, Culture, and Power in St. Petersburg, 1900–1914* (Berkeley and Los Angeles, 1993).

22. S. D. Krolevets, "Promysly krest'ianskogo naseleniia," *Statisticheskii obzor Kaluzhskoi gubernii za 1901 god* (Kaluga, 1902), no. 1, p. 112.

23. P. Timofeev (P. Remezov), *Chem zhivet zavodskii rabochii* (St. Petersburg, 1906), translated in Bonnell, *The Russian Worker*, pp. 28–30.

24. Zhbankov, *Bab'ia storona*, pp. 26–27.

25. V. O. Mikhnevich, *Iazvy Peterburga. Opyt istoriko-statisticheskogo issledovaniia nravstvennosti stolichnogo naseleniia* (St. Petersburg, 1886), p. 403. For an introduction to the lives of Russia's self-made millionaries, see Thomas Owen, *Capitalism and Politics in Russia: A Social History of Moscow Merchants, 1855–1905* (Cambridge, 1905); and Ch. M. Ioksimovich, *Manufakturnaia promyshlennost' v proshlom i nastoiashchem* (Moscow, 1915).

26. Cited from an unpublished *zemstvo* correspondent's report in Vorob'ev, *Otkhozhie*, p. 118.

27. See the provocative discussion in Von Geldern, "Life in Between: Migration and Popular Culture in Late Imperial Russia," 365–83.

28. Kniazev, *Zhizn' molodoi derevni*, p. 21.

29. From V. Mel'nikov-Pecherskii, *V lesakh* (Moscow, 1958), 2: 161–62. This edited translation appeared in James Lawrence West, "The Moscow Progressivists: Russian Industrialists in Liberal Politics, 1905–1914" (Ph.D. diss., Princeton University, 1974), pp. 50–51.

30. GME, f. 7, op. 1, d. 11, ll. 6 ob, ll. 51–52.

31. GME, f. 7, op. 1, d. 5, l. 9. (Vladimir Province and District, 1898).

32. Ibid., l. 13. (Vladimir Province and District, 1898). On the social topography of greetings, see the work of the anthropologist Raymond Firth, "Bodily Symbols of Greeting and Parting," in *Symbols Public and Private* (London, 1973).

33. GME, f. 7, op. 1, d. 5, l. 11–12. (Vladimir Province and District, 1898). Of course, sycophantic behavior should not be construed as a reflection of a peasant's private feelings. The important element here is the role of public behavior or rites and gestures that celebrated wealth, *not* the private transcripts of peasants in conversation among themselves, with inevitable scandalmongering, backbiting, and the like. See the discussion in James Scott, *Domination and the Arts of Resistance*.

34. GME, f. 7, op. 1, d. 5, l. 9–10 (Vladimir Province and District, 1898). For similar statements on peasant pride, see GME, f. 7, op. 1, d. 3, l. 23; d. 11, ll. 6 ob.–7; d. 28, l. 41; d. 518, l. 9; and d. 525, l. 11 ob.

35. Sergei Nedeshev, report on peasants in Vladimir District, 1898. GME, f. 7, op. 1, d. 5, l. 30.

36. Extract from a letter from peasant woman Anna Zinov'eva to her husband Polien Petrovich, a peasant-worker from Kostroma (1880s). Cited in Zhbankov, *Bab'ia storona*, pp. 114–15.

37. Unpublished correspondent's report cited in I. M. Krasnoperov, "Mestnye i otkhozhie promysly krest'ianskogo naseleniia," *Sel'skokhoziaistvennyi obzor Tverskoi gubernii za 1894-i god* (Tver, 1895), pt. 2, p. 17.

38. The inventory and various legal documents are in TsGIAgM, f. 62, op. 1, d. 139. Further information was drawn from K. Nistrem, ed., *Ukazatel' selenii i zhitelei uezdov Moskovskoi gubernii. Sostavlen po offitsial'nym svedeniiam i dokumentam* (Moscow, 1852), p. 127; A. P. Shramchenko, ed., *Spravochnaia knizhka Moskovskoi guvernii, (opisanie uezdov), sostavlennaia po offitsial'nym svedeniiam Upravliaiushchim Kantseliarieiu Moskovskogo Gubernatora* (Moscow, 1890), p. 78; *Naselennyia mestnosti Moskovskoi gubernii* (Moscow, 1913), p. 79.

39. Icons were "traded" or "given away" at markets, as compensation for the efforts of the dealer. See the description in I. A. Slonov, *Iz zhizni torgovoi Moskvy* (Moscow, 1914), pp. 235–37.

40. Quoted in Ostrovyi, "Promysly," p. 47.

41. Smirnov, "Ruchnoi tkach," p. 204.

42. Ostrovyi, "Promysly," p. 43.

43. Kharizomenov, *Promysly Vladimirskoi gubernii*, 2: 17.

44. Gertsenshtein, "K voprosu ob otkhozhikh promyslakh," p. 153.

45. K. A. Solov'ev, *Zhilishche krest'ian Dmitrovskogo kraia (Severnaia chast' Moskovskogo okruga)* (Dmitrov, 1930) p. 141.

46. Ibid., pp. 53–109. See also Isaev, "V Iaroslavskoi gubernii," p. 179; S. P. Tolstov, "Russkie krest'ianskie postroiki," *Etnografiia* 4, no. 2 (1927): 364–65; *Krest'ianskie postroiki Iaroslavsko-Tverskogo Kraia* (Leningrad, 1926).

47. The census took an inventory of 7,488 dwellings of former manorial peasants: 90.54 percent (6,780) had thatched roofs, 8.86 percent (664) wooden shingled roofs, and only 0.6 percent (44) roofs made of sheet metal. For 12,952 dwellings of former state peasants: 81.72 percent (10,585) had thatched roofs, 17.74 percent (2,298) had roofs made of wooden shingles, and 0.53 percent (69) had sheet-metal roofs. See Tsentral'nyi Statisticheskii Komitet, *Statistika pozemel'noi sobstvennosti i naselennykh mest Evropeiskoi Rossii po dannym obsledovaniia, proizvedennogo statisticheskim uchrezhdeniem Ministerstva Vnutrennykh Del, po porucheniiu statisticheskogo Soveta*, no. 2, *Gubernii Moskovskoi Promyshlennoi oblasti* (St. Petersburg, 1881), p. 24, table 5.

48. Corrected data drawn from insurance agency statistics in the Dmitrov Museum, evaluated and summarized by Solov'ev, *Zhilishche krest'ian*, p. 54.

49. Based on an ethnographic investigation conducted in 1929. Peasant houses constructed after 1917 continued these same trends, with an ever-greater proportion of new peasant homes with metal roofs. See ibid., pp. 55–56.

50. I. Shchelgov, in Liakhi village, Melenki District, Vladimir Province. GME, f. 7, op. 1, d. 43, l. 9.

51. Isaev, "V Iaroslavskoi gubernii," p. 174. Cf., "Kerosin v derevne," *Sovremennyi mir (Mir Bozhii)*, 1904, no. 6, pp. 50–51.

52. Isaev, "V Iaroslavskoi gubernii," p. 177.

53. Father F. Kazanskii, Shuia District, Vladimir Province. GME, f. 7, op. 1, d. 63, l. 3 ob.

54. On the popular culture of portrait photography in America, see the pathbreaking work by Shirley Teresa Wajda, "'Social Currency': A Domestic History of the Portrait Photograph in the United States, 1839–1889" (Ph.D. diss., University of Pennsylvania, 1992).

55. Based on a survey of portraits at the Arkhiv kinofotodokumentov (located in Krasnogorsk, Russia), the Gosudarstvennyi Istoricheskii Muzei (in Moscow), the provincial museum in Nerekhta (Kostroma), and antiquarian bookstores and private collections.

56. Isaev, "V Iaroslavskoi gubernii."

57. See the tables that trace the transformation of peasant diets (and household budgets) in the Central Industrial Region in A. I. Petrovskii, "Prodovol'stvennyia i kormovyia normy," *Statisticheskii obzor Kaluzhskoi gubernii za 1897 god* (Kaluga, 1898), pp. 59–70; M. P. Nikitin, "Krest'ianskiia prodovol'stvennyia i kormovyia normy," *Statisticheskii obzor Kaluzhskoi gubernii za 1901 god* (Kaluga, 1902), no. 1, pp. 46–58; V. Maslov, "Opisanie derevni Volkovoi, Peterburgskogo uezda," *Izvestiia Rossiiskogo Geograficheskogo Obshchestva* (1875), no. 2, p. 474. Also see R. E. F. Smith and David Christian, *Bread and Salt: A Social and Economic History of Food and Drink in Russia* (Cambridge, 1984).

58. On the consumer fetishism of Russian women generally, see Christine Ruane, "Clothes Shopping in Imperial Russia: The Development of a Consumer Culture," *Journal of Social History* 28, no. 4 (Spring 1995): 765–82.

59. From an unpublished report of a *zemstvo* correspondent cited in Krasnoperov, "Krest'ianskii kredit," p. 57.

60. Isaev, "V Iaroslavskoi gubernii," p. 180.

61. Engel, *Between the Fields and the City,* pp. 81–82.

62. Balov, "Ocherki Peshekhon'ia," p. 69. For similar reports throughout the Central Industrial Region, see GME, f. 7, op. 1, d. 11, l. 7; d. 28, ll. 22–23, 49; d. 518, l. 9; d. 525, l. 11 ob.

63. Christine Ruane, "Clothes Make the Comrade: A History of the Russian Fashion Industry," *Russian History/Histoire Russe* 23, nos. 1–4 (1996), pp. 319–20. Compare Iu. L. Elets, *Podval'noe bezumie: k sverzheniiu iga mod* (St. Petersburg, 1914), pp. 135–36.

64. From an unpublished report of a *zemstvo* correspondent cited in Krasnoperov, "Krest'ianskii kredit," p. 56.

65. From an unpublished report of a *zemstvo* correspondent cited in Krasnoperov, "Krest'ianskii kredit," p. 57. On the urbanization of peasant wedding ceremonies, see G. V. Zhirnova, "Nekotorye problemy i itogi izucheniia svadebnogo rituala v russkom gorode serediny XIX–nachala XX v (na primere malykh i srednykh gorodov RSFSR)," in K. V. Chistova and T. A. Bernshtam, eds., *Russkii narodnyi svadebnyi obriad: issledovaniia i materialy* (Leningrad, 1978), pp. 32–47; and M. N. Shmeleva, "Ob osnovnykh tendentsiiakh razvitiia material'noi kul'tury russkogo gorodskogo naseleniia za poslednee stoletie. (Iz opyta izucheniia malykh i srednikh gorodov srednei polosy RSFSR)," *Sovetskaia etnografiia,* 1974, no. 3, p. 33.

66. From an unpublished report of a *zemstvo* correspondent cited in Krasnoperov, "Krest'ianskii kredit," p. 56.

67. Ibid., p. 56.

68. Ibid., p. 57. Ironically, in some regions, the costs of ostentatious peasant weddings intended to produce a good impression on neighbors grew so expensive that the local rates of elopement skyrocketed. See Balov, "Ocherki Peshekhon'ia," pp. 58–59.

69. See the full text of the letter in Zhbankov, *Bab'ia storona,* pp. 114–15. Emphasis added.

70. Gertsenshtein, "K voprosu ob otkhozhikh promyslakh," p. 153. Timothy Mixter has noted similar "elite" criticisms of "irresponsible" peasant spending habits among Saratov agricultural workers: "Of Grandfather-Beaters and Fat-Heeled Pacifists: Perceptions of Agricultural Labor and Hiring Market Disturbances in Saratov, 1872–1905," *Russian History/Histoire Russe* 7, pts. 1–2 (1980): 139–68.

71. GME, f. 7, op. 1, d. 5, l. 23.

72. Ibid.

73. Balov, "Ocherki Peshekhon'ia," p. 69.

74. Ibid., p. 69.

75. I. Shchelgov, in Liakhi village, Melenki District, Vladimir Province. GME, f. 7, op. 1, d. 43, l. 10.

76. Balov, "Ocherki Peshekhon'ia," p. 69. The French historian Alain Corbin has identified a direct correlation between urban self-identification and scent. See his *The Foul and the Fragrant: Odor and the French Social Imagination* (Cambridge, 1986).

77. Isaev, "V Iaroslavskoi gubernii," p. 177.

78. Ibid., p. 176.

79. Ibid., p. 176. On the significance of clocks in early modern English households, see Lorna Weatherill, "The Meaning of Consumer Behaviour in Late Seventeenth- and Early Eighteenth Century England," in Brewer and Porter, *Consumption and the World of Goods,* pp. 209–13.

80. For a general survey, see G. A. Dikhtiar, *Vnutrennaia torgovlia dorevoliutsionoi Rossii* (Moscow, 1960). On the change in peasant consumption patterns, see Ekonomicheskii otdel Vserossiiskogo soiuza gorodov, *Normy potrebleniia sel'skogo naseleniia po dannym biudzhetnykh issledovanii* (Moscow, 1915). On the development of market matrices and the transformation of local and regional infrastructures, see the classic article by G. William Skinner, "Marketing and Social Structure in Rural China," *Journal of Asian Studies* 24, no. 1 (November 1964): 3–43; no. 2 (February 1965): 195–228; no. 3 (May 1965): 363–99.

81. I. V. Krasnoperov, "Torgovlia i promyshlennost'," *Statisticheskii ezhegodnik Tverskoi gubernii za 1899 god* (Tver', 1900), p. 93.

82. Ibid., p. 92.

83. Ibid., pp. 93–94.

84. While most hiring contracts carried punitive charges of 25–100 rubles in fines for a peasant-worker's early departure from the contract, nonfulfillment of exclusive concession agreements for local tavern- and storeowners approached 150–300 percent of the annual rent in the event of violation by either party.

85. See this and other sales contracts in TsGIAgM, f. 705, op. 1, d. 257. This contract, dated 12 February 1872, appeared on ll. 176–77.

86. A peasant in a nearby village sold his home for fifty-six rubles silver in August 1868. TsGIAgM, f. 705, op. 1, d. 829. 1868 g., no. 7. The success of peasant communes to raise needed funds through sales of village concessions to outsiders largely accounted for the rapid growth of indirect taxes of the Russian autocracy during the last quarter of the nineteenth century. Essentially, the imperial state expropriated the income bases of the village communes, further strapping village coffers even as state demands on local officials continued to grow. See the discussion in "Nashi vnutrennniia dela," *Nabliudatel'*, 1887, no. 3, sect. 2: 45–69. See also the data and discussion in Stephen Wheatcroft, "Crises and the Condition of the Peasantry in Late Imperial Russia," in Esther Kingston-Mann and Timothy Mixter, eds., *Peasant Economy, Culture, and Politics of European Russia, 1800–1921* (Princeton, 1991), pp. 158–66.

87. TsGIAgM, f. 705, op. 1, d. 829, ll. 76–78. "Kniga Stepanovskogo Volostnogo Pravleniia na zapisku sdelok i dogovorov kak mezhdu krest'ianami tak i s postaronnami litsami (3 ianvaria 1867–28 okt 1878)," 11 May 1868.

88. For an excellent study of the vodka trade to 1860, see David Christian, *Living Water: Vodka and Russian Society on the Eve of Emancipation* (Oxford, 1990). Also see I. G. Pryzhov, *Istoriia kabakov v Rossii v sviazi s istoriei russkogo naroda*, 2d ed. (Kazan', 1914), first edition published in 1868. Excerpts and materials for unpublished volumes 2 and 3 of this classic study of Russian taverns are located in Pryzhov's personal collection at Rossiiskii Gosudarstvennyi Arkhiv Literatury i Iskusstva (hereafter, RGALI), f. 1227, Ivan Gavrilovich Pryzhov (1827–1885 gg.), op. 1, d. 5 ("Grazhdane na Rusi"), ll. 1–496; and d. 13 ("Istoriia kabakov v Rossii"), ll. 1–125.

89. Krasnoperov, "Torgovlia i promyshlennost'," p. 94.

90. V. A. Chernevskii, *K voprosu o p'ianstve vo Vladimirskoi gubernii i sposobakh bor'by s nim (Po offitsial'nym dannym i otzyvam korrespondentov tekushchei statistiki)* (Vladimir, 1911), p. 24.

91. Quoted in ibid., p. 24.

92. Usadskaia *volost'*, Melenki District. From an unpublished report of a *zemstvo* correspondent cited in ibid., p. 24.

93. Russia, Ministerstvo finansov, *Statistika po kazennoi prodazhe pitei, 1902–1909.* See Chervenskii, *K voprosu o p'ianstve,* p. 9.

94. In a survey of 776 correspondents in Vladimir Province, 74 percent indicated that side-work and factory work were the main factors accounting for the rise in peasant drinking. Chernevskii, *K voprosu o p'ianstve,* p. 24.

95. Most accounts fail to distinguish between inns, taverns, saloons, speakeasies, or tea rooms, and one frequently finds these terms used interchangeably to describe the same type of establishment. Consequently, I use the phrase *village saloon* for all these social institutions collectively.

96. GME, f. 7, op. 1, d. 11, ll. 5 ob.–6.

97. A. Lebedev, Kaluga District, Kaluga Province. GME, f. 7, op. 1, d. 518, l. 8. See also, d. 11, ll. 5 ob.–6.

98. GME, f. 7, op. 1, d. 518, l. 8.

99. GME, f. 7, op. 1, d. 43, l. 12.

100. GME, f. 7, op. 1, d. 525, l. 25–26.

101. Comparative Western studies of saloons and cafés have focused on their central role in the working-class milieu of urban areas, where they functioned as "clubs" for members of the lower classes prior to the birth of modern union halls. The saloons served the varying purposes of information centers, meeting places, and the like which were tolerated by even the strictest government decrees otherwise prohibiting working-class assembly or organization. See Jon M. Kingsdale, "The 'Poor Man's Club': Social Functions of the Urban Working-Class Saloon," *American Quarterly* 25 (1973): 472–89; James S. Roberts, "The Tavern and Politics in the German Labor Movement, c. 1870–1914," in Susanna Barrows and Robin Room, eds., *Drinking: Behavior and Belief in Modern History* (Berkeley and Los Angeles, 1991). On French cafés, see in the same volume the essay by Susanna Barrows, "'Parliaments of the People': The Political Culture of Cafés in the Early Third Republic," pp. 87–97.

102. "Gazeta v derevne," *Moskovskaia guberniia v sel'sko-khoziaistvennom otnoshenii (s oktiabria 1904–noiabr' 1905)* (Moscow, 1906), p. 175.

103. Derived from descriptions in GME, f. 7, op. 1, d. 11, ll. 6; d. 518, l. 7; d. 525.

104. Isaev, "V Iaroslavskoi gubernii," p. 176.

105. "Gazeta v derevne," p. 175.

106. Ibid., p. 175.

107. Ibid., pp. 170–78.

108. Ibid., p. 175.

109. Ibid., p. 175.

110. Petr Ivanovich Kamanin, Domnino village, Liakhovskaia *volost',* Melenki District, Vladimir Province. GME, f. 7, op. 1, d. 28, ll. 36–37.

111. Numerous observers have noted substantially higher literacy rates in high-migration villages. On peasant reading habits, see Jeffrey Brooks, *When Russia Learned to Read: Literacy and Popular Literature, 1861–1917* (Princeton, 1985); and Ben Eklof, *Russian Peasant Schools: Officialdom, Village Culture, and Popular Pedagogy, 1861–1914* (Berkeley and Los Angeles, 1986).

112. "Gazeta v derevne," p. 176.

113. Ibid., p. 178.

114. On efforts to gauge newspapers to peasant understanding, see James H. Krukones, "'To the People': The Russian Government and the Newspaper *Sel'skii Vestnik (Village Herald)*, 1881–1917" (Ph.D. diss., University of Wisconsin, 1983); and Brooks, *When Russia Learned to Read.*

115. S. M. Dubrovskii and B. B. Grave, comps., *Agrarnoe dvizhenie v 1905–1907 gg.* [Materialy departamenta politsii] (Moscow-Leningrad, 1925), p. 70.

116. D. I. Rikhter, "Podmoskovnoe," in *Agrarnoe dvizhenie v Rossii v 1905–1906 gg.* (Trudy Imperatorskogo Vol'nogo Ekonomicheskogo Obshchestva), 2 vols. (St. Petersburg, 1908), 1: 8–9. For a summary of the relationship between peasant labor migration and village activism in 1905, see Perrie, *Agrarian Policy.*

117. Roberts, "The Tavern and Politics," pp. 98–99, 101.

118. For a comparative perspective on the adaptation of traditional cultures to modern, organized, self-sustaining political organization, see the discussion in Frances Fox Piven and Richard Cloward, *Poor People's Movements: Why They Succeed, How They Fail* (New York, 1977).

119. An important and critically perceptive guide to the Western debate over the past twenty years is provided by Steven L. Hoch, "On Good Numbers and Bad: Malthus, Population Trends, and Peasant Standards of Living in Late Imperial Russia," *Slavic Review* 53, no. 1 (Spring 1994): 41–75. My own analysis of the transition from a needs-oriented to an acquisition-oriented culture in high-migration villages is consistent with Hoch's rejection of the so-called rural crisis argument.

To date, Stephen Wheatcroft has offered the best description of aggregate changes in peasant consumption habits throughout European Russia. See "Crises and the Condition of the Peasantry in Late Imperial Russia," with important correctives by Hoch, "On Good Numbers and Bad."

120. James C. Scott, *The Moral Economy of the Peasant* (New Haven, 1976); Donald McCloskey, "English Open Fields as Behavior Towards Risk," *Research in Economic History* 1 (Fall 1976): 124–70, and "The Prudent Peasant: New Findings on Open Fields," *Journal of Economic History* 51, no. 2 (June 1991): 343–55; Samuel Popkin, *The Rational Peasant* (Berkeley and Los Angeles, 1979).

121. I. Kh. Ozerov, *Politika po rabochemu voprosu v Rossii za poslednie gody (Po neizdannym dokumentam)* (Moscow, 1906) p. 106.

122. From original worker broadsheets and leaflets reproduced in ibid., pp. 104–05. (1905). The two samples are representative of thousands of such broadsheets collected in GARF, f. 1741, "Kollektsiia nelegal'nykh izdanii (listovok i broshiur), otlozhivshikhsia v politseiskikh i sudebnykh organakh dorevoliutsionnoi Rossii (1850–1917 gg.)," op. 1–2. Also see samples reproduced in A. M. Pankratova and L. M. Ivanov, eds., *Rabochee dvizhenie v Rossii v XIX veke: Sbornik dokumentov i materialov*, 4 vols. (Moscow-Leningrad, 1950–1963).

123. Kniazev, *Zhizn' molodoi derevni*, p. 21.

124. Reginald E. Zelnik, *Law and Disorder on the Narova River: The Kreenholm Strike of 1872* (Berkeley and Los Angeles, 1995), pp. 288–89. Emphasis added.

125. Ibid., pp. 122–24. On codes and signals, see F. G. Bailey, *Gifts and Poison*, p. 10: "Messages are conveyed in a variety of ways: the spoken word, the gesture, the nod, the failure to greet, the banging down of coins on the counter, the timidity of a knock at a door and other

slight cues of this kind, which may well remain invisible to someone not familiar with the culture."

126. Summarized from reports in Ozerov, *Politika po rabochemu voprosu,* pp. 107–08. The grievances focused on the decline in wages and the strict quality control procedures that reduced payment on a lot of good piece-work. The special issue was related to the rumors (which proved to be accurate) of a 25 percent wage increase at the neighboring factory of Savva Morozov. The action was settled when the factory inspector arbitrated in the director's office a meeting between the director and his staff with a committee of twenty elected workers.

127. Vorob'ev, "Iz zhizni Ivanovo-Voznesenskikh rabochikh," p. 70, referring to a strike in May 1905. For workers' physical and mortal threats to wealthy bosses, see examples in GARF, f. 1741, op. 1, nos. 5973, 10036, 18366, 18370, 30892, 31519. Cf., Daniel R. Brower et al., "Labor Violence in Russia in the Late Nineteenth Century: A Discussion," *Slavic Review* 41, no. 3 (1982): 417–53; and Theodore H. Friedgut, "Labor Violence and Regime Brutality in Tsarist Russia: The Iuzovka Cholera Riots of 1892," *Slavic Review* 46, no. 2 (Summer 1987): 245–65.

Lawrence Bennett Glickman, in "A Living Wage: Political Economy, Gender, and Consumerism in American Culture, 1880–1925" (Ph.D. diss., University of California at Berkeley, 1992), has described a "modern moral economy": the demands of American workers for a "living wage," defined as "wages that would reward workers commensurate with their needs as consumers." Evidently, Russian workers at the turn of the century had come to expect the same thing.

128. Neueberger, *Hooliganism,* p. 278. On the decaying atmosphere between haves and have-nots in urban areas, also see Haimson, "The Problem of Social Stability"; and Stephen Frank, *Crime, Cultural Conflict, and Justice in Rural Russia, 1856–1914* (forthcoming), chap. 9, "Savages at the Gates: Bandits, Hooligans and the Last Crime Wave."

129. M. N. Shustova, "Dnevnik (1870–1878)," Rossiiskaia Gosudarstvennaia Biblioteka, Otdel rukopisi, f. 218, kartonka 173, ed. khr. 5, ll. 59 ob.–60.

130. Emphasis added. Lev Tolstoi, "Derevnia i gorod," *Russkoe bogatstvo,* 1885, no. 12, p. 156. Tolstoi's account is likewise filled with numerous anecdotes relevant to this study: his manservant's obsession with acquiring a pocket watch, for instance (pp. 145–67).

Chapter 7. A Culture of Denunciation

1. See the full text of the communiqué from the Moscow governor's office to the Metropolitan of Moscow from 23 October 1872, in TsGIAgM, f. 203, "Moskovskaia dukhovnaia konsistoriia," op. 341, d. 124, ll. 1–2.

2. These cases are preserved in TsGIAgM, f. 203, "Moskovskaia dukhovnaia konsistoriia." The typical file contains either a peasant's written denunciation (in rare cases) or a written summary of such denunciations prepared by a parish priest or the local superintendent. In addition, I have relied on unpublished ethnographic collections, most notably: Gosudarstvennyi Muzei Etnografii Narodov SSSR. Sektsiia Rukopisei (hereafter, cited as GME), f. 7, "Materialy 'Etnograficheskogo Biuro' V. N. Tenisheva, 1897-1901," a remarkable collection of over eighteen hundred files, with original reports from three hundred correspondents, who

responded to over four hundred questions. I have also used police files of the Russian Ministry of Internal Affairs in Rossiisskii Gosudarstvennyi Istoricheskii Arkhiv, St. Petersburg (hereafter, cited as RGIA), f. 1284, "Departament Obshchikh Del Ministerstva Vnutrennykh Del"; and in local village police and court records preserved in TsGIAgM.

Boris Litvak has proposed that I present these cases in a time series so as to uncover distinct patterns in the evolution of religious denunciations. However, that task would have been fruitless in this case. In the 1950s, when the Moscow City Archive was moved to a new building, the collection of the Moscow Spiritual Consistory was deliberately decimated, reducing the size of the priceless collection from over a million files, to just over 150,000. While the inventories of the original collection reveal tens of thousands of cases of religious denunciations, only several hundred cases still remain in the files for the period under investigation. Any statisical survey would therefore fail to reflect the true chronological patterns of denunciation.

3. In the pages below I draw no distinction between various forms of religious sectarianism in Russia. This is to a large degree merely a reflection of the popular and official belief among Orthodox believers, for whom all forms of heresy were equally repugnant. For a more nuanced treatment, see Robert O. Crummey, *The Old Believers and the World of Antichrist: The Vyg Community and the Russian State 1694-1855* (Wisconsin, 1970); A. I. Klibanov, *History of Religious Sectarianism in Russia, 1860s-1917* (Oxford, 1982); and T. I. Butkevich, *Obzor russkikh sekt i ikh tolkov*, Second Edition (Petrograd, 1915).

4. See James Cracraft, "Opposition to Peter the Great," in Ezra Mendelsohn and Marshall S. Shatz, eds. *Imperial Russia, 1700–1917: State, Society, Opposition. Essays in Honor of Marc Raeff* (Dekalb, Illinois, 1988), pp. 29–30, and *The Church Reform of Peter the Great* (Stanford, 1971), pp. 238–40.

5. For an example of the standard oath, see "Prisiaga proizvodimym v sviashchenniki stavlennikam," TsGIAgM, f. 206, op. 1, d. 163, ll. 6–7.

6. See the version in *Kostromskiia eparkhialnyia vedomosti*, Year 8, no. 13 (July 1894): 273–76. The Russian title was "Odin iz predmetov, zasluzhivaiushchikh osobennogo vnimaniia sel'skikh pastyrei." The same theme was heard in the Church's survey of the causes of hooliganism in Russian society: the majority of Russian Orthodox bishops identified a direct relationship between hooliganism and peasant migration for side-earnings. See the collected reports in RGIA, f. 796, "Kantseliariia Sinoda," op. 195, d. 3223, passim. A partial and incomplete summary of the reports was published in P. A. Blagoveshchenskii, *O bor'be s khuliganstvom. Iz eparkhial'noi zhizni* (St. Petersburg, 1914).

7. *Kostromskiia eparkhialnyia vedomosti*, Year 8, no. 13 (July 1894): 276.

8. Ibid., p. 273.

9. Ibid., p. 275.

10. On ritual integration of *otkhodniki* into community life, see T. A. Bernshtam, *Molodezh' v obriadovoi zhizni russkoi obshchiny XIX–nachala XX v.: polovozrastnoi aspekt traditsionnoi kul'tury* (Leningrad, 1988), pp. 210–11.

11. *Kostromskiia eparkhialnyia vedomosti*, Year 8, no. 13 (July 1894), pp. 275–76. For other priests' calls for such integration of peasant-workers into the village ritual process, see the discussion in Blagoveshchenskii, *O bor'be s khuliganstvom*, pp. 6–7, 10–11.

12. R. I. Moore, "Popular Violence and Popular Heresy in Western Europe, c. 1000–1179,"

in W. J. Sheils, ed., *Persecution and Toleration,* Papers of the Ecclesiastical Historical Society (London, 1984), p. 49.

13. TsGIAgM, f. 203, op. 342, d. 31, ll. 11–14 *passim.* The file is a full summary of the judicial and Church proceedings against Petrov. For a detailed inventory of Petrov's books, see the report on ll. 21–22. The possession of a prohibited book aggravated Petrov's case; he was found guilty of violating article 550 of the criminal code.

14. TsGIAgM, f. 203, op. 371, g. 1886, d. 10, l. 1 ob. (Moscow District).

15. Different researchers have found conflicting evidence on this point. While in theory, a close watch was kept on confession and communion registers, the practice varied considerably. In my work in Moscow Consistory, I found numerous cases in which nonreporting or reports that reflected a marked decline in parish attendance provoked investigation by the local superintendent. In her work in Vologda Province, in contrast, Vera Shevzov has found that the local consistory was more or less indifferent to such annual reports and intervened only in particularly egregious cases when the recusant's conduct had drawn the attention of others. Vera Shevzov, "Popular Orthodoxy in Late Imperial Rural Russia (Orthodox Christianity, Vologda, Rural Life)" (Ph.D. diss., Yale University, 1994). Cf., I. S. Belliustin, *Description of the Clergy in Rural Russia: The Memoir of a Nineteenth-Century Parish Priest* (Ithaca, 1985), pp. 173–78.

16. For a description of the powerful role of parish priests in *svidetel'stva* or affidavits, see the report of I. Shchelgov, the elder from Liakhi village in Melenki District, Vladimir Province. GME, f. 7, op. 1, d. 41, l. 4.

17. TsGIAgM, f. 203, op. 371, d. 18, l. 1.

18. Gregory L. Freeze, *The Parish Clergy in Nineteenth-Century Russia: Crisis, Reform, Counter-Reform* (Princeton, 1983), pp. 459–60.

19. Ibid., pp. 64–65.

20. Ibid., pp. 58–59.

21. TsGIAgM, f. 203, op. 342, d. 106, l. 1 ob.

22. TsGIAgM, f. 203, op. 393, g. 1896, d. 42, l. 2 ob. (Bronnitsy). For related cases of evasion, see f. 203, op. 349, g. 1877, d. 53 (Serpukhov District).

23. TsGIAgM, f. 203, op. 364, g. 1882, d. 25, l. 10 (Volokolamsk District). For other examples of lying to priests, see op. 347, g. 1876, d. 49, l. 6 (Vereia District).

24. Two young brothers who were accused of deviation successfully defended themselves against the charges by presenting such evidence. See TsGIAgM, f. 203, op. 371, g. 1887, d. 10, ll. 1, 3 (Moscow District). For similar cases, see op. 341, g. 1871, d. 25, ll. 8–9, 15 ob. (Vereia District).

The certificates were routinely used for prewedding investigations and were generally required in all marriages taking place outside the native parish of either the bride or the groom. For an excellent illustration of the difficulty of marrying without such documentation, see the case in TsGIAgM, f. 203, op. 349, g. 1874, d. 85 (Moscow District).

25. TsGIAgM, f. 203, op. 347, g. 1875, d. 20, l. 1 (Moscow District).

26. See the Kolomna District police report on Martynov's activities, TsGIAgM, f. 203, op. 393, d. 8, ll. 1, 3, 5. In defense of his own failure to report Martynov's conversion, his parish priest argued that Martynov had deviated to the *raskol* only at age fifty and now refused to return to the Church out of "stubbornness" (l. 7). For a similar case, see op. 366, g. 1885, d. 76.

27. As Gregory Freeze has shown, parish priests did often come to resemble their parishioners. Quoting Count Benkendorf, Freeze wrote: "The young priest, sent into the countryside, is dependent upon [local] society, goes to seed, and acquires the visage, character, and even the habits of the *muzhiki* around him. In thoughts and feelings, he merges with that *soslovie* which provides him his sustenance. Poverty and dependency upon the peasantry forces him to encourage the [social] aspirations and passionate desires of his flock; hence the government cannot rely upon parish clergy." *Parish Clergy in Nineteenth-Century Russia*, p. 58.

28. Ibid, p. 461.

29. The works of E. P. Thompson and Natalie Zemon Davis have been particularly influential in leading historians to investigate the cultural codes imbedded in the way even the most unruly mob conducted its violence. See E. P. Thompson, "The Moral Economy of the English Crowd in the Eighteenth Century," *Past and Present* 50 (February 1971): 76–136; Natalie Zemon Davis, "The Rites of Violence," *Society and Culture in Early Modern France* (Stanford, 1965), pp. 152–88. For an insightful review and critical appraisal of their work, see Suzanne Desan, "Crowds, Community and Ritual in the Work of E. P. Thompson and Natalie Davis," in Lynn Hunt, ed., *The New Cultural History* (Berkeley and Los Angeles, 1989), pp. 47–71. More recently, see Pierre Bourdieu, "Rites as Acts of Institution," in J. G. Perestiany and Julian Pitt-Rivers, eds., *Honor and Grace in Anthropology* (Cambridge, 1992), pp. 79–90.

30. Robin Briggs, *Communities of Belief: Cultural and Social Tension in Early Modern France* (Oxford, 1989), p. 3. On the critical role of a bad reputation ("ill fame") leading to prosecution for witchcraft in early-modern Europe, see Keith Thomas, *Religion and the Decline of Magic*, pp. 526–34.

31. From the report of the local ecclesiastical superintendent: TsGIAgM, f. 203, op. 342, d. 106, ll. 1 ob., 9.

32. See the grieving letters of fathers of recusants in TsGIAgM, f. 203, op. 342, d. 106, ll. 3–3 ob. (1873); op. 347, d. 21, ll. 1–2 (1875–1876).

33. TsGIAgM, f. 203, op. 342, d. 106, l. 2.

34. Ibid., l. 24 (police report from 20 December 1873).

35. Ibid., l. 25 ob.

36. Petition for annulment on the grounds of her husband's adultery, dated 28 April 1905. TsGIAgM, f. 203, op. 412, d. 16, l. 1–1 ob. Literally thousands of such cases appear in the secret section of each provincial governor's collection. See, for example, the 400 cases in TsGIAgM, f. 17, "Kantseliariia Moskovskogo Gubernatora," op. 66 *(tainyi otdel)*. The cases represent a vast, unexplored channel into the horrors of Russian domestic violence: each file includes a statement in the aggrieved wife's own words, followed by police investigation and testimony of witnesses.

37. TsGIAgM, f. 17, op. 66, d. 632, ll. 1–2 (woman's handwritten denunciation, dated 15 July 1896, as dictated to a third person). Sabina's petition for a legal separation and separate passport from her husband was granted in September 1896.

38. TsGIAgM, f. 203, op. 412, d. 36, ll. 1, 8–8 ob. (October–November 1905). Although she paid several rubles in fees and special stamps, Guseva's case was eventually rejected almost eight months later on technical grounds, since she was from a district outside the jurisdiction of the Moscow Spiritual Consistory.

39. TsGIAgM, f. 203, op. 412, d. 26, l. 1–1 ob., 16.

40. Ibid. The couple eventually reunited. Following strict procedures, the Moscow Spiritual Consistory ordered that the unhappy pair live together for two months, at the end of which they still remained unreconciled. However, the priest handling the case pressed for reconciliation after he learned the following in a sworn statement from Evdokeia, given in Lavrov's presence: "I want to live in Christian wedlock with my husband Ivan Lavrov. I promise to reform my behavior—I will neither fornicate nor drink [vodka]. I first sinned with him, Ivan Lavrov, when I was 12 or 13 or 14 years old. In this way, I consider him the culprit for my degradation, and he knows this. ([Priest's aside:] Evdokeia said this in the presence of Ivan.) Later when he was married to his first wife he also sinned with me" (l. 17). Despite repeated written appeals for over a year by the angry Lavrov, the Spiritual Consistory dragged out the case. Just when an annulment was about to be granted, Lavrov informed the authorities that he and Evdokeia had been reconciled and withdrew the petition for annulment.

41. Thomas, *Religion and the Decline of Magic*, pp. 527, 530.

42. Mironov, "Traditsionnoe demograficheskoe povedenie," p. 84. For a similar notion, see A. F. Kistiakovskii, "K voprosu o tsenzure nravov u naroda," *Zapiski Imperatorskogo Russkogo Geograficheskogo Obshchestva po otdeleniiu etnografii*, no. 8, (St. Petersburg, 1878).

43. M. M. Gromyko, "Traditional Norms of Behavior and Forms of Interaction of Nineteenth-century Russian Peasants," *Soviet Anthropology and Archeology* 30, no. 1 (Summer 1991): 76.

44. Gaudin, "Governing the Village," p. 162. Cf. the discussion of the social role of peasant reputations in F. G. Bailey, "Gifts and Poison," p. 4.

45. Scott, *Domination and the Arts of Resistance*, p. 131.

46. On rumors, see examples in TsGIAgM, f. 203, op. 347, g. 1875, d. 20, l. 1; f. 203, op. 349, g. 1877, d. 53, l. 1–1 ob. The priest would investigate and then file a formal complaint to the appropriate authorities.

47. Max Gluckman, "Gossip and Scandal," *Current Anthropology* 4, no. 3 (June 1963): 308.

48. Ibid., p. 312.

49. GME, f. 7, op. 1, d. 11, ll. 5 ob.–6 ob.

50. TsGIAgM, f. 203, op. 349, g. 1877, d. 53, l. 1. (Serpukhov District).

51. Ibid., l. 8. In a resolution of 12 March 1877, the commune confirmed the basic facts of the case: that Skvortsov and his family had been born and raised in Orthodoxy, and that Skvortsov had left the faith (l. 4.). The preceding discussion was drawn from the description in the local superintendent's report, ll. 6–7.

52. TsGIAgM, f. 142, "Moskovskii okruzhnyi sud," g. 1890, op. 1, d. 162, ll. 2–2 ob., 28, 42–43, 47–49. See also the examples in *Stanovlenie revoliutsionnykh traditsii piterskogo proletariata. Poreformennyi period, 1861–1883 gg.* (Leningrad, 1987). For other examples, see TsGIAgM, f. 203, op. 368, g. 1886, d. 6, ll. 1–1 ob., 3–6; op. 364, g. 1884, d. 80; and op. 352, g. 1878, d. 11, l. 1. On communal banishment in rural Russia, see the pathbreaking work by Corinne Gaudin, "Governing the Village," pp. 150–83.

53. TsGIAgM, f. 203, op. 341, d. 25, l. 1.

54. *Samosud* as a weapon to impose community control over peasants is discussed in Stephen P. Frank, "Popular Justice, Community, and Culture among the Russian Peasantry, 1870–1900," *Russian Review* 46, no. 3 (July 1987): 239–65; Frank, *Crime, Cultural Conflict,*

and Justice in Rural Russia, chap. 8; and Cathy A. Frierson, "Crime and Criminality in the Russian Village: Rural Concepts of Criminality at the End of the Nineteenth Century," *Slavic Review* 46, no. 1 (Spring 1987): 55–69. On peasant shaming rituals, see Christine Worobec, *Peasant Russia,* pp. 139–43, 148–49.

55. The report comes from Ioakimanskaia *volost',* Shuia District, Vladimir Province. GME, f. 7, op. 1, d. 58, l. 11. The source of the account, the shamed woman's parish priest (Father Kazanskii), added: "Only such girls who are not at all afraid of people's gibes and condemnation, and who freely 'carouse' *(guliat')* with several 'playmates' *(igral'shchiki)* at the same time undergo public condemnation or punishment and ridicule from the boys." Elena later married, but even then continued to "lead her former life, in spite of the frequent beatings [she suffered] from her husband." The practice of shaming a woman by tying her skirt above her head was a common form of public humiliation in the Russian village. See Engel, *Between the Fields and the City,* pp. 101, 139.

56. See the sample of an anonymous denunciation written in pencil on a torn piece of paper of a fellow worker and Old Believer accused of interfering in the religious life of other workers. RGIA, f. 1284, op. 208, g. 1853, d. 465. Also, TsGIAgM, f. 203, op. 368, g. 1886, d. 6, ll. 1–1 ob., 3–6; op. 352, g. 1878, d. 11, l. 1.

57. TsGIAgM, f. 203, op. 346, d. 11, ll. 1–1 ob.

58. Ibid., l. 10.

59. See the police report to the local superintendent on 9 January 1875. Ibid., l. 19.

60. The text of the tsarist gendarme's oath explicitly required Russian policemen to track religious dissidents. See the sample on permanent display in the Muzei Ministerstva Vnutrennykh Del (Museum of the Ministry of Internal Affairs), Moscow.

61. I. A. Golyshev, "Vospominaniia Ivana Aleksandrovicha Golysheva (1838–1878)," *Russkaia starina,* 1879, no. 24, p. 755.

62. For an illustrative case of a parish priest in conflict with the local police constable regarding the proper enforcement of religiosity, see in TsGIAgM, f. 203, op. 371, d. 8, ll. 1–2, 5.

63. The passage is taken from a leaflet entitled "On the Essence and Significance of the Schism in Russia," an extreme right-wing pamphelet issued by the Holy Synod in 1881, and quoted by Savich in the reference below. For descriptions of night raids against religious dissenters and nonconformists, see various issues of the Old Believer journal *Starobriadets.* For the typical case, see P. N. Vasil'evskii, "Istoriia staroobriadcheskikh obshchin: Elesinskii staroobriadcheskii prikhod (Nizhegorodskoi gubernii)," *Starobriadets,* 1907, no. 6, pp. 693–99.

On the relationship between militant Orthodox brotherhoods and Black Hundreds activity, see the article by A. P. Savich, "K istorii staroobriadchestva (po materialam arkhiva N. I. Subbotina)," *Zapiski otdela rukopisi GBL,* no. 2 (1939): 84–88. The archives of the brotherhood and its leaders are preserved at the Otdel Rukopisi (Manuscripts Department) of the Russian State Library, f. 294, "N. I. Subbotin," and f. 39, "Bratstvo Sv. Petra, Mitropolita Moskovskogo." The founder of the brotherhood was Father Nikolai Ivanovich Subbotin, professor of religion at the Moscow Spiritual Academy. He directed its central organization until his death in 1905. See "Bratstvo dlia oslableniia raskola v Moskve," *Vladimirskiia eparkhial'nyia vedomosti,* 1869, no. 7 (1 April), pp. 341–42.

64. See the large number of denunciations of priests for laxity in parish spiritual life in RGIA (Petersburg), f. 796, "Kantseliariia Sinoda." It seems likely that the Right terror that

emerged in Russia during the last two generations of the Old Regime was a direct response to the growing ineffectiveness of state and Church authorities: the vacuum from above helped to provoke and sustain "right-thinking" vigilante action from below. In this lay a powerful factor in the polarization of forces and the decay of a moderate alternative that characterized the last decade of the Old Regime.

65. Events reconstructed from the denunciation, investigation, and testimony in TsGIAgM, f. 203, op. 371, g. 1886–1887, d. 8, ll. 1–2, 5. The complaint was signed by Father Mikhail Sareevskii, Ivanovskoe village, in the Church of Predtechevskaia. The lesson of this case is also telling. Soon after a formal investigation began, it became clear that Kamenskii had managed to intimidate the key witnesses who, apparently out of fear, refused to verify the testimony they had initially given.

The chain of events was, of course, completely different from Kamenskii's point of view: he argued that before acting, he had consulted yet another peasant woman known to him, a certain Evdokeia Kuzvlina, who worked at the nearby Mazurin factory. Allegedly, Kuzvlina told Kamenskii that Pestova was drunk.

In May 1887, the prosecutor in Moscow circuit court dismissed the case, which by this time relied only on hearsay evidence (since none of the principal witnesses would support Father Sareevskii's charges). Even Pestova testified that she had heard nothing about having been beaten that day while she lay unconscious and implied that this had been Father Sareevskii's idea a few days later. The nervous friend, Semenova, was even more forthright: she absolutely refused to testify that constable Kamenskii had been excessive in any way. Several witnesses, even the Church guard Zaitsev, likewise retracted their initial testimony in the court.

66. TsGIAgM, f. 2330, op. 1, "Iudinskaia kollektsiia," ed. khr. 984–86, "Dnevnik Moskovskogo kuptsa Petra Vasil'evicha Medvedeva, 1854–1864 gg." Passage from ed. khr. 984, l. 12 ob. (22 June 1854).

67. "Promysly i nezemledel'cheskie zarabotki krest'ian Moskovskoi gub. v 1898–99 g." *Statisticheskii ezhegodnik Moskovskoi gubernii za 1899 god* (Moscow, 1900), sec. 2, p. 24. Kurochkin's full report is reproduced on pp. 22–25.

68. Ibid., p. 25.

69. Ibid., p. 24.

70. From the *zemstvo* correspondent's report in Lunevskaia *volost'*, Mosal'sk District. Cited in Ostrovyi, "Promysly," pp. 47, 48–49. On deals between village officials and hiring agents or employers, see several hundred cases of garnisheed wages in TsGIAgM, f. 710, op. 1, g. 1902, d. 111.

71. "Mestnye i otkhozhie promysly v 1899–1900 g. g.," *Obzor Vladimirskoi gubernii v sel'skokhoziaistvennom otnoshenii za 1900 god* (Vladimir, 1903), p. 329.

72. "Promysly i nezemledel'cheskie zarabotki krest'ian Moskovskoi gub. v 1899–1900 g.," *Statisticheskii ezhegodnik Moskovskoi gubernii za 1900 god* (Moscow, 1900), sec. 2, p. 21.

73. TsGIAgM, f. 203, op. 347, d. 21, l. 22 (May 1876).

74. TsGIAgM, f. 203, op. 364, g. 1884, d. 80, l. 1–2 (July 1884). The letter was signed by twenty-one male adults, who represented twelve clans in the village. Almost half the "signatories" were illiterate, so that signatures were placed by others next to each illiterate's "X."

75. As the text of the petition reveals, the law had been successfully applied at other times

in the history of this mixed Orthodox and Old Believer village (ll. 1–2). In a similar case in 1874, a village elder of the Old Belief was removed from his position after a formerly Orthodox peasant failed to baptize his newborn son and refused to return to Orthodoxy or even to sign an affidavit in which he recanted the blasphemous act. See ibid., op. 346, d. 29, ll. 14–15, 18 ob.

76. There is an enormous and fascinating comparative literature on religious denunciations as a means by which to gain the upper hand in nonreligious conflicts. Carol F. Karlsen has demonstrated that in colonial New England the most vulnerable to anathematization for witchcraft were "those women [who] were aberrations in a society with an inheritance system designed to keep property in the hands of men." *The Devil in the Shape of a Woman: Witchcraft in Colonial New England* (New York, 1987), p. 101.

77. Basil Sanson, "When Witches Are Not Named," in Max Gluckman, ed., *The Allocation of Responsibility* (Manchester, 1972), pp. 193–226.

78. Peter J. Wilson, "Filcher of Good Names: An Enquiry Into Anthropology and Gossip," *Man* 9 (1974): 100. Also see Bailey, "Gifts and Poison."

79. J. G. Peristiany, ed., *Honour and Shame: The Values of Mediterranean Society* (Chicago, 1965), p. 11. On patterns of litigation over defamation in early modern England, see the provocative J. A. Sharpe, *Defamation and Sexual Slander in Early Modern England: The Church Courts at York,* Borthwicke Papers 58 (York, 1980).

80. Scott, *Domination and the Arts of Resistance*, p. 131.

81. Cf., N. A. Minenko, "The Living Past: Daily Life and Holidays of the Siberian Village in the Eighteenth and First Half of the Nineteenth Centuries," *Soviet Anthropology and Archeology* 30, no. 1 (Summer 1991): 6–71.

82. TsGIAgM, f. 62, op. 1, t. 1, d. 334, ll. 22–23 (September 1893).

83. Ibid., l. 11.

84. I. A. Golyshev, "Vospominaniia," p. 354, with cases following.

85. In Russian provincial police files, there was always a special secret section containing investigations regarding "political reliability" of locals, usually peasants. For examples, see TsGIAgM, f. 479, "Dmitrovskoe uezdnoe politseiskoe upravlenie," op. 3, g. 1886, d. 28, "Predpisaniia Moskovskogo gubernatora o sbore svedenii o nravstvennykh kachestvakh, ob obraze zhizni i politicheskoi blagodezhnosti otdel'nykh lits" (Instructions of the Moscow governor regarding the collection of information about the moral qualities, about the way of life and political reliability of individuals).

86. TsGIAgM, f. 17, op. 66, d. 12, l. 11 ob.–12 (14 October 1888). The real issue seems to have been the poor living conditions for workers and Suvirov's failure to fulfill explicit promises made to Osipov and his family.

87. E. E. Evans-Pritchard, *Witchcraft, Oracles, and Magic Among the Azande* (Oxford, 1937), p. 110.

88. From the text of a review of the case in the Moscow circuit court. TsGIAgM, f. 17, op. 66, g. 1895, d. 617, l. 4.

89. Ibid., ll. 3–4.

90. From the memo of the minister of internal affairs to the Moscow governor-general, 9 December 1895. Ibid., ll. 7–8.

91. Samoilov, *Vospominaniia*, 1: 73.

92. TsGIAgM, f. 203, op. 342, d. 31, ll. 11–14 passim. Observations on the basic relationship between religious dissent and popular protest are not new. For related works, see Michael Cherniavsky's classic "The Old Believers and the New Religion," in *The Structure of Russian History* (New York, 1971), pp. 140–88; A. I. Klibanov, "Problems of the Ideology of Peasant Movements (1850s–1860s)," *Russian History* 11, nos. 2–3 (1984): 168–208; and V. G. Kartsov, *Religioznyi raskol kak forma antifeodal'nogo protesta v istorii Rossii* (Kalinin, 1971), pts. 1–2. For comparative perspectives, see Christopher Hill, *Antichrist in Seventeenth-Century England* (Oxford, 1971).

On the link of religious sectarianism with worker activism, David Pretty, "The Saints of the Revolution," has identified numerous parallels between working class militancy and schismatic religious preferences: "Worldviews anchored in schismatic religion facilitated conversion to social democratic activism and eased adaptation to underground and conspiratorial work. Old Belief by definition was, for all its innate conservatism, oppositional, rejecting the authority of both the official church and the tsarist regime" (pp. 276–304); see also David Pretty, "Neither Peasant nor Proletarian." Cf., Zelnik, "'To the Unaccustomed Eye'"; Mark D. Steinberg, "Workers on the Cross: Religious Imagination in the Writing of Russian Workers, 1910–1924," *Russian Review* 53, no. 2 (April 1994): 213–39; and Kimberly Page Herrlinger, "Class, Piety, and Politics: Workers, Orthodoxy, and the Problem of Religious Identity in Russia, 1881–1914" (Ph.D. diss., University of California at Berkeley, 1996).

93. Lynne Viola has identified peasant-workers as a particularly high-risk group for denunciation and dekulakization after 1927. See "The Second Coming: Class Enemies in the Soviet Countryside, 1927–1935," in J. Arch Getty and Roberta Manning, eds., *Stalinist Terror: New Perspectives* (Cambridge, 1993), pp. 65–98.

94. Autograph letter of 6 March 1928, f. 396, op. 6, d. 61, ll. 155–56. For a similar case, see RGAE, f. 7486, "Ministerstvo Zemledeliia SSSR," op. 37, d. 65, l. 37.

95. See also the denunciation of selected fellow villagers by M. N. Kozlov in Tula Province, RGAE, f. 7486, op. 37, d. 65, ll. 78–80. Cf. ll. 87–88.

96. In contrast, Sheila Fitzpatrick's study of peasant denunciations in the late 1930s does *not* show peasant labor-migrants were a major target. See her article and introduction in Sheila Fitzpatrick and Robert Gellately, eds., *The Practice of Denunciation*, special issue of *Journal of Modern History* 68 (December 1996). And Fitzpatrick's book: *Stalin's Peasants: Resistance and Survival in the Russian Village After Collectivization* (Oxford, 1994), pp. 233–61.

There is no fundamental contradiction between the different findings: there is considerable evidence to suggest that peasant labor-migrants had been transformed into permanent workers as a direct result of the first two Five-Year Plans. See Hoffmann, *Peasant Metropolis*.

GLOSSARY

blagodetel: benefactor

chuzhoi: an outsider, not of the village; something alien (cf. *svoi*)

desiatina: Imperial Russian land measure equivalent to 2.7 acres

domokhoziain: peasant household chief (pl. *domokhoziaieva*)

dvor: peasant household

etapnik: peasant returned "under guard" to his village

gliadia po cheloveku: "depending on the person"

kabak: village saloon (*kabatchik:* saloon-keeper)

krugovaia poruka: mutual responsibility for dues and obligations (initially of fiscal duties, but later for contracts as well)

kulak: derogatory term for an abusive wealthy peasant; literally "fist"

mir: village assembly

muzhik: a Russian male peasant (pl. *muzhiki*)

nalevo: "on the sly," "under the table," illicitly

napitrit'sia: peasant slang meaning to live in Petersburg so long that you get sick to death of life there

nerazdel'naia sem'ia: the indivisible (peasant) family unit

otkhod, otkhodnichestvo: peasant labor migration for side-earnings (versus *pereselenie:* permanent peasant relocation to a new region)

otkhodnik: peasant labor-migrant

Piter: popular jargon for "Peter," or St. Petersburg

pitershchik: popular expression for a peasant-worker who works in St. Petersburg; sometimes used more generally to describe any peasant-worker who worked outside the village

po etapu: literally, "under guard," referring to a peasant's forced return to his or her village

pomoch: mutual aid among fellow villagers

raskol: "schism" in the Russian Orthodox Church in the seventeenth century

raskol'nik: schismatic, Old Believer, religious dissenter (pl. *raskol'niki*) *shinok:* village low bar, speakeasy (after 1894, village bars operating illegally, in violation of the state vodka monopoly)

starosta: village elder

starshina: volost or cantonal elder

svoi: one's own, a village insider (cf. *chuzhoi*)

traktir: tavern

tysiachnik: "thousandaire." (a wealthy person)

volost: canton, subunit of the *uezd* (district) and of the *guberniia* (province)

vytrebovanie: forced return of a peasant labor-migrant. Cf. *etapnik*

zemliachestvo: the phenomenon of peasants from the same village or *volost* clustering in factories, skills, or neighborhoods outside the village; the ties that bind those peasant-workers

zemliak: a fellow villager or peasant from the same village or region

znakomstvo: acquaintanceship, "connections," generally: acquaintanceship networks

BIBLIOGRAPHY

Archival Sources

Gosudarstvennyi Arkhiv Iaroslavskoi Oblasti (GAIaO)

Kollektsiia rukopisei. Dnevniki [Iaroslavskogo krest'ianina-otkhodnika] I. G. Andreeva, 1905–1914 gg. [in 17 parts], ed. khr. 527, 670, 1065, 1071, 1135, 1161–71, 1394.

Gosudarstvennyi Arkhiv Rossiiskoi Federatsii
(GARF, formerly TsGAOR SSSR)

f. 1741. Kollektsiia nelegal'nykh izdanii (listovok i broshiur), otlozhivshikhsia v politseiskikh i sudebnykh organakh dorevoliutsionnoi Rossii (1850–1917 gg.), op. 1–2.

Gosudarstvennyi Muzei Etnografii Narodov SSSR.
Sektsiia Rukopisei (GME), St. Petersburg

f. 7. Materialy "Etnograficheskogo Biuro" V. N. Tenisheva, 1897–1901.

Muzei Ministerstva Vnutrennykh Del, Moscow

Rossiiskii Gosudarstvennyi Arkhiv Literatury i Iskusstva
(RGALI, formerly TsGALI), Moscow

f. 1227. Ivan Gavrilovich Pryzhov (1827–1885 gg.).

Rossiiskaia Gosudarstvennaia Biblioteka (RGB),
Otdel Rukopisi (formerly, GBL)

f. 39. Bratstvo Sv. Petra, Mitropolita Moskovskogo.
f. 218, kart. 173, ed. khr.1–5. M. N. Shustova, "Dnevnik (1870–1878)."
f. 294. N. I. Subbotin.

Rossiiskii Gosudarstvennyi Arkhiv Ekonomiki
(RGAE, formerly TsGANKh SSSR), Moscow

f. 396. Redaktsiia "Krest'ianskoi gazety" izdaniia TsK RKP(b).

f. 7486. Ministerstvo Zemledeliia SSSR.

Rossiiskii Gosudarstvennyi Istoricheskii Arkhiv
(RGIA, formerly TsGIA SSSR), St. Petersburg

f. 796. Kantseliariia Sinoda.

f. 1284. Departament Obshchikh Del MVD.

f. 1405. Osobaia pasportnaia komissiia Ministerstva Vnutrennykh Del.

Tsentral'nyi Gosudarstvennyi Istoricheskii Arkhiv goroda Moskvy
(TsGIAgM), Moscow

f. 16. Kantseliariia Moskovskogo General-Gubernatora

f. 17 Kantseliariia Moskovskogo Gubernatora.

f. 62. Moskovskoe gubernskoe prisutstvie.

f. 66. Moskovskoe gubernskoe po krest'ianskim delam prisutstvie.

f. 179. Moskovskoe gorodskoe obshchestvennoe upravlenie.

f. 203. Moskovskaia dukhovnaia konsistoriia.

f. 217. Preobrazhenskaia bol'nitsa dlia dushevnobol'nykh (1791–1917 gg.).

VOLOSTNYE PRAVLENIIA PO UEZDAM MOSKOVSKOI GUBERNII

BOGORODSKII UEZD

f. 705. Volostnye pravleniia Bogorodskogo uezda Moskovskoi gubernii (Ignat'evskoe volostnoe pravlenie).

BRONNITSKII UEZD

f. 746. Rozhdestvenskoe volostnoe pravlenie.

f. 808. Chulkovskoe volostnoe pravlenie.

f. 2237. Usmerskoe volostnoe pravlenie.

DMITROVSKII UEZD

f. 795. Timinovskoe volostnoe pravlenie.

f. 815. Il'inskoe volostnoe pravlenie.

MOSKOVSKII UEZD

f. 8. Nogatinskoe volostnoe pravlenie.

f. 378. Tsarinskoe volostnoe pravlenie.

MOZHAISKII UEZD

f. 579. Borodinskoe volostnoe pravlenie.

f. 581. Elmanovskoe volostnoe pravlenie.

PODOL'SKII UEZD

f. 600. Dobriatinskoe volostnoe pravlenie.

f. 601. Klenovskoe volostnoe pravlenie.

ZVENIGORODSKII UEZD

f. 515. Pavlovskoe volostnoe pravlenie.

f. 747. Sharapovskoe volostnoe pravlenie.

f. 748. Iaguninskoe volostnoe pravlenie.

FONDY MOSKOVSKOGO GUBERNSKOGO ZEMSTVA

f. 184. Moskovskaia gubernskaia zemskaia uprava.

f. 199. Moskovskii gubernskii statisticheskii komitet.

UEZDNYE ZEMSKIE UPRAVY MOSKOVSKOI GUBERNII

f. 11. Moskovskaia uezdnaia zemskaia uprava.

f. 12. Bogorodskaia uezdnaia zemskaia uprava.

f. 187. Volokolamskaia uezdnaia zemskaia uprava.

f. 188. Dmitrovskaia uezdnaia zemskaia uprava.

f. 194. Serpukhovskaia uezdnaia zemskaia uprava.

Tsentral'nyi Gosudarstvennyi Arkhiv Kinofotodokumentov SSSR (TsGAK SSSR), Krasnogorsk

Selected Primary Sources

Abramov, Ia. V. "Krest'ianskii kredit." *Otechestvennye zapiski,* 1884, no. 1, sec. 2, pp. 1–34.

Agrarnoe dvizhenie v Rossii v 1905–1906 gg. Trudy Imperatorskogo Vol'nogo Ekonomicheskogo Obshchestva. 2 vols. St. Petersburg, 1908.

Andreev, F. "V zashchitu krest'ianskoi sem'i." *Severnyi vestnik,* 1889, no. 4.

Artynov, Aleksandr Iakovlevich. "Vospominaniia krest'ianina sela Ugodicha, Iaroslavskoi gubernii, Rostovskogo uezda (S predisloviem A. A. Titov)." *Chteniia v Imperatorskom Obshchestve Istorii i Drevnostei Rossiiskikh pri Moskovskom Universitete,* 1882, bk. 1 (January–March), pp. 1–88; bk. 3 (July–September), pp. 89–160.

Barykov, V. I., A. V. Polovstev, and P. A. Sokolovskii, eds. *Sbornik materialov dlia izucheniia sel'skoi pozemel'noi obshchiny*. St. Petersburg, 1880.

Baskin, G. I. "Mestnye i otkhozhie promysly." *Obzor Vladimirskoi gubernii v sel'skokhoziaistvennom otnoshenii za 1897 god*. Vladimir, 1898.

Blagoveshchenskii, N. A. "Sborshchiki podatei." *Ekonomicheskii zhurnal*, 1889, nos. 10–11, pp. 33–52.

Blagoveshchenskii, V. P. *Melkii kredit v derevne*. Moscow, 1906.

Bogolepov, I. P. "Kustarnye, otkhozhie i fabrichnye promysly v Moskovskoi gubernii v zimu 1887–88 g." *Statisticheskii ezhegodnik Moskovskoi gubernii za 1888 god*. Moscow, 1888.

Bonnell, Victoria E., ed. *The Russian Worker: Life and Labor Under the Tsarist Regime*. Berkeley and Los Angeles, 1983.

Brzheskii, Nikolai Kornilovich. "Krest'ianskie semeinye razdely i zakon 18 marta 1886 goda." *Russkoe ekonomicheskoe obozrenie*, 1900, no. 4, pp. 39–79; no. 5, pp. 68–110; no. 6, pp. 48–82.

———. *Krugovaia poruka sel'skikh obshchestv (Soobrazheniia redaktsionnykh komissii po sostavleniiu polozhenii 19 fevralia 1861 g. i pravitel'stvennye vzgliady za vremia s 1861 po 1895 god)*. St. Petersburg, 1896.

———. "Nanimateli i rabochie v sel'skom khoziaistve." *Russkoe ekonomicheskoe obozrenie*, 1898, no. 10.

———. *Natural'nye povinnosti krest'ian i mirskie sbory*. St. Petersburg, 1906.

———. *Nedoimochnost' i krugovaia poruka sel'skikh obshchestv (Istoriko-kriticheskii obzor deistvuiushchego zakonodatel'stva, v sviazi s praktikiiu krest'ianskogo podatnogo dela)*. St. Petersburg, 1897.

———. *Obshchinnyi byt i khoziaistvennaia neobespechennost' krest'ian (Po povodu predstoiashchego peresmotra krest'ianskikh polozhenii)*. St. Petersburg, 1899.

———. "Obychnyi poriadok nasledovaniia krest'ian." *Russkoe ekonomicheskoe obozrenie*, 1899, no. 6, pp. 1–24; no. 7, pp. 1–23.

———. *Ocherki agrarnogo byta krest'ian*. St. Petersburg, 1908.

———. *Ocherki iuridicheskogo byta krest'ian*. St. Petersburg, 1902.

Bulgakov, A. A. *Sovremennye peredvizheniia krest'ianstva. Napravleniia, razmery i usloviia krest'ianskikh dvizhenii Moskovskoi gubernii po novym tsifrovym dannym za desiatiletie 1894–1903 gg*. St. Petersburg, 1905.

Chernenkov, N. N., comp. "Krest'ianskii kredit v Moskovskoi gub. po soobshcheniiam gg. korrespondentov." *Statisticheskii ezhegodnik po Moskovskoi gubernii za 1889 g*. Moscow, 1889.

———. "Nekotoryia svedeniia o krest'ianskikh obshchestvennykh zaimakh v Moskovskoi gubernii (po issledovaniiam 1876–1878 gg.)." *Statisticheskii ezhegodnik po Moskovskoi gubernii za 1889 g*. Moscow, 1889.

Chernevskii, V. A. *K voprosu o p'ianstve Vladimirskoi gubernii i sposobakh bor'by s nim.* Vladimir, 1911.

Chernobrovtsev, S. V. *Melkii kredit v derevne Vladimirskoi gubernii (po otzyvam derevenskikh zhitelei).* Vladimir, 1913.

Chervinskii, P. "Ekonomicheskiia skitaniia." *Otechestvennye zapiski,* 1880, no. 7, pp. 71–116.

Dadonov, V. "Russkii Manchestr" (Pis'ma ob Ivanovo-Voznesenske)." *Russkoe bogatstvo,* 1900, no. 12, pp. 46–67.

Dement'ev, E. M. *Fabrika, chto ona dala naseleniiu i chto ona u nego beret.* Moscow, 1893.

Diubiuk, Evgenii. "Fabriki v derevne (pis'mo iz Vladimira)." *Sovremennyi mir,* 1911, no. 4 (April), pp. 274–81.

Dobrotvorskii, N. "Iukhnovskie zemlekopy." *Severnyi vestnik,* 1887, no. 6, sec. 2, pp. 54–77.

———. "Torgovyia krest'ianskiia arteli." *Severnyi vestnik,* 1886, no. 3 (March), sec. 2, pp. 131–39.

Dobrotvorskii, N. A. "Krest'ianskie iuridicheskie obychai v vostochnoi chasti Vladimirskoi gubernii (uezdy: Viaznikovskii, Gorokhovetskii, Shuiskii, i Kovrovskii)." Pts. 1–4. *Iuridicheskii vestnik,* 1888, no. 6/7, pp. 322–49; 1889, no. 6/7, 1891, no. 10, pp. 197–208; 1891, no. 11, pp. 326–63.

Dokumenty po istorii krest'ianskoi obshchiny, 1861–1880 gg. A. M. Anfimov and B. G. Litvak, eds. Vol. 1. Moscow, 1983. Vol. 2. Moscow, 1984.

Dolivo-Dobrovol'skii, A. N. "Tkatskoe proizvodstvo." *Kustarnaia promyshlennost' Rossii. Raznye promysly.* Vol. 1. St. Petersburg, 1913.

Druzhinin, N. M., ed. *Krest'ianskoe dvizhenie v Rossii v XIX–nachale XX veka.* 10 vols. Moscow, 1960–1968.

Dubrovskii, S. M., and B. B. Grave, comps. *Agrarnoe dvizhenie v 1905–1907 gg.* [Materialy departamenta politsii]. Moscow-Leningrad, 1925.

Elets, Iu. L. *Podval'noe bezumie: k sverzheniiu iga mod* (St. Petersburg, 1914).

Ermolov, A. S. *Neurozhai i narodno bedstvie.* St. Petersburg, 1892.

Eropkin, A. "Pervyi god podatnoi reformy." *Narodnoe khoziaistvo. Nauchnoe obshchestvennyi zhurnal,* 1901, no. 2, pp. 54–74; no. 3, pp. 47–74.

Firsov, B. M., and I. G. Kiselev, eds. *Byt velikorusskikh krest'ian-zemlepashtsev. Opisanie materialov etnograficheskogo biuro Kniazia V. N. Tenisheva (na primere Vladimirskoi gubernii).* St. Petersburg, 1993.

Fortunatov, A. F. "Chastota neurozhaev na krest'ianskikh nadelakh." *Vestnik sel'skogo khoziaistva,* 1906, no. 29 (16 July 1906), pp. 1–4.

———. "Rzhanie nedorody na krest'ianskikh nadelakh za 10-tiletie 1896–1905," *Russkie vedomosti,* 1906, no. 177 (12 July 1906), p. 3.

Gertsenshtein, M. Ia. "Melkii Kredit." *Nuzhdy derevni po rabotam komitetov o nuzhdakh sel'skokhoziastvennoi promyshlennosti.* Vol. 2. St. Petersburg, 1904.

Golubev, P. "Podat' i narodnoe khoziaistvo." *Russkaia mysl'*, sec. 2, 1893, no. 5 (May), pp. 137–50; no. 6 (June), pp. 47–67; no. 7 (July), pp. 1–29.

———. "Podatnye ocherki." *Russkoe bogatstvo*, 1894, no. 1, sec. 2, pp. 1–26.

Golyshev, I. A. "Vospominaniia Ivana Aleksandrovicha Golysheva (1838–1878)." *Russkaia starina*, 1879, no. 24, pp. 753–72; no. 25, pp. 353–66.

Goremykin, I. L. *Svod uzakonenii i rasporiazhenii pravitel'stva ob ustroistve sel'skogo sostoianiia i uchrezhdenii po krest'ianskim delam.* 2 vols. St. Petersburg, 1903.

Grigor'ev, M. I. *Melkii kredit v Iaroslavskoi gubernii (Istoricheskii ocherk razvitiia uchrezhdenii melkogo kredita, obzor ikh deiatel'nosti i svodka materialov ankety)* Iaroslavl', 1912.

Guliaev, A. M. "Krest'ianskii dvor." *Zhurnal Ministersva Iustitsii*, 1899, no. 4 (April), pp. 53–99.

Iablonskii, A. A. "Vliianie urozhaia 1896 g. na blagosostoianie naseleniia." *Obzor Vladimirskoi gubernii v sel'skokhoziaistvennom otnoshenii za 1896 god.* Vladimir, 1897.

Iakushkin, Evgenii Ivanovich. *Obychnoe pravo: Materialy dlia bibliografii obychnogo prava.* 4 vols., parts 1/2. Iaroslavl', 1875. Parts 3/4. Moscow, 1908–1909.

———. "Volostnye sudy v Iaroslavskoi gubernii." *Iuridicheskii vestnik*, 1872, no. 3, sec. 2.

———, with S. P. Nikonov. *Grazhdanskoe pravo po resheniiam Krestobogorodskogo volostnogo suda Iaroslavskoi gubernii i uezda.* Iaroslavl', 1902.

Ianson, Iu. E. *Opyt statisticheskogo issledovaniia o krest'ianskikh nadelakh i platezhakh.* St. Petersburg, 1881.

Ianzhul, I. I. *Fabrichnyi byt Moskovskoi gubernii. Otchet za 1882–1883 g.* St. Petersburg, 1884.

I———. Kh———. [pseud.]. "Pomoch'." *Russkoe bogatstvo*, 1879, no. 1.

Iaroslavl' (Province). *Obzor Iaroslavskoi gub.* Vol. 2. *Otkhozhie promysly krest'ian Iaroslavskoi gub*, ed. A. R. Svirshchevskii. Iaroslavl, 1896.

———. *Statisticheskoe opisanie Iaroslavskoi gubernii.* Vol. 5., *Iaroslavskii uezd.* Iaroslavl', 1907.

———. *Istoriko-statisticheskie tablitsy po Iaroslavskoi gubernii za 1862–1898 gg.* Vol. 8 of *Statisticheskii sbornik po Iaroslavskoi gubernii.* Iaroslavl', 1901.

———. *Otkhozhie promysly krest'ian Iaroslavskoi gubernii (po dannym o pasportakh za 1896–1902 g. g.).* Vol. 19 of *Statisticheskii sbornik po Iaroslavskoi gubernii.* Iaroslavl', 1907.

———. *Sel'skokhoziaistvennyi obzor za [1898–1912] g.* 13 vols. Iaroslavl', 1899–1914.

Ioksimovich, Ch. M. *Manufakturnaia promyshlennost' v proshlom i nastoiashchem.* Moscow, 1915.

Isaev, Andrei Alekseevich. "V Iaroslavskoi gubernii (iz putevykh zametok)." *Otechestvennye zapiski*, 3d ser., 251, no. 8 (August 1880): 172–91.

———. "Znachenie semeinykh razdelov krest'ian. Po lichnym nabliudeniiam." *Vestnik Evropy*, 1883, no. 7, pp. 333–49.

Kanatchikov, S. I. *A Radical Worker in Tsarist Russia: The Autobiography of Semën Ivanovich Kanatchikov.* Trans. and ed. Reginald E. Zelnik. Stanford, 1986.

———. *Iz istorii moego bytiia*. 2 vols. Moscow-Leningrad, 1929.

Kandinskii, V. "O nakazaniiakh po resheniiam volostnykh sudov Moskovskoi gubernii." In Nikolai Kharuzin, ed. *Sbornik svedenii dlia izucheniia byta krest'ianskogo naseleniia Rossii. Trudy etnograficheskogo otdela imperatorskogo obshchestva liubitelei estestvoznaniia, antropologii i etnografii*. Bk. 9, vols. 1–2. Moscow, 1889–1890.

Kartsev, E. E. "Ekonomicheskie etiudi. Otkhozhii promysel." *Nabliudatel'*, 1882, no. 3.

Karyshev, Nikolai Aleksandrovich. "Narodno-khoziaistvennye nabroski: otkhozhie promysly Smolenskoi gubernii." *Russkoe bogatstvo*, 1897, no. 6, pp. 173–89.

Kasperovich, G. "O kredite dlia remeslennikov." *Vestnik finansov, promyshlennosti i torgovli*, 1914, no. 1, pp. 10.

"Kharakteristika iavleniia vremennoi priostanovki i zakrytiia predpriiatii v russkoi promyshlennosti." *Vestnik finansov, promyshlennosti i torgovli*, 1914, no. 24, pp. 522.

Kharlamov, I. N. *Sbornik statisticheskikh svedenii po Smolenskoi gubernii*. Vol. 1, part 2. *Viazemskii uezd*. Moscow, 1886.

Kirillov, L. A. "K voprosu o vnezemledel'cheskom otkhode krest'ianskogo naseleniia." *Trudy Imperatorskogo Vol'nogo Ekonomicheskogo Obshchestva*, 1899, vol. 1, bk. 3, pp. 259–99.

Kolesnikov, V. A. *Prichina krest'ianskikh semeinykh razdelov*. Iaroslavl', 1898.

Kolobov, V. M., comp., Vikhliaev, P. A., ed. *Sel'skii kredit v Moskovskoi gubernii*. Moscow, 1914.

Korolenko, S. A., comp. *Sel'skokhoziaistvennye statisticheskie svedeniia po materialam, poluchennym ot khoziaev*. 12 vols. St. Petersburg, 1884–1905. Vol. 5, *Volnonaemnyi trud v khoziaistvakh vladel'cheskik i peredvizhenie rabochikh, v sviazi s statitistiko-ekonomicheskim obzorom Evropeiskoi Rossii v sel'skoi-khoziaistvennom i promyshlennom otnosheniiakh*. St. Petersburg, 1892.

Kostroma (Province). Kostromskoe Gubernskoe Zemstvo. Otsenochno-statisticheskoe Otdelenie. *Materialy dlia otsenki zemel' Kostromskoi gubernii*. 15 vols. Kostroma, 1900–1916.

———. *Sbornik statisticheskikh svedenii po Kostromskoi gubernii*. Vol. 1. *Sel'skokhoziaistvennyi obzor Kostromskoi gubernii po svedeniiam tekushchei statistiki za 1896–1905 i 1902–1905 gg*. Kostroma, 1908.

———. *Statisticheskii ezhegodnik Kostromskoi gubernii za [1907–1909] god. Sel'skoe khoziaistvo i krest'ianskie promysly*. Kostroma, 1908–1912.

Krasnoperov, I. V. "K voprosu o prichinakh nedoimochnosti krestianskogo naseleniia. (Platezhi, nedoimki i dolgi krest'ian Nikolaevskogo uezda, Samarskoi gubernii)." *Iuridicheskii vestnik*, 1889, vol 3, bk. 2 (October), pp. 435–49.

Krasnoperov, I. M. "Krest'ianskii kredit." *Sel'skokhoziaistvennyi obzor Tverskoi gubernii za 1897 god*. Tver', 1898.

———. *Sel'skokhoziaistvennyi obzor Tverskoi gubernii za 1894-i god*. "Mestnye i otkhozhie promysly krest'ianskogo naseleniia." Tver', 1895. Part 2, pp. 1–18.

———. "Mestnye i otkhozhie promysly i zaniatiia naseleniia v 1900–1901 g." *Statisticheskii ezhegodnik Tverskoi gubernii za 1901 god*. Tver', 1902.

———. "Mestnye i otkhozhie promysly krest'ianskogo naseleniia," *Statisticheskii ezhegodnik Tverskoi gubernii za 1898 god* (Tver', 1899),

———. "Otkhozhie promysly." *Statisticheskii ezhegodnik Tverskoi gubernii za 1897 god.* Tver', 1898.

"Krest'ianskii kredit." *Novoe vremia,* 8 September 1898, no. 8093, pp. 1–2.

"Krest'ianskie vybory v Kostromskoi gubernii." *Moskovskiia vedomosti,* 1864, no. 134 (18 June), p. 2.

Krestovnikov, A. N. *Pitanie krest'ian Kostromskoi gubernii po dannym biudzhetnogo issledovaniia 1908–9 gg.* Kostroma, 1912.

Lagovskii, F. N. *Narodnye pesni Kostromskoi, Vologodskoi, Novgorodskoi, Nizhegorodskoi i Iaroslavskoi gubernii.* Kostroma, 1923.

Lenin, Vladimir Il'ich. *Collected Works.* 5th ed. Moscow, 1964.

Lenskii, B. "Otkhozhie nezemledel'cheskie promysly v Rossii." *Otechestvennye zapiski,* 1877, no. 12, pp. 207–58.

———. "Semeinye razdely." *Delo,* 1881, no. 11.

Leont'ev, A. A. *Volostnoi sud i iuridicheskie obychai krest'ian.* St. Petersburg, 1895.

"Letnii otkhod v 1896 godu." *Sel'sko-khoziaistvennyi obzor Nizhegorodskoi gubernii za 1896 god.* Nizhnii Novgorod, 1897.

Liadov, Ivan Matveevich. "Iuridicheskie obychai krest'ian Shuiskogo uezda." *Ezhegodnik Vladimirskogo gubernskogo statisticheskogo komiteta.* Vol. 1, no. 2. Vladimir, 1877.

Lichkov, L. S. "Krest'ianskie semeinye razdely." *Severnyi vestnik,* 1886, no. 1, pp. 84–108.

———. "Krugovaia poruka i obshchinnoe zemlevladenie." *Russkaia mysl',* 1886, no. 10, pp. 33–34.

Lozina-Lozinskii, M. A. "Nechto o zakondatel'nom poriadke i krest'ianskom dvore." *Pravo,* 1899, no. 46 (14 November), pp. 2197–201.

Make-ov, L. V. "Arendnaia sdacha nadel'noi zemli." *Ekonomicheskii zhurnal,* 1889, no. 4, pp. 27–41.

Makarenko, A. "Otkhozhie i kabal'nye rabochie." *Iuridicheskii vestnik,* 1887, no. 4 (April), pp. 727–40.

Maksimov, Evgenii. "O krugovoi poruke v sel'skikh obshchestvakh." *Ekonomicheskii zhurnal,* 1893, no. 4, pp. 13–24.

Maslov, Petr. *Agrarnyi vopros v Rossii: Uslovie razvitiia sel'skogo khoziaistva v Rossii.* 2 vols. St. Petersburg, 1905–1908.

"Mestnye i otkhozhie promysly v 1899–1900 g. g." *Obzor Vladimirskoi gubernii v sel'skokhoziaistvennom otnoshenii za 1900 god.* Vladimir, 1903.

Mikhnevich, V. O. *Iazvy Peterburga. Opyt istoriko-statisticheskogo issledovaniia nravstvennosti stolichnogo naseleniia. Istoricheskie etiudy russkoi zhizni,* vol. 3. St. Petersburg, 1886.

Miller, E. E. "Promysly i vnezemledel'cheskie zarabotki krest'ianskogo naseleniia za 1894/5 g." *Statisticheskii ezhegodnik Moskovskoi gubernii za 1895 god.* Moscow, 1896.

M. N. R. "Sud v derevne (Iz dnevnika byvshego mirovogo sud'i)." *Nabliudatel'*, 1882, no. 2, pp. 95–124; no. 3, pp. 45–62.

Nikol'skii, V. *Opyt analiza dannykh zemskoi tekushchei statistiki (Podennye platy vo Vladimirskoi gubernii pri sel'skokhoziaistvennom naime rabochikh v 1896–1900 gg.).* Vladimir, 1905.

"Nishchenstvo." *Statisticheskii ezhegodnik Moskovskoi gubernii za 1910 god.* (Moscow, 1911), 3: 78–91.

Novikov, Aleksandr I. *Zametki zemskogo nachal'nika.* St. Petersburg, 1899.

Novikov, Andrei Alekseevich. *Iz zapisok agronoma [1880–1906 gg.].* Vladimir, 1908.

Nuzhdy derevny po rabotam komitetov o nuzhdakh sel'skokhoziaistvennoi promyshlennosti. (Sbornik statei). 2 vols. St. Petersburg, 1904.

Obzor Iaroslavskoi gubernii za [1900–1912]. Prilozhenie k vsepoddaneishemu otchetu. Iaroslavl', [1901–1913].

Orlov, V. *Krest'ianskoe khoziaistvo.* No. 1. *Formy krest'ianskogo zemlevladeniia v Moskovskoi gubernii.* Moscow, 1879.

———. *Moskovskii uezd. Statisticheskie svedeniia o khoziaistvennom polozhenii Moskovskogo uezda.* In *Sbornik statisticheskikh svedenii po Moskovskoi gubernii. Otdel khoziaistvennoi statistiki.* No. 1. Moscow, 1877.

Ostrovyi, K. M. "Promysly." *Statisticheskii obzor Kaluzhskoi gubernii za 1897 god.* (Kaluga, 1898), pp. 34–59.

Pakhman, S. V. *Obychnoe grazhdanskoe pravo v Rossii. Iuridicheskie ocherki.* 2 vols. St. Petersburg, 1877–1879.

Peskov, P. A. *Fabrichnyi byt Vladimirskoi gubernii: otchet za 1882–1883 g.* St. Petersburg, 1884.

Petrov, V. V. "Promysly i vne-zemledel'cheskie zarabotki v zimu 1890–91 g." *Statisticheskii ezhegodnik Moskovskoi gubernii za 1891 god.* Moscow, 1891.

———. "Promysly i vne-zemledel'cheskie zarabotki v zimu 1891–1892 g." *Statisticheskii ezhegodnik Moskovskoi gubernii za 1892 g.* Moscow, 1892.

———. "Promysly i vnezemledel'cheskie zarabotki v zimu 1893–94 goda." *Statisticheskii ezhegodnik Moskovskoi gubernii za 1894 g.* Moscow, 1895.

Pogozhev, A. V. *Uchet chislennosti i sostava rabochikh v Rossii.* St. Petersburg, 1906.

Pokrovskii, F. "O semeinom polozhenii krest'ianskoi zhenshchiny v Kostromskoi gubernii po dannym volostnogo suda." *Zhivaia starina*, 1896, sec. 1, pp. 457–76.

Polnoe sobranie zakonov Rossiiskoi imperii. St. Petersburg, 1830–1916.

Prokopovich, Sergei Nikolaevich. *Agrarnyi vopros i agrarnoe dvizhenie.* Rostov, 1905.

———. "Krest'ianstvo i poreformennaia fabrika." *Velikaia Reforma: Russkoe obshchestvo i krest'ianskii vopros v proshlom i nastoiashchem.* Vol. 6. Moscow, 1911.

———. *Mestnye liudi o nuzhdakh Rossii.* St. Petersburg, 1904.

"Prom. Kost. 1913." *Vestnik finansov, promyshlennosti i torgovli*, 1914, no. 19, pp. 295.

"Promysly i vne-zemledel'cheskie zarabotki v zimu 1888–89 gg." *Statisticheskii ezhegodnik Moskovskoi gubernii za 1889 g.* Moscow, 1889.

"Promysly i vnezemledel'cheskie zarabotki krest'ianskogo naseleniia za 1895–6 god." *Statisticheskii ezhegodnik Moskovskoi gubernii za 1896 g.* Moscow, 1897.

"Promysly i vnezemledel'cheskie zarabotki krest'ianskogo naseleniia za 1896–97 godu." *Statisticheskii ezhegodnik Moskovskoi gubernii za 1897 god.* Moscow, 1897.

"Promysly i nezemledel'cheskie zarabotki krest'ian Moskovskoi gub. v 1898–99 g." *Statisticheskii ezhegodnik Moskovskoi gubernii za 1899 god.* Moscow, 1900.

"Promysly i nezemledel'cheskie zarabotki krest'ian Moskovskoi gub. v 1899–1900 godu." *Statisticheskii ezhegodnik Moskovskoi gubernii za 1900 god.* Moscow, 1900.

"Promysly i nezemledel'cheskie zarabotki krest'ian Moskovskoi gub. v 1902–1903 godu." *Statisticheskii ezhegodnik Moskovskoi gubernii za 1903 god.* Moscow, 1904.

"Promysly i vnezemledel'cheskie zarabotki krest'ian Moskovskoi gub. v 1909–1910 g." *Statisticheskii ezhegodnik Moskovskoi gubernii za 1910 god.* Moscow, 1911.

Promysly Vladimirskoi gubernii. 5 vols. Vladimir, 1882–1884.

Prugavin, Viktor Stepanovich. *Ocherki kustarnoi promyshlennosti Rossii po poslednim issledovaniiam chastnykh lits, zemstv i komissii.* Moscow, 1882.

Rabochee dvizhenie v Rossii v XIX veke: Sbornik dokumentov i materialov. Ed. A. M. Pankratova and L. M. Ivanov. 4 vols. Moscow-Leningrad, 1950–1963.

Rikhter, D. I. "Podmoskovnoe." *Agrarnoe dvizhenie v Rossii v 1905–1906 gg.* Trudy Imperatorskogo Vol'nogo Ekonomicheskogo Obshchestva. 2 vols. St. Petersburg, 1908.

Rudnev, S. F., and Kablukov, N. A. "Promysly i vnezemledel'cheskie zarabotki v zimu 1892–3 goda." *Statisticheskii ezhegodnik Moskovskoi gubernii za 1893 g.* Moscow, 1893.

Russia. Komissiia dlia issledovaniia polozheniia sel'skogo khoziaistva v Rossii (P. A. Valuev, predsedatel'). *Doklad vysochaishe uchrezhdennoi komissii dlia issledovaniia nyneshnego polozheniia sel'skogo khoziaistva i sel'skoi proizvoditel'nosti v Rossii.* St. Petersburg, 1873.

———. Komissiia po issledovaniiu kustarnoi promyshlennosti v Rossii. *Trudy.* 16 vols. St. Petersburg, 1879–1887.

———. Komissiia po preobrazovaniiu volostnykh sudov. *Trudy.* 7 volumes. St. Petersburg, 1873–1874.

———. Ministerstvo finansov. Departament okladnykh sborov. *Sushchestvuiushchii poriadok vzimaniia okladnykh sborov s krest'ian. Po svedeniiam, dostavlennym podatnymi inspektorami za 1887–1893 gg. (Materialy dlia peresmotra uzakonenii o vzimanii okladnykh sborov).* 2 vols. St. Petersburg, 1894–1895.

———. Ministerstvo vnutrennykh del. Zemskii otdel. *Materialy po izdaniiu zakona 8 iunia 1893 goda o peredelakh mirskoi zemli v mestnostiakh v kotorykh vvedeno polozhenie o zemskikh nachal'nikakh. Zakonodatel'nye materialy po voprosam otnosiashchimsia k ustroistvu sel'skogo sostoianiia.* St. Petersburg, 1900.

———. *Svod zakliuchenii gubernskikh soveshchanii po voprosam, otnosiashchimsia k peresmotru zakonodatel'stva o krest'ianakh.* 4 vols. St. Petersburg, 1897.

———. *Trudy redaktsionnoi komissi po peresmotru zakonopolozhenii o krest'ianakh.* 6 vols. St. Petersburg, 1903–1906.

———. *Ukazatel' uzakonenii, otnosiashchikhsia k ustroistvu sel'skogo sostoianiia s 1858 po 1896 god.* St. Petersburg, 1897.

———. *Zakonodatel'nye materialy po voprosam otnosiashchimsia k ustroistvu sel'skogo sostoianiia.* 2 vols. St. Petersburg, 1899–1900.

———. Otdel sel'skoi ekonomii i sel'skokhoziaistvennoi statistiki. *Sel'skokhoziastvennye statisticheskie svedeniia v [1906–1917] god: po otvetam, poluchennym ot khoziaev.* St. Petersburg, 1906–1917.

———. *Polozhenie o nuzhdakh sel'skokhoziaistvennoi promyshlennosti: na osnovanii vsepoddanneinikh otchetov general-gubernatorov, gubernatorov i nachal'nikov oblastei za 1902 god.* St. Petersburg, 1904.

Samoilov, Fedor Nikitich. *Po sledam minuvshego.* 2d ed. Moscow, 1948.

———. *Vospominaniia ob Ivanovo-Voznesenskom rabochem dvizhenii.* 4 vols. Moscow, 1921–1927.

Sazonov, G. P. "Ekspluatatsiia artelei. Zametki i vpechatleniia." *Russkaia mysl',* 1882, no. 7, pp. 141–76; no. 8, pp. 40–61; no. 9, pp. 125–46.

———. "Formy narodnogo kredita: kabala." *Severnyi vestnik,* 1887, no. 11 (November), pp. 1–31.

———. "Formy narodnogo kredita: kabala." *Severnyi vestnik,* 1887, no. 12 (December), pp. 1–26.

———. "Kabala." *Severnyi vestnik,* 1887, no. 9 (September), pp. 1–36.

———. "Kabala v otkhozhem promysle." *Nabliudatel',* 1889, no. 3 (March), pp. 28–56; no. 4 (April), pp. 137–59.

———. "Kredit pod produkty i inventar'." *Severnyi vestnik,* 1887, no. 7 (July), pp. 1–44.

———. *Krest'ianskaia zemel'naia sobstvennost' v Porkhovskom uezde [Pskovskoi gubernii].* St. Petersburg, 1890.

———. "Narodnyi kredit i rostovshchichestvo (Doklad Imperatorskomu Vol'no-Ekonomicheskomu Obshchestvu 21 marta 1887 goda)." *Severnyi vestnik,* 1887, no. 4, pp. 118–46.

———. *Neotchuzhdaemost' krest'ianskikh zemel' v sviazi s gosudarstvenno-ekonomicheskoi programmoi.* St. Petersburg, 1889.

———. "O neotchuzhdaemosti krest'ianskikh zemel'." *Nabliudatel',* 1888, no. 3, pp. 41–73.

———. "Prodazha-pokupka produktov, kak kreditnaia sdelka." *Severnyi vestnik,* 1887, no. 6, pp. 1–14.

———. "Rabstvo 'Svobodnogo Truda.'" *Nabliudatel',* 1887, no. 11, pp. 18–36; no. 12, pp. 135–50.

———. *Rostovshchichestvo-kulachestvo: nabliudeniia i issledovaniia.* St. Peterburg, 1894.

"Selo Teikovo Shuiskogo uezda Vladimirskoi gubernii." *Zhurnal Ministerstva Vnutrennykh Del,* 1855, pt. 11, sec. 5, pp. 34–38.

Semenov (Tian-Shanksii), V. P., ed. *Rossiia. Polnoe geograficheskoe opisanie nashego otechestva*. Vol. 1. *Moskovskaia promyshlennaia oblast' i verkhnee povolzh'e*. St. Petersburg, 1899; vol. 2, *Sredne Russkaia chernozemnaia oblast'*, St. Petersburg, 1902.

Semevskii, V. I. "Neobkhodimost' otmeny telesnykh nakazanii." *Russkaia mysl'*, 1896, no. 2, pt. 2, pp. 1–27; no. 3, pt. 2, pp. 33–66.

Shashkov, S. "Kustar' i kulak." *Slovo*, 1881, no. 2 (February), pp. 25–52.

Shchepot'ev, S. A. "Krugovaia poruka v bytovom i fiskal'nom otnoshenii." *Severnyi vestnik*, 1886, no. 7, sec. 2 (July), pp. 1–19; no. 8, sec. 2 (August), pp. 1–24.

Shrag, Il'ia. *Krest'ianskie sudy Vladimirskoi i Moskovskoi gubernii*. Moscow, 1877.

Shvanebakh, P. K. *Nashe podatnoe delo*. St. Petersburg, 1903.

Slonov, I. A. *Iz zhizni torgovoi Moskvy*. Moscow, 1914.

Smirnov, Aleksandr Vasil'evich. "Chto chitaiut v derevne." *Russkaia mysl'*, 1903, no. 7, pp. 107–16.

———. "Fabrika i fabrichnyi rabochii," *Russkaia mysl'*, 1902, no. 5, pp. 152–67.

———. "Iz nabliudenii zemskogo statistika." *Russkoe bogatstvo*, 1904, no. 4, pp. 1–20.

———. "Ruchnoi tkach ili fabrika." *Russkaia mysl'*, 1903, no. 9, pp. 199–207.

———. "Sostoianie mestnykh i otkhozhikh promyslov naseleniia Vladimirskoi gubernii vesnoi i letom 1899 goda." *Obzor Vladimirskoi gubernii v sel'skokhoziaistvennom otnoshenii za 1899 god*. Part 3. Vladimir, 1900.

———. "Zemledelie i zemledelets tsentral'noi promyshlennoi gubernii." *Russkaia mysl'*, 1901, no. 7, pp. 173–86.

Sobolev, A. *Svadebnyi obriad v Sudogodskom uezde Vladimirskoi gubernii*. Vladimir, 1912.

Sobol'ev, M. N. "Bor'ba s rostovshchichestvom." *Severnyi vestnik*, 1893, no. 3, sec. 3, pp. 1–18.

———. "Rostovshchichestvo." *Entsiklopedicheskii slovar'*. St. Petersburg, 1897.

———. "Sel'skii rostovshchicheskii kredit v Rossii po dannym zemsko-statisticheskoi literatury." *Sbornik pravovedeniia i obshchestvennykh znanii*. Vol. 1. St. Petersburg, 1893.

Sokolov, V., ed. "Stachka tkachei Ivanovo-Voznesenskoi manufaktury v 1895 g." *Krasnyi Arkhiv* 72 (1935): 110–19.

"Sostoianie fabrichnykh promyslov." *Obzor Vladimirskoi gubernii v sel'skokhoziaistvennom otnoshenii za 1905 god*. Vladimir, 1906.

"Sostoianie mestnykh i otkhozhikh promyslov naseleniia Vladimirskoi gubernii vesnoi i letom 1898–99 g." *Obzor Vladimirskoi gubernii v sel'skokhoziaistvennom otnoshenii za 1899 god*. No. 1. Vladimir, 1900.

"Sostoianie mestnykh i otkhozhikh promyslov (ne fabrichnykh)." *Obzor Vladimirskoi gubernii v sel'skokhoziaistvennom otnoshenii za 1905 god*. Vladimir, 1906.

"Sostoianie mestnykh i otkhozhikh vnezemledel'cheskikh promyslov vo Vladimirskoi gubernii v 1907 godu." *Obzor Vladimirskoi gubernii v sel'skokhoziaistvennom otnoshenii za 1907 god*. Vladimir, 1909.

"Sostoianie promyslov za pervuiu i vtoruiu polovinu 1905 g. (tekst)." *Obzor Vladimirskoi gubernii v sel'skokhoziaistvennom otnoshenii za 1905 god.* Vladimir, 1906.

Sudeikin, Vasillii. "Dosrochnyi vykup krest'ianskikh zemel'." *Ekonomicheskoe obozrenie,* 1886, no. 7, pp. 25–40.

Svirshchevskii, A. P., ed. *Otkhozhie promysly krest'ian Iaroslavskoi gubernii. Obzor Iaroslavskoi gubernii.* Vol. 2. Iaroslavl', 1896.

Tenishev, (Prince) Viacheslav Nikolaevich. *Programma etnograficheskikh svedenii o krest'ianakh tsentral'noi Rossii.* Smolensk, 1897.

Tenishev, V. V. *Administrativnoe polozhenie Russkogo krest'ianstva.* St. Petersburg, 1908.

———. *Pravosudie v Russkom krestianskom bytu (dobytykh etnograficheskimi materialami Kniazia V. N. Tenisheva).* Briansk, 1907.

Terner, F. G. *Gosudarstvo i zemlevladenie.* 2 vols. St. Petersburg, 1896–1901.

———. "Krest'ianskii kredit." *Vestnik Evropy,* 1899, no. 1 (January), pp. 83–112.

———. "Krest'ianskie platezhi i sposoby ikh vzyskaniia." *Vestnik Evropy,* 1895, no. 10 (October), pp. 441–83.

Tillo, A. A. *Kustarnye i otkhozhie promysly Kostromskoi gubernii.* St. Petersburg, 1883.

Titov, Andrei Aleksandrovich. *Iuridicheskie obychai sela Nikola-Perevoz, Sulostskoi volosti, Rostovskogo uezda [Iaroslavl' Province].* Iaroslavl', 1888.

———. *Svedeniia o kustarnykh promyslakh po Rostovskomu uezdu Iaroslavskoi gubernii, sobrannye i sostavlennye v 1878 g.* Moscow, 1879.

Tolmachev, M. S. *Krest'ianskii vopros po vzgliadam zemstva i mestnykh liudei.* Moscow, 1903.

Tolstoi, Lev. "Derevnia i gorod," *Russkoe bogatstvo,* 1885, no. 12, pp. 145–67.

Trirogov, V. *Obshchina i podat' (sobranie issledovaniia).* St. Petersburg, 1882.

———. "Kabala v narodnom khoziastve." *Otechestvennye zapiski,* 1879, no. 5.

Tsimmerman, Roman Emel'evich (Gvozdev). *Kulachestvo-rostovshchichestvo: ego obshchestvenno-ekonomicheskoe znachenie.* St. Petersburg, 1899.

Tugan-Baranovsky, M. I. *The Russian Factory in the Nineteenth Century.* New York, 1970.

Vesnin, A. "Ob otmene krugovoi poruki sel'skikh obshchestv." *Narodnoe khoziaistvo: Nauchnoe obshchestvennyi zhurnal,* 1901, no. 8 (October), pp. 1–37.

Vesin, L. P. "Znachenie otkhozhikh promyslov v zhizni russkogo krest'ianstva." *Delo* 19, no. 7 (November 1886): pp. 127–55; 20, no. 2 (February 1887): pp. 102–24.

Vessel', N. "Gosudarstvennyi zemel'n. i sel'sko-khoziaistven. kredit." *Severnyi vestnik,* 1885, no. 3, pp. 194–222.

"Vidy na zhitel'stvo, vydannye krest'ianskomu naseleniiu Moskovsk. gub. v 1880–1885 g. g." *Statisticheskii ezhegodnik Moskovskogo gubernskogo zemstva 1886 g.* Moscow, 1886.

Vikhliaev, P. A. "Ob ustoichivosti vnezemledel'cheskikh otkhozhepromyslovykh zarabotkov sel'skogo naseleniia." *Narodnoe khoziaistvo,* 1900, no. 3, pp. 73–90.

———. *Ocherki iz russkoi sel'skokhoziaistvennoi deistvitel'nosti.* St. Petersburg, 1901.

———. "Ustoichivost' vnezemledel'cheskikh otkhozhe-promyslovykh zarabotkov sel'skogo naseleniia v Rossii." *Narodnoe khoziaistvo* 1, no. 3 (1900): 73–90.

———. *Zemledel'cheskoe khoziaistvo i promysly krest'ianskogo naseleniia: promysly*. Moscow, 1908.

Vorob'ev, Klementii Iakovlevich. *Otkhozhie promysly krest'ianskogo naseleniia Iaroslavskoi gubernii: Statisticheskii ocherk*. Iaroslavl', 1903.

Vorob'ev, N. I. "Iz zhizni Ivanovo-Voznesenskikh rabochikh." *Obrazovanie*, 1906, no. 3, sec. 2, pp. 16–52.

Voronov, N. I. *Zapiski o sobytiiakh Vladimirskoi gubernii*. Vladimir, 1907.

Vorontsov, Vasilii Pavlovich [V. V.]. "Arteli dlia podriadnykh i naemnykh rabot." *Novoe slovo*, 1895, no. 1 (October), pp. 65–101; 1896, no. 11 (August), pp. 33–49; 1896, no. 12 (September), pp. 1–16.

———. *Itogi ekonomicheskogo issledovaniia Rossii po dannym zemskoi statistiki*. Vol. 1. *Krest'ianskaia obshchina*. Moscow, 1892.

———. "Iz oblasti krest'ianskogo khoziaistva." *Nabliudatel'*, 1885, no. 7, pp. 147–69.

———. "Iz praktiki narodnogo kredita." *Nabliudatel'*, 1884, no. 11 (November), pp. 20–40.

———. "Kredit v kustarnom proizvodstve." *Nabliudatel'*, 1886, no. 1, pp. 40–61.

———. *Ocherki kustarnoi promyshlennosti v Rossii*. St. Petersburg, 1886.

———. *Progressivnyia techeniia v krest'ianskom khoziaistve*. St. Petersburg, 1892.

———. "Semeinye razdely i krest'ianskoe khoziaistvo." *Otechestvennye zapiski*, 3d ser., 266, no. 1 (1883): 1–23; no. 2 (1883): 137–61.

———. "Zimnaia naemka." *Nabliudatel'*, 1885, no. 2, pp. 42–70.

Zarudnyi, M. I. *Zakony i zhizn': itogi issledovaniia krest'ianskikh sudov*. St. Petersburg, 1874.

Zhbankov, D. N. *Bab'ia storona: statistiko-etnograficheskii ocherk. Materialy dlia statistiki Kostromskoi gubernii*. Vol. 8. Kostroma, 1891.

———. "K voprosu o plodovitosti zamuzhnikh zhenshchin." *Vrach*, 1889, no. 13.

———. "O gorodskikh otkhozhikh zarabotkakh v Soligalicheskom uezde Kostromskoi gubernii." *Iuridicheskii vestnik*, 1890, no. 9, pp. 130–48.

———. *Otkhozhie promysly v Smolenskoi gubernii v 1892–1895 gg.* Smolensk, 1896.

———. *Vliianie otkhozhikh promyslov na dvizhenie narodonaseleniia Kostromskoi gubernii po dannykh 1866–1883 gg.* Kostroma, 1887.

———. "Vliianie otkhozhikh promyslov na dvizheniia naseleniia za 1866–1890 gg." *Vrach* 16, no. 24 (1895): 636–40; no. 25 (1895): 679–705.

Zhbankov, D. N., and Iakovenko, Vl. I. *Telesnyia nakazaniia v Rossii v nastoiashchee vremia*. Moscow, 1899.

Z. N. "O krest'ianskikh semeinykh razdelakh." *Pravo*, 1901, no. 12.

Selected Secondary Sources

Aleksandrov, V. A. *Sel'skaia obshchina v Rossii (XVII–nachala XIX v.).* Moscow, 1976.

Alekseichenko, G. A. "Prigovory sel'skikh skhodov kak istochnik po istorii krest'ianskoi obshchiny v Rossii vtoroi poloviny XIX veka (Po materialam Tverskoi gubernii)." *Istoriia SSSR,* 1981, no. 6, pp. 116–25.

Anan'ich, B. V. "Iz istorii zakonodatel'stva o krest'ianakh (vtoroi poloviny XIX veka)." In *Voprosy istorii Rossii XIX–nachala XX veka.(Mezhvuzovskii sbornik).* Leningrad, 1983.

Anderson, Barbara A. *Internal Migration During Modernization in Late Nineteenth-Century Russia.* Princeton, 1980.

———. "Who Chose the Cities? Migrants to Moscow and St. Petersburg Cities in the Late Nineteenth Century." In *Population Patterns in the Past,* ed. Donald Lee. New York, 1977.

Anfimov, A. M. *Ekonomicheskoe polozhenie i klassovaia bor'ba krest'ian Evropeiskoi Rossii, 1881–1904.* Moscow, 1984.

———. *Krest'ianskoe khoziaistvo Evropeiskoi Rossii: 1881–1904.* Moscow, 1980.

———. "Nekotorye dannye ob izmeneniiakh ekonomicheskogo polozheniia krest'ian raznykh razriadov v kontse XIX v." In *Problemy sotsial'no-ekonomicheskoi istorii Rossii: sbornik statei k 85-letiiu so dnia rozhdeniia akademika Nikolaia Mikhailovicha Druzhinina.* Moscow, 1971.

Anfimov, A. M., and P. N. Zyrianov. "Nekotorye cherty evoliutsii Russkoi krest'ianskoi obshchiny v poreformennoi period (1861–1914 gg.)." *Istoriia SSSR,* 1980, no. 4, pp. 26–41.

Arora, Mandakini. "Boundaries, Transgressions, Limits: Peasant Gender Roles in Tver' Province, 1861–1914." Ph.D. diss., Duke University, 1995.

Atkinson, Dorothy. *The End of the Russian Land Commune, 1905–1930.* Stanford, 1983.

Bailey, F. G., ed. *Gifts and Poison: The Politics of Reputation.* Oxford, 1971.

Baker, Anita B. "Deterioration or Development? The Peasant Economy of Moscow Province Prior to 1914." *Russian History/Histoire Russe* 5, no. 1 (1978): 1–23.

Balashov, S. "Rabochee dvizhenie v Ivanovo-Voznesenske (1898–1905 gg.)." *Proletarskaia revoliutsiia,* 1925, no. 9, pp. 144–75.

Bater, James H. "The Journey to Work in St. Petersburg, 1860–1914." *Journal of Transport History* 3, no. 2 (September 1974): 214–33.

———. *St. Petersburg: Industrialization and Change.* London and Montreal, 1976.

———. "Transience, Residential Persistence, and Mobility in Moscow and St. Petersburg, 1900–1914." *Slavic Review* 39, no. 2 (June 1980): 239–54.

Berlin, S. L. "Naemnyi trud v krest'ianskom zemledel'cheskom khoziaistve Moskovskoi gubernii kontsa XIX–nachala XX veka." In *Ezhegodnik po agrarnoi istorii vostochnoi evropy 1970 g.* Riga, 1977.

Bernshtam, T. A. *Molodezh' v obriadovoi zhizni russkoi obshchiny XIX–nachala XX v.: polovozrastnoi aspekt traditsionnoi kul'tury.* Leningrad, 1988.

Bernstein, Laurie. *Sonia's Daughters: Prostitutes and Their Regulation in Imperial Russia.* Berkeley and Los Angeles, 1995.

Bobroff, Anne Louise. "Working Women, Bonding Patterns, and the Politics of Daily Life: Russia at the End of the Old Regime." 2 vols. Ph.D. diss., University of Michigan, 1982.

Bonnell, Victoria E. *Roots of Rebellion: Workers' Politics and Organizations in St. Petersburg and Moscow, 1900–1914.* Berkeley and Los Angeles, 1983.

Bradley, Joseph. *Muzhik and Muscovite: Urbanization in Late Imperial Russia.* Berkeley and Los Angeles, 1985.

Brooks, Jeffrey. *When Russia Learned to Read: Literacy and Popular Literature, 1861–1917.* Princeton, 1985.

Brower, Daniel R. et al. "Labor Violence in Russia in the Late Nineteenth Century: A Discussion." *Slavic Review* 41, no. 3 (1982): 417–53.

Brym, Robert J., and Evel Economakis. "Peasant or Proletarian? Militant Pskov Workers in Petersburg, 1913." *Slavic Review* 53, no. 1 (Spring 1994): 120–39.

Budaev, D. I. *Smolenskaia derevnia kontsa XIX–nachala XX v.* Smolensk, 1972.

———. "Polozhenie sel'skokhoziaistvennykh rabochikh Smolenskoi gubernii po dogovoram o naime." In *Sotsial'no-politicheskoe i pravovoe polozhenie krest'ianstva v dorevoliutsionnoi Rossii.* Voronezh, 1983.

Bushnell, John. "Peasants in Uniform: The Tsarist Army as a Peasant Society." *Journal of Social History* 13 (1980): 563–74.

Christian, David. *Living Water: Vodka and Russian Society on the Eve of the Emancipation.* Oxford, 1990.

Crisp, Olga. "Labour and Industrialization in Russia." In *The Cambridge Economic History of Europe,* vol. 7. Cambridge, 1978.

Czap, Peter, Jr. "The Influence of Slavophile Ideology on the Formation of the Volost Court of 1861 and the Practice of Peasant Self-Justice between 1861 and 1889." Ph.D. diss., Cornell University, 1959.

———. "Marriage and Peasant Joint Family in the Era of Serfdom," In *The Family in Imperial Russia: New Lines of Historical Research,* ed. David Ransel. Urbana, Ill., 1978, pp. 103–23.

———. "Peasant-Class Courts and Peasant Customary Justice in Russia, 1861–1912." *Journal of Social History* (Winter 1967): 149–78.

———. "The Perennial Multiple Family Household, Mishino, Russia 1782–1858." *Journal of Family History* 7, no. 1 (Spring 1982): 5–26.

Dikhtiar, G. A. *Vnutrennaia torgovlia dorevoliutsionoi Rossii.* Moscow, 1960.

Diubiuk, Evgenii. "Fabrichnaia promyshlennost' i rabochii klass Kostromskoi gubernii v deviatisotykh godakh." In *1905 god v Kostrome,* ed. Ia. A. Andreev. Kostroma, 1926.

———. "Obrabatyvaiushchaia promyshlennost' Kostromskogo kraia." In *Proshloe i nastoiashchee Kostromskogo kraia*. Kostroma, 1920.

Donnorummo, Robert Pepe. "The Peasants of Central Russia and Vladimir: Reactions to Emancipation and the Market, 1850–1900." Ph.D. diss., University of Pittsburgh, 1983.

Druzhinin, N. M. "The Liquidation of the Feudal System in the Russian Manorial Village (1862–1882)." *Soviet Studies in History* 21, no. 3 (Winter 1982–1983): 14–67.

Dubrovskii, S. M. *Krest'ianskoe dvizhenie v revoliutsii 1905–1907 gg*. Moscow, 1956.

Economakis, Evel G. "Patterns of Migration and Settlement in Prerevolutionary Petersburg: Peasants from Iaroslavl and Tver Provinces." *Russian Review* 56, no. 1 (1997): 8–24.

———. "Patterns of Peasant Recruitment and the Making of the St. Petersburg Industrial Working Class." Ph.D. diss., Columbia University, 1994.

Egiazarova, N. A. *Agrarnyi krizis kontsa XIX veka v Rossii*. Moscow, 1959.

Eklof, Ben. "Peasant Sloth Reconsidered: Strategies of Education and Learning in Rural Russia Before the Revolution." *Journal of Social History* 14, no. 3 (Spring 1981): 355–85.

———. *Russian Peasant Schools: Officialdom, Village Culture, and Popular Pedagogy, 1861–1914*. Berkeley and Los Angeles, 1986.

Emeliakh, L. I. *Antiklerikal'noe dvizhenie krest'ianstva v period pervoi Russkoi revoliutsii*. Moscow-Leningrad, 1965.

Engel, Barbara Alpern. *Between the Fields and the City: Women, Work and Family in Russia, 1861–1914*. Cambridge, 1994.

———. "Peasant Morality and Pre-Marital Relations in Late Nineteenth-Century Russia." *Journal of Social History* 23, no. 4 (1990): 695–714.

———. "Russian Peasant Views of City Life." *Slavic Review* 52, no. 3 (Fall 1993): 446–59.

———. "St. Petersburg Prostitutes in the Late Nineteenth Centuries: A Personal and Social Profile." *Russian Review* 48, no. 1 (January 1989): 21–44.

———. "The Woman's Side: Male Out-Migration and the Family Economy in Kostroma Province." *Slavic Review* 45, no. 2 (Summer 1986): 257–71.

———. "Women, Work, and Family in the Factories of Rural Russia." *Russian History/Histoire Russe* 16, nos. 2–4 (1989): 223–38.

Engelstein, Laura. *Moscow 1905: Working-Class Organization and Political Conflict*. Stanford, 1982.

Fedorov, Vladimir Aleksandrovich. "Barshchina i obrok v tsentral'no-promyshlennykh guberniiakh Rossii v pervoi polovine XIX v." In *Ezhegodnik po agrarnoi istorii vostochnoi evropy 1964 god*. Kishinev, 1966.

———. *Krest'ianskoe dvizhenie v tsentral'noi Rossii. 1800–1860 (Po materialam tsentral'no promyshlennykh gubernii)*. Moscow, 1980.

———. "K voprosu o genezise kapitalizma v doreformennoi Rossii (po materialam krest'ianskikh promyslov Kostromskoi gubernii)." *Vestnik Moskovskogo Universiteta,* 9th ser. *Istoriia*. 1964, no. 5, pp. 55–68.

———. "Krest'ianin-otkhodnik v Moskve (konets XVIII–pervaia polovina XIX v.)." In *Russkii gorod (issledovaniia i materialy),* vol. 1. Moscow, 1976.

———. "Krest'ianin-otkhodnik v Moskve (vtoraia polovina XIX v.)." In *Russkii gorod (issledovaniia i materialy),* vol. 6. Moscow, 1983.

———. *Pomeshchich'i krest'iane tsentral'no- promyshlennogo raiona Rossii (kontsa XVIII–pervoi poloviny XIX v.).* Moscow, 1974.

———. "Pomeshchich'i krest'iane tsentral'no-promyshlennogo raiona Rossii nakanune padeniia krepostnogo prava." Dokt. istoricheskikh nauk, Moscow State University, 1969.

———. "Semeinye razdely v Russkoi poreformennoi derevne." In *Sel'skoe khoziaistvo i krest'ianstvo severo-zapada RSFSR v dorevoliutsionnyi period. (Mezhvuzovskii sbornik nauchnykh trudov).* Smolensk, 1979.

Field, Daniel. *Rebels in the Name of the Tsar.* Boston, 1976.

Frank, Stephen P. "Confronting the Domestic Other: Rural Popular Culture and Its Enemies in Fin-de-Siècle Russia." In *Cultures in Flux,* ed. Stephen Frank and Mark D. Steinberg. Princeton, 1994.

———. *Crime, Cultural Conflict, and Justice in Rural Russia, 1856-1914.* Forthcoming.

———. "Popular Justice, Community and Culture Among the Russian Peasantry, 1870–1900." *Russian Review* 46, no. 3 (July 1987): 239–65.

———. "'Simple Folk, Savage Customs?' Youth, Sociability, and the Dynamics of Culture in Rural Russia, 1856–1914." *Journal of Social History* 25, no. 4 (1992): 711–36.

Freeze, Gregory L. "Handmaiden of the State? The Church in Imperial Russia Reconsidered." *Journal of Ecclesiastical History* 36, no. 1 (January 1985).

———. *The Parish Clergy in Nineteenth-Century Russia: Crisis, Reform, Counter-Reform.* Princeton, 1983.

Friedgut, Theodore H. "Labor Violence and Regime Brutality in Tsarist Russia: The Iuzovka Cholera Riots of 1892." *Slavic Review* 46, no. 2 (Summer 1987): 245–65.

Frierson, Cathy A. "Crime and Criminality in the Russian Village: Rural Concepts of Criminality at the End of the Nineteenth Century." *Slavic Review* 46, no. 1 (Spring 1987): 55–69.

———. "Peasant Family Divisions and the Commune." In *Land Commune and Peasant Community in Russia,* ed. Roger Bartlett. New York, 1990.

———. *Peasant Icons: Representations of Rural People in Late Nineteenth-Century Russia.* Oxford, 1992.

———. "*Razdel:* The Peasant Family Divided." *Russian Review* 46 (1987): 35–52.

Gaudin, Corinne. "Governing the Village: Peasant Culture and the Problem of Social Transformation in Russia, 1906–1914." Ph.D. diss., University of Michigan, 1993.

Genkin, L. B. "Nezemledel'cheskii otkhod Iaroslavskoi i Kostromskoi gubernii v pervoi polovine XIX v." *Uchenye Zapiski Iaroslavskogo Gosudarstvennogo Pedagogicheskogo Instituta.* Vol. 9. Iaroslavl', 1947.

———. *Pomeshchich'i krest'iane Iaroslavskoi i Kostromskoi gubernii pered reformoi i vo vremia reformy 1861 g.(k voprosu o razlozhenii feodal'no-krepostnicheskoi sistemy i genizise kapitalizma v Rossii)*. Uchenye Zapiski Iaroslavskogo Gosudarstvennogo Universiteta.

Gerschenkron, Alexander. "Agrarian Policies and Industrialization: Russia, 1861–1917." In *The Cambridge Economic History of Europe*, vol. 6. Cambridge, 1965.

Glickman, Rose L. *Russian Factory Women: Workplace and Society, 1880–1914*. Berkeley and Los Angeles, 1984.

———. "'Unusual Circumstances' in the Peasant Village." *Russian History/Histoire Russe* 23, nos. 1–4 (1996): 215–29.

Gliksman, Jerzy G. "The Russian Urban Worker: From Serf to Proletarian." In *The Tranformation of Russian Society: Aspects of Social Change Since 1861*, ed. Cyril F. Black (Cambridge, 1960).

Gluckman, Max. "Gossip and Scandal." *Current Anthropology* 4, no. 3 (June 1963).

Grigor'ev, V. I. *Predmetnyi ukazatel' materialov v zemsko-statisticheskikh trudakh s 1860-kh godov po 1917 g*. Moscow, 1926.

Gromyko, M. M. "Obychai pomochei u russkikh krest'ian v XIX v. (K probleme kompleksnogo issledovaniia trudovykh traditsii)." *Sovetskaia etnografiia*, 1981, no. 4, pp. 26–38; no. 5, pp. 32–46.

———. *Traditsionnye normy povedeniia i formy obshcheniia russkikh krest'ian XIX v*. Moscow, 1986.

Herlihy, Patricia. "Joy of the Rus': Rites and Rituals of Russian Drinking." *Russian Review* 50, no. 2 (March 1991): 131–47.

Herrlinger, Kimberly Page. "Class, Piety, and Politics: Workers, Orthodoxy, and the Problem of Religious Identity in Russia, 1881–1914." Ph.D. diss., University of California, Berkeley, 1996.

Hickey, M. "Russian Migrant Workers in Helsinki on the Eve of World War I." *Journal of Baltic Studies* 26, no. 4 (Winter 1995): 361–74.

Hoch, Steven L. "On Good Numbers and Bad: Malthus, Population Trends, and Peasant Standards of Living in Late Imperial Russia." *Slavic Review* 53, no. 1 (Spring 1994): 41–75.

———. *Serfdom and Social Control in Russia: Petrovskoe, a Village in Tambov*. Chicago, 1986.

———. "Serfs in Imperial Russia: Demographic Insights." *Journal of Interdisciplinary History* 13, no. 2 (Autumn 1982): 221–46.

Hoffmann, David L. *Peasant Metropolis: Social Identities in Moscow, 1929–1941*. Ithaca, 1994.

———. "Land, Freedom, and Discontent: Russian Peasants of the Central Industrial Region Prior to Collectivisation." *Europe-Asia Studies* 46, no. 4 (1994): 637–48.

Iakovlev, A F. *Ekonomicheskie krizisy v Rossii*. Moscow, 1955.

Johnson, Robert Eugene. "Family Relations and the Rural-Urban Nexus: Patterns in the Hinterland of Moscow, 1880–1900." In *The Family in Imperial Russia: New Lines of Historical Research*, ed. David L. Ransel. Urbana, Ill., 1978.

———. "Peasant Migration and the Russian Working Class: Moscow at the End of the Nineteenth Century." *Slavic Review* 35, no. 4 (December 1976): 652–664.

———. *Peasant and Proletarian: The Working Class of Moscow in the Late Nineteenth Century.* New Brunswick, 1979.

———. "Strikes in Moscow: Rural-Urban Ties as a Factor of Social Unrest." *Russian History/Histoire Russe* 5, no. 1 (Spring 1978).

Kadek, M. E. "Sel'skoe khoziaistvo Iaroslavskoi gubernii v nachale XX veka." In *Trudy Iaroslavskogo Pedagogicheskogo Instituta.* Vol. 1, no. 2, pp. 1–39. Iaroslavl', 1926.

Kantor, R. "K kharakteristike ekonomicheskogo polozheniia rabochego elementa v Ivanovo-Voznesenske (1871 g.)." In *Arkhiv istorii truda v Rossii,* bk. 5, pt. 2. Petrograd, 1922.

Kirianov, Iu. I. *Zhiznennyi uroven' rabochikh Rossii (konets XIX–nachalo XX v.).* Moscow, 1979.

Koenker, Diane. *Moscow Workers and the 1917 Revolution.* Princeton, 1981.

Kolpenskii, V. "Otkhozhie promysly krest'ian po ofitsial'nym dannym 90-kh godov 19-go veka." In *Arkhiv istorii truda v Rossii,* bk. 11/12. Petrograd, 1924.

Korelin, A. P. *Sel'skokhoziaistvennyi kredit v Rossii v kontse XIX–nachale XX v.* Moscow, 1988.

Kozlova, N. V. "Krepostnoi trud na Serpukhovskoi manufakture Kishkinykh v 30–40-e gody XVIII veka." *Voprosy istorii* 1983, no. 3, pp. 178–79.

Krest'ianstvo tsentral'no-promyshlennogo raiona (XVIII–XIX vv.). Kalinin, 1983.

Kruze, E. E. *Peterburgskie rabochie v 1912–1914 godakh.* Moscow-Leningrad, 1961.

Kuchumova, L. I. "Sel'skaia pozemel'naia obshchina Evropeiskoi Rossii v 60–70-e gody XIX v." *Istoricheskie zapiski* 106 (1981): 323–47.

Kuznetsov, S. V. "Khoziaistvennye traditsii v zemledelii russkikh krest'ian nechernozemnogo tsentra vtoroi poloviny XIX v." Kand. ist. nauk, Moscow State University, 1992.

Lewin, Moshe. "Popular Religion in Twentieth-Century Russia." In *The Making of the Soviet System.* New York, 1985.

Lindenmeyr, Adele. "The Ethos of Charity in Imperial Russia." *Journal of Social History* 23, no. 4 (1990): 679–94.

Macey, David A. *Government and Peasant In Russia, 1861–1906.* Illinois, 1987.

———. "The Russian Bureaucracy and the 'Peasant Problem': The Pre-History of the Stolypin Reforms, 1861–1907." Ph.D. diss., Columbia University, 1976.

Mandel, James I. "Paternalistic Authority in the Russian Countryside, 1856–1906." Ph.D. diss., Columbia University, 1978.

Manning, Roberta Thompson. *The Crisis of the Old Order in Russia: Gentry and Government.* Princeton, 1983.

Matossian, Mary. "The Peasant Way of Life." In *The Peasant in Nineteenth Century Russia,* ed. Wayne S. Vucinich. Stanford, 1968.

Matveeva, E. V. "Formirovanie proleteriata v tekstil'noi promyshlennosti Kostromskoi gubernii (80–90-e gg. XIX v.)." In *Uchenye Zapiski Kostromskogo Gosudarstvennogo Pedagogicheskogo Instituta,* no. 24. *Istoriia.* Kostroma, 1971.

———. "K voprosu o sviazi rabochikh-tekstil'shchikov Kostromskoi gubernii s zemlei v 90-e gody XIX veka." In *Promyshlennost' i proletariat gubernii Verkhnego Povolzh'ia v kontse XIX–nachale XX vv. Mezhvuzovskii sbornik nauchnykh trudov,* no. 44. Iaroslavl', 1976.

Meierovich, M. G. "Fabrichno-zavodskaia promyshlennost' Iaroslavskoi gubernii v nachale XX v." In *Vestnik Iaroslavskogo Universiteta,* no. 1. Iaroslavl', 1972.

———. "O proiskhozhdenii promyshlennykh rabochikh Iaroslavskoi gubernii (kontsa XIX–nachala XX v.)." *Vestnik Moskovskogo Universiteta,* 9th ser., 1969, no. 6, pp. 26–42.

———. "Ob istochnikakh popolneniia fabrichno-zavodskogo proletariata v epokhu imperializma (na materialakh Iaroslavskoi gubernii)." *Istoriia SSSR,* 1980, no. 5, pp. 151–68.

Merriman, John M. *The Margins of City Life: Explorations on the French Urban Frontier, 1815–1851.* New York, 1991.

Milogolova, I. N. "Semeinye razdely v Russkoi poreformennoi derevne (na materialakh tsentral'nykh gubernii). *Vestnik Moskovskogo Universiteta,* 8th ser., *Istoriia,* 1987, no. 6, pp. 37–47.

———. "Sem'ia i semeinyi byt russkoi poreformennoi derevni, 1861–1900 gg. (na materialakh tsentral'nykh gubernii)." Kand. ist. nauk., Moscow State University, 1988.

Mints, L. E. *Otkhod krest'ianskogo naseleniia na zarabotki v SSSR.* Moscow, 1925.

Mironov, Boris Nikolaevich. "The Russian Peasant Commune After the Reforms of the 1860s." *Slavic Review* 44, no. 3 (Fall 1985): 438–67.

———. "Traditsionnoe demograficheskoe povedenie krest'ian v XIX–nachale XX v." In *Brachnost', rozhdaemost', smertnost' v Rossii i v SSSR. (Sbornik statei),* ed. A. G. Vishnevskii. Moscow, 1977.

Mixter, Timothy. "Of Grandfather-Beaters and Fat-Heeled Pacifists: Perceptions of Agricultural Labor and Hiring Market Disturbances in Saratov, 1872–1905." *Russian History/Histoire Russe* 7, pts. 1–2 (1980): 139–68.

———. "Migrant Agricultural Laborers in the Steppe Grainbelt of European Russia, 1830–1913." Ph.D. diss., University of Michigan, 1992.

———. "The Hiring Market as Workers' Turf: Migrant Agricultural Laborers and the Mobilization of Collective Action in the Steppe Grainbelt of European Russia, 1853–1913." In *Peasant Economy, Culture, and Politics in European Russia, 1800–1921,* ed. Esther Kingston-Mann and Timothy R. Mixter. Princeton, 1991.

Mogul, Jonathan. "In the Shadow of the Factory: Peasant Manufacturing and Russian Industrialization, 1861–1914." Ph.D. diss., University of Michigan, 1996.

Munting, R. "Outside Earnings in the Russian Peasant Farm: The Case of Tula Province, 1900 to 1917." *Journal of Peasant Studies* 3 (1976): 428–46.

Nagaev, A. S. "Iz istorii sel'skikh promyshlennykh tsentrov podmoskov'ia (vtoraia polovina XIX veka)." In *Voprosy obshchestvennogo i sotstial'no-ekonomicheskogo razvitiia Rossii v XVIII–XIX vekakh (po materialam tsentral'nykh gubernii). Sbornik.* Riazan', 1974.

Neuberger, Joan. *Hooliganism: Crime, Culture, and Power in St. Petersburg, 1900–1914.* Berkeley and Los Angeles, 1993.

———. "Popular Legal Cultures: The St. Petersburg *Mirovoi Sud.*" In *Russia's Great Reforms, 1855–1881,* ed. Ben Eklof, John Bushnell, and Larissa Zakharova. Bloomington, 1994.

Pallot, Judith, and Denis J. B. Shaw, *Landscape and Settlement in Russia, 1613–1917.* New York, 1990.

Pankratova, A. M. "Proletarizatsiia krest'ianstva i ee rol' v formirovanii promyshlennogo proletariata Rossii (60–90e gg. XIX v.)." *Istoricheskie zapiski* 54 (1955): 194–220.

Pearson, Thomas S. *Russian Officialdom in Crisis: Autocracy and Local Self-Government, 1861–1900.* Cambridge, 1989.

Peristiany, J. G., ed. *Honour and Shame: The Values of Mediterranean Society.* Chicago, 1965.

——— and Julian Pitt-Rivers, eds. *Honor and Grace in Anthropology.* Cambridge, 1992.

Perrie, Maureen. *The Agrarian Policy of the Russian Socialist-Revolutionary Party from its Origins Through the Revolution of 1905–1907.* Cambridge, 1976.

———. "The Russian Peasant Movement of 1905–1907: Its Social Composition and Revolutionary Significance." *Past and Present* 57 (November 1972): 123–55.

Pershin, Pavel Nikolaevich. *Agrarnaia revoliutsiia v Rossii.* Vol. 1, *Ot reforma k revoliutsii.* Moscow, 1966.

Phillips, Laura Lynne. "Everyday Life in Revolutionary Russia: Working-Class Drinking and Taverns in St. Petersburg, 1900–1929." Ph.D. diss., University of Illinois, Champaign-Urbana, 1993.

Plaggenborg, S. "Tax Policy and the Question of Peasant Poverty in Czarist Russia, 1881–1905." *Cahiers du monde russe i sovietique* 36, nos. 1–2 (January–June 1995): 53–69.

Pliushchevskii, B. G. "Krest'ianskii otkhod na territorii Evropeiskoi Rossii v poslednie doreformennye desiatiletiia (1830–1850 gg)." Kand. ist. nauk, Leningrad State University, 1974.

———. "Organizatsiia krest'ianskikh otkhozhikh promyslov v krupnykh votchinnykh khoziaistvakh nechernozemnogo tsentra (vtoraia chetvert' XIX v.)." In *Voprosy istorii Urala.* Perm, 1966.

———. "Prinuditel'naia kontraktatsiia v otkhozhikh krest'ianskikh promyslakh russkoi derevni v 1830–1850 gg." In *Uchenye zapiski Udmurtskogo gosudarstvennogo pedagogicheskogo instituta,* no. 15. Izhevsk, 1967.

———. "Vnegubernskii otkhod krest'ian v 1830–1850 gody i ego vozdeistvie na sotsial'noe rassloenie Viatskoi derevni." In *K voprosu o formirovanii kapitalizma v Rossii.* Kirov, 1974.

———. "Vozdeistvie otkhozhikh promyslov na sotsial'no-psikhologicheskii sklad russkogo krest'ianstva." In *Sotsial'no-politicheskoe i pravovoe polozhenie krest'ianstva v dorevoliutsionnoi Rossii.* Voronezh, 1983.

Pretty, David. "Neither Peasant nor Proletarian: The Workers of the Ivanovo-Voznesensk Region, 1885–1905." Ph.D. diss., Brown University, 1997.

———. "The Saints of the Revolution: Political Activists in Ivanovo-Voznesensk and the Path of Most Resistance." *Slavic Review* 54, no. 2 (Summer 1995): 276–304.

Ransel, David L., ed. *The Family in Imperial Russia: New Lines of Historical Research.* Urbana, Ill., 1978.

———. *Mothers of Misery: Child Abandonment in Russia.* Princeton, 1988.

Rashin, A. G. *Formirovanie promyshlennogo proletariata v Rossii. Statistiko-ekonomichesikie ocherki.* Moscow, 1940.

Reichman, Henry. *Railway and Revolution: Russia, 1905.* Berkeley and Los Angeles, 1987.

Rozhkova, M. K. "Fabrichnaia promyshlennost' i promysly krest'ian v 60–70-kh godakh XIX v. (po materialam Bogorodskogo uezda Moskovskoi gubernii)." In *Problemy sotsial'no-ekonomicheskoi istorii Rossii: sbornik statei k 85-letiiu so dnia rozhdeniia akademika Nikolaia Mikhailovicha Druzhinina.* Moscow, 1971.

———. *Formirovanie kadrov promyshlennykh rabochikh v 60–nachale 80-kh godove XIX v. (Po materialam Moskovskoi gubernii).* Moscow, 1974.

Robinson, G. T. *Rural Russia Under the Old Regime.* London, 1932.

Rozov, E. K. *Krest'iane i krest'ianskoe khoziaistvo Tverskoi i Novgorodskoi gubernii v seredine XIX–nachale XX veka.* Kalinin, 1974.

Ruane, Christine. "Clothes Make the Comrade: A History of the Russian Fashion Industry." *Russian History/Histoire Russe* 23, nos. 1–4 (1996): 311–44.

———. "Clothes Shopping in Imperial Russia: The Development of a Consumer Culture." *Journal of Social History* 28, no. 4 (Spring 1995): 765–82.

Rudolph, Richard L. "Family Structure and Proto-industrialization in Russia." *Journal of Economic History* 40 (1980): 111–18.

Ryndziunskii, P. G. *Gorodskoe grazhdanstvo doreformennoi Rossii.* Moscow, 1958.

———. *Krest'iane i gorod v kapitalisticheskoi Rossii vtoroi poloviny XIX veka (Vzaimootnoshenie goroda i derevni v sotsial'no-ekonomicheskom stroe Rossii).* Moscow, 1983.

———. *Krest'ianskaia promyshlennost' v poreformennoi Rossii (60–80e gody XIX v.).* Moscow, 1966.

———. *Utverzhdenie kapitalizma v Rossii, 1850–1880 gg.* Moscow, 1978.

Schneer, Matthew. "The Markovo-Republic—A Peasant Community During Russia's First Revolution, 1905–1906." *Slavic Review* 53, no. 1 (Spring 1994): 104–19.

Scott, James C. *Domination and the Arts of Resistance: Hidden Transcripts.* New Haven, 1990.

———. "Resistance Without Protest and Without Organization: Peasant Opposition to the Islamic *Zakat* and the Christian Tithe." *Comparative Studies in Society and History* 29, no. 3 (July 1987): 417–52.

———. *Weapons of the Weak: Everyday Forms of Peasant Resistance.* New Haven, 1985.

Shanin, Teodor. *The Awkward Class.* Oxford, 1972.

———. *Russia as a Developing Society: The Roots of Otherness.* Vol. 2, *Russia 1905–1907: Revolution as a Moment of Truth.* London, 1986.

Sharpe, J. A. *Defamation and Sexual Slander in Early Modern England: The Church Courts at York.* Borthwicke Papers 58 (York, 1980).

Shevzov, Vera. "Popular Orthodoxy in Late Imperial Rural Russia (Orthodox Christianity, Vologda, Rural Life)." Ph.D. diss., Yale University, 1994.

Shinn, William. "The Law of the Russian Peasant Household." *Slavic Review* 20 (1961): 601–21.

Simonova, M. S. "Otmena krugovoi poruki." *Istoricheskie zapiski* 83 (1969): 159–95.

Smirnova, G. K. "Klassovaia bor'ba krest'ian Iaroslavskoi gubernii v poreformennyi period." *Uchenye zapiski Vologodskogo Pedagogicheskogo Instituta*. Vol. 19, *Istoricheskii*. Vologda, 1954.

Steinberg, Mark D. *The Culture of Class Relations in the Russian Printing Industry, 1867–1907.* Berkeley and Los Angeles, 1992.

Steinberg, Mark D. "The Urban Landscape in Workers' Imagination." *Russian History/Histoire Russe* 23, nos. 1–4 (1996): 47–65.

———. "Workers on the Cross: Religious Imagination in the Writing of Russian Workers, 1910–1924." *Russian Review* 53, no. 2 (April 1994): 213–39.

Stepanova, E. S. "Razvitie otkhozhikh krest'ianskikh promyslov v Riazanskoi gubernii 70–80-kh godov XIX veka." In *Voprosy obshchestvennogo i sotstial'no-ekonomicheskogo razvitiia Rossii v XVIII–XIX vekakh (po materialam tsentral'nykh gubernii). Sbornik*. Riazan', 1974.

Stichter, Sharon. *Migrant Laborers*. Cambridge, 1985.

Svavitskii, Z. M., and Svavitskii, N. A. *Zemskie podvornye perepisi, 1880–1913: Pouezdnye itogi*. Moscow, 1926.

Tikhonov, Boris Vasil'evich. "Migratsii fabrichno-zavodskikh rabochikh v Shuiskom uezde Vladimirskoi gubernii (po materialam zemskoi perepisi 1899 g.). In *Istoricheskaia geografiia Rossii XII–nachala XX v. Sbornik statei k 70-letiiu professora Liubomira Grigor'evicha Beskrovnogo*. Moscow, 1975.

———. *Pereseleniia v Rossii vo vtoroi polovine XIX v. (po materialam perepisi 1897 g. i pasportnoi statistiki)*. Moscow, 1978.

Vainshtein, Al'bert L'vovich. *Oblozhenie i platezhi krest'ianstva v dovoennoe i revoliutsionnoe vremia; opyt statisticheskogo issledovaniia*. Moscow, 1924.

Vasil'ev, B. N. "Formirovanie promyshlennogo proletariata Ivanovskoi oblasti." *Voprosy istorii*, 1952, no. 6, pp. 99–117.

———. "Formirovanie tekstil'nogo proletariata v Shuiskom raione." Diss. dokt. ist. nauk, Moscow State University, 1949.

———. "K kharakeristike formirovaniia proletariata v Rossii (po materialam Vladimirskoi, Kostromskoi i Iaroslavskoi gubernii). In *Uchenye Zapiski Shakhtinskogo Pedagogicheskogo Instituta*. vol. 2, pt. 2. Shakhta, 1957.

Vinogradov, V. A. "Istochniki dlia izucheniia mirovozzreniia poreformennogo krest'ianstva." In *Istochnikovedenie otechestvennoi istorii. Sbornik statei, 1979*. Moscow, 1980.

———. "Krest'ianskoe dvizhenie v Tverskoi gub. v 1861–1881 godakh." Diss. kand. ist. nauk, Moscow State University, 1970.

Vishnevskii, A. G., ed. *Brachnost', rozhdaemost', smertnost' v Rossii i v SSSR. (Sbornik statei)*. Moscow, 1977.

Vladimirskii, Nikolai Nikolaevich. *Kostromskaia oblast'. (Istoriko-ekonomicheskii ocherk)*. Kostroma, 1959.

———. *Ot domashnego tkachestva k sotsialisticheskomu tekstil'nomu proizvodstvu*. Kostroma, 1949.

———. *Otkhod krest'ianstva Kostromskoi gubernii na zarabotki*. Izdanie Kostromskogo Gubstatotdela. Kostroma, 1927.

Vodarskii, Iaroslav Evgen'evich. *Promyshlennye seleniia tsentral'noi Rossii v period genesiza i razvitiia kapitalizma*. Moscow, 1972.

Von Geldern, James. "Life in Between: Migration and Popular Culture in Late Imperial Russia." *Russian Review* 55, no. 3 (April 1996): 365–83.

Von Laue, Theodore. "Russian Labor between Field and Factory." *California Slavic Studies* 3 (1964): 33–66.

———. "Russian Peasants in the Factory." *Journal of Economic History* 23 (1961): 61–80.

Vorderer, Susan M. "Urbanization and Industrialization in Late Imperial Russia: Ivanovo-Voznesensk, 1880–1914." Ph.D. diss., Boston College, 1990.

Vvedenskii, R. M. "Pasportnaia politika russkogo tsarizma i ee vliianie na krest'ianskoi otkhod." In *Sotsial'no-politicheskoe i pravovoe polozhenie krest'ianstva v dorevoliutsionnoi Rossii*. Voronezh, 1983.

Vyskochkov, L. V. "Vliianie Peterburga na khoziaistvo i byt gosudarstvennykh krest'ian Peterburgskoi gubernii v pervoi polovine XIX v." In *Staryi Peterburg: istoriko-etnograficheskie issledovaniia*. Leningrad, 1982.

———. "Gosudarstvennye krest'iane S.Peterburgskoi gubernii v doreformennoi period (1836–1866)," Kand. ist. nauk, Leningrad State University, 1980.

Wheatcroft, Stephen. "Crises and the Condition of the Peasantry in Late Imperial Russia." In *Peasant Economy, Culture, and Politics of European Russia, 1800–1921*, ed. Esther Kingston-Mann and Timothy Mixter. Princeton, 1991, pp. 128–72.

Weissman, Neil B. *Reform in Tsarist Russia: The State Bureaucracy and Local Government, 1900–1914*. New Brunswick, 1981.

Wilson, Peter J. "Filcher of Good Names: An Enquiry Into Anthropology and Gossip." *Man* 9 (1974).

Worobec, Christine D. *Peasant Russia: Family and Community in the Post-Emancipation Period*. Princeton, 1991.

Wortman, Richard. *The Crisis of Russian Populism*. Cambridge, 1967.

Zaionchkovskii, Petr Andreevich. *Krizis samoderzhaviia na rubezhe 1870–1880 godov*. Moscow, 1964.

———. *Otmena krepostnogo prava v Rossii*. 3d ed. Moscow, 1968.

———. *Rossiiskoe samoderzhavie v kontse XIX stoletie (Politicheskaia reaktsiia 80kh–nachala 90kh godov)*. Moscow, 1970.

Zelnik, Reginald E. *Labor and Society in Tsarist Russia: The Factory Workers of St. Petersburg, 1855–1870.* Stanford, 1971.

———. "Russian Bebels: An Introduction to the Memoirs of Semen Kanatchikov and Matvei Fisher." *Russian Review* 35 (1976): 249–89, 417–47.

———. "'To the Unaccustomed Eye': Religion and Irreligion in the Experience of St. Petersburg Workers in the 1870s," *Russian History/Histoire Russe* 16, nos. 2–4 (1989): 297–326.

———. *Law and Disorder on the Narova River: The Kreenholm Strike of 1872.* Berkeley and Los Angeles, 1995.

Zyrianov, Pavel Nikolaevich. *Krest'ianskaia obshchina Evropeiskoi Rossii v 1907–1914 gg.* Moscow, 1992.

———. *Pravoslavnaia tserkov' v bor'be s pervoi Russkoi revoliutsei, 1905–1907.* Moscow, 1984.

INDEX

abandonment, 33–34, 38–39, 77–79, 109–11, 216
abolition of serfdom, 11, 34–35, 41–43, 52, 144–45. *See also* Emancipation statute; redemption payments; serfdom
absence (from the parish) *(za otluchku)*, 195, 271n24. *See also* omission; spiritual negligence *(neradenie)*
address bureaus, 103
adultery *(nezakonnoe sozhitel'stvo)*, 200, 205. *See also* marriage, noncanonical
advances, of wages, 94, 108–10, 122. *See also* contracts; credit; wages
advertisements, 145–51
age, 27, 67
agoraphobia, 128–29
agrarian crisis, 135–40
agrarian revolution, 6, 179
agriculture, 20, 26–27, 119, 135–39
Akimov, Aleksei, 205
alcohol, 31, 33, 126, 131, 173–74
allotments *(nadely)*, 51–56, 132
ambivalence, toward the city, 262n19; toward the market, 116, 125; toward migration, 2, 17, 34
anathematization, 202, 186–204
Andreev, Ivan, 125–26
Anfimov, A. M., 250–51n47
annulment *(rastorzhenie braka)*, 198–99
anomie, 16, 32–33, 126–31, 227–28n5
anthropology of the personal, 1–10, 98, 185
anthropomorphization, 5, 9–10, 185, 187–88
anxiety, 29–34, 79–84, 129–31
apostasy. *See* "falling away"; Old Believers; scofflaws
apprenticeship, 15–16, 25–26, 38, 71–72, 96, 106–07, 129, 153–54, 209
arbitrariness, in communal manipulation, 215; in corporal punishment, 215; in labor relations, 121; parental, 83–84; and passports, 58, 66; of patriarchal control over women, 198–99; in taxation schemes, 21
architecture (peasant cottages), 160–63
Arkhangel Province, 22–24
Arkhipov, Ivan, 212
arrears, 46–47, 59–63
arson, 46

artels, 103, 107, 187
assimilation, 41. *See also* cooptation
auctions, 62–63, 159. *See also* boycotts
autocracy, 42–43, 45–46

babaia storona ("the woman's side"), 25–26. *See also* women
Bailey, Connor, 101
Bailey, F. G., 10
banishment, 188, 203, 212, 216
begging, 75, 214
behavior, 9–10, 77–79, 201–02
Belov, Pavel, 218
benefactors, 90–102. *See also* kulaks; patronage
Bessarabia, 22–24
bifurcation, 6, 15, 73–74, 135–36, 244n86
Black Hundreds, 177, 206–07
blagochinnye (ecclesiastical superintendents in the Orthodox Church administration), 193, 198
Blagolev, Father Viktor, 195
blasphemy, 186–87
blessings, 190–91
bootmakers, 131
boycotts, 47, 63
bribery, 46, 58, 212
brickmakers, 110
brotherhoods, 206–07
Brzheskii, N. K., 35, 50, 111, 238n17
Bulgakov, A. A., 117
bunt, buntarstvo (riotousness; spontaneous or random violence), 8
bureaucracy, 42–43
Bureau of Peasant Affairs, Moscow, 80–88
Burliuk, David, 151
Burylin, Stepan, 214–15

capitalism, viii, 7, 11. *See also* kulaks; Lenin, Vladimir I.
carpenters, 118, 211
cash transfers *(denezhnye pakety)*, 82, 133–34. *See also* support
Central Agricultural Region (CAR), 15, 20, 36, 52, 104, 139. *See also* regional differences
Central Industrial Region (CIR), 1, 15, 17, 20, 24, 26, 35–36, 38–39, 42–43, 46, 47, 52–55, 57,

307

Central Industrial Region *(continued)*
    59–61, 90–91, 97, 101, 102, 104, 106, 116,
    119, 125, 132, 136–40, 145, 176, 180. *See also*
    regional differences
ceremonies, 11–13. *See also* weddings
certificates *(svidetel'stva)*, 195–96. *See also* absence
    (from the parish)
character: and corporal punishment, 77–78; and
    moral typing, 208–11; and passports, 58–59;
    and slander, 201, 212–13, 215
chastushka (peasant ditty), 72–73, 154–55, 169–70,
    182, 187
childhood, 8. *See also* apprenticeship; child labor
child labor: 24, 39, 42, 129, 153–55
children *See* apprenticeship; childhood; child
    labor; stress
chuzhoi, 41–42. *See also* "little community";
    odnosel'chane; outsiders; *svoi*
city, 143, 145–52
class, 6–8, 181–85. *See also* kulaks; Lenin, Vladimir I.
clothing, 30–31, 166–70, 257n14
clubs: peasant, 166–69, 174–75, 184–85; working
    class, 115. *See also* taverns
clustering, 114–17
cobblers, 110, 131
coercion, 42–43, 46–50, 238n17; and communal
    resistance, 45–50; family, 63–64, 70–75;
    limits to, 77; influence of proximity, 132;
    and moral typing, 208–11
collective defense schemes, 41–42
collectivization, 218
collusion, 43, 107–08, 113–14
Columbia University Labor History Project,
    123–24
commoditization, 5–6. *See also* advertisements;
    consumerism; clothing
commune, 1–2, 5, 9–11, 17–19; as distributor of bur-
    den, 52; as extension of the state bureaucracy,
    45–50, 247n5; as a labor broker, 104–14; as a
    lender, 90–93, 248n8; as a mitigator, 45–50;
    threatened by migration, 38–39; unproduc-
    tive members of, 85–88, 214. *See also* fami-
    lies; households; patriarchalism
Communion, Holy: as Christian duty, 190; com-
    munion and confession registers *(ispovednye
    vedomosti)*, 193, 196, 271n15; as test to root
    out religious deviants, 190–91, 196
community, 1–2; changing concept of, 4; re-
    silience of, 41–42; and social control, 9–10,
    14–16; theories of, 213. *See also* character,
    and slander; "good name"; reputation
Confession, 32–33; as Christian duty, 190, 196,
    203; and confidentiality, 189
conflict, 30–34; between generations, 36–37; and
    denunciations, 212, 276n76; labor, 121–25,
    181–85. *See also* denunciations
consent, parental: and marriage, 198; and pass-
    ports, 56–58, 74–75, 81–84. *See also* patriar-
    chalism
conspicious consumption, 156–59, 168

consumerism, 30–34, 143–71; peasant logic of, 157,
    168–69
contractors, 106, 100
contracts: books, 106; and debt control, 91–96; fa-
    vors as, 106; forward *(zaprodazhi)*, 94; hir-
    ing, 105–14; leave, and passports, 58, 81–82,
    103–04; oral versus written, 106–07; peas-
    ant-workers' insistence on, 111; for village
    retail concessions, 172. *See also* advances; fa-
    vors; hiring agents; *pomoch*
conversion: forced, 198; illegal, 192
coopers, 125
cooptation, 5, 41–43, 45–50, 104, 213–15. *See also*
    collusion
corporal punishment, 16, 75, 77–79, 187, 245n111;
    as act of impugning reputation, 215; as state-
    sponsored violence, 245–46n112; village offi-
    cials exempt from, 48
corruption, 30–34; of husbands denounced by
    wives, 198–99; *isporchennyi* (corrupted),
    32–33; *izbalovannyi* (spoiled), 12, 30–32; and
    occupation, 208–11; religious struggle
    against, 189–90; of wives denounced by
    husbands, 199–201
cosmetics, 169–70
cottage manufacturers *(kustari)*, 6, 100
cottages, 160–63
courtship, 71–73. *See also* marriage; weddings
credit, 16, 90–95, 102, 126, 156, 168
creditors, 2, 90–101, 213–14. *See also* credit; pa-
    tronage
Crisp, Olga, 7–8, 121
cross, 191–92, 202
cultural crisis, 29–39
culture: of acquistion, 143–85; of denunciation,
    186–218; theory of, vii, 6, 98
customary law *(obychnoe pravo)*, 2, 43, 57
cycles, economic, 119–20, 139

Dadonov, V., 37, 54, 122
deception, 195, 212
delinquents, 46. *See also* corporal punishment;
    scofflaws; taxation
delusion, 197–98
demography, 70–75, 135
denunciations, 186–218; and labor migration,
    215–16; as theater, 212. *See also* social control
departure fee. *See* leave charges
dependents, 28–39, 233n44. *See also* denuncia-
    tions; patriarchalism; social control
derevenskii ("bumpkin culture"), 70–75, 128, 144,
    151. *See gorodskoi*
D'iakonova, Elizaveta, 128, 150
diaries, 126, 128, 184–85, 208
diet, 30–31, 163
disobedience *(nepovinovenie)*, 46
distraint *(opis)*, 61–63
divorcement, from agriculture, 7, 136. *See also* so-
    cial division of labor
Dobrotvorskii, N., 112

domokhoziaistvo. See patriarchalism
Don Region, 22–24
dreams, 94–95, 127, 150–59, 184–85
drunkenness, 190. *See also* alcohol; taverns
Duma, 179–80, 196–97
dvor (peasant household unit), 17–18. *See also* family; household

ecclesiasiatical courts, 192
Ecclesiasiatical Regulation (1722), 189
economic crisis, 1, 119–22, 180–81
elder *(starosta)*, 77–79, 113, 186–87, 212. *See also* patriarchalism
Emancipation statute, 11, 49–50, 53. *See also* abolition of serfdom
embezzlement, 48
employers: and village controls, 70; ethos of, 100; and collusion with local authorities, 43; and hiring, 105–14; and reputations of workers, 215. *See also* contracts; patriarchalism
endogamy, 73–74, 217
enemies of the people, 218
"energetic measures," 47, 245–46*n*112, 247*n*5
Engel, Barbara Alpern, 166
entertainment *(magarych, privalnaia, ugoshchenie)*, 93, 159
enticements, 14, 30–34, 37–38, 128, 145–51; and immorality, 210, 212. *See also* delusions
envy, 184–85, 218
etapniki (peasants returned to their villages "under guard," *po etapu*), 75–76, 187, 214. *See also vytrebovanie*
Evans-Pritchard, E. E., 216
evasion, 194–95
evil, 188, 190, 198, 215
exile, 212
exitlessness *(beziskhodnost)*, 13–14, 75, 83–84, 91, 126
exploitation, 91
extortion, 53, 65
"extraordinary measures," 43, 107

factory: development of industry, 7, 132; *fabrichnye* (factory workers), 210; factory work, 7–9, 11–12, 15, 27, 28–34, 37–38, 53–54, 57, 81–82, 103, 114–17, 127–28, 139–40, 152, 155, 163–65, 178–79, 181–83, 186–87, 191, 200, 204, 207–08, 214–15; and hiring and controls, 70, 105–14; and recessions, 119–21. *See also* layoffs
"falling away" *(otpadenie)*, 195, 217. *See also uklonenie*
families, and migrants, 27–38; as channels for community coercion, 70–75, 214; and denunciations, 197–200; and reputations across generations, 201. *See also* households; patriarchalism
farmwork, 15, 25–27, 120–21, 124–28, 131–40
fasting, 32, 190
favors *(odolzhenie)*, 96, 110. *See also* credit; debt; patronage

Fedorov, Grigorii, Iakov, and Mikhail, 197–98
Fedorova, Anna, 66
Fedorova, Dar'ia, 192
Fedorova, Praskov'ia, 205
feuds, 201–02, 212
Florova, widow, 192
food. *See* diet
forced return of migrant laborers. *See etapniki; vytrebovanie*
Fortunatov, A. F., 136–38
fraud, 240–41*n*20
Freeze, Gregory L., 194, 272*n*27
"frolics," 100
funeral service *(otpevanie)*, 186–87
furniture, 162

gambling, 33
Gautier, Théophile, 146–47
Geertz, Clifford, vii
gender, 24–26, 166–70
generation crisis, 14, 28–38. *See also* patriarchalism
Gerasimov, Mikhail, 151
Gerasimov, Vasilii, 182–83
gestures, 156, 182–83, 201
Gluckman, Max, 201
Golikov, Aleksandr, 88
Golyshev, Ivan, 205–06, 215
"good name," 10, 98, 168, 213. *See also* reputation
gorodskoi (of the city), 128; *po gorodski* (the city as a fashion-setter), 144, 152–57, 160. *See also derevenskii*; urban style, emulation of
gossip, 128, 174, 201, 204
Governing Senate *(Pravitel'stvuiushchii Senat)*, 56, 236–37*n*3
grain, 119
greed, 65
Grigor'ev, Iakov, 195
Grigor'ev, Petr, 65
Gromyko, M. M., 97, 115, 200–01
Grossman, Vasilii, 118
guliatskii obrok (wanderer's tax), 54–55, 214. *See also* leave charge
Gur'ev, Father Viktor, 192
Guro, Elena, 150
Guseva, Luker'ia, 199

hardship, 13. *See also* labor migration
harvest failures, 136–39
health, 27–28, 125–26, 214; mental, 129–30
hegemony. *See* information
Helmsman (Kormchii), 189–90
hereditary proletariat, 7
heresy, 197, 212. *See also* Old Believers; recusants; scofflaws
Hindus, Maurice, 89
hingemen, 5
hiring, 16, 103–14. *See also* contracts
hiring agents, 1, 105–14. *See also* contracts
Hobsbawm, Eric, vii
holidays, 97, 120–21, 127, 131, 159, 162, 190–91, 203

Holy books, 191–92
Holy Synod, 193, 205
honor. *See slava*
hooliganism, 151–52, 184, 187
hospitality *(gostepriimstvo)*, 95–101. *See also* contractors; employers; entertainment; patronage; village elites
house decorators, 124
households, 16; bifurcated, 6; budget data for, 131–40, 163; divisions of, 34–38, 81, 235n61; inventories of, 27, 135–36, 157–59, 161; size of, 35–36. *See also* families
husbands, 198–200
hybrid, 6, 17, 43, 50

Iakovenko, Vladimir, 129
Iakushev, Vasilii, 186–87
Iakushkin, E. I., 57
Iaroslavl Province, 21–24, 26, 35, 48, 57–58, 61, 64, 72, 75–76, 103, 116, 121, 126, 128, 135–36, 139, 145, 154, 162, 171, 176
Iartseva, Marfa, 198–99
iconoclasm, 183
icons, 162, 186–87, 191
illiteracy, 151–52
immorality. *See* corruption
industrialization, 132
information, 176–80; hiring contractors and secrecy, 109; imparting to priests, 189; manipulation of by village elites, 215; and *zemliaki*, 116–17
injury, 126
inquisitiveness, 176–80
insecurity, 4, 33–34, 119–28, 190
insularity, 101, 217
insults, 188, 199
insurance. *See* safety net
interest rates (on debts), 90–93
interregnum, 4, 42–43, 236–37n3
inversion ritual, 99, 183
Isaev, Andrei A., 35, 171, 176
isolation, 16, 128–31, 188
Ivanov, Lev, 192
Ivanov, Nikolai, 68
Ivanova, Evdokiia, 195
Ivanovo-Voznesensk, 13, 37, 54, 122, 124, 126–27, 146, 217

James, William, 91
job security, 118–26
Johnson, Robert Eugene, 8, 127–28, 244n86
justice, 181–85. *See also samosud*

kabaki. *See* taverns
kabal'nye rabochie. *See* labor, forced
Kaluga Province, 21–23, 26, 31, 38, 47–48, 57, 59, 100, 102, 108, 110, 159, 174, 192, 211
Kamenskii, 207–08, 275n65
Kanatchikov, Semën, 11–14, 38, 74–75, 114, 117, 121–22, 128–29, 131, 145–46, 227–28n5

Karasev, 197
Karidalin, A. N., 109–10
Karlsen, Carol F., 276n76
kerosine, 162
Khitrovo market, 105, 199
khlebosol'nyi khoziain ("bread and salt patron"), 95–101. *See also* patronage
kinship, 10
Kisliakov, Ermil and Vasilii, 86–87
Klimov, 56
Konovalov, Kuzmich, 155
Kostroma Province, 20–26, 37–38, 47–48, 52, 57–59, 63–64, 70–72, 75, 79, 103, 111, 116, 125, 128, 155, 168
kowtowing to authority, 64–70
Kreenholm, 182
Krestov, V. D. 175
krugovaia poruka. *See* mutual responsibility
Krylov, Petr, 67
Kudin, N. A., 157–59
Ku Klux Klan, 206
Kukushkin, Vasilii, 186–87
kulaks (wealthy peasants): and state, 42; as benefactors, 90–101, 119; *kulaki-otkhodniki*, 218; sociology of (Lenin's stratification thesis), 119, 185, 250–51n47; and labor migrants in the Soviet era, 218; as targets of denunciations, 212; trouble identifying, 249n25. *See also* contractors; credit; employers; patronage; village elites; *znakomstvo*
kumovstvo (godparenthood), 95
Kurochkin, A. A., 177, 209–10
Kursk Province, 22–24

labor: division of, 24–26; forced, 108; in *pomoch*, 96–100; social division of, 6–7, 136. *See also* contractors; contracts; employers; hiring
labor contractors. *See* contractors
labor migration *(otkhod)*, and Orthodox Church, 189–90; and recession, 118–21; statistics on, 21–27, 242n45; and strikes, 121–25
labor principle *(trudovoe nachalo)*, 81–82
land: claims after 1905, 240–41n20; excess obligations and *otkodniki*, 19–21, 42–43; psychological attachment to, 126–27; rental of, 53. *See also* credit, land
return to, 27; as safety net, 55. *See also* taxation
land purchases, 135–40
Larkin, Jack, 100
Lashmanov, F., 47–48, 175
Lavrov, Ivan and Evdokeia, 200, 273n40
layoffs, 121–23, 124–26
leaflets, 181–82
leave charge *(otpusknoe, spusta)*, 53–54
leave contract *(podpiska)*. *See* contracts, leave, and passports
Lebedev, A., 174
leisure, 130–31
Lenin, Vladimir I., 6–7, 136, 185, 250–51n47
Leont'ev, Aleksandr, 18

letters, 63–70, 74–75, 117, 199
literacy, 147–52, 176–80
"little community," 5, 45–50, 101, 201, 216, 254*n*95
little tradition, 6
livestock, 139
loans, 90–95, 248*n*8
localism: and lending strategies, 90; and local solutions, 16, 42–44; and passport restrictions, 58–59; and state cooptation of local controls, 45–50
Lukacs, Georg, 5
lumber industry, 109, 113

machine industry, 12, 186
magarych. See entertainment
Makhonin, S. Ia., 177
malevolence, 212. See also envy; evil
marginalization, 6, 119, 212
market economy, 13, 19
market middlemen, 1–2. See also contractors
markets. See consumerism; hiring; Khitrovo market
marriage, 16; age at, 70–71; and bifurcation of peasant households, 70–75; noncanonical, 193–94; and reputation, 71, 213; seasonal character of in high-migration villages, 71. See also matchmakers; weddings
Matveev, Nikofor, 203
Martynov, Boris, 196
Marx, Karl, 11, 100
Maslov, Petr, 1
matchmakers, 71
material culture, 152–71
Mayer, Arno, 5
McCloskey, Donald, 180
mediation, 5, 208, 213
Medvedev, Petr, 208
melancholy, 127–31
Mel'nikov-Pecherskii, V., 155
migration. See labor migration
Mikhnevich, O. V., 154
military service, 233*n*40, 246*n*124
Ministry of Internal Affairs (MVD), 34–23
Mironov, Boris, 9, 2
Mirovich, D. A., 122
mirovoi sud'ia (peace justice), 112
missionary activities, 192
mixed economy, 6. See also hybrid
money lenders, 92–95
moral codes, 189, 197
moral economy, 12, 180
morality, 30–34. See also corruption
moral typing, 30–34, 75–77, 208–11
Morozov, Vikula, 183
Moscow City, 38, 65–66, 69, 103, 127–28, 145–46, 191, 195, 197–99, 202, 204–05, 209, 216
Moscow Metropolitan, 198
Moscow Province, 20–23, 26, 31, 34–35, 38–39, 45–47, 54–55, 57–59, 70, 73–74, 76, 79, 81, 88, 104, 106, 110, 114–16, 119–20, 122–23, 129, 140, 157–58, 176, 186, 190–91, 195–98, 200, 203, 207–09, 212, 214–16
Moscow Spiritual Consistory, 188, 199, 201, 203, 205, 216, 269*n*2
murder, 46, 199
mutual responsibility *(krugovaia poruka)*, 49, 51–52, 77, 90, 238*n*17, 247*n*2, 247*n*5; and hiring, 107–08; and taxation, 15, 18–19, 49, 51–52, 90
myths: about land, 12; "good master," 94–95; and social control, 76–77; social mobility, 152–59, 180–81

napitrit'sia, 126
Nedeshev, Sergei, 156–57
Nedokhodovskii, 31
neotdelennye chleny (inseparable members), 18, 81
nerazdel'naia sem'ia (indivisible family unit), 18, 57
Neuberger, Joan, 184
newspapers, 176–80. See also reading; taverns
Nikolaev, Vasilii, 193
Nikonov, Mikhail, 66–67, 69
1905 Revolution, 124–25, 178–80
Nizhnii Novgorod Province, 21–23, 47, 55, 58
nobility, 20. See also land; redemption payments
nonconformity, 200, 216–17, 277*n*92. See also Old Believers
norms: community imposition of, 200–02, 209–10, 216; peasant labor-migrants' propensity to challenge, 216–17; sexual, 204, 274*n*55; subordination of Church authority to village, 197
nostalgia, 128–31
Novgorod Province, 22–24
novichki ("hayseeds"), 128

oath *(prisiaga)*, 189, 205
obrok (quitrent), 20, 145, 261*n*5, 261*n*5
obychnoe pravo, See customary law
odinochki (lone workers), 73, 214
odnosel'chane (fellow villagers, neighbors), 47, 54, 65, 82, 94, 97, 101, 103, 114, 189, 200, 212, 216. See also patronage; *znakomstvo*
Old Believers (religious sectarians), 188, 191–92, 202–04; and language of denunciations, 216–17; and langauge of rebellion, 217–18; as nonconformists, 216–18
Olonets Province, 22–24
omission, 193. See also spiritual negligence
Omviiskii, Father Aleksei, 195
opinion, 45–50, 98–99, 101, 206
opportunists, 4, 43
opportunity, 213–14
Orenburg Province, 22–24
Orlov Province, 22–24
osedlost (settled base, place where one can make a living), 199, 214
Osipov, 215
ostracization, 188, 214–15. See also banishment; shunning

otkhod (labor migration), 14, 20–27, 215–16
otrezki (reduced allotments), 20. *See also* land
outsiders: suspicion toward, 1, 42; and social control, 213–15; village use of, 188. *See also chuzhoi*

parental authority, 45–46. *See also* family; households; patriarchalism
parishes, 188–97
Parusnikov, Father Mikhail, 202
passports: and families, 74–75; regulation of, 16; restrictions of, 56–61; term of, 58–61. *See also* coercion; taxation
"paternalistic vigilance," 74, 245–46n112
patriarchalism *(domokhoziaistvo)*, 11–13, 17–19, 41; crisis of, 29–39; and passports, 56–57; challenges to, 79–88; and social mobility, 153–57; and state authority, 45–50
patron-client relations. *See also* credit; employers; patronage; *pomoch*; village elites; *znakomstvo*
patronage, 95–101, 108, 110, 119, 126, 159, 213–14. *See also slava; znakomstvo*
Pavlova, Fekla, 129–30
peasantization, 117, 226n11
"peasantness," 7–9
peasant-workers *(otkhodniki)*, 12, 64–65, 216; and contracts, 111; identity of, 41–42; and isolation in cities, 16, 128–31; and job security, 118–26; and money, 32; nervous disorders among, 129–30; perceived as agents of change, 139–40, 217; and rebellion, 217–18; support for agriculture of, 135–40. *See also* labor migration
peat workers, 110, 122
Penza Province, 22–24
pereselentsy (settlers), 15, 239n5
Perestiany, J. G., 213
perfume, 170
"pernicious moral influence," 187. *See also* corruption; evil; malevolence; social control
persecution, 206
personal contacts. *See znakomstvo*
Pestova, Evdokia, 207–08
Peter the Great (I), 189
petitions, 45–46, 82–88, 123, 198, 203, 212, 214
Petrov, Fëdor, 191
phenomenology, 16
pilgrimage, 25, 115, 190
Piskarev, Vasilii and Konstantin, 81–82
pocket watches, 168–69, 171
podriadchiki. See contractors; employers; hiring
Pogozhev, A. V., 139–40
Pokrov Psychiatric Hospital (Moscow), 129
Poliakov, Iakov, 186–87
police and policing, 50, 69–70, 102–04, 177–79, 186–87, 191–94, 199, 204–08, 212, 215–16
"political unreliables," 215, 257n14
pomoch, 96–101. *See also* favors
Popkin, Samuel, 180
population growth, 21

Populists, 131
portrait photographs, 162–65
power, 6
prayer, 11–12, 113, 190–91
Preobrazhenskaia Hospital for the Insane (Moscow), 129–30, 258n41
Pretty, David, 257n14, 277n92
priests, 32–33, 187–97, 272n27; community opinion on, 196–97, 202, 203–04; factors undermining authority, 194; as officials, 189; and police, 204–08, 217; as sources: 156, 159, 174, 190–93, 195–96, 201–04, 207–08, 275n65. *See also* Communion, Holy; Confession
processions, 190–91
proletarian culture, 6
property, 212
protest, 180–85. *See also* resistance, everyday forms of
proverbs, 12, 15, 227–28n5
Pskov Province, 20
psychology, 6–8, 125–31
pustyrniki (peasants who abandoned their obligations), 76

railway workers, 67, 123
raskol. See Old Believers
razdel. See households, division of
razluchenie (forced separation of spouses in a non-canonical marriage), 198
reading, 176–80
rebellion, language of (and peasant-workers), 217–18
recession, 13, 119–20, 139
reciprocity, 96, 98
recusants. *See* "falling away"; *uklonenie*; scofflaws
redemption payments *(vykup)*: and redemption operation, 239n6; reduction of in 1880s, 139, 220–21; and regional differences, 20, 39, 136–39
Redfield, Robert, 254n95
regional differences: and communal attitudes toward allotment size, 52; commune as labor broker, 102–03; consumer revolution, 160–180; economic cycles, 119–20; harvest failures, 136–39; and hiring market, 104–06; importance of agriculture in household income, 119; migration patterns, 15; in 1905, 124; and passport term, 59–61; and peasant commune, 46; peasant household size, 35–36; proportion of peasant-worker support for agriculture, 135–40; and redemption patterns, 20, 39, 230–31n14; and wage disparities, 98; and *zemliak* clustering, 116–17
reification, 5
religious beliefs, 188
religious deviants, 190–97
religious dissent, 192
renunciation (of faith), 191
reputation, 9–10, 66–67; building and impugning, 212–13; and denunciations, 186–218;

reputation *(continued)*
  impugned by employers, 215; impugned by village elites, 215; and marriage, 71–72; and moral typing, 200, 208–11; and opportunity, 213–14; and passports, 58–59; and priests, 193; and religion, 200; wealth and status, 156–57. *See also* character, and slander
resettlement, 38–39, 42
resistance, 46–50; everyday forms of, 5, 46–50, 63, 225*n*4
resolution (communal) *(prigovor)*, 202–03, 212
retail trade, 171–75
Riazan Province, 21–23, 26, 49, 57, 76, 102, 105–06, 110, 199
Rikhter, D. I., 179
risk aversion, 180–81
rites of denunciation, 197
rituals, 11–12, 131; as tests to root out religious deviants, 190–91; surfeit of in Orthodox parishes, 194
Roberts, James S., 179
Rogozhskii cemetery, 192, 204
Ruane, Christine, 166
rumors, 70, 116–17, 177–79, 196, 201
rural crisis debates, 180–81
rural-urban ties, 7, 114–17, 119–40
Russo-Japanese war, 124
Rylova, Arafima, 197–98

Sablin, Stepan, 199
Sablina, Ekaterina, 199
sacraments, 192, 195, 198. *See also* Communion, Holy; Confession
safety net, 2, 27, 55, 125–26, 132–40. *See also* land
St. Petersburg (city and province), 37, 63–64, 72–73, 81, 98–99, 103, 109, 115–16, 118, 121, 126, 141, 145–52, 154, 157, 168, 179, 182, 184–85
saloons. *See* taverns
salvation, 205–06
Samara Province, 22–24
Samoilov, Fëdor, 13, 15, 124, 126–27, 129–30, 146, 217
samosud (peasant vigilante justice), 204, 206
samoupravlenie (peasant self-government), 42–43. *See also* localism
Sanson, Basil, 212
Sapozhnikov, 172
Sareevskii, Father Mikhail, 207–08, 275*n*65
Sazonov, G. P., 112
schismatics *(raskol'niki)*, *See* Old Believers
scofflaws, 77–79, 188 *See also* abandonment; corruption; *etapniki*; social control; *vytrebovanie*
Scott, James C., 6, 180, 213, 243*n*72
scutchers, 211
sectarianism. *See* Old Believers
security *(obespechenie)*, 18, 125
seduction, religious *(sovrashchenie)*, 193, 202, 205. *See also* advertisements; consumerism; delusions
Semenova, Evdokeia, 207

serfdom, 2, 17–21, 34–35, 42–43, 52, 106, 143–45, 239*n*6. *See also* abolition; land; nobility; redemption payments
Sergeev, Timofei, 192
sexual relations, 200, 204
shaming, 188, 204, 245*n*111
Shchelgov, I., 174–75
Shelagin, P. P., 176
shoemakers, 125
shopping, 171–75
shunning, 201. *See also* banishment, ostracization
Shuster, U. A., 109
Shustova, Masha, 184–85
Siberia, 15, 239*n*5
sickness, 126, 128
Simbirsk Province, 22–24
Skundova women, 196
Skvortsov, Vasilii, 202–03
slander: religious *(khula)*, 192; in village life, 201. *See also* character, and slander; "good name"; reputation
slava (honor, status), 155–56, 212. *See also* character, and slander; reputation
Smirnov, Father, 196
Smolensk Province, 20–24, 38, 56, 61, 76, 94, 107
social control, 51–88, 201–02, 212–15
Society of the Archangel Michael, 206
Sokolov, Father Dmitrii, 190–91
Sokolov, Father Mikhail, 156, 174, 201–02
songs. *See chastushka*
sorrowful repast *(pechal'nyi pir)*, 12–13, 227*n*7
soslovie, 42
speakeasies *(shinki)*, 173–74
"species peasant," 6
Spiridonov, 216
spirituality, 189–90
spiritual negligence *(neradenie)*, 196. *See also* absence (from the parish);, omission
stalking, 199–200
starosta (village elder). *See* elder
status, 212. *See also slava*
Steinberg, Mark, 130, 262*n*19
Stishinskii, A. S., 57
Stolypin reforms, 42, 45, 55, 57
stonemasons, 211
stratification, 213. *See also* Lenin, Vladimir I.
street signs, 145–51
stress, 128–31
strikes, 121–25, 217
Struve brothers, machine construction mill (Moscow), 186
subsistence orientation, 17, 119, 121, 125, 132–40, 180–81
superiaga (joint tilling of land), 96. *See also pomoch*
superstition, 10
support, 131–34
surety, 100–01
Suvirov, Vladimir N., 215
svoi (insider), 41–42. *See also chuzhoi; odnosel'chane;* outsiders; *zemliachestvo*

sycophancy (towards officialdom), 64–70
symbiosis, 136

Tabeev, Father Vasilii, 159
tactical mobility, 136–40
Tarasov, Grigorii, 204
Tatarinov, P., 141
Taurida Province, 22–24
taverns, 173–75, 176–80, 267*n101*
taxation, 15, 18–19, 49, 51–56, 90; and allotment size, 132; arbitrariness of, 21, 85–88; and coercion, 56–61; and corporal punishment, 77–80; and passports, 56–64; sources for understanding, 229–30*n11;* and state officials, 45–50; wealthy peasant noncompliance of, 47. *See also* coercion; delinquents; *guliatskii obrok* (wanderer's tax); leave charge; letters; mutual responsibility; patriarchalism; *vytrebovanie*
tea rooms. *See* taverns
Tenishev Collection, 269–70*n2*
textile workers, 200, 217
Third World, 116, 193
threats, 46–48, 188, 199, 212, 216
tiaglo, 17
Tikhonov, Boris V., 70, 76
Timofeev, P., 152
Tolstoi, Lev, 185
trade and traders. *See* consumerism
Trofimov, Iakov and Petr, 87
Tukhmanov, Mikhail, 85–86
Tula Province, 21–23, 26, 48, 59, 78, 120, 123, 129
Tver Province, 20–23, 26, 49, 57, 62–63, 73, 91–94, 103, 108, 115–16, 157, 172–73, 207, 218
tysiachniki ("thousandaires"), 153–54

Ufa Province, 22–24
ugoshchenie. See entertainment
uklonenie (religious deviation), 188, 194
unemployment, 119–21, 123–25. *See also* insecurity; layoffs
Union of Russian People, 206
uprootedness, 6
urbanization, 110
urban-rural migration, 132. *See also* rural-urban ties
urban style, emulation of, 30–34, 144–71, 183–85
usury, 11, 91–92. *See also* credit; interest; loans

vendettas, 212. *See also* envy; feuds; malevolence
Viatka Province, 20, 47
vigilantism. *See samosud*
Vikhliaev, P. A., 136, 139

village elites, 95–101, 215. *See also* credit; creditors; elder; employers; patriarchalism; patronage
"village origins," 7–9
Vinogradov, Father Matvei, 203–04
violence, 8, 183–84, 188, 203
Vladimir Province, 20–23, 26–27, 29–30, 32–33, 35, 36, 49, 52–54, 56, 62–63, 74, 97, 102, 104, 109–11, 113, 119–20, 124–25, 132–34, 156–57, 159, 173, 175, 183, 200–01, 204–06, 211, 217
Vologda Province, 22–24, 99
volost courts, 238*n17*
Volynia Province, 22–24
von ("out there"). *See chuzhoi;* corruption
Von Laue, Theodore, 8
Vorob'ev, Klementii, 135–36, 139
Voronezh Province, 22–24
Vorontsov-Dashkov, 51, 238*n17*
vykup (redemption operation). *See* redemption payments
vytrebovanie (forced return under guard to a peasant's native village), 75–77, 103–04, 211; for religious deviation, 203. *See also etapniki*

wage labor, 2, 29–30
wages, 105, 120, 210–11, 275*n70. See also* advances; contracts; hiring
waiters, 209
Wajda, Shirley, 162
wealth, 144–45, 152–70, 260–61*n4*
weavers, 154
Weber, Max, vii
weddings, 70–75, 131, 166–67, 190, 198. *See also* marriage
windows, 160–61
wives, 198–200, 212, 272*n36*
women, 24–26, 166–70
woodcutters, 13
workers, 7–8

Zaionchkovskii, P. A., 20
Zaitsev, I. M., 122–23
Zasulich, Vera, 11
Zelnik, Reginald, 182–83
zemliachestvo (*zemliaki,* peasants from the same village or region), 8, 103, 114–17, 130–31, 187, 254*n95;* and leisure, 115, 131
zemstvo, 129, 176, 178
Zhbankov, D. N., 27–28, 37–38, 70–72, 75, 125, 128, 131
Zhuravlev, Father Aleksei, 193
znakomstvo (acquaintanceship, personal contacts), 9–10, 94, 101, 106, 114–15, 126, 213–14